Genel Yayın: 618

POLITICAL SCIENCE

SUNA KİLİ
THE ATATÜRK REVOLUTION
A PARADIGM OF MODERNIZATION

© TÜRKİYE İŞ BANKASI KÜLTÜR YAYINLARI, 2003

GRAPHIC DESIGNER
BİROL BAYRAM

PAGE DESIGN
TÜRKİYE İŞ BANKASI KÜLTÜR YAYINLARI

Translated by
Sylvia Zeybekoğlu

FIRST EDITION: JANUARY 2003
SECOND EDITION: MARCH 2007
THIRD EDITION: JUNE 2007

ISBN 978-975-458-376-2

PRINT
ŞEFİK MATBAASI
(0212) 472 15 00
MARMARA SANAYİ SİTESİ M BLOK 291
İKİTELLİ 34306 İSTANBUL

TÜRKİYE İŞ BANKASI KÜLTÜR YAYINLARI
İSTİKLAL CADDESİ, NO: 144/4 BEYOĞLU 34430 İSTANBUL
Tel. (0212) 252 39 91
Fax. (0212) 252 39 95
www.iskultur.com.tr

Suna Kili

The Atatürk Revolution

a paradigm of modernization

TÜRKİYE İŞ BANKASI
Kültür Yayınları

In commemoration of
the 125th year anniversary of the birth of
Mustafa Kemal Atatürk

Those who have grasped the purpose of the revolution will always be able to safeguard it.

Mustafa Kemal Atatürk

İnkılabın hedefini kavramış olanlar daima onu muhafazaya muktedir olacaklardır.

Mustafa Kemal Atatürk

TABLE OF CONTENTS

I

INTRODUCTION

II

OTTOMAN SOCIETY AND STATE STRUCTURE

III

THE STATE OF AFFAIRS IN TURKEY
AT THE BEGINNING OF THE REVOLUTION

IV

THE ATATÜRK PARADIGM OF MODERNIZATION

V

USING THE PARADIGM TO TRANSFORM THE STRUCTURE OF SOCIETY AND STATE

VI

ATATÜRKISM AND THE ATATÜRK PRINCIPLES

VII

THE ATATÜRK REVOLUTION:
THE INTERPLAY BETWEEN PRINCIPLES AND POLITICAL EXIGENCIES
May 1919-January 2007

VIII

EPILOGUE
The Atatürk Paradigm of Modernization; Turkey and The European Union, Cyprus, Globalization, Republic and Democracy

Foreword To The Second Edition

As the author I was solely responsible for the updating of the second edition of this book, which included the writing of the new material directly in English. While updating the book I emphasized those aspects of the Atatürkist paradigm of modernization and Atatürkism which have particular relevance for our world today.

Developments in the world especially since September 11, 2001, has reinforced the credibility and the validity of the Atatürkist paradigm of modernization. Moreover, it is important to note that the Islamic world has to be thankful to the Atatürk Revolution for two major reasons. Firstly, although the population of Turkey is in the main Moslem, as a result of the successful implementation of the radical Atatürk reform program, the Turkish Republic became a laïc state. And secondly, also as a result of the successful implementation of the Atatürk reform program, democratization of the Turkish state and society became a reality. The Atatürkist paradigm of modernization has discredited the argument that a basically Moslem country cannot become a laïc and democratic state. Hence, the Atatürkist paradigm of modernization constitutes a bridge of peace between the East and the West and the North and the South.

Atatürkism is a system of thought which involves total commitment to modernization and nation-building. Establishing a nation-state, nation-building, creating a national culture and disseminating this culture among the populace is a primary objective throughout all the stages of modernization. With its republican, national, populist and laïcist content the Atatürkist system of thought has retained this objective throughout the implementation of all the reform laws. Atatürkism is the system of thought of the Turkish Enlightenment.

The Atatürk Revolution involved the recognition and the strengthening of the Turkish nation. The Atatürk Revolution aimed at Turkish nation-building. In view of the ethnic and religious controversies in many countries such as Iraq and Lebanon, the modernizing, nation-building message of Atatürk has become even more pertinent.

The two "Red Lines" of contemporary Turkey are also the Atatürkist "Red Lines". The constitutional commitment to the indivisibility of the Turkish state, as regards its territory and nation, and to laïcism constitute the main components of these two "Red Lines". In this context, for a thorough understanding of Atatürkism and the Atatürk paradigm of modernization it is important to understand the difference between secularism and laïcism. Secularism as implemented in such countries as the USA and Great Britain involves the separation of state and religion. However, as implemented in France and as embraced by Atatürkism, laïcism is not merely separation of state and religion. Laïcism gives the state the right to intervene in case religion begins to meddle in politics, in matters of the state.

The Atatürkist system of thought is primarily republican. A "republic" in fact involves the nationalization and popularization of the political regime. In order to achieve a more modern structure, it is indispensable that a republic adopts a laïc order which in fact embraces as first principles rationality and science. In a truly republican regime political authority has to rest on a laïc foundation. On the other hand, Atatürkist system of thought is not compatible with the contemporary understanding and implementations of globalization. This incompatibility does not merely stem from the commitment of Atatürkism to nation-state and to national identity. This incompatibility also rises from the commitment of the Atatürkist system of thought to the "social state". Public good, unconditional sovereignty of the people are important components of the Atatürkist system of thought. Belief in the necessity of an equitable distribution of the national wealth, egalitarian implementations and humanist values constitute also integral parts of both the Atatürkist paradigm of modernization and the Atatürkist system of thought. Atatürkism involves commitment to social justice. Because of the afore-mentioned reasons, Atatürkist understanding of republicanism and the Atatürkist system of thought are in contradiction with the contemporary implementations of globalization which shove aside common good and which undermine equality between peoples and between nations.

In view of and within the context of the above-mentioned arguments, it is important to note that the Atatürkist paradigm of development and modernization has a special message for the developing countries and perhaps with a renewed sense of urgency. The Atatürkist paradigm of modernization is neither Capitalist nor Marxist. *It is a third way.* It is a *"national"* paradigm of development, of modernization. And as such it has great relevance for the problems confronted by the developing countries in the contemporary world. What is the economic aspect of this paradigm which is of particular importance for the developing countries that lack the capital needed for growth? In the 1930's Turkey implemented an economic policy which strengthened the public initiative in economic development leading to capital accumulation. And the resources of the country were activated within the context of economic planning. In the formulation and implementation of this economic plan the "iron fist" approach was not employed. And Turkey pursued a successful policy of industrialization in the years between 1929-1939. And if this economic policy were to be continued, Turkey, most probably, would have reached the level of an economically developed country.

The developing countries, which confront economic difficulties may benefit from the economic experience of Turkey in the 1930's. For this reason, the sections of the book dealing with étatism and economic planning in the Atatürk era have special significance for the contemporary world.

In her history Turkey has experienced both grandeur and defeat. Fully cognizant of the historical experiences of Turkey and the realities of the world, Atatürk believed that "peace at home and peace in the world" was the only effective principle to follow. Given the political and economic realities of the contemporary world, we could say that the Atatürkist paradigm of modernization has gained new relevance.

SUNA KİLİ
January 31st, 2007

Foreword To The First Edition

This book was prepared for the Türkiye İş Bankası Cultural Publications "Atatürk series" on the occasion of the 100th commemoration of the birth of Atatürk in 1981. The request from Türkiye İş Bankası to prepare such a book came almost two years prior to that date.

I deliberately chose the subject of the book as "The Atatürk Revolution: A Paradigm of Modernization" for two major reasons: Firstly, I had worked, in the main, on the ideological aspect of the Atatürk Revolution and had published in this field. My book on *Kemalism* (1969), Robert College Publication, is an example of such a study. And I thought it would be appropriate to do research on the "paradigm" of modernization systematized and implemented by Atatürk. I also aimed at comparing this paradigm with the two other important paradigms of development and modernization; namely, the Capitalist and the Marxist. Secondly, at the time when this book was published the world was still deeply experiencing the conflict between the Capitalist and Marxist paradigms of modernization. The paradigm of modernization of the Atatürk Revolution was a "third" way, a third paradigm, the reality of which has been recognized by quite a few scholars and leaders of the world. Moreover, the paradigm of modernization of the Atatürk Revolution and Atatürkism continue to be sources of inspiration, especially for the developing countries of the world.

The essential characteristic of the paradigm of modernization of the Atatürk Revolution is that it is "national". It is based on the accumulation of historical, economic, political, social experiences of a country. And as such it has a better chance of success than superficially imposed models, paradigms of development, of modernization which, for the most part, are not in tune with the realities of a given country.

In order to assess adequately both Atatürkism and the paradigm of modernization of the Atatürk Revolution, it is necessary to understand *devrimcilik* -a concept closely associated with the Atatürkist system of thought. *Devrimcilik* is translated into English as reformism or revolutionism. It means rapid, fundamental, and whenever necessary, radical change although it does not necessarily connote the idea of violence. Atatürkist *devrimcilik is national in character*. Moreover, Atatürkist principle of *devrimcilik* gives both the "paradigm" of modernization and the Atatürkist system of thought a chance to grow and to be abreast with the times, without abandoning their basic commitments and values.

In view of the ongoing intense debate in Turkey regarding globalization, membership in the European Union, and the relationship between democracy and republicanism, I thought it to be necessary to add a new section to the Book on the afore-mentioned questions. Moreover, I thought that all these questions should also be analyzed from the perspective of the Atatürk paradigm of modernization and the Atatürkist system of thought . All this necessitated the writing of a new Chapter; namely, Chapter VIII, and the rewriting of Chapters VI and VII, and also the addition of some new pages, which as the author I wrote directly in English. As the author I also translated into English most of the speeches and statements of Atatürk as well as those documents of the Atatürk Revolution which are included in the book.

I owe special thanks to Mr. Ersin Özince, the CEO of the Türkiye İş Bankası, who suggested that this book should be translated into English.

I hope that this book shall help the foreign reader to understand the underlying reasons for the Turkish people's commitment both to Atatürkism and the paradigm of modernization of the Atatürk Revolution.

SUNA KİLİ
January 25, 2003

I

INTRODUCTION

1. Characteristics of the Era

One of the leading characteristics of the twentieth century has been the worldwide spread of the aspiration for national independence.

Most of the nearly 200 countries in the world today did not exist at the beginning of the twentieth century. In fact, there were no more than fifty, spread out over five continents. Most of the growth in the number of countries in the interim has come through the collapse of colonialism. The effect of this is most glaring in Africa and Asia, where nearly every country there was once a colony of a Western power and has since acquired its independence due to national struggle. And even while never formally colonized, the Ottoman Empire had been subject to the expansionistic and imperialistic designs of the powerful Western states, to which it eventually succumbed. When this happened, the Empire inevitably disintegrated, leaving its former territories in the Middle East, the Arab peninsula, and North Africa to have to grapple with the dynamics of their own "independence." However, most of them, at least initially, were unable to attain complete independence. Possessing an abundance of natural resources, with the collapse of the Ottoman Empire,these countries were confronted with yet another kind of subjugation: they were transformed into economic satellites of the Western powers who were intent on enhancing their own politico-economic positions.

This subjugation gave rise to conditions that would form the nucleus for yet another struggle. During the course of colonialism, inhabitants of subjugated countries had undergone a kind of "depersonalization" at the hands of their oppressors. Similarly, they had to face the consequences of the underdevelopment colonialism had imposed on their territories. Thus, there grew an increasing desire for statehood. However, not only did they want independence, they also wanted to acquire [national] "identities" of their own. Both of these desires paralleled a sense of wanting to "catch up" with the very states that had restricted their freedom and had contributed to their current status. Therefore, once the conditions were ripe, this colonial legacy produced a pervasive aspiration for statehood among the various countries and peoples of the world. Fueled by an ever-increasing nationalistic fervor that had been inspired (even if latently) by the historical experience of the French Revolution, it came to engulf the entire colonial world.

There was still another source of inspiration for the rapid expansion of independence movements in the 20th century. This was the anti-imperialist Turkish National Struggle carried out in the aftermath of World War I against the Western powers, and the ensuing Atatürk Revolution. An analogy can be drawn between it and the French Revolution. The latter had given rise to a nationalism that was to spread throughout the European continent and stretch to the Balkans. The desire for independence was awakened within the Balkan nations that existed under the cloak of Ottoman imperial power. Similarly, the Turkish War of Independence and Atatürk's subsequent victory over colonialism spawned the tide of succeeding independence movements in the 20th century.

Starting out as an aspiration to break free from foreign domination and blossoming into a full-blown passion, the desire for independence in colonized societies grew to be the definitive feature of the era. States would come to be constituted within delineated boundaries and identified by their own flags. These new states came to join the ranks of other states within international organizations of independent states and acquired the right to vote within these bodies. But it soon became apparent that clearly marked boundaries and the unfurling of a nationally recognized flag were not going to be sufficient for independence. The truth was that regardless of the paradigm or system adopted for the creation of a state, the powerful states in the world would continue to exercise some form of control. This control manifested itself through an international system fostering the maintenance of dominant-subordinate relations between strong and weak states, leading to a redefinition of what it meant to be independent. In the greater sense of the term, independence meant "complete independence." In order to be fully free - to be able to live in a wholly free manner - it would be necessary to become "modern." Regardless of the term used to define them - "backward," "undeveloped," "under-developed" – the objectives of poor countries struggling to overcome their poverty have gone beyond simply "being independent" to one of "being modern."

a) The Road to Independence,
Modernization and Development

While an important prerequisite to complete independence is *political* independence, independence needs to be addressed in terms of the broader sense of *complete* independence.

Historically, colonialism has had functional and utilitarian components. Altering the terms of a colonial regime once it had been established was no simple task. Colonial powers held colonies because they were important factors contributing to their economic and political power: Given that a colonial power came to a country in search of natural resources, both above and below the ground, it is only natural that, once finding them, it would establish itself there. It would then proceed to avail itself of those resources and, at the same time, come to make use of domestic labor power, either through employment or slavery. It was simply in its interest to do so. Aiming at transferring all local resources to the home country, the colonial power thereby enriches itself, enabling it to develop its own economy to the greatest extent possible. Throughout the course of world politics, it has been the aim of a colonial power to grow and enhance its position within the global realm of dominant states. Thus, they were not to be easily convinced to alter the terms of such a relationship, even if their colonies requested it.

Colonial policies had a number of unexpected consequences: the dynamics of colonial administration, the ports, roads, electricity, means of communication, and the establishment of small-scale industries necessary for economic functioning gave rise among the local populace to new demands and aspirations, which must be included among the factors that contributed to the rise of independence movements. The colonial powers were confronted by an inevitable dilemma created by this phenomenon. In order to manage the extraction of natural resources, they needed to set up a colonial order. But in trying to maintain that order, the changes they introduced became a source of new needs - at least among the masses. At the same time, these conditions also created among the local elites a sense that they wanted to become "liberated," freed from the grip the colonial regime had imposed upon them. They wanted to nationalize resources and land, and to drive out the colonialists. One of the conditioning factors for this was the education that local elites received. Naturally, the colonial power would want to build local support, which they were able to do by establishing somewhat mutually advantageous relationships with certain families and powerful individuals. Education was one way in which this was effected. By providing the opportunity for the children of these families and individuals to be educated in schools run by the colonial powers, bonds could be forged between the elites and the foreign powers. Through the inculcation of Western values, this education had the effect of creating a generation of intellectuals who were "admirers of the West" and who were disposed to Western culture, its political institutions and traditions. Furthermore, it made possible the formation of local administrative personnel ready to put these institutions and forms of political administration into effect in their own country. In nearly all colonized societies, the same phenomenon repeated itself: the core of political opposition to colonial rule was made up of local elites who had received their education in the schools of the colonial powers, and it was they who came to exercise political power once independence was achieved.

Regardless of particular set of politico-economic variables characterizing individual countries, the first step toward emancipation was the struggle for political independence. This was the case not only in colonized societies that were once autonomous and had their own statehood tradition, but also in societies that were once tribal and had no such history. However, the key to the successful transition to *complete* independence and modernization made possible initially by *political* independence entails the political, social, cultural, and economic transformation of the entire society. Mustafa Kemal, leader of the Turkish National Struggle, offered a definition of this notion of "complete independence" in October 1919:

What is meant by complete independence is complete independence and complete freedom in all areas – political, financial, economic, legal, military and cultural. The absence of independence in anyone of these areas means that the nation and country are lacking independence in its true sense.[1]

A colonial society can achieve *de facto* political independence. It may even have its own flag and other accoutrements of statehood. But it is impossible to speak of an independent state if the mines, roads, ports, industries and means of communication within the boundaries of that state are still controlled by the former colonial power; if foreign soldiers and military forces continue to protect the interests of that power; if foreigners are still given special treatment in courts of law; if foreigners guiity of crimes are not taken to court; if the schools in the country conduct education in the language of the colonial power; or if these schools maintain the traditions and culture of the colonial period.

This is actually an accurate litmus test against which it can be determined whether in fact a society has attained independence on the political front. The challenges, both domestic and international, that these societies encounter in their struggle to transform political independence into complete independence are greater and more difficult than those faced during the period of struggle for independence.

For the most part, domestic challenges stem from the traditional structure of society. Predominantly rural, with agriculture and animal husbandry carried out under primitive conditions, the only urban dwellers are those who run the companies belonging to the colonial state, their employees and those who provide services to them. The only businesses run by locals are the ones in which foreigners take no interest. There is also a small group of "elites" - individuals and families that benefit from collaboration with the colonial power. In terms of infrastructure, the communication and transportation networks are skewed toward specific regions of material interest to the colonial power, thus not being set up according to the economic and social needs of the local population. With respect to the provision of state services, it is the needs of the colonial power and not those of the country and society as a whole that are taken into consideration. They are made available in light of what will ensure benefits to the colonizer at the least cost. In all regards, poverty, primitive living conditions, illiteracy and lack of schooling are the basic characteristics of underdeveloped societies. Disease is rampant; health services are limited. A large gap exists in society between the local populace and the narrowly based intelligentsia. Because the latter lead lives, for the most part, intimately intertwined with foreigners, they bear the wrath of the local population who live in poverty. While both belong to the same country and are members of the same society, the gulf existing between them is one of alienation. The great injustices in the distribution of land and income have created domestic strife and enmity. Moreover, once the colonial power has departed, a vacuum is created with respect to jobs and services requiring skill and expertise, which is difficult to fill. The main reason for this is that the training and creation of cadres that would be able to do so had been intentionally obstructed by the former colonial power. The people, predominantly the large numbers living in rural areas, have no interest whatsoever in the administration of the state. This vast segment of society, fettered by religious and magical beliefs, is at the beck and call of tribal chiefs, religious nobles, performers of witchcraft and those who own the land. Rather than bear the brunt of their animosity and risk death, the poor prefer to do with what they have.

On a number of fronts, the resources available to the country and state are extremely circumscribed. Not only is there disunity among the various segments of society, division and conflict is rampant. This is aggravated even more from abroad in the post-colonial period. Moreover, in taking the steps necessary to achieve independence, new governments face opposition from elements in society that are negatively affected by those measures.

Therefore, among the greatest problems facing societies that have wrenched themselves from the grip of colonialism and occupation are "unity," "authority," and "equality."

Without first assuring unity, without establishing authority, and without making efforts to ensure equality, it is impossible to protect newly independent societies from convolutions, internal contradictions and conflict. This is why the issue of modernization is so important to them.

Researchers from various disciplines tend to approach the study of modernization from different perspectives. Naturally, they all propose that modernization is the solution to the problems addressed in their fields. But this assumption is flawed. Failing to understand that modernization cannot be addressed within the limited framework of particular disciplines, but rather, that it requires a more holistic approach, the proposals they make on the basis of their research have limited value.

An equally serious inaccurate assumption made by researchers, most of whom come from developed societies, is that they can apply knowledge they have regarding the conditions of their own societies and peoples to other societies that have rather different structures. Their reductionism, however, quite naturally results in reaching erroneous conclusions.

Another mistake commonly made is to put all under developed and backward countries into the same category and then trying to extrapolate, compare and contrast what are essentially rather unique constellations of characteristics. For example, Pakistan or Bangladesh is compared with Turkey, Iran with Nigeria, or Indonesia with Ghana from the point of their being "underdeveloped." This error is compounded by, once having placed them into the category of underdevelopment, focusing on a single issue such as religion. What results is a distortion in analysis and understanding. Failing to draw the appropriate conceptual boundaries with respect to various factors, sound scientific research is thus undermined.

There is yet another misconception, actually related to the second, which has to do with the misapplication of paradigms. What is of particular concern here is the attempt to apply in the short term, development paradigms that actually took centuries to unfold in rather different historical contexts. Such paradigms are viewed as unassailable prototypes that, provided that they are applied appropriately, will breed success. Thus, when the inevitable incoherence, lack of continuity, indecisiveness, and regression ensue in the countries that are attempting to do so, it is the countries rather than the paradigms that are held accountable.

However, recognition of these fallacies has given rise to more consistent, more scientific approaches to the study of the phenomenon of underdevelopment. Similarly, investigation and resolution of problems associated with modernization have begun to emerge.

Modernization, or "being modern," for a state, nation or a person is must be viewed as a holistic concept. It is nearly impossible to deal with the problems of modernization by overly concentrating on a narrow aspect of the problem. To emphasize particular dimensions such as the political, economic, organizational, institutional, ethical, or educational, to the exclusion of others, unavoidably leads to failure. Solutions are not easily come by and problems are made even more intractable the further the holistic nature of the phenomenon is disregarded. Of course, there is no practical way to simultaneously address the problems inherent to modernization. The most rational approach is to devise a plan whereby the extant social conditions of a country are evaluated, with solutions arrived at through a prioritization of needs. In this way, the best interests of the nation and society will be served. Given that each underdeveloped country has its own unique condition, a similarly unique modernization paradigm can be proposed and implemented.

Modernization does not simply entail the breaking down of barriers to development in the areas of politics, economics, culture, religion, sects, ethnic structure, government, participation in government, law and customs. Mere escape from forms of dependency does not guarantee modernization, either. All the same, it cannot be denied that modernization brings an important degree of personal freedom.

Just as modernization does not result from the mere adoption of Western politico-institutional models, the laws that make those institutions function do nothing to contribute to modernization if other factors are missing. Even establishing replicas of Western-style parliaments and electoral systems will be relatively ineffective in achieving the objectives of modernization in the absence of more fundamental changes.

Contrary to general notions, modernization is also more than just the formation of an industrial society in which industrialization is achieved through the use of the latest technologies, inventions and techniques. Merely enhancing the material resources available to the state, society or particular people within it will have little effect if the more fundamental dynamics of modernization are not set in motion.

In the final analysis, modernization is more than window dressing; it aims at a much more rudimentary level - that of the emancipation of man in all areas of life. In a modernized society, the individual will be able to hold his head up honorably and confidently conduct his relations with other members of society, as well as the state. This behavior is the expression of his system of beliefs and values, which is distinct from that of traditional society. He uses reason and science - as reflected in scientific and laïc thought - as a guide in conducting worldly affairs. Quintessentially, modernization is the construction of a social order that will respond positively not only to man's material needs but to his spiritual ones as well.

If the term "modern" in the expression "being modern" only meant having reached the same level of advancement in all areas as that attained by the most developed countries and being like them, entirely different problems would arise in the course of discussing and seeking answers to the *problematique*. Indeed, upon examining the societies of such former colonial powers in the West as the United States, Great Britain, France or Germany, or a Scandinavian country such as Norway, or perhaps Japan of the Far East, it is clear that from the point of view of "freedom" and "what is desirable," there remain quite a few unresolved problems, deficiencies and obstacles to be overcome. And what's more, the new difficulties created by that development and "progress" have made man, to some extent, even more alienated from himself. They have created in man a certain "discontent" - this, in spite of ever-growing material wealth.

Thus, characterizing modernization in terms of the "emancipation of mankind" and the "enhancement of his welfare," serves to underscore the ultimate reality intrinsic to the phenomenon. Short of being utopian, is it unrealistic to anticipate a day when man will finally attain this kind of freedom? Despite the controversy over the experience, modernization has been marked by an unending pursuit of the good, the developed, and the better. Even if bringing these ideas to fruition is difficult, to the extent to which they are seen as aspirations that are common to all societies in the world, they constitute a collection of shared symbols that will ultimately benefit mankind.

England is usually cited as the first society to have become modernized. But it did so without having patterned itself after a pre-existing "archetype." On the contrary, it modernized as a consequence of internal and external events that were peculiar to its own society and country. Today there no longer exists a single paradigm of development. It is possible to speak of many different models, including ones used by the former Soviet Russia, China and Japan. Despite what they have in common, the differences among them are obvious.[2]

b) The Capitalist Development Paradigm

Ethnic and tribal groups within former colonies or Empires that have ceased to exist have a difficult decision to make. While having fought for and acquired political independence, they still face the daunting process of nation-building. This requires them to choose an appropriate paradigm to serve as the basis for guiding the change that their societies must undergo. But just how is this to be done? What paradigm will be chosen? How will political, social and economic development be ensured? The easiest path to take in making this choice is to take an already existing paradigm, one currently used by one of the developed countries, and attempt to implement it as is or modify it so as to suit the distinct conditions of the societies intent on using- it. Since development is one of their most important goals, this manner of choosing a development paradigm may seem appropriate at first. Nevertheless, rather than producing benefits, it is the first step leading to a blind ally.

Historically, for newly independent societies looking for a paradigm of development, there have been basically two to choose from: the capitalist model of developed Western societies and the Marxist (socialist) one.

The Western capitalist system is based on the principle of the "free market and price mechanism." In this system, the state does not interfere with economic initiative; it takes no part in price formation. The state assumes no entrepreneurial role in the either the economy or in industrial management. Decisions concerning the production are made independently of the state. It has no role in determining what is to be produced, how much is produced or by whom. The form assumed by the relations between capital and labor is beyond the purview of the state. Nor is how the distribution of income is to come of any concern. The outcomes in all these areas are determined by the "free market and price mechanism," which is based on "free competition," devoid of state interference. Equilibrium within this order is based on what is called "supply and demand" - the balance between goods offered for sale and goods consumers want to buy. Individual "property rights" is a prerequisite of the capitalist system. Under no condition can these rights be rescinded.

However, it is important to bear in mind that the capitalist system has not remained in this pristine condition. Over time, it has met with changes in light of new circumstances. The Industrial Revolution and the continual exploitation of labor; the elimination of small-scale industry and handicrafts by the Industrial Revolution and mechanization; the growth of unemployment; the domination of the economy by companies in various areas of production through the formation of trusts, cartels and monopolies; economic depressions; the oppression of people under the weight of all this; and finally, within this milieu, the emergence of socially conscious, more humanistic theories, had the effect of necessitating state intervention as part of the paradigm. The organization of labor through the formation of unions and the legalization of the right to strike and conduct collective bargaining that resulted; the creation of a more socially favorable income distribution through the use of various forms of taxation by the state; its assumption of management responsibilities in the area of industry; the enactment of statutes prohibiting the formation of monopolies; the social consciousness of at least certain political parties - whether in the determination of prices and wages, the provision of services or in income distribution – all had, in the end, the effect of transforming the concept of the state from one of "spectator state" to one of "welfare state." Nevertheless, this development took place over a lengthy period in some countries, at the end of an intense struggle conducted by the working class - one fraught with difficulties, prolonged conflict and bloody clashes. This new conception of the state emerged in light of an awakening class consciousness and was in part developed to counter the theory of revolutionary socialism espoused by Karl Marx and Frederick Engels, which had called attention to the shortcomings of the capitalist system. In other words, it arose to prevent what this theory had supposed to be the "inevitable shortcoming" or "inevitable outcome" of that system. According to Marxist theory, it was the very structure of the capitalist system that lent itself to such inadequacies and produced such adverse consequences. The contradictions resulting from practices inherent in the system would engender pervasive crises, the consequence of which would be the formation of a dictatorship of the working class through revolution. The end result would be the destruction of the capitalist system.

Today, even while the Western development paradigm allows for at least partial state intervention in the economy, such intervention is contingent upon the investment practices of large corporations, direction by monetary institutions and the implementation of decisions made by them. Moreover, the multinational corporations, operating beyond national borders, have spread to nearly all countries - conducting such activities as making industrial investments, exploiting natural resources both above and below ground, and marketing goods. Developed Western countries have witnessed a dramatic increase in capitalist accumulation, the invention of new techniques of production, and in the number of specialists required to employ these techniques. Every year, a sum greater than that of the budgets of most developing countries is spent on research and the development of new techniques and inventions. The "assistance" provided to countries attempting to develop, such as the establishment of investment regimes, only serves to hinder the formation of free decision-making in those countries, thus making them even more dependent on the existing power structure of the Western capitalist system.

Something else that must be taken into consideration is the lengthy period of time it took for Western capitalist societies to reach their stage of development. Moreover, the contributions of the past colonialization of what are today underdeveloped countries to the development of the West should not be disregarded.

In addition to its economic component, however, the Western paradigm of development has a political one, which includes political organization and system. The role of political parties in the development the West has been great. They are themselves the result of enormous political transformations that Western countries have undergone. Political parties emerge within the context of political, cultural, social and economic changes peculiar to each society. In large part because of the factors behind their emergence, they also shape and direct these changes. To the extent that these institutions serve to give direction to societies, alter their social structure, and in the meantime, function to enlighten the masses, political parties have been the driving forces behind political socialization. Because political parties in the West have appeared as the result of socio-economic development and transformation, they have assumed efficacious roles in the development of Western societies. In this regard, there is a direct link between political parties and Western political development. The Western model of development is based on nation-building, which is the inauguration of modernization. An important point that should not be overlooked in examining Western development and modernization is that they occurred in consecutive stages, with one stage reaching completion before another would begin. The execution in contemporary developing countries of a gradual form of development that occurs in successive stages is impossible. Present-day societies desiring development are obliged to squeeze into a short period of time what took centuries in the West. Today there exists a vast network of means of communication that broadcasts continually worldwide. Becoming aware of the opportunities presented by the modern era, people in underdeveloped countries acquire new aspirations, new hopes and new expectations. Within such an environment, proposing to poor, "underdeveloped" countries a form of development that took the West hundreds of years to accomplish will only make things more difficult when it comes to solving issues concerning administrative-bureaucratic cadres.

Political scientists conducting research on political development and the problems associated with it have determined that such development consists of several important stages.[3] According to them, societies undergoing political change confront six important crises that they have to resolve to complete their development. From this perspective, these crises are to a great extent obligatory. These crises, the necessary stages that have to be overcome, are those involving identity, legitimacy, penetration, participation, organization-integration, and distribution.

To be able to ascertain the place and importance of each of these problems of development in the process of modernization, it is necessary to clarify the contents of each.

Identity: Members of the same society need to come to share the belief that their society forms a nation and that the country in which they live is their home. Furthermore, they need to be able, to the extent possible, to identify themselves with a common purpose and country. A person needs to have a sense of contentment as an individual of a nation - of being a citizen of that country. In a society consisting of people who have attained a consciousness of national identity, "unity" will have reached its pinnacle. Identity is in essence the psychological and social sense of shared nationhood.

Legitimacy: Everyone living in a society must accept as legitimate and coherent the constitutional order, the form of government and the political order of the state. Legitimacy is, in fact, the problem of authority and of constitutional issues in the organization and division of authorities.

Penetration: Penetration is the capacity of the government to reach into the society in order to facilitate change and mobilize resources. Penetration is intimately connected with the growth and development of a particutar economy.

Participation: The role of mass participation in the decision-making process of a society has a great influence on the extent to which decisions made for that society are acceptable, legitimate and efficacious. In this way, decision-making is no longer the monopoly of a narrowly based minority of elites and bureaucrats. It is extended to the whole of society. By allowing for the all members of society to participate in reaching decisions having import for that society, their implementation will more easily be socially accepted, thereby reducing to a minimum conflict and internal contradictions. Enfranchisement of the individual, his being transformed from subject to citizen, is the prerequisite of participatory society. Participation, in the main, involves this change in status of the individual.

Organization-Integration: In every society, there are conflicting interests and groups with which reconciliation is difficult. The need for personal efforts and individual initiatives is unquestionable. By co-

ming together and forming, for example, unions, cooperatives, associations and parties, those who share common ideas and pursuits,
and who have mutual interests can ensure that social conflicts can be
dealt with in a more coherent, conscious and routinized fashion. In
addition, they can more easily defend and obtain their rights and interests in the face of opposition by other social groups and forces. At
the same time, organizing forms a consensus among conflicting and
contradictory social interests. This saves the society from having to
deal with continual discord. Organization, then, involves the building
of political parties, the integration of interest articulation and interest
aggregation functions.

Distribution: One of the most important functions of a state is
providing the conditions for a prosperous economy and the equitable distribution of national income among individuals as the economy
grows. Perhaps one of the most important prerequisites for a member
of a society to identify with a nation, for him to consider as legitimate the political order under which he lives, and in his believing in and
trusting its state, is his receiving his just share of the social product
and the resulting income. In the final analysis, distribution is the capacity of the political system to effect mainly economic development
but is also the distribution of material security and justice.

These are the difficulties that had to be overcome in the development of the Western political system. Occurring over the long haul
and through stages, their resolution gave rise to both an increase and
complexity in the functions of state. One of the reasons for this was
simply the transformation of social requirements over time. Another,
however, had to do with the differentiation resulting from the changing needs of industrial society. It was also consequence of the ongoing structural and functional needs of a society undergoing development . All of these contributed to the increasing complexity of society and state - a complexity that increasingly necessitated the development of areas of specialization.

The Western paradigm of development proposes an identification
of nation with society within a pluralist, liberal parliamentary order;
a form of government that is strong and efficacious and enthusiasti-
cally accepted by citizens; a decision-making mechanism carried out

through the participation of the whole of society; the formation of a balanced functioning of the political system through the organizing of society; and the assumption of responsibility in division and sharing of state income and services. These are to take place within a capitalist economic structure.

What needs to be emphasized, however, is that the countries of the West became modern countries only after a protracted fashioning of their paradigm of development, complemented by the benefits obtained through colonialism. It is this paradigm, however, that they are currently proposing to countries aspiring and struggling to achieve development. It needs to be pointed out that endemic to these countries are bottlenecks and contradictions stemming from their economic, political, social, and cultural structures. Applying this model in its entirety and across the board is impossible. In fact, the on-going conflict between blacks and whites in the United State, the Quebecois and Flemish problem in Canada and Belgium, respectively, demonstrate that despite their being developed, a consciousness of national identity has still to be acquired by the whole of society. Upon attaining emancipation from colonial rule, countries failed to consider race, culture or tribal distinctions in determining national borders- and this in societies that had not even begun nation-building. Therefore, it can be said that most important sources of the frequently seen conflicts in Africa, for example, have been tribal and ethnic distinctions.

The creation of a strong and effective government will remain impossible unless nation-building is completed, legitimacy of the political order is adopted by the entire society, and national unity is established.

Therefore, it is inappropriate to apply the Western paradigm to societies where cultural, religious, social and tribal distinctions remain, which have not undergone nation-building, and where educational problems and economic and social bottlenecks have not been resolved. In trying to create a system based on pluralist political parties, the resulting political parties that are rooted in distinctions within society will make it even more difficult for a newly independent state to deal with the first and most important matter, which is unity. This will undoubtedly only serve to fuel the division and renting of society.

The economic elements of the Western development paradigm are the product of, and function to meet, the requirements of the capitalist system. The driving impetus of this system is the accumulation of big capital and superior technology, together with the existence of a strong private entrepreneurial sector. To apply the same capitalist model of development to a newly independent country, where most of the existing economic units are either owned or controlled by foreigners, will not have the same effect. Not only will it intensify exploitation under the aegis of independence, but it will also enable foreign capital to continue its production in more profitable sectors, resulting in the country simply becoming a market for foreign capital.

A natural consequence of this is the impoverishment and underdevelopment of the society. It will continue to be exploited. The aspirations hoped to be met, and the problems expected to be solved, through independence will intensify. This will have the effect of completely obstructing complete independence and will not allow for development or modernization.

c) The Marxist Development Paradigm

According to the theory developed by Karl Marx, societies go through different stages in their evolution. Sequentially, these are primitive (communal) communism, slavery, feudal and capitalist. These stages determine the social and political institutions of societies, their currents of thought, organizational forms, and mode and means of production. The transformation of the mode and techniques of production, enable new forces, which clash with the old, to appear. The resolution of this conflict produces new organizations and new formations; in short, a new superstructure. The value of a good produced is determined by the cost of the labor used to produce it. This numerical equivalent of this labor forms the market exchange value of the good produced. In this theory, despite the value of a good being determined in this fashion, because capitalists strive to keep their rates of profit high, they pay wages at the lowest rate possible - just to maintain their worker's physical survival. By investing even more in pursuit of greater earnings, they continue to exploit the worker. This development within capitalism will create internal contradictions, which will give rise to increasing impoverishment of the working class. With expanding destitution, capital will accumulate in the hands of the few. The army of the unemployed appears, followed by great economic crises. Taking advantage of these crises, and having nothing to lose but their lives, the working class wages a bloody revolution. It overthrows the capitalist class and brings capitalism to its end. The final step is the establishment of a working class socialist rule. A "dictatorship of the proletariat" is set up in place of the capitalist state that has been destroyed. Under the dictatorship of the proletariat, after a temporary socialist period, society reaches its final stage - that of communism. At this stage, the state comes to an end and society is no longer class based. Everyone contributes to production according to his skills and talents and receives his share based on need. According to the theory, there is no "property right." The means of production are completely public and collectively owned.

The theorist of the system, as well as all those who followed him, expected this transformation to occur in Western capitalist countries and within advanced industrial societies, but what they had anticipated did not transpire. The first revolution - its first actual practical application - occurred in Russia. In the aftermath of World War II, the Soviets set up "Peoples' Republics" in the Eastern European countries occupied by the Russian army. This was done under conditions that were completely contrary to theory. The most important Socialist Peoples' Republic to be established was that of the agrarian-based Chinese example. In the course of their struggle for independence, some Southeast Asian and African countries set up new socialist dictatorships, and "democratic" republics. They were thus symbolic of their identification with the socialist opposition to capitalism and its promulgation. The socialist system of Fidel Castro's Cuba on the American continent is one such example of this phenomenon.

What became obvious from this phenomenon was that the "dictatorship of the proletariat" that was to be brought about through bloody revolution of the working class in a capitalist society did not occur. Rather, it was under completely different circumstances that these socialist regimes were established. Not only that – the socialist paradigm became as diverse as there were "socialist" regimes.

The most powerful examples of the Socialist system based upon the Marxist development paradigm within all this diversity are the (former) Union of Soviet Socialist Republics and the present-day Chinese Peoples' Republic - notwithstanding the fact that the latter has been increasingly opening up to the outside and has begun adopting some aspects of the capitalist system.

Intrinsic to the system and seen in the examples provided, all rights and freedoms are restricted under such regimes. Personal freedoms are not granted. Opportunities for independent political, professional and similar types of organizations are not provided. Consent is given to the establishment of a single political party. Whether officially "communist" or functioning under another name, it serves as the "official" political institution. Membership in this party is not open to everyone but a high voter turnout and the casting of votes for the candidates picked by the party is mandatory. The army, party and bureaucracy are integrated into one unified whole. The espousing, writing or propagation of ideas other than those determined by the state, party or party oligarchy as official ideology is prohibited. The theory demands the hegemony of the working class but in practice, the working class and workers generally are not permitted to step outside the bounds of decisions made by the higher echelons of the party. Decisions cannot be debated publicly. Only a very select group of members can participate in the decision-making process. There is intense internal oppression and a powerful police force operating under the supervision of the party oligarchy.

The economy and industry are completely under state control. Land is nationalized and collectives are established on the basis of collective labor management. The system pushes aside personal interests and rights and places public and social interests first. Development is to be carried out through a central plan regime operating through decrees. The share of what is produced, either in the form of an exchange for labor or wages determined by general planning, is usually rather low. Education is developed in line with the official ideology determined by the party.

The political systems of the "Socialist Peoples' Republics" created in such countries as Poland, Czechoslovakia, Hungary, Romania and Bulgaria in the aftermath of World War II, as a consequence of the occupation and compulsion by the Soviet army, were all rather similar. Another important deadlock for these countries was the bloody crushing by the Soviets of freedom movements that appeared from time to time in Poland, Czechoslovakia and Hungary - or at the very least, the prospect of such a possibility was always lurking around the corner. National sovereignty in these countries was transformed into the sovereignty of Soviet Russia. The army-backed state-party-army triumvirate is what maintained unity and authority. Society could in no way escape from the realities of this system. Its legitimacy was forced upon it as a fait accompli.

Because of its powerful support for national liberation movements, the Marxist development paradigm had a particular appeal to societies having recently achieved political independence from their colonial status. However, given that the social, economic, cultural and ethnic structures of these societies are at odds with those envisioned by the paradigm, its application in them is next to impossible. Nearly all of these countries, most of which also consist of ethnic groups, are without strong armies, state traditions or bureaucracies. Authority capable of creating unity has not been established. This opens the door to the frequently seen military interventions, spawned by domestic upheavals and supported and encouraged by the West, which are not development or modernization oriented in the slightest. This impasse, arrived at when societies attempted to apply the Marxist development paradigm, is no different than that reached by application of the Western capitalist paradigm. On the other hand, toward the end of the 1980s, the dissolution of the Soviet Union began, with its final dispersal occurring in 1991. The collapse of the Soviet Union brought about the establishment of a variety of states on territories once belonging to it, as well as the independence of Eastern European countries that had lived under Soviet occupation and repression. At this moment in time, Russia and all these other countries are, to varying degrees, undergoing the pangs of making the transition to democracy and the capitalist system.

d) Common Characteristics of Developed Countries

Developed countries share characteristics that bring them into greater confluence with one another - or, perhaps more accurately make them resemble one another. By considering this seemingly contradictory thesis from another perspective, these common characteristics will come to light. The most important variable giving rise to distinctions between countries is not *form* of government but rather *degree* of government.[4] Disparities between developed countries resulting from differences in form of government are much less than those between developed and underdeveloped countries. Among the most important of these differences are the extent to which unity is guaranteed within national borders; the degree to which social integration carried out within the framework of national objectives; the scope of established authority; and the capacity of the existing state and government to make decisions and carry them out. Forms of government may be different but in spite of these differences, if general controversy in society as to the legitimacy of a particular form of government is absent; if an effective bureaucracy has been established; if consensus between individuals with respect to principles and objectives has been reached; if general social acceptance and concurrence vis-à-vis those governing society with respect to how this is being done exists, these characteristics common to those societies cannot be - or at least should not be - denied.

It is possible to see these characteristics both in the developed capitalist countries of the West and in the formerly Marxist governments of Eastern Europe, despite the differences in form of government.

The presence of these common characteristics in both groups of countries in spite of their different forms of government is derived from the effectiveness of their political systems.

Those working within the state bureaucracy are competent specialists who are well positioned to administer the provision of services. The functional distinction between job and office makes possible the uninterrupted provision of an extensive range of services in all its complexity to both state and society even when there are changes in government.

In addition to all of the aforementioned characteristics, irrespective of their political systems, developed countries have a high rate of literacy. National income is above the global norm. They have advanced and administratively efficient industrial, transport and communications systems and facilities. Moreover, they have a sufficient number of good quality healthcare facilities, specialists and technocrats to meet the needs of society. The vast majority of their population has moved from rural areas to the cities. Developed countries have also experienced a rapid rate of urbanization. Having made the shift to high-tech farming, agriculture has begun to be more productive.

Despite differences in forms of government in these systems, their shared characteristics have come to form the criteria of development.

e) Common Characteristics and Dilemmas of Developing Countries

Just as development in developed countries evolves around a set of common characteristics, irrespective of form of government, so does underdevelopment in developing countries. The fact is, however, that what distinguishes each society and country from one another are variables ranging from historical, cultural, religious, political and social conditions to geographical and environmental, and from foreign relations to the structure of its economy. Nevertheless, despite such variations in conditions, characteristics and degree of underdevelopment, it is possible to determine mutual attributes as well as the impediments created by them.

The traits shared by underdeveloped countries are diametrically opposed to those shared by developed ones.

In addition to the structurally related problems experienced by newly emancipated countries as they struggle with nation-building, political socialization, the development of the economy and industrialization - in other words, its "growing pains," there are the bottlenecks associated with efforts to modernize.

These bottlenecks appear irrespective of the paradigm used - Western capitalist or single-party Marxist.

Regardless of the religious, ethnic, social and economic divisions in societies, during times of struggle for national independence, nearly everyone in society unites behind the leader of the struggle as well as those coalesced around him. Depending on the nature of the conjuncture and the leader's personality, leadership may turn into charisma. But after independence, that charisma is not going to be sufficient in the long term to satisfy societies. During struggles for independence, societies are indoctrinated under the banners of future-oriented ideals and promises of gratification and a more comfortable life, which serve to mobilize them. Upon the awakening of aspirations, the hope and expectations of society are rallied behind the leader. These hopes and expectations revolve around problems having political, economic and social dimensions that are not easily solved. Prior to independence, it is the leader and his companions who are impatient; afterwards, it is the society and the people. Society wants reform, it wants jobs. It wants bread. It wants freedom. On the other hand, society and country have suffered exploitation for ages; they have been left impoverished. They have been deprived of the very possibilities for the success whose short-term achievement had been promised prior to independence.

Many demarcations exist between the various strata of society. These include, economic, ethnic, cultural, religious differentiation. In the post-independence period, these distinctions may come to exert a centrifugal force on social unity.

Under the conditions existing in such underdeveloped countries, a comprehensive application of the Western paradigm is very difficult. This is particularly so from the point of view of its human, economic, cultural and political makeup since it entails the legitimatization of political parties, unions, and associations as functional elements. Even attempting to do so is enough to produce new conflicts, disjunctions, opposition to change and reactionary forces.

The fundamental difficulty encountered by newly independent countries is modernization. The task of modernization is finding solutions to the aforementioned problems. However, in attempting to overcome them within a very short period of time, only creates new problems - regardless of which development paradigm is used. The ongoing influence of developed countries on, and their superiority over, underdeveloped ones stems from the fact that in spite of political independence, the latter are still economically dependent on the former.

The real root of the political instability, chaos, the inability to form an effective government, and the frequently seen military interventions is the desire for emancipation from the restrictions imposed by underdevelopment.

A society that has adopted a Western-type development paradigm naturally places importance on the political institutions it advocates. For example, it will want to allow for the formation of political parties based on different currents of thought. In this way, those ideologies and/or currents of thought can be represented through parliamentary participation. Furthermore, it will want basic rights and freedoms to be legally guaranteed. Nonetheless, because civic consciousness has not reached the whole of society, traditional elements continue to exercise influence in society, the level of education is very low, and political socialization has not been achieved, the formation of political parties and the right of everyone of a minimum age to vote - essential elements of the system - can have consequences contrary to those expected. Social forces based on religious, sectarian, ethnic and ideological distinctions will appear with party formation. This will create even more confusion and serve to undermine the sought after social unity and integration. This rapid transformation will create a situation that is contrary to the aim of development. In other words, in an attempt to avoid such an undesirable state of affairs, the principle of political freedom, which is at the heart of the paradigm, may be compromised. An example of this includes the setting up of a single party and thus postponing the matter of the development of a pluralist political system, which will give rise to an intense debate over political freedoms and create new problems and conflicts in society. It then becomes a question of whether elections should be held or rather, should effort be concentrated on creating a laïc society that is free from traditionalism, and, subsequently, establish and develop a stable public order in which free elections can be held.

It is possible to analyze the Turkish Revolution in these terms. After the founding of the Republic, Turkey experienced two unsuccessful attempts at transition to a multiparty system. The first party of the era was the Republican People's Party, which supported the leader of the radical reform movement, Mustafa Kemal. The establishment of the "Progressive Republican Party" and the "Free Republican Party" followed in 1924 and 1930, respectively. Both of these parties were closed as a result of the counter-revolutionary forces that they unleashed. These two cases make much clearer the problem confronted by Turkey and the means it had to choose from to deal with it. The question was whether it was wise to permit the expression of all ideas and the subsequent assumption of power by parties representing them or whether this would have the result of producing a counter-revolution a few short years down the line.

A British political scientist has raised the question as to what would have happened "if the Turks had switched to a multiparty regime in 1930, when the setting was inappropriate." He responds by saying "only the insane would attempt what had already been tried."[5]

The situation in societies that adopted the Marxist development paradigm was no different. This was the case in European countries like Poland, Czechoslovakia, Hungary, Romania and East Germany, which were occupied by the armies of the Union of Soviet Socialist Republics and forced to adopt Marxist systems. It also included both large and small states with Marxist regimes, such as the People's Republic of China and Cuba, respectively. The price paid by these nations and the individuals within them for development was great. As for the countries forced into adopting a Marxist system after occupation, despite their appearance of independence after World War II, they remained under the control and subjugation of the Soviet armies, which had remained on their soil. Decisions were not made according to the interest of the nation or national will but rather according to that of the Soviet-directed Marxist system. From time to time, the bloody repression of dissent and demands for freedom in Poland, Hungary and Czechoslovakia by the Soviet armies is striking evidence of this. The fundamental natural of the Marxist system is that it rejects the teleologically oriented notion of freedom being the ultimate goal that is achieved once socio-economic development and industrialization have occurred. Marxist theory calls for the hegemony of the working class under which the class rules by decree; no rights to other classes or segments of society are recognized. Marxist development entails the abolishment of a class-based society, to be replaced at the end of the developmental process by a communist one. Development in the communist society assumes an elimination of different ideologies and beliefs. It does not allow for the free expression of any such differences or the participation of those expressing them in government. Nevertheless, in practice -contrary to the theorized hegemony and dictatorship of the working class- a new ruling class was born. Because of their responsibilities in the party machinery, bureaucracy, army and economy, the upper level administrative personnel acquired privileges. This is clearly pointed out by one of leading theorists of the Yugoslav Marxist revolution, Milovan Djilas, who was subsequently imprisoned for his criticism of its practice there. According to Djilas, this class forms the party but as this class gets bigger and stronger, it begins to manipulate the party for its own ends, which results in the weakening of the party. This is the inevitable fate of every communist party in power. Parties are generally institutions consisting of intellectually and economically empowered classes and segments of society. It is rather odd for a political party to have formed a class. A class having such powers of control over people is unprecedented in history. After industrialization, there are two things left for this class to do. One is to increase outright tyranny and the other is to plunder.[6]

The use of tyranny, repression, oppression, and fear, by discounting and outright denying the fundamental rights and freedoms of the individual, by seeing individuals as simply cogs in the machine of development and industrialization, even if assumed that this will bring about desired results for society, requires practices that are not consistent with human nature, his existence or the concepts of individual rights and freedoms derived from man's very humanity.

This phenomenon, which has been a subject of rather heated public debate in both developed and underdeveloped countries having a Marxist system of government, is one of the most important practical problems facing Marxist systems.

In Marxist theory, there is no recognition of property rights. It conceives of a collectivist order and mode of production. This requires societies of newly independent countries that have adopted Marxist paradigm of development to abolish, both legally and practically, property rights in all their forms, regardless of the extent to which

they actually exist and how just they may be. Carrying out such policies in a country where national unity and authority has not been established gives rise to opposition to the new regime by segments of
society consisting of powerful people, families, tribes and clans. This
can generate additional difficulties for the fledging Marxist regime, as
was seen in the Allende example in Chile, where, through the support
and assistance of foreign powers, the regime can be overthrown. The
unfolding of such a set of circumstances works against the efforts of
a newly independent state at modernizing, thus contributing to its being dragged into a dependence upon the powerful Western developed
state that has come to exercise control over it. A similar situation may
result in the case of a country that wants to adopt the Marxist paradigm and seeks help and support from a powerful developed Marxist
state. As can be seen in the historical instance of Afghanistan, the country may find its very independence at risk. What these examples demonstrate is that doubt and antipathy are likely to be produced and
promoted in societies attempting to develop in the shadow of dominating powerful industrialized states, regardless of system of origin.
Because of their fear, less powerful states will try to distance themselves from the influence and control of the more powerful states. The
national interests of the two groups of states are, for the most part,
incompatible. This is particularly evident in the case of weaker states
that adopt the Marxist model of development. Historically, not only
have they been in need of assistance from powerful Marxist states but
also they have, quite naturally, posed a challenge to the majority of
developed Capitalist states. Thus, the major difficulty of less powerful, Marxist, states is overcoming the disproportionate influence of
stronger states - both Marxist and Capitalist.

2. In Pursuit of a National Development Paradigm

The need to implement a *national* model of modernization becomes clear once the results of the uncritical application of either the
Western-type or Marxist models are assessed. The social, cultural,
historical, ethnic, religious and economic structures that characterize
a particular nation create unique obstacles and difficulties that must

be overcome in especially tailored ways. Thus political elites and government officials must exercise care in choosing an appropriate model of development given the existing parameters in their nation.

It is virtually impossible today to read an academic journal in any
of the social sciences and not come across the terms "development,"
"modernization," "industrialization," or "Westernization." Generally, the meanings of these terms are so close to one another as to
overlap. Nevertheless, it must be emphasized that they have two common dimensions. The first is that poor countries wish to become wealthy by expanding their productive capacities. The second, related to
the first, is that the role and behavioral patterns available to them are
becoming increasingly differentiated and complex.[7]

Interest in the subjects of modernization and development, especially in the post-World War II era, began intensifying as new states came to emerge. The main issue was the problem of how these countries would be able to develop.

According to the American political scientist Sigmund, writing at
the beginning of the 1960s, endemic throughout the countries of Asi-
a, Africa and Latin America of that time, were crises of modernization. Thus, political independence was not their only goal. The "anti-
colonial revolutions" occurring there also had as their aim the end of
Western domination. They were simultaneously social and economic
revolutions. The driving force behind them were the Westernized elites in those countries. Struggling to create modern states and industrialized economies, they wanted to bring their countries into the modern world.[8]

Contemporary developing countries have not been exposed to the
variety of ideologies such as those that vied with one another and influenced the political life of 19th century Europe. Nevertheless, the
most prominent ideology that was to find its way into the contemporary context was that of modernizing nationalism.[9]

The fundamental goal of national leaders anywhere has been the
realization of national development, the prerequisite of which is national independence. National leaders speak of freedom but it is more in a national than in an individual sense. Freedom is sought not for
the individual but rather for the nation.[10]

Turkey is a good illustration of this phenomenon. In the early days of the Atatürk Revolution, reforms were made, bearing in mind the impact they would have on both society and the nation as a whole. Tunaya underscores the point that the Revolution gave "priority to nation rather than the individual. In this way, the circumstances that would enable the individual Turk to live and progress would also set the stage for national independence. Dealing with the human element from the point of view of democracy is only now receiving priority."[11]

However, when national leaders in developing countries speak of development, what they actually mean is *economic* development. Proponents of national movements are aware of the contrast between the pervasive poverty, disease and illiteracy in their own countries and wealth, welfare and services that exist in developed countries. For them, the most important distinction is not between communism and pluralistic democracies. Rather, it is the distinctions between rich and poor, countries with developed economies and technologies and those with underdeveloped ones. The key to eliminating these distinctions in standards of living is economic development - chiefly industrialization. Development and industrialization will create social equality, educational opportunity, and adequate conditions for the maintenance of health - in short, the formation of a modern welfare state.[12]

According to Sigmund, for a number of economic and moral considerations, developing countries intent on laying the foundations for industrialization reject the capitalist model of development in favor of the socialist. However, this should not be seen as a blind and comprehensive imitation of the Soviet paradigm. In fact, what developing countries are after is the creation of an identity distinct from either East or West. They propose to approach economic development in a different way, one that distances itself from the oversights and shortcomings of both the Communist and the Western capitalist systems. Despite their confidence in economic planning and support of centralized supervision of the economy, developing countries allow room for private initiative. The main reasons why they do not prefer Western capitalism is its continuous cutthroat competition, extreme individualism, and the insufficient importance given to human and social values. On the other hand, they are critical of the excessive communalism of communism and its hard and rigid collectivism, its repression of the individual, its materialism, and its support of rather narrowly defined interests, e.g., of one or a group of countries (the former communist block ones).[13]

Socialism in new nations has been fueled by the desire for social equality and rapid economic growth, as well as by negative attitudes toward foreigners. Even though influenced by Marxist-Leninist theory, movements have not been inclined to completely accept it. Theirs has tended to be a socialism having a national basis - one that is void of the notion of class struggle within the context of economic relations. They have espoused the ideal of the workingman. For people and societies that are not independent and do not know what it is like to live as a nation, not only becoming a nation, but one that is independent, is an extraordinary historical phenomenon. To create a nation and bring about the development of the country, the national leader must concentrate on national unity, e.g., the unity of its people, and not on the interests of any particular class.[14]

All national leaders know that a strong government is a prerequisite for modernization and development. To ensure the goals of modernization, they tend to rely on single hegemonic party rule and powerful government. The leaders of countries aiming at modernization stress that the authoritarian aspects of their administrations is temporary. In the past, Atatürk used this type of temporary, authoritarian model - one that was followed by an orderly transition to democracy.[15]

In spite of certain authoritarian elements, the single-party in these countries is democratic in structure and intent. It is a mass organization open to all citizens. In this way, it is very different from the party of elites envisioned by Lenin.

Political parties in developing countries form a driving force behind development programs. At the same time, they assume the public relations role of relaying the sentiments and demands of the people to the leadership.[16]

According to Sigmund, while national leaders are oriented toward modernization, many of them feel the need to protect elements of traditional culture and the customary values that represent them. For example, Nehru frequently referred to the "spiritual solitude" of elites.

Most of the time, elites in developing countries are confronted with both accepting and rejecting the values of traditional civilizations.[17]

The cultural "renaissance" of developing countries is to some extent a rejection of Western culture, which was formerly portrayed as a desirable paradigm. Attempts are made at strengthening national pride and self-respect, which complete the process of nation-building.[18]

Barring special circumstances, developing countries of Asia, Africa and the Middle East preferred non-alliance in foreign politics, paying careful attention to remain outside of the Eastern and Western Blocks.

It is possible to call the values and beliefs of developing countries as a whole a modernizing national ideology. This ideology is distinct from Western liberalism and Soviet collectivism. It has a funcrion: to assist in the modernization of traditional society and, in order to achieve this goal, to demonstrate that demanding self-sacrifice from the people is appropriate and correct. With respect to the contents of ideology, it avails itself of the ideas and experiments of the systems of both East and West.

In general, developing countries have accepted some aspects of the Marxist perspective and rejected others. While they acknowledge economic factors as being the most important, they do not adopt Marxist determinism. According to the nationalist perspective, political forces are sufficient for economic control and for remaining dominant over them. The abolition of the state is not sought. Furthermore, assuming that there are spiritual aspects to life, Marxist materialism is rejected. Marx's examination of "class" is found to be inadequate. There is more to history than simply the struggle between the "proletariat and the "bourgeoisie." Rural dwellers, intellectuals and soldiers are also important. Allegiance to nation, not class, is the most fundamental and vital symbol. Some nationalists in new states have even denied the existence of class distinction.

Modernizing regimes have need of an ideology to guide the formulation of policies. This is because the reforms required bringing about effective social and economic transformation must be based on the interest of the characteristics of the country and the interests of the whole nation - not just certain groups or classes. This resembles Atatürk's ideology more than it does that of Marx.[19]

For any underdeveloped country or society to be able to initiate development or modernization movement, to be able to make the transition from a traditional to a modern social structure requires its independence and liberation from colonial rule. Two other equally vital prerequisites are for political leaders to share such a goal and for "unity" and "authority" to be ensured in society so as to be able to take the first steps toward development.

The 20th century, notably the years following the Second World War, was a period during which nearly all countries acquired political independence. Regardless of size, all of these countries wanted to climb out of poverty, develop, and modernize and to live without being subservient to rich countries and subject to their control. In order to develop and modernize, what leaders of these underdeveloped countries, most of which acquired independence through a struggle for independence -very few as a result of international politics and influence- had to do, above all, despite structural differences between them, was establish a legitimate public order, "unity," and "authority." Political instability is one of the major problems confronting every country and regime, especially countries struggling with the developmental process. In order to ensure sound and unfailing development, a leadership cadre having certain essential characteristics and capabilities is essential. It must be committed to the establishment of "authority" and political stability in the pursuit of modernization and reform, in doing so, it must be efficacious and strong. In addition, it has to be able to make and implement decisions that are consistent with the means through which modernization is to be achieved. Those decisions must also be appropriate to the realities of the society in question, its structure and conditions. Finally, this leadership cadre must be able to make sound decisions that address the requirements of the society, given existing resources, which satisfy the people. Regimes of countries in which these are absent exist under the fear of continual revolutions, military interventions and domestic and foreign intervention. In order to be able to limit "authority," it first has to exist. One of the elements in the shortest supply in developing countries is authority. In less developed countries, governments are at the "mercy" of alienated intellectuals, and rioting students.[20] They either acquiesce to the demands made upon them and continue to exist - being dragged along in the process, or they are toppled.

Before a successful, sound process of modernization can be initiated and maintained, first a consistent *national* model for development must be chosen. There also needs to be a policy oriented toward change so as to put the model into practice. By making the necessary practical, social, economic and cultural reforms, the state must reach the goals sets out by the policy.

Changes in social values and behavior, as well as the development and spread of the means of communication, should be ensured by these reforms. Ties to person, family, tribe, group, religion and sect ought to be transformed into ties to nation. Society, public order and life, by becoming the focal point of authority in society, should be laïcized. Organizations having specified functions have to be set up and developed. Appointment of individuals should be made on the basis of his achievements, abilities, skills and productivity rather than on personal connections. Finally, making assignments and granting rewards, and sharing material and symbolic resources must be more equitable and just.

A system or regime may claim to be attempting to modernize. However, if a major part of its citizenry is without schools, teachers, the doctors, medicine and care necessary for health, in effect - all that is required to maintain a humane existence; if the state does not make its presence felt, it is meaningless to speak of the constitution, laws or system of that country. In such an environment, the presence or lack of classical freedoms, judicial autonomy, freedom of the press, or autonomous institutions, and issues of elections and parliaments are of concern to a very small minority and go no further than being subjects of debate among this minority. This demonstrates that the system operates in the name of, and for, this minority. Hence, the system becomes transformed into one of futility, which contributes to its collapse.

In summary, a paradigm of modernization can be successful, effective and continual only to the extent that, through its modes and application, 1) it brings a "consciousness of citizenship" to all individuals and segments of society, ranging from urban laborers to rural villagers, young and old, men and women, from student to civilian and military bureaucrats, teachers, and from businessmen and industrialists to people working in an assortment of occupational fields; 2) it ensures that "blessings" and "tribulations" are shared; and 3) it sees to it that resources are distributed in a fair and equitable manner. Such a practice and development will instill a new social sensitivity in individuals and bring the entire society into the system.

If this is not achieved, the system will collapse, or as in the case of most South American countries, and in new states in Africa acquiring independence, and in Pakistan, a succession of military interventions will ensue ... or, as in the case of Iran in 1925, a change in "dynasty" will occur. When the new "dynasty" is unsuccessful, it collapses or else, as in the case of Turkey, in place of an Empire, there emerges a new regime based on a national ideology and a determination to put it into practice.

In the aftermath of World War II, countries attaining independence and their rulers who were leading the struggle to modernize did not have many alternative development paradigms from which to choose that could be applied comprehensively to their societies. The Western type, Marxist and Japanese development models were such that they were at odds with the structures, exigencies, and conditions of these societies and would thus only contribute to even bigger problems. Apart from these paradigms, the only other model of modernization available was that of the new Turkish Republic that had been founded under the leadership of Mustafa Kemal Atatürk, it was set up in Anatolia and Thrace, the former lands of the Ottoman Empire, which had emerged defeated from World War I and had suffered occupation by the Western powers.

Mustafa Kemal, leader of the Anatolia-based National Struggle, said in 1922 - in the midst of the years of the War of Independence - that this war, undertaken by the Turkish nation - shared with "all subjugated nations" the same problem and called upon all Eastern countries to take up arms to fight for their rights and emancipation:

> Although all of our friends have expressed it before, I feel the necessity to confirm again that the struggle of Turkey today does not pertain to Turkey alone. If the present struggle of Turkey were only in her name only and for her sake it

could, perhaps, be shorter, less bloody, and could be over sooner. Turkey is showing determination and making a great effort. Because what she defends is the
cause of all oppressed nations and of the whole East, and until it is won, Turkey
is sure that all the nations of the East will march together witn her. To attain all
this, Turkey will not follow the requirements of history books, but the requirements
of history.[21]

This subject was also addressed by Mustafa Kemal in 1933 at the
10th year anniversary of the founding of the Turkish Republic, which
had been founded after the successful conclusion of a War of Independence and was in the midst of efforts to modernize. Reiterating his
call for the rights of Eastern countries, he restated his unshakable belief that they would emerge victorious from their own wars of independence, thus serving as a source of inspiration for these countries:

> As I look at the sun that will now rise from the East today, I see the break of
> day. I see from afar the awakening of all the Eastern nations. There are many
> brotherly nations that shall attain their independence and freedom. Their rebirth
> will be in the direction of progress and welfare. These nations shall be victorious
> in spite of all the hardships and obstacles, and shall reach the future awaiting
> them.
> Colonialism and imperialism shall be annihilated from the face of this earth,
> and in their place, a new era of harmony and cooperation between nations shall
> prevail, regardless of differences of color, race, and creed.
> I am telling you all this not as the President but only as an individual member
> of the Turkish nation.[22]

There is much evidence supporting the argument that this appeal
made by Atatürk was in fact a source of inspiration for the elites of
countries undertaking revolutions of their own in an attempt to break free from their colonial status. Some of these elites who looked on
in admiration at Atatürk's Revolution and the Turkish War of Independence are among those who assumed leadership roles in their own
countries' wars of independence and later came to form the cadre of
ruling elites after independence. The elites of these countries, as well
as many foreign scholars, have indicated that the paradigm of moder-

nization championed by the Atatürk Revolution was of a kind upon which the modernization efforts of other countries could be patterned. And this is a matter of great relevance even for contemporary Turkey - given all the challenges that remain to the ongoing success of the Revolution. In the presence of many different currents of thought, the implementation of a *national* model of modernization within the context of the rule of law assumes even greater importance.

Muhammed Ali Cinnah, the leader who worked toward the establishment of a national state during Pakistan's struggle for independence, raised the following question to the Moslems of India: "As long as there's an exemplary leader such as Atatürk, how can Indian Moslems continue to accept their present state of affairs?"[23]

Nehru, India's greatest leader after Ghandi, saw Atatürk as the "creator of the modern era" in the East: "Kemal Atatürk, or rather what we knew him by then - Kemal Pasha, was my hero when I was young. When I read about his great reforms, I was impressed. I had great appreciation for the general efforts undertaken by Atatürk in modernizing Turkey. His dynamic, unyielding and untiring nature had a big impact on me as a person. He is one of the creators of the modern era in the East. I continue to consider myself one of his greatest admirers."[24]

For Habib Burgiba, the leader of Tunisia's national struggle for independence, the Atatürk Revolution was a source of inspiration:

> The Battle of Sakarya and the victory that ensued, became the greatest recollection I had had during my 20 years. At that time, I thought to myself: I wonder if I couldn't mobilize my nation in such a way? Couldn't I equally instill this liberating leap forward, this unyielding passion in the same spirit?
>
> Atatürk's death demonstrated to the stunned world just what could be accomplished by a nation that had risen above servitude. This example would not be forgotten. His eternal tour de force would remain a shining example and source of inspiration to those ruling over the destinies of nations that have become sovereign.
>
> The personality of Mustafa Kemal became a gauge against which the revolts of the masses and peoples' struggles would be measured. These struggles grew after his death. They spread to the Third World that existed between the Eastern and Western blocks - releasing it from colonial repression.[25]

In addition to these national leaders who saw the Atatürk Revolution as a source of inspiration, there are Western scholars who share this view. They stress that Atatürk's paradigm of national modernization was a genuine source of inspiration for countries escaping from colonialism.

The famous British historian, Arnold J. Toynbee believed that Atatürk was "more than a national hero." Commenting on Atatürk, he said, "Atatürk was a pioneering figure. What he was able to accomplish in Turkey after 1920 came to serve as an example to other leaders who wanted to help their nations and countries."[26]

Moreover, French scholar, Maurice Duverger, considered Atatürkism[27] as a system. Indicating that it had become an exemplary paradigm - particularly after 1945, he described it as an alternative that would show the way to the countries of the Third World:

> Mustafa Kemal's achievement was carried out throughout Turkey up until the beginning of World War II. There was no one who did not applaud the effort expended to transform an old country into a modern nation. The success in question acquired the status of example after 1945. Kemalism became more than simply another page taken from the history of Turkey; it assumed a leadership role for a political system. This was because it offered a path to a third type of state that had not yet come under the influence of Moscow or Peking. For countries only partially developed, this system offered them a second alternative to Marxism.[28]

Duverger characterized the Atatürkist model of revolutionary reform as an alternative model of development. The most prominent aspect of the Atatürk paradigm of modernization is that it is national. As such, it is a paradigm of modernization that is based on the historical, cultural, social and economic conditions of a particular society. This model was a copy of neither the Western nor the Soviet Russian model. By taking the specific realities of the country and society into consideration, it used a pragmatic approach to come up with novel means to address its problems. It is not dogmatic. It sees society as a living entity —something that changes. And because of that change, new needs are continually arising. In order to meet these needs, the paradigm suggested new ways of doing things based on pragmatic considerations. What makes this system of thought revolutionary is its recognition of just this requirement of pragmatism and being open to change. Modernization is not undertaken simply because developed countries have done so. Rather, it is carried out because it is in the interest of the country and society to do so. The development paradigm comes not from the advice, pressure or coercion of another (developed) country. On the contrary, it is the expression of the will of the nation demonstrated through the votes of its representatives and subsequently put into effect. As a system, the Atatürkist modernization paradigm is oriented toward the West. Accordingly, it works toward setting up Western-style institutions in all areas of life, including law, government, social life, education, and technology. Property rights are recognized in the means of production. Nevertheless, through the principle of étatism, the state is given the responsibility to direct the economy toward the interest of society, thus creating a guided economy. Given these conditions, it became imperative for the state to establish a national industry and to provide roads, water and electricity, and meet needs in the areas of communications, health and agriculture as part of the responsibilities laid out for it under modernization. This aspect is in tune with the prerequisites of the "social state," with its promotional role of the state, and mode of guided industrialization. But it should be borne in mind that the principle of étatism was not espoused simply out of ideological considerations. On the contrary, Atatürk and his cadre's approach to economic affairs was pragmatic. Due to the lack of adequate capital, an entrepreneurial class and skilled labor, étatism was adopted as a pragmatic means to activate the resources of the country, thereby realizing economic growth.

The Atatürk paradigm of modernization adopted Western political institutions and embraced the pluralist principle of political party formation. However, due to socio-political exigencies existing in Turkey at the time, a single-party system was initially instituted. It was conceived of as a temporary measure to stem the tide of reactionary religious forces and keep them from undermining the fledgling (laïc) Republic. In reality, despite the existence of a single-party system, the Atatürk paradigm is essentially pluralist in orientation. It works toward creating the conditions that will enable a pluralist system to function. Yet, at the same time, it makes certain not to abandon the structure and fabric of society to a natural process of change. Rather, it works to speed up the process by initiating, forging and strengthening elements contributing to a transformation from a unitary society to a pluralist one, and from a single-party to a multi-party regime.

In summary, the Turkish Republic had been founded upon the successful conclusion of a War of Independence. It had been pursued against the imperialist Western powers that had occupied Anatolia and wanted to deprive Turks of their right to exist as a state. The Atatürkist system of thought was formulated to modernize the country and nation of this new Turkish Republic. The War of Independence, along with the radical reforms implemented and the system of thought developed by the leader of the Revolution would serve as a source of inspiration for the colonized "oppressed nations" of the East. By following the same path, they would attain their own independence. Thus, the Atatürk paradigm of modernization became, in effect, a "third" way, in contrast to the Western and Marxist paradigms.

Although the Turkish nation fought Western imperialism, the objective of their struggle was to reach the "level of contemporary civilization" that existed in the West.

While the Turks received support during their War of Independence from the Soviet government in Russia at that time, in contrast to Soviet "expectation," the leaders and politicians of the new Turkish state did not adopt the Marxist development paradigm.

The Atatürk paradigm took Western political institutions as the basis for its system. While recognizing the property rights in economic development and supporting the role of capitalist private initiative, it also gave the state obligations to take initiative in the area of production, and to assume roles of economic manager and industrialist.

Organizationally, it was through the Republican People's Party that Atatürk principles and reforms were applied in the political and social spheres. This party had its origins in the "Society for the Defense of Rights of Anatolia and Thrace," which had been created during the War of Independence. Being a dynamic component of the Revolution, it was the only party to represent the entire nation.

The Atatürk paradigm adopted the Western political system but it did not want to accept the reality of the existence of class and class distinction that existed in Western societies. Instead of referring to class conflict, avoiding even the use of the term "class," it preferred to establish harmony and balance between classes. Employing the expression "a classless social body," it adopted the most effective term of that time, "People," and aimed at establishing a "People's Government" – a "People's State."

Beginning with the War of Independence, the Atatürk paradigm emphasized the significance of every single action and policy for the formation of nation, national unity, nationalism, and the *consciousness* of "nation." Nearly everything that could be done was done to reinforce this sense of nation and nationalism.

Beginning with the preparatory and organizational stage of the War of Independence, the Atatürkist approach was to base every decision made on the will of the people, e.g. the National Will. All policy was to be formulated and carried out in the name of the people, as reflected in the votes of their representatives. Unconditional sovereignty of the nation was the leading ideological commitment of the Atatürkist system of thought.

In a society where religious elements were ubiquitous, the Atatürkist system of thought chose to underplay spiritual and sectarian forces, symbols and other religious images during the years of the War of Independence. It chose instead to work toward the establishment of laïc society based on reason and knowledge.

With these basic features, Atatürkism and its paradigm of modernization, to be discussed in detail in the following sections, formed an alternative to the pure Western and Marxian development paradigms. It was one that was distinctly "national" and that conformed to the unique structure and conditions of Turkish society. It also came to serve as a kind of "scheme" for countries that were later to wage their own wars of national independence.

Pakistan and India in Asia, and the countries of Southeast Asia, nearly all the states of Black Africa, Tunisia, Algeria and Libya in North Africa, Iraq and Syria in the Middle East, as well as many other countries obtained their independence long after the Turkish War of Independence - most of them in the years following World War II. Regional and border proximity gave rise to mutual support, ties of solidarity and shared aspirations - as well as common areas of ideology, propaganda and influence in the countries of Southeast Asia. Apart from a few exceptions, following their independence, most of the new states in this region adopted neither the pure Capitalist paradigm of the West nor the Marxist paradigms of either the Soviet Union or the People's Republic of China.

Studies carried out on the modernization and economic development strategies followed by these countries support this conclusion. Moreover, these countries received support and attention in international organizations, world public opinion and by the Soviets and Chinese throughout their anti-imperial struggles with Western powers. And while they accepted economic assistance from those very countries, instead of their political systems, they chose those of the West. Moreover, instead of their paradigms of economic development, they preferred a "socialism" that was tailored to their own needs. While they accepted foreign assistance, capital and technology, they wanted to do so in a way that benefited their countries' conditions and structures. Furthermore, in contrast to the Western political system, they adopted, for the most part, single-party regimes. Despite opposing the imperialism of the West, their aim was to catch up with the West. And while they received assistance and support from Marxist countries, they feared coming under the influence of Russia and China. They also denied class distinctions and, in addition to allowing private initiative, they gave the state an obligatory role in development as entrepreneur, manager, and industrialist. Yet, some countries -principally those of Black Africa- were unable to achieve even language unity due to their inability to escape from their tribalism. This, of course, reflects their social and ethnic makeup and, contrary to their modernization goals, remains a critical problem that has to be overcome.

Apart from ideological, political and national interests, the crux of the matter is this: while it may appear that the former Marxist or the present capitalist states - both the colonialists of, the past, and new ones of today - simply seek to provide their own paradigms as a so-

II

OTTOMAN SOCIETY
AND
STATE STRUCTURE

The Turkish National Struggle was fought and won under the leadership of Atatürk, it was through his direction that the War of Independence was won, the new Turkish state set up, and the Revolution paving the way for modernization was realized. At no time during their history were Turks without a state. Nor were they ever colonized. And while it is true that exploitation under the Capitulations, particularly during the period of decline of the Ottoman Empire, was commensurate with the weakening of the state, Turks did not become a colony of another state. Repeatedly throughout Turkish history, whenever one Turkish state has reached the end of its viability, another has been set up in its vestiges.[29]

Under the Ottoman Empire, Turks had spread to the interior of Europe, North Africa, all of Mesopotamia as far as the Red Sea, countries of the Middle East and the north of the Black Sea. Over the final two hundred years of the Empire, the Turks suffered one defeat after another until World War I, when they suffered their ultimate trouncing. Subsequently, the lands of Anatolia, identified as homeland, were overrun and occupied by enemy powers. These European intruders essentially wanted to partition the country and share it amongst themselves. Nevertheless, this case was going to be no different from previous eras. The Turks would find the strength whereby they would be able to retain some form of a state. Even if powerless, they would have a state through which they would be able to maintain their sovereignty. But at this stage in Turkish history, the issue was not simply the setting up of just any state order. What became of the utmost concern was the issue of salvaging the state and retaining its viability. How could Turks come to live as an *honorable* nation? A new order and regime needed to be established. The Christian West and Russia had an accretion of religious, political and historical experience with Turks. Furthermore, they had designs and future-oriented objectives with respect to them. They wanted to share amongst themselves what remained of the Empire they had nicknamed as the "Sick Man" of Europe and to wipe the Turks as a state entity off the stage of history. Everyone, including the rulers of the Empire and intellectuals, knew this and were looking for ways to "save the state." The historical, social, political, economic, cultural and religious factors contributing to Turkish decline, as well as the solutions, actions and policies designed to stop it can be analyzed against the backdrop of history. In brief, these include the assessment of the conditions under which the War of Independence began and the sort of social structure, conditions and ideological milieu within which the Atatürk Revolution was formed, as well as the clarification of the principles of the Atatürk modernization paradigm and the reasons behind its regime.

1. The Characteristics of the State and Society

The Turkish Republic was founded upon the former territory of the Ottoman Empire in Anatolia and Thrace. Its form and system of government and policies were future oriented from its very inception. But the founders of this state are one of the oldest nations in the history of mankind. The structure and fabric of this new state structure, its political, cultural and economic features and aspects, were formed within the framework of the system of thought of its founder, Atatürk.

Of course, any new ideology, system of thought, action and innovation is conditioned by the dynamics inherent within a given society. These dynamics include existing currents of thought. Thus, in this regard, it is impossible to completely abstract the Atatürk Revolution from the currents of thought and universal ideologies of the society in which it was found. Nevertheless, the Revolution was not simply an extension of the reform movements of the Ottoman period - a natural consequence that would have "happened in any case," as assessments, especially those developed in the West over the last few decades and which have found expression in Turkey, would have it. On the contrary, it was a national movement that aimed at transforming, renovating, modernizing and developing a society by using its political, economic, social and cultural structure in its entirety. Furthermore, it envisioned this being accomplished through commitment to continual change. One of the reasons behind the realization of the Revolution, of course, was that such a personality as Atatürk – an individual who was powerful, committed, brave, rational and had trust in his nation - was its leader. Still another reason is that throughout history, the Turkish nation has demonstrated state formation capability such that even in the face of the collapse of the Ottoman Empire, they retained their characteristic desire for statehood, independence and freedom, and the sense of nation inherent within the identity of individuals. Mustafa Kemal's greatness, reflected in his leadership and skill, derives not only from his recognition and knowledge of his nation, its deep-seeded passion for independence. It comes also from his ability to transform this passion and these characteristics at the right time into action taken for national independence. Such inconsistent misjudgements as "reform movements had begun during the Ottoman era anyway; they would have continued - in any case, they would have been carried out" can only be interpreted as a denial of the extraordinariness of the Atatürk Revolution and the singularity of the War of Independence.

Surveying the structure and problems of the society that existed prior to the Atatürk Revolution; investigating the reform efforts and extant ideas of the period; and examining why they were unsuccessful in rescuing the Ottoman Empire will reveal the importance of National Struggle and the factors that gave rise to Atatürkism.

Founded in 1299, and having existed as a state for a period of 600 years, the Ottoman Empire exhibits certain peculiarities with respect to structure of its state and society, form of government, mode of production, commerce, property regime, culture, religion, language, history, and the human element within its borders.

a) The State Regime

The bedrock of the 600-year Ottoman regime was its theocratic state. Theocracy was also the basis for the state in medieval Europe, where religion and church dominated society. Power to rule the world, men and their affairs came from God. Regardless of how a ruler came to occupy a position of authority within the state, his power to "command" or "govern" came from God. Since commands issued within the world order were designed to perpetuate that order and were made in the name of God, to oppose them meant the same thing as opposing God. Likewise, within the Islamic states of the East, sovereignty was theocratic in essence. Based upon the holy "Koran," according to Islam, the "Prophet," the founder and disseminator of Islam, is God's "envoy" on earth. This was interpreted to mean that the "Caliphs" who followed after the death of the Prophet were considered the "representatives" of God's emissary, Mohammed. The Prophet and the Caliphs that came after him received their powers from God and commanded in his name. Islam, with its body of regulations, is as much a basis for social order and form of government as it is a religion. This conception continued under the Ottoman State, where sovereigns were thought of as "shadows" of God. After the Ottoman Sultan Yavuz Sultan Selim took possession of Egypt in 1517 and assumed the role of Caliph of the Islamic world, the religious basis for the order intensified. Religious regulations became the criteria upon which all organs and functions of society were evaluated. The Sultan was the head of government. The *Veziri aza-m* (Prime Ministers), ministers, provincial governors, and *sipahi* (cavalry soldiers) assisted him in governing the country.

b) The Property Regime

According to Islam, the earth and all of its lands belong to God. The right to rule over, regulate and manage land, and to authorize others to use it is the prerogative of the Caliph-Sultan. The Ottoman system created a division of labor on the land located within the borders of the Empire between the *beylerbeyi* (provincial governors) and *sancakbeyi* (yeoman), who were considered extensions of the central administration. This division was carried out in such a way as to meet the needs of the state and of the "central power" that formed and fed all aspects of its military apparatus. Land was partitioned into "fiefdoms," known variously - depending on size - as *has, zeamet,* or *tı-mar,* which were given to those with positions and responsibilities within the state apparatus. Nevertheless, this land did not belong to these people; they were unable to directly manage the land they held.They were obliged to give fief to villagers and *reaya* (subjects) in exchange for a modest rent and had no rights to make villagers leave the lands. To be able to farm this land, villagers had to pay rent to the fief owner as well as tax to the state. The rent that the fief owners received from the villagers farming the land was not simply for meeting their own personal needs. It had to be used as well to prepare a certain number of soldiers who would be made available to the army in time of war and "military campaigns," which included arming, training and feeding them. During the periods of Ottoman State grandeur, this property regime functioned without failure and formed the real basis for the economy.

As the state became weaker, this property regime began to grow corrupt. Land increasingly fell into the hand of the people who had been given the right to use it. Villagers who were farming the land in exchange for the payment of rent began to be crushed under the oppression of governors, powerful families and individuals.

c) The Economic Structure

There was little industrialization in Ottoman society to speak of. In the cities, there were handicraft workshops and small enterprises that made weapons, tools and equipment for the army. The latter were the preserve of the state. Production was almost completely based on agriculture. With the Capitulations, which were first granted by Sultan Murat Hüdavendigar in 1365 to the Raguza Republic in the form of special economic privileges, new commercial relations emerged in the economy. Subsequently, trade centers of foreign mariner merchants appeared in coastal towns of the Empire - and as an extension of them, new markets. This had a two-fold consequence. First, the economy increasingly fell under the control of foreigners. Second, a sector of domestic merchants doing business with them developed.

Apart from taxes and the revenue derived.from fiefs, another major source of income for the state was the "booty" obtained during times of war, the taxes collected from those countries and the gold it received from the commercial mini-states in lieu of providing protection and granting privileges to them.

d) The Social Structure

The principality set up by Osman Bey in the vicinity of Söğüt gradually expanded to take in all of Anatolia. Spreading beyond Anatolia, it grew to encompass the entire Arab Peninsula and stretched as far as North Africa, the Balkans, the interior of Europe, the Crimea, and Iran. Within this expanding Empire were groups coming from different religions, sects and ancestry and speaking different languages. The military prowess of the state enabled it to impose strict control on these peoples having different ancestries, languages, religions and cultures - making it possible for them to live together. However, there was no policy of Turkification or Islamization in the countries to which the Empire spread. Rather, they were seen as countries and societies that provided the Empire with revenue and products, and that paid taxes. From the point of view of language, religion and culture, the people of these countries were free. By virtue of the *millet*[30] system, traditions, customs, habits, languages, religions, and cultures were easily maintained. This was the state of the human element making up the population of the Empire.

2. The Collapse of the Empire

Growing and developing at such a rate, the Ottoman Empire had become one of the world's most powerful states. Nonetheless, by the beginning of the 17th century, it began to experience a period of increasing decline. After an initial hiatus, this decline rapidly grew over the years. The Empire began losing land and its borders contracted. Its population began to decrease. A weakening of its economic strength was set in motion. Those countries that had previously feared the Ottoman armies and had been defeated by them in due course began to wage wars of independence. As a result, they were able to establish new independent states. Moreover, states that had earlier feared the Ottoman State, once having become strong, began referring to it as the "Sick Man" of Europe. Conspiring amongst themselves, they hoped to share its legacy. In the end, the Empire was confronted with an utter collapse.

There are economic, political, religious, cultural, ethnic, domestic and foreign factors contributing to this collapse. Fundamentally, these domestic and international factors are derived from problems interlocking and reinforcing one another at various junctures.

a) The Development of the West

The development of the nation-state in Europe that began in the 13th century grew rapidly in subsequent centuries. The most important examples of this are France and England. The transformation of a fragmentalized, traditional political structure consisting of feudal principalities into a nation-state, which gave rise to a powerful centralization of political and economic resources, was propelled by Kings and the national bureaucracy and national armies they set up.

During previous centuries, absolute monarchy had been the dominant form of government in Europe. The English and the French Revolutions in the 17th and 18th centuries, respectively, were steps taken toward democratization. The provision of freedoms in the political arena and a move away from absolutism were components of this.

Together with the transition from a traditional feudal social structure to nation-state, a national economy began to develop. This naturally gave rise to first a commercial revolution and then an industrial one. As a consequence of the two, an industrial bourgeoisie emerged and began to develop.

Beginning in the 19th century, the social aspect of democracy acquired significance, which resulted in social and economic rights appearing on the political agenda. There is no question that the Industrial Revolution and the working class it created had a great impact on making the structure of the social and economic systems more democratic, freer and more equitable.

One of the fundamental economic factors behind development in the West was the overseas expansion of England, France, Spain, Portugal, Holland, Belgium - and later Germany. Through this expansion, whereby countries were colonized, they not only acquired markets, natural resources and labor power from them, but also, by placing the economies of these countries at their service, they exploited them and their peoples.

b) Foreign Factors

This expansion of the West became one of the most important factors behind the decline of the Ottoman Empire: It contributed to the weakening of its economy, the loss of control of its commerce to foreigners, the transformation of the country into a market for the West, the increasing elimination of domestic small-scale industry, and the degeneration of the state.

Another major factor that gave rise to the disintegration and contracting of the Empire was spreading of the wave of nationalism, which had begun with the French Revolution, to the various *millets* within its borders. On the other hand, while this phenomenon of decline was due in part to this upsurge in nationalism, it was encouraged and speeded up by the Western colonial powers. There was an effort being made to break off communities in the Balkans and the Middle East and establish them as separate, independent states. While the Western states were laying the foundation for this, they were instrumental in helping the Christian "nations" within the Empire to obtain independence. However, when it came to the independence of the Moslem Arabs in the Middle East, not only did the Western states hamper efforts made to bring this about - despite having previously promised it, they brought these countries under the mandate system and turned them into semi-colonial entities.

Still another foreign factor was religion. Nearly everyone in Christian Europe saw a powerful Moslem state as a threat, historically, culturally and economically but also from the point of view of religion. This "Crusades" mentality continues to be reflected in the modern world. The weakening, disintegration, decline, increasing elimination and the dividing up of its lands would be in the interest of the expansionist Western states. The existence of a powerful state in the vicinity and along the way to Indian and Indochina -and its colonies there - was in all respects pernicious. Religious sentiment provided the support for what was essentially an economic motive.

These and similar foreign factors, which had the effect of intensifying domestic ones, led to a growth in the enormity of problems. They contributed to disintegration in the face of an expanding West, which ultimately brought about the collapse of the Empire.

c) Domestic Factors

There were also a number of domestic political, economic, ethnic, and religious reasons behind the collapse of the Ottoman Empire. The most important of these was the failure on the part of the traditional Ottoman State to transform itself into a nation-state. It did not undertake the reorganization of social, economic, political and state institutions within a laïc framework that met the requirements of such an entity. This is not to discount various attempts made at reform in an effort to salvage the institution of "Caliph-Sultan" and to avoid suffering defeat at the hands of Western states. Nonetheless, they were all superficial and they in no way reflected an appreciation of what development entailed in the West. They thus were unable to achieve any real transformation that might have led to a similar kind of development.

There were other domestic factors, apart from the political, ethnic and religious ones, that contributed to the collapse of the Ottoman Empire. These included the degeneration of the land regime, an increase in foreign debt, the existence of the Capitulations, the failure to industrialize, the contraction of the Empire arising from a loss of land and, along with this, the inability to meet state expenses.

Most notably during the period of Ottoman expansion, revenues derived from conquests made up a significant part of Ottoman finance. Provisions were procured through booty obtained from these conquests as well as revenues received from countries conquered. However, with the stagnation and subsequent decline experienced by the Empire, all this was lost. Moreover, as a natural consequence of contraction, the difficulty of finding land and work for those who withdrew from these lands into the confines of the Empire became an issue.

The decline in the usual, customary revenue of the state that resulted from this contraction gave rise to the need to impose new taxes or increase existing ones. All along those who had been paying taxes had been the *reaya*. As taxes increased, discontent grew and the central power lost much of its control over the periphery. This resulted in a rise in distinct concentrations of power in *sipahi* regions previously under state control not unlike that which had existed in feudal Europe. This led to a wavering and ultimate elimination of central authority and its ability to impose its will in these areas. As the state's authority and ability to impose its will weakened, local powers within the state's borders began to emerge. The emergence of these local powers was the most important factor contributing to the further weakening of the state, usurpation of its duties and the breakdown of order.

The "privileges" or Capitulations, which the Ottoman Sultans had initially provided as a kind of "protection," increased to such an extent that it led to the complete collapse of the Empire's commerce and fledgling crafts and industries; in short, its entire economy. Goods produced by the Industrial Revolution in the West were sold in the cities of the Empire without the imposition of tax or customs. It gave rise to a situation where the economy of the country was completely dependent upon the outside. The inability of the state revenues to cover expenses resulted in foreign indebtedness.

The rebellion within the borders of the country of Christian communities having different ancestries; the secessions from the Empire that came with the wave of nationalism; the rapprochement with other states by Moslem communities having different ancestries for the purpose of seceding; and the general discontent among Turkish groups brought the regime face to face with practically insolvable problems.

Among the reasons for the collapse of the Ottoman Empire, the impact of religious fanaticism was extremely important. Religious zealots objected to innovation; they opposed every kind of reform movement simply on the grounds of personal interest. Some of the most grievous examples of reasons for the collapse of the state include the actions taken by a religious fanaticism that was allowed a legitimate voice in the life of the state. This was a fanaticism that would render the setting up of a printing press as a "sin;" inquiry into whether or not the "quarantine" requested in the case of such contagious diseases as plague and cholera was contrary to religion; first opposing the "fez" and then opposing the "hat" when the later was proposed to replace the former.

One of the most significant consequences of the religious influence was that contrary to the laïcization of education that had occurred in Europe, which provided the basis for the development and modernization of all areas of society, the religious basis of education continued in the schools of the Empire. This strict religious practice formed the greatest, most powerful obstacle to the transfer of Western technology to Ottoman society.

The source of all this rigidity, resistance and desire to preserve the status quo was the class of *Ulema,* who had great weight in Ottoman society and the state regime. Those dealing with *Sharia* (the body of religious legal codes) and *fıkıh* (Islamic jurisprudence) - men of rank within the *ulema* - the *müderris* (high ranking instructors of Islamic sciences), *Kadı* (judge of Islamic law), and *kazasker* (chief military Islamic judge) - were all cut out from the same fabric. Contrary to being true scholars, they were the biggest reason behind the backwardness of the society.

3. Attempts at Reform

It was only toward the end of the 18th century that ways of salvaging and maintaining the Ottoman State and its society began to be considered. It was then that attempts were made to implement reforms in light of the development achieved in the West. The advances made there were envied but the Ottoman State had developed a regime that was based on conquest and preparation for war. They were ill prepared to do what was necessary to even begin such a process of development. Rulers were under the misconception that all they had to do to catch up with the West was evaluate problems as it always had, e.g., in militaristic terms, which meant providing new weapons and techniques to the army. In this way, they could not only compete with the West but also regain historical supremacy over it. Beginning at the time of Abdülhamit I, this mentality led to a tradition of bringing of experts from Europe and having them train the army. It was thought that the revitalization of the army was all that was needed to stop the collapse of the Empire and bring back the old days.

In a similar vein, Selim III wanted to have new army units that would be trained using European methods existing alongside the Janissaries. Several reforms were initiated. Nevertheless, these efforts fell victim within a short time to the reaction of the Janissaries and the religious fanatics. They were subsequently brought to an end by the revolt led by Kabakçı Mustafa. Selim III established the first artillery school *(Mühendishane-i Berri-i Hümayun)* and naval academy *(Mü-*

hendishane-i Bahri-i Hümayun) of the Ottoman era. Those responsible for the bringing about a curtailment of his efforts at reform were the Janissaries and the *Ulema*. As a consequence of the collaboration of these two, Selim the 3rd was assassinated.

States and those at their helm, regardless of country, have always feared undisciplined armed powers that recognized no authority or higher command. The Janissaries of the Ottoman era, most conspicuously during times of decline, became a source of "trouble" for administrators. No matter what the occasion, they revolted. After Mahmut II took power, he felt that it was time for the state's worst nightmare - the Janissaries - be eliminated and replaced with a new army. He wanted to establish an army that would be trained according to Western standards and be loyal to the state, thus ensuring the continuity of state authority. Accordingly, the institution of the Janissary was abolished in 1826. This reform, which has come down in Turkish history as *"Vak'a-i Hayriyye,"* had the effect of neutralizing the local notables of Anatolia and Roumelia. Mahmut II. A large number of legal reforms contributed to the creation of a new disciplinary code applicable to civil servants. One of the most serious problems confronting the Empire during Mahmut II's time was the intensification of the wave of nationalism, which entailed the rebellion against the state by nations contained within the borders of the Empire, the emergence of Greece as an independent state, followed by other Balkan nations.

a) The Tanzimat Proclamation

After the death of Mahmut II, Sultan Abdülmecit became head of state. Under the influence of Mustafa Reşit Pasha, he had a legal document, variously known as the *Tanzimat Fermanı* or the *Gülhane Hattı Hümayunu* or the *Gülhane Hattı Şerifi* (since it had been proclaimed in Gülhane Park), prepared. This document placed importance on personal rights, and was designed to ensure the life, property, honor and domicile of an individual. No longer would anyone receive illegal punishments. Equality would be ensured for all with respect to life, property, honor and residence. Everyone - Christian and Moslem alike - would be subject to the same laws. During this period, there was also the desire to adopt certain laïc laws from the West so as to reform the state regime. This, however, was not an easy task since the state was already being challenged on a number of fronts. For example, the Christian communities within the borders of the Empire, having come under the influence of the rising tide of nationalism, had developed the desire for statehood. This gave rise to attempts to secede from the Empire, thus undermining the authority of the Ottoman State. Moreover, the admiration of the West during this period gave rise to the granting of new privileges to Western states. Further undermining the autonomy of the State were the new and larger loans that had been sought as a way out of the state's financial bottlenecks.

This period was one during which relations with the West and the presence of Western ideas intensified in the Ottoman country. Western-style parliamentary democracy was endorsed and efforts made toward its practical implementation. It was at this time, too, that the first steps toward a "Constitutional Regime" were taken. The notion that a person derived his sovereignty by virtue of divine right was being challenged. The institution of the Sultanate was still recognized but it was to be kept in check in the name of the people. This novel idea had been promulgated by the "Young Ottomans, who were later referred to as "Young Turks" (the expression used in Western circles to refer to the leaders of the "Constitutional Period" movement). Abdülaziz, who was head of state at this time, and those in his entourage were suspicious of this new development. As a result of this mistrust, its leaders - Namık Kemal, Ziya Pasha - and their close associates were forced to flee the country. This struggle, which was conducted both at home and abroad, led to Murat V, who had succeeded Abdülaziz to the "throne," being deposed. He was replaced by Abdülhamit II, who had promised to fulfill all the demands made by the Young Ottomans.

b) Constitutional Sultanate

The first constitutional regime during the Ottoman era was set up in 1876. From then on, a constitution would form the basis for the state. Government would consist of two legislative bodies: the Council of Deputies and the Senate, to be elected by the people and the Sultan, respectively. The first Constitution was prepared by Mithat Pasha and later accepted by Abdülhamit. While it is true that a Constitution existed and two legislative bodies had been set up on the basis of it, all power and authority continued to remain in practice with the Sultan. This Constitution, among other things, gave to him the right to convene and close sessions of the Parliament and suspend it as well. Under these conditions, it was no easy task for the representatives of the people to oversee the Sultan. Nevertheless, he drew criticism at the first session of Parliament. This development led the suspicious, calculating, and scheming Abdülhamit to look for an opportunity to disband Parliament. Not having to look very far, he used the outbreak of the Turco-Russian War (1877-1878) as an excuse to do just that on February 14, 1878.

After this first experiment in parliamentary government, Abdülhamit exiled - under the flimsiest of pretexts - whomever he felt suspicion toward and rid the army of "undesirable" elements. He set up and maintained what was to be a 30-year regime of despotism. Intellectuals, who feared this closed, oppressive regime, fled to Western countries and continued their struggles there. Secret societies were set up during this period and intensive efforts were begun both at home and abroad to bring down Abdülhamit. It was at this time that the İttihat ve Terraki Cemiyeti (the Committee of Union and Progress) was set up. In subsequent years, this committee would become transformed into a political party, assume responsibility for the administration of the country, lead Turkey into World War I and establish a military-backed regime.

At the end of a struggle that had mainly depended on the army and its young officers, army units in Thrace rebelled. Marching upon Istanbul, they forced Abdülhamit to reinstate the Constitution. In 1908 the Parliament was reconvened. However, Abdülhamit was unable to allow himself to be humiliated by this defeat. The following year, secretly supported and encouraged by Abdülhamit, the "31 March Affair," which was a reactionary and fanatical opposition to the Constitution, erupted. In response, the army units from Thrace (the Harekât Ordusu) arrived in Istanbul to subdue the rebellion and deposed Abdülhamit. The Committee of Union and Progress took over government, ushering in, in due course of time, an oppressive regime that did not allow for any type of dissent. There was no fully democratic, laïc Constitution in sight. The Union and Progress and the Freedom and Alliance Parties continued their all out wrangling. In the meantime, the country had to deal with the advent of new wars. The wars in Tripoli, 1911-1912, and the Balkans, 1912-1913 led to even more problems and difficulties for the state. The collapse of the state, which had entered World War I on the side of the Germans, accelerated the historical demise of the Ottoman Empire.

4. Ideological Inquiries and Currents of Thought

During the last years of the rapid decline of the Ottoman State, a number of ideological currents claiming to offer ways of salvaging the State and maintaining its viability surfaced. These were "Ottomanism," "Islamism," "Turkism," "Entrepreneurship-Federalism in Government," "Westernism" and "Socialism." But since none of them was modern in content, logically consistent or conformed to social reality, they were not effective. They all failed in their attempt to keep the Empire intact. All of ideologies, and the measures they advocated, had one thing in common: their failure to advance beyond a unidimensional approach to issues and problems. They did not go beyond offering superficial solutions to problems - regardless of whether they had to do with the state or those inherent within particular ideologies themselves. The only consistent, progressive and modern idea among these ideological movements was "Turkism." However, with its transformation into "Turanism," it too met with failure.

a) Ottomanism

This current of thought envisaged the creation of an "Ottoman Nation," consisting of people living within the borders of the Empire - regardless of ancestry or religion - as the way to salvage the Ottoman State. Whether Turk, Armenian, Jew, Albanian, Arab, or Bulgarian, all would become one within the melting pot of the Ottoman State. This would quell attempts at separatism and independence created by nationalism. Everyone would work toward the resurrection of the Ottoman State. Within this state, everyone would be equal - Ottoman subjects having the same rights and no one having any special privileges. The prerequisite for this "lawful" government, with the right of "representation" of all the *millet*s in the Parliament.

b) Islamism

This current of thought originated prior to the Tanzimat and gained strength during the First and Second Constitutional periods with the recognition of new rights to non-Moslems. It held that the only reason for the degeneration of the state was the failure to apply religious codes in their entirety. Its adherents believed that the best, most developed and most efficacious state and social order is one that has adopted Islam. Islamic code, without concession, should be incorporated within state policies and social life. A union of all Islamic countries all over the world should be set up. Since the Moslem Caliph is the Ottoman Sultan, the creation of such a union would enable the Ottoman State to regain its former prowess and respect. The Moslem Ottoman Empire would be based on religious power and codes.

In time, Abdülhamit II became fully committed to Islamism. Thus the policies of the Ottoman State during the reign of Abdülhamit were oriented in this direction. He even went as far as considering the creation of Turco-Arab Empire. Accordingly, he attempted to obtain Arab support by showing them great interest and granting them several favors.

This is the reason why advocates of contemporary "Islamism" and those endorsing the notion of "Islamic Union" demonstrate a special kind of respect to Abdülhamit by referring to him as "exalted sovereign" and "the abode of paradise."

c) Turkism

Turkism, which began with the study and investigation in the areas of language, history and literature, was not able to spread much during the periods dominated by Ottomanism and Islamism. It blossomed after the 2nd Constitutional Period, when it became obvious that these other currents of thought were not going to be adequate to rescue the Empire. During the years that Ottomanism and Islamism continued as state policy, it had been impossible for the idea of "Turkism" to develop as a political movement. According to its leaders, a nation consists of a unity in language, religion, race and ideal. The state can only remain standing if it is based upon a society that is unified in this way. The rescue of the Ottoman State would be possible only through the creation of a sense of unity and national identity of Turks living within the Empire. One of the main reasons for the weakening of the Ottoman State had been the attempt by different linguistic, religious and ancestral communities to create their own states. The way to prevent this and to strengthen the state was the revitalization of Turkish nation. Through the intellectual contributions of the scholar Ziya Gökalp to the development of Turkism during the 2nd Constitutional period, Turkism grew more dynamic. Undoubtedly, Turkism was the current of thought that was to prove the most consistent and useful to the National Struggle, directed as it was to the creation of a nation. However, its adherents began to get caught up with the belief that Turks outside their own country needed to be rescued and brought within the borders of the Empire. They thus came to embrace the notion of a union of Turks, which was the ideal of "Turan." This, however, was inconsistent with the original intent of Turkism. While it is true that strength of a state is enhanced when it is founded upon a coherent nation-state, the consciousness of nation, e.g., the consciousness of "Turkishness," had not appeared in the mind or heart of the great majority of Turks. In fact, it was not until the days when the Ottoman State was about to collapse that such a consciousness emerged. Up until then, the religious structure of the state and the extension of religious codes to all aspects of society had not left room for the possibility of a notion of being Turkish or being part of a Turkish nation. The state did not see its Turkish and Moslem citizens as part of a Turkish nation but rather as individuals of an *ümmet* (members of the same religious community - in this case, one believing in and bound to the Prophet). The nationalist movements undertaken by the Christian communities in the Balkans and, perhaps even more important than these, the efforts made at nation-building by the Arabs, who were themselves Moslem, did not wake up the Ottoman Sultans and statesmen from their slumber. Nationalism had failed to become part of the repertoire of notions available to those running the Ottoman State until its last days. It was a few intellectuals who had gotten the nationalist movement off the ground and it was they who then worked to keep it going.

d) Westernism

This current of thought originated not as a political ideology as such but rather as an attempt to resemble the West by adopting such reforms as a national army and the training of soldiers according to Western standards. It spread within Ottoman Turkish society under the increasing influence of the new liberal ideology put forth by the French Revolution. But it was without social, scientific or economic content and was more a superficial and formalist imitation of the West. The Ottoman Sultans and their *sadrazams* (Grand Viziers), who had been defeated by the West and had subsequently lost land, thought that all that needed to be done to reach the level of the West was to purchase new weapons, have ships built, have new weapons made, change the uniforms worn by soldiers, and to set up a *Meclis-i Ayan* (Senate) that was under their control and a *Meclis-i Mebusan* (Assembly of Deputies), which was in effect without power or importance. It gradually became obvious that such a superficial application of what was "Western" to institutions, along with the corresponding changes did not prevent collapse. Consequently, following the First Constitutional Period, apart from those running the state, Westernism assumed a political content among the intelligentsia that had ties with the West. Rather than being seen simply in terms of a parroting of the West, it began to be understood as constituting a holistic political, cultural, social and economic order. Nonetheless, in spite of these developments, following both the First and Second Constitutional Periods, its adherents failed to realize that being Western involved a question of total modernization and change. They did not see that radical reforms were needed to solve these problems. That this required social change and that nationalism had to be one of the goals of Westernism remained beyond their conceptual schemata.

e) Entrepreneurship and
Federalism in Government

Another group of intellectuals, under the leadership of Prince Sabahattin, saw the salvation of the Ottoman Empire in "entrepreneurship
and federalism" The number of its supporters grew after the Second
Constitutional Period. Through such publications as "How the Ottoman Empire Can be Saved," their leader, Prince Sabahattin tried explaining how the Empire could be "rescued." The advocates of this movement gathered together as part of the "New Generation Club" they
founded and began disseminating their ideas to youth. In their opinion,
the Ottoman State held together an Empire consisting of a very large
country populated by many different peoples of different religions speaking different languages, which was difficult to govern. The root of the
problem was seen to be the lack of importance placed on the education and development of the individual. The viability of the state was
thought to depend on functional capacity of individuals in society. The
individual ought not to work for the state or society but rather the state and society ought to work for the individual. Prince Sabahattin wanted to apply his individualist perspectives, which he borrowed from
such Western social scientists as Le Play and Edmond Demoulins, to the
Ottoman State. This radical individualist understanding led him and his
supporters to work toward the transformation of the Empire into a fe-
deral state. Otttoman territory should be divided up into regions that
would be granted relative autonomy, even if not independence. These
autonomous regions would still be bound to the Ottoman State and its
Sultans but would be organized on the basis of, for example, production, economic activity, industry and public works and allowed to function freely in these areas. In this way, the minorities and *millet*s within
the Empire would continue to maintain a conflict-free existence. Moreover, the individuals making up these would become wealthier, develop and contribute to the strengthening of the state.

f) Socialism

Among the currents of thought existing during late Ottoman era -
even if not as influential as some of the others - was the socialist one.

It was, however, unable to expand beyond a limited circle of intellectuals. The spread of its ideas was sought through articles written in the newspapers, *İştirak* and *İnsaniyet*, published by Hüseyin Hilmi. In 1910, the "Ottoman Socialist Party," which had been founded by Hüseyin Hilmi, Namık Hasan, Pertev Tevfik, İbnîl Tarih İsmail Faik, Baha Tevfik, Hamdi Suphi, was shut down after being active for a short period of time. It was ascertained that some Deputies during the 2nd Constitutional Period were actively involved in espousing socialism. Even so, socialist ideas failed to spread and reach a broad level of consciousness. During this period, Dr. Refik Nevzat opened a branch of the Ottoman Socialist Party in Paris in 1911. Through the Party's newspaper, *Beşeriyet*, attempts were made to spread the idea that the establishment of a socialist regime in the Ottoman Empire was the only way for it to attain the same level of development as existed in the West.[31]

5. The Culmination of Ottoman Endeavors at Reform

How was it that despite all these currents of thought, soul-searching, and initiatives the Ottoman State could not be saved? Why were these struggles and ideas unable to prevent its bankruptcy? Did they have the effect of slowing down - at least in part - the collapse of the Ottoman State or did they solely act to speed it up? Did these currents of thought have any real effect on the Ottoman state and society? If so, to what extent were they beneficial?

In order to be able to answer these questions, it is necessary to provide a general critique of these ideological movements so as to determine the degree to which the ideological milieu prior to the War of Independence in Turkey was consistent. In this way, it will be possible to understand the influences and reactions that Atatürkism confronted.

Apart from their aim to revitalize the Ottoman State, the currents of thought that emerged during the late Ottoman Empire share a number of common characteristics. First, they wanted to have policies formulated and implemented that were inconsistent with their guiding principles. Second, they were unable to recognize that the problems before them had certain common characteristics. This resulted in their failure to approach those problems in a radical and holistic fashion. Third, they assumed that a state and social structure that was completely void of modern features could be maintained through ancillary support. Finally, they really did not know the West; they had no real idea as to the meaning or content of the term "modernization."

If we elaborate on the subject and go into more detail in our critique of each current of thought, we can more easily find the answers to "what for" and "how come."

Ottoman society consisted of a variety of ethnic, religious and sectarian groups. Even when the state was at its most powerful, through its *millet* system, it left these groups alone with respect to their languages, religions, cultures, sects, and traditions. It provided the conditions whereby they could continue to exist in relative autonomy. In an era where the State had begun to collapse and *millets,* under the influence of the wave of nationalism that had begun to spread universally, had begun to see themselves as nations, it was impossible to pretend that the Empire could be seen a homogenous entity - "clan," "family," or "dynasty" - called "Ottoman." Having acquired a self-consciousness, a nation assumes the status of a living entity, which is nearly impossible to eliminate.

Besides the fundamentally scientific inconsistency of the Ottomanist movement, its rise served as an impetus - quite contrary to its goals - to the development of nationalist struggles within ethnic groups. What ethnic group would want to be "Ottomanized," e.g., obliterated in the name of the state? The leaders of this movement were so far removed from being able to understand this that they were completely bewildered by the collapse of the state.

The collapse of the Ottoman State cannot be reduced to a question of "being Ottoman" or "not being Ottoman." What weakened the state and caused its demise was not only the behavior of ethnic groups within its borders, their struggle for independence and secession from the Empire. Because of its backward structure, form of government and conceptual orientation, the Ottoman State would have failed even if all the people inside its borders had accepted being Ottoman.

Ottomanism was itself a misplaced current of thought. At a time when the wave of nationalism had reached its highest crests universally, during an era in which ethnic groups were being inflamed, to propose or see as possible the eradication of nation was simply not reasonable since it had no basis in reality.

The superiority of the West was not derived from a denial of the existence of nation. On the contrary, it came from the establishment of the nation-state and was strengthened by it. These countries became prosperous by transferring the natural resources, both above and below the ground, and the manpower of its colonies to their own countries. By using these resources and exploiting manpower, before and after the Industrial Revolution, they experienced technological development. Moreover, the structures of society and the state underwent a reorganization commensurate with the changing temporal and human requirements brought about by development and the process of change.

Religion is a social institution. However, along with this social institution is the reality of "nation." Religion has not been able to maintain unity even within its own *ümmet* (religious community). Sects emerge and their followers become enemies of one another. Sectarian strive was not alien to the Ottoman State. Perhaps the leaders of Islamism could be excused for not knowing about the religious wars in Europe but not being aware of or forgetting the presence of sectarian strife in their own history is an inexcusable oversight. Considering the history of discord and fighting between members of the same nation who are from different sects, the idea supported by Islamism that other nations could somehow be brought together under the command of the Ottoman Sultan, who at the same time continued as Caliph, thereby resulting in an increase in strength was simply fantasy. Europe did not rise and develop because of religious unity or the gathering of all Christians under one banner. On the contrary, it grew in strength because it carried out religious reform, removing the influence of religious codes, priests and upper-level ecclesiastical officials from society and state. The nation-state, free from theocratic influence, prevailed in Europe, with the only remaining theocratic state confined to the Vatican, under the leadership of the "Pope."

In addition to a lack of historical consciousness, the leaders of Islamism acted in ways that conflicted with what they themselves advocated. Their actions contributed to the minorities of other religions and *millets*, as well as other Moslem nations - particularly the Arabs, into war with the Ottoman State.

Neither Ottomanism nor Islamism was modern. Universally, among the developed, powerful states of the time, there was not a single state or country whose social structure was based on religion. Moreover, those undergoing development, seeing that a religious state structure was an impediment to further development, did away with it, turning instead to a laïc, liberal regime based on science.

Within the ideological movements of the day, leaving aside the later deviations and its inability to be holistic, the most modern, relatively consistent, future-oriented movement was Turkism. It was the most important current of thought influencing the "Anatolian" struggle toward nation-building and the decision to establish a nation-state. Through their investigation of the attitude of the Ottoman State toward the Turkish language and views of Turkish people on its lands, the leaders of the movement were able to get a clear conceptualization and understanding that national consciousness was one of the greatest forces for a state. The ideas espoused by Turkism were appropriate for the era and was for this reason modern. The sociologist, Ziya Gökalp, took pains to study in detail the contents of Turkism so as to reveal its scientific basis. Beginning with Ottomanism, he progressed to Turkism. In the years following the Second Constitutional Period, he proposed that nationalism went through three-stages: *Türkiyecilik, Oğuzculuk* and *Turancılık* (Pan-Turanism). According to Gökalp, the goal of *Türkiyecilik* was the unification of all Turks within the borders of Turkey into a single nation; that of *Oğuzculuk* was the unification of the Oğuz Turks, within which the Turks of Turkey were included; and *Turancılık* was the unification of all Turks, regardless of lineage or where they lived in the world. In later years, especially after World War I, he said that Pan-Turanism was a "far off ideal" and emphasized the need for the unification of and the creation of a nation out of the Turks of Turkey. In Gökalp's opinion, Turkification was a stage on the road to becoming a nation. In order to develop, changes were needed within the state and social order. Law and science had to be independent vis-à-vis religion. State functions and those of religion were separate and should not be confused with one another. The source of national culture was the people. Turkism was at the same time populism. According to Gökalp, "Turkification, Islamification and Modernization" were distinctly discrete methods. Nevertheless, there was no need for conflict between them. What was of value was their reconciliation. While searching for national culture and bringing it to the fore, it was necessary to graft Western civilization to it.

In the end, Gökalp recommended Anatolian nationalism for Turkey and attempted to delineate its contents. However, just as previously propagated ideas before it, such as *Oğuzculuk* and *Turancılık,* it became inconsistent with its original intent and unrealistic. Moreover, the content of this current of thought, during both the Ottoman and Turkish Republic periods, was such that it drew disapprobation from foreign circles. Instead of rescuing, protecting or strengthening a state, this current of thought was confronted by foreign pressure and even aggression.

The dream of *Turan,* rather than strengthening the Ottoman State, accelerated its demise. The idea of uniting Turks, bringing them together within the boundaries encompassed by the Ottoman State, and including their lands as part of Ottoman "property" may have been an attractive one. Nevertheless, in reality it was contrary to the intent of the policy that had motivated it in the first place - that of saving the Ottoman State.

This critical approach sheds light on why the Ottoman State failed to be salvaged and why it collapsed. Furthermore, it helps clarify whether or not any of these movements contributed to a new formation or transformation and if so, the extent to which they did.

In summary, the most important factor in the collapse of the Ottoman State was the failure to create a nation-state and move away from traditional society to a modern one. In addition, the location and geographical position of the country, combined with the ongoing wars - initially to expand and broaden its borders and later to protect countries within them - led to situations that lent itself in all ways to secession, dissolution and fragmentation of the social structure. Moreover, remaining on the sidelines of the Industrial Revolution in the West, together with drying up of opportunities for accumulation and investment produced by the capitulations led to economic weakness. The self-imposed isolation of the administrative class from the outside and the degeneration of the "Ulema," which led them to resist all innovation, and the increasing dependence of the economy were also significant factors.

The currents of thought that emerged to counter this collapse could not forestall it. Nor did they contribute to the ideological platform of the National Struggle. However, once Turkism began to be transformed into a movement aspiring to the building of a nation-state having limited national boundaries, it led intellectuals to think about and look for answers to the question of what could be done. These ideas contributed to the raising of new generations open to debate and receptive to the creation of a milieu, which would contribute to the acceleration of development and change.

The generations raised within these currents of thought of the final period of the Ottoman Empire consisted of people who came to assume positions as national representatives in the Turkish Grand National Assembly. It is only natural and inevitable that ideological movements contradictory to one another would be present in this Assembly. In fact, especially toward the end of the war years, the signs of these disparities became more apparent.

III

THE STATE OF
AFFAIRS IN TURKEY
AT THE BEGINNING OF
THE REVOLUTION

To be able to decide whether movements aimed at modernization and radical reform are successful, to see the extent of the ground covered, and to understand the degree to which change has been achieved, it is necessary to understand the characteristics of the country and society where the radical reforms are being undertaken. Hence, it is beneficial to broadly outline the state of affairs that existed in Turkey at the beginning of the Atatürk Revolution with respect to its economic characteristics, industries, demographic composition and features, ideological differences existing in society and the domestic and foreign difficulties confronted by the Revolution.

1. Economic Characteristics And Industries

Toward its demise, the Ottoman Empire experienced wars, defeats and continual loss of land. The Sevres Treaty, which was signed by the officials of the Empire but which failed to be put into effect due to the success of the War of Independence, intended to break up Anatolia - leaving the Turks with only Central Anatolia.

The economy, especially in the years following the *Tanzimat,* fell subject to the dynamics of Western capitalism, which resulted in it becoming dependent, indebted and continually running a deficit.

According to estimates made by the statistician Vedat Eldem, based on prices current in 1914, at the beginning of World War I, Gross National Product was 24.107 million *kuruş*. Of this, 13.060 million *kuruş* came from agriculture while 2.443 million *kuruş* came from industry. Inter-regional income distribution was markedly disparate. Per capita income was very low and its inter-regional distribution was extremely inequitable. While the national average was 1.072 *kuruş,* it was 1.160 in Roumelia and the Islands, 1.934 in Istanbul and Çatalca, 1.130 in Syria, 1.205 in Lebanon, 1.192 in Jerusalem, and 745 in Iraq. The growth of national income over a 25-year period (1890 =

100) was 56% while the annual rate of growth was only 2%. During the same period, the annual rate of population growth was 1%. Consequently, growth in real terms actually fell to 1%. In contrast, a growth rate of 3.3% was realized in the United States between 1913-1914, 3.1% in Germany between 1875 and 1913, 2.4% in England between 1875-1909 and 4.1% in Japan between 1883-1912.

The low level of national income during the last years of the Ottoman Empire naturally had a negative effect on investments, which, in terms of GNP, reached 7.8% in 1907-1908, 8.9% in 1913-1914, and only 6.2% in 1914-1915.

The Empire ran a constant trade deficit. This deficit had reached 226.1 (1910 = 100) in 1913-1914, which was equivalent to 2.2024 million kuruş at the time. 59.4% of imports were comprised of industrial goods, followed by 25% grains and 7% raw materials. On the other hand, exports consisted of 45% grains, 38.4% raw material and 13% construction goods. 31.1% of the industrial goods, which led imports, were made up of clothing and 10% investment goods. This qualitative and quantitative composition of foreign trade demonstrates rather dramatically the external dependence of the economy and the exploitation by foreign economies.

The Ottoman State took out its first foreign loan during the Crimean War. By 1914, the total debt owed by the Empire to various countries totaled 153,7 million Ottoman liras. Leading the list of countries to which debt was owed was France, accounting for 49% of the debt. This was followed by Germany at 20%, Belgium at 11%, and England at 7%.

One of the main problems of the economy of the Empire concerned foreign capital and trade. In 1910, within the borders constituted by the National Pact (Misak-ı Milli),[32] there was 5 billion 711 million kuruş in foreign capital. In 1914, a total of 3.112.000.000 Ottoman liras were transferred to foreign countries. This sum consisted of 228 million kuruş in profits accrued to foreign capital, 2,024 million in foreign trade deficit, with the remainder being composed of interest on foreign debt. These figures demonstrate that 14.8% of GNP was going to foreign countries. Areas in which foreign capital was invested included industry, electricity, tramways, water and commerce - led by railroads at 58%.

This was the composition of the economy taken over by the Atatürk Revolution and the Republic.[33]

In 1915, there were 282 facilities of varying sizes operating in industry, the most important being in food, agricultural products, textiles, leather, forestry, paper, printing, and chemicals. Of these facilities, 155 were in Istanbul, 62 in Izmir, and 65 in other provinces. 22
of them were state-owned, 28 were incorporated, while the rest were
owned by individuals. According to 1915 figures, 14.060 workers
were employed in these workplaces, with an average daily income of
14,2 *kuruş* for those working in the food industry, 17,7 in agriculture, 13,9 in leather, 16 in forestry, 6.8 in textiles, 13.6 in paper and
printing, and 11,1 *kuruş* for those working in the chemical industry.
The total production value of these workplaces was 757.046.755 *kuruş*, in 1922, the total number of workplaces in the country, including
workshops and home-based businesses was 32.721, employing
75.411 workers, for an average of 2,3 workers per establishment.

Available qualitative and quantitative evidence indicate that industrialization was absent in the country.

2. The Composition and Characteristics of the Population

Population censes were taken in the Ottoman Empire in 1831,
1844, 1859 and 1882, and in 1912, an agricultural census based on
provincial annuals *(salnâme)* was conducted. While these censes are
far from representarive, they do provide some indication as to the demographic makeup of the Empire.

According to calculations and estimates made by the statistician
Eldem, the population (as a total of the provinces remaining within
today's borders) in 1913 was 15.821.000. He found an annual rate of
population increase in 1913 of 0.8%. The 29-year period between
1884 and 1913 witnessed an average annual population increase of
0.77%. While it is certain that these figures - since they are based on
estimates - are far from accurate and sound, they do provide a rough
picture. It goes without saying that wars, health conditions and disease, and migrations had a major impact on repressing population
growth rates.

It is known that during the last few years of the Empire, 80% of the population lived in rural areas and were involved in agriculture and animal husbandry. Nevertheless, there are no documents available that might indicate the composition of this population in terms of age, occupation, and gender. Minorities such as the Greeks, Jews and Armenians had an influential role within the economic life of the general population.

According to figures published in the 1879 statistical yearbook of the Statistics Department of the Commerce and Public Works Ministry, there were 14.212.000 Moslems, 2.570.000 Orthodox, 1.042.000 Armenians, 830.000 Bulgarians, and 216.000 Jews living within the confines of the Ottoman Empire - in Roumelia, Istanbul, Anatolia, Syria and Iraq. Further, statistics show that, among the total population of Ottoman citizens, there were 1.076.000 speakers of Albanian, 2.055.000 speakers of Greek, 1.370.000 speakers of Armenian, 764.000 speakers of Serbian, 3.607.000 speakers of Arabic, 9.819.000 speakers of Turkish, 1.478.000 speakers of Kurdish, and 355.000 Jews.

Those living in rural areas were spread out in small communities and scattered settlements. The economy in rural areas was closed. People generally tried producing what they needed to subsist. The country was completely devoid of water, roads, bridges, schools and healthcare facilities. 14% of villagers risked contracting malaria, 9% syphilis, and 72% typhoid.

The literacy rate in rural areas was around 7%. Life in towns outside cities such as Istanbul and Izmir, while somewhat better than in rural areas, was still dominated by a general prospect of poverty.

Undoubtedly, the total population having this composition and these characteristics decreased even further during World War I and the War of Independence. The loss of male labor power contributed to an increase in poverty. This was the condition in which the citizens of the new Turkish Republic found themselves.[34]

3. Ideological Differences

The arrival of Mustafa Kemal in Samsun on 19 May 1919 inaugurated a period of congresses that led up to Ankara being selected as the seat of government. It was there that the Anatolian National Struggle founded the Turkish Grand National Assembly, which was to reflect the national will. Even so, the leader of this movement did not start out with an altogether consistent and harmonious "cadre." During those days, there was but a single goal that had to be reached regardless of issue or problem: to save the motherland from the enemy and acquire national independence. The only way that this could be realized was for everyone, every idea, every segment and group in society to take its place in this national struggle and support and assist each other. Having started out like this, the intention was to continue in this fashion until the end was reached. However, before reaching its desired conclusion, signs of division - political factionalism - began to appear.

It is important to understand the conditions with which the Atatürk Revolution had to contend as it began to materialize. Without having an awareness of the obstacles that Mustafa Kemal had to overcome to realize his radical reforms, as well as the nature of the political divisions and ideological movements that influenced the post-Republican period as well it is impossible to appreciate the fact that they continue to be debated even today.

A group that appeared in the Assembly as a result of the Çerkez Ethem affair was the *Kuvayı Seyyare*. Void of any ideological content, it was clearly a power struggle conducted by cliques over "seats." For a variety of reasons, some Deputies belonging to other groups that appeared in later schisms supported the "Ethem clique" for their progressive ideas. Ethem fled and sought asylum with the Greeks. Subsequently, he, his brothers and some of his supporters were prosecuted by the Ankara Court of Independence, which issued the death penalty to some and imprisonment at hard labor to others. Still others were acquitted. Among those receiving prison sentences were Deputies who were leaders of the "Green Army," the "Clandestine Communist Party," the "People's Communist Party," and the "People's Party." The "Unionists" were a major power within the Assembly. Even the groups supporting the "Defense of Right" were split among themselves.

The Unionists: Appearing in 1889, the Committee of Union and Progress began as a clandestine organization, which received its support mainly from officers and intellectuals. Later it became transformed into a political party. After the Second Constitutional Period, it was to make its mark on the fate of the country and the Empire. The party had had many supporters due to its extended past. Nevertheless, because of having emerged defeated at the end of World War I, the respect afforded the Unionists significantly declined. Even though they had fallen out of favor, experienced veteran Unionists continued their efforts secretly. They wanted to take over the direction of the Anatolian National Struggle and regain control of the newly established state. It is known that there were about forty Unionists in the Grand National Assembly, some of whom had severed ties with Unionism and supported Mustafa Kemal. One group was caught up in "scheming." They would support Mustafa Kemal until the war was won and then they would replace him with Enver Pasha, who was waiting in Russia. In reality, they were in continuous contact with him. Enver Pasha had tried every way to move into Anatolia and had even held discussions with the new Soviet government.

Unionist Deputies, taking into consideration every possibility, saw fit to be part of a variety of political groupings during this period. The presence of Unionists was unusually great among such left-wing groups as the "People's Party," the "Communist Party," the "People's Communist Party," and the "Green Army." This dispersal to left-wing groups is due in part to the orientation of the "Party of Populist Councils," whose founding had been planned by Enver Pasha. The majority of Unionists were ruthless enemies of Mustafa Kemal.

It is only natural for political movements that have become firmly entrenched and functional in the life of a society to have an impact on neighboring societies. Historically, this has been the case with Marxist regimes. Relations between Marxist regimes and neighboring countries have generally been intense. This was no different during the period of National Struggle in Anatolia. Many individuals had close relations with Soviet Russia and sought assistance and support. Their organization and movements, carried out both clandestinely and overtly, were directed toward leftist-oriented alliances. This was the case not only in Anatolia but in the Assembly as well. Nearly all of them had as their policy the establishment of a connection between the principles of Islamic social justice and those of Bolshevism, or the creation of an identity based on them. Their dream was the creation of a new order for the Moslem Turks of Anatolia.

The Green Army: The Green Army was a clandestine organization that began operation in May 1920. Its general secretary was the former Unionist, Minister of Finance Hakkı Beyiç, who had participated in the Sivas Congress[35] and had been elected to the Board of Representatives. He entered the Turkish Grand National Assembly as a representative from Denizli. Who the other key members of the organization were is still a matter of debate. During the trial of one of them, Tokat Deputy Nazım, at the Ankara Independence Court, said that there were a total of 14 key members - all of them Deputies, three of whom were state ministers. Not having been founded in accordance with the law governing organizations, the organization was illegal. Nevertheless, it was known in Ankara - and especially in governmental circles - who belonged to it, what it did and how it operated. The organization had a 32-article bylaw. Apart from this, from time to time, it published communiqués and secretly distributed them throughout the country. The driving force of the organization was Çerkez Ethem and his *Kuvayı Seyyare.*

The publishing arm of the organization was the *Star of the New World,* edited by Arif Oruç and published in Eskişehir. The expression, "Workers and Poor of the World, Unite" appeared in the caption of the newspaper. The activities of the Green Army ended with the legal establishment of the Turkish Communist Party in Ankara on 18 October 1920.

The goals of the Green Army - it political, economic, and social programme - were laid out in the by- laws of the organization:

> • The Green Army is committed to the elimination of unjust tyrannical and oppressive practices exercised in Turkey by capitalists and all forms of expansionist, imperialistic forces.
> • The Green Army is devoted to ensuring that all individuals in the country benefit from land and general wealth commensurate with their labor as well as material and moral capabilities.
> • It considers land to be a public good and a vital need no different from water, air, light and heat, which is to be regulated by the government and managed publicly.

• In order to ensure that income and benefits accumulated from capital and derived from liquid assets go to all individuals in society and not just a few individuals and families, it calls for the active involvement of the government in the economy.

• The Green Army recognizes a government by the people that operates as a cooperative venture.

• The Green Army acknowledges that those who assist humanity the most and who are its soundest elements are people who make their living through physical and mental toil.

• The Green Army respects family life.

• The Green Army believes that a return to the "age of bliss" (according to the Sunni sect of Islam, the period of the reign of the first four Caliphs was a happy one in which genuine Islam was in force. It is necessary to return to this period. Islamic socialists consider this period and its practices as an ideal) and its authenticity is necessary and that the vain and insatiable passions coming from the West have to be thrown out of Asia. The only way of accomplishing this is following the way of God.

• Education must be free of charge, compulsory and with board, and provided in light of the common social values of society.

• The Green Army considers expansionism as the most serious ofcrimes and officially authorizes the death penalty for its supporters alone.

• The Green Army possesses a sincere fraternity and alliance with the Red Revolutionary Army (in Soviet Russia).

• The symbol of the Green Army is the green flag. Islamic fraternity will be formed under this flag and the union of people under red and green flags will usher in a joyous revolution and a renewed period of genuine bliss.

• The Green Army is run in Turkey by a clandestine central administration. Just as it is linked to all countries having Green Army organizations, it also has relations with Moscow and the center of the red army.

• Those who are members of the Green Army who betray our objectives for expansionism will be summarily executed. Death penalties will be issued by the central administration and carried out through special clandestine means.[36]

The goals of the Green Army are quite unambiguous. it is clear that while it supports the Soviets, it wants to be able to imbue communism with a religious content, taking into consideration the conditions and Islamic beliefs of the country, just as all socialist movements in Islamic countries do. Documents published right up to today provide evidence that the organization had relations with Soviet Russia.

The Communists: The Soviet government provided material assistance during the years of the War of Independence. Naturally, this was to have an effect on Turkey. Two "Turkish Communist Parties" were founded. One of these was legal; set up under the directives of Mustafa Kemal by close associates of his, and placed under his supervision, it was considered politically indispensable due to rapprochement with Soviet Russia. The other party - the Turkish Communist Party, was illegal. After working covertly for a time, it surfaced and assumed the name, "Turkish People's Communist Party."

The legal communist party was founded on 18 October 1920 with two objectives. The Marxist revolution that occurred in neighboring Russia had put into place a regime that had shown close interest and provided support and assistance to the Turkish national independence movement. By virtue of the good relations that existed between Ankara and Moscow, it was hoped that by setting up a legal communist party, covert organizations would be brought to an end. Another purpose of the party was to bring into line initiatives that were deviating from the goals of the National Struggle. Deputies included among those assigned to be founders of the legal Communist Party, set up with the knowledge and upon the orders of Mustafa Kemal, were Tevfik Rüştü (Aras), Mahmut Esat (Bozkurt), Yunus Nadi (Abalıoğlu), Kılıç Ali, Hakkı Behiç (Bayiç), Topçu İhsan, Refik (Koraltan), Mahmut Celâl (Bayar), Eyüp Sabri, and Süreyya (Yiğit). This was a step taken to be able to say to Soviet officials who, at that time, supported and encouraged covert, illegal pro-Soviet organizations in Turkey "stop providing clandestine support and encouragement ... we have founded this party legally." It was also a way to control the leaders and supporters of the communist movement in the country. The party was founded and its program prepared, but the conception of communism this party had was different from the one in Russia. In articles written in the newspapers *Hakimiyeti Milliye* ("National Sovereignty") and *Yenigün* ("New Day"), both under the control of Mustafa Kemal, the following theme was emphasized: "our understanding of the proper regime for Turkey does not conform to yours; we do not desire the kind of bloody revolution led by the working class that you advocate; the characteristics and conditions in our country are different; we want a system that uniquely suits our temperament - one that is bloodless. We want to establish a nation-state based on the sovereignty of the people" The legal Communist Party, like the "Green Army," tried to form a bridge between communism and the social justice perspectives of Islam. After a few months of ostentatious initiatives and publications, it became silent.

After the Soviet Revolution in Russia, the new officials in Moscow also worked hard at creating an administration in Turkey that would not only parallel their own interests but also could be under their control. Thus, one of the reasons for their support of and assistance to the Anatolian National Struggle was the existence of a Turkish State between Russia and the West. Another important reason for Soviet Russia supporting the National Struggle was so that Turkey would be in a strong enough position to block foreign vessels going through the straits to the Black Sea. This behavior was realistic, appropriate and rational - both theoretically and within the context of historical concerns over access to the open sea. With this in mind, the leaders of Soviet Russia sent many persons to Turkey to help in the establishment, encouragement and support of a communist regime in Anatolia. Ranging from the Soviet representative, Şerif Manatof to Mustafa Suphi, many individuals worked to realize this idea. The illegal Turkish Communist Party that became active at the beginning of the summer of 1920 was an organization set up as a consequence of this policy.

According to the view expressed in the bylaws of this party, it would work toward the assistance of nations and classes in their opposition to poverty and oppression; the abolition of property rights; and the nationalization of capitalist, wealth-producing resources, such as land, banks, factories, buildings, railroads, maritime transportation and commerce. This was to be done by the leadership of the workers carried out within general policy of the organization in Russia. It was known for certain that the party was pro-Soviet. It was active until the end of 1920. It subsequently appeared as the legal "Turkish Populist Communist Party." Thus a clandestine party became legal with the formation of this party. According to some, there is a possibility that the Turkish Populist Communist Party was active prior to becoming a legal entity.

The Turkish Populist Communist Party was founded on 7 December 1920 and was active for two to three months. Its activities were halted during the days that Çerkez Ethem sought refuge with the Greeks. Among the founders of the party were Tokat Deputy Nazım, Bursa Deputy Sheik Servet, Afyonkarahisar Deputy Mehmet Şükrü, Veterinary Major Salih (Hacıoğlu), and Ziynetullah Nuşirevan. The goals of this party were the same as the other illegal communist parties. However, for a Communist revolution and regime, workers were not enough; villagers were included as part of the ruling and revolutionary classes. They also had the idea of taking advantage of the social conventions of Islam. Because it was claimed that the party cooperated with Çerkez Ethem and his bothers and was working to overthrow the government and leaders of the National Struggle, their activities were prohibited.

The Turkish People's Communist Party became politically active once again during the spring of 1922, but after it attempted to set up a pro-Soviet government, it was closed down under the Rauf Bey government.

The Fragmentation of the Society for the Defense of Rights: Turkish Grand National Assembly during its first term was characterized as a "hybrid committee" with respect to the ideas, objectives - both concealed and disclosed, illusions, pursuits, social and political origins, and ambitions reflected there. Each Deputy committed himself to the "National Pact." Everyone was a champion of the "Defense of Rights". Be that as it may, as time passed after the initial opening of the Assembly and issues began to be discussed there, the real views, passions, and objectives of its members began to come to light and debates intensified. The leadership of the movement was mainly concerned with the regime that was to be set up once victory was achieved and who was to head it. A large group unquestionably saw Mustafa Kemal as its natural leader. However, there were other groups that had different people, administrators and regimes in mind. At a time when the National Front was facing its greatest threats, Mustafa Kemal was being subjected to extensive criticism in the Assembly. It was clear that paths would part sooner or later but it was still uncertain as to just when this would come about. The most opportune time had not yet arrived. After the reading of the "Populist Programme," various groups formed within the Assembly and began making decisions as to the course to follow in the days ahead. Among these groups, those emphasized in Mustafa Kemal's "Speech"[37] were the "Solidarity Group," the "Independence Group," the "Defense of Rights Group," the "People's Group," and the "Reform Group." The members of the Independence Group were mostly revolutionary youth while those of the People's Group were leftist-oriented Deputies. The conservatives united in the Solidarity Group with some of the Unionists and Ottoman reformers commg together in the Reform Group.[38]

On 10 May 1921, as the turmoil, formation of alliances and dissension was in full swing, Mustafa Kemal and his supporters formed a new group, followed in the next few days by an opposition group. This gave rise to the division in the Assembly among the supporters of the "Society for the Defense of Rights," which, from here on will be referred to as the "First Group," and the "Second Group."

The First Group: The charter of the First Group, whose 14-member executive committee was chaired by Mustafa Kemal, consisted of 16 articles. The main article of the charter contained two points. First, that the Group was dedicated to the principles of the National Pact and second, that it intended to employ all the material and spiritual resources at the disposal of the nation to obtain a peace that would ensure national unity and independence. This was to be done by making all the organizations and institutions in the country - both public and private - work toward the same goal. The Group was to aim at determining which organizations were constitutionally appropriate for the state and nation and take the measures necessary to create them.

This group was to serve as the basis for the "Anatolian and Roumelian Defense of Rights Group" that Mustafa Kemal had hoped to establish in what was to be the final Ottoman Assembly in Istanbul. However, it was some four months before this happened since Deputies who had gone to Istanbul failed to keep their word. The Group had 262 members.[39] The First Group became a political party upon the forming of the People's Party on 9 September 1923.

The Second Group: This group was a rival front within the Assembly that was formed by Deputies who were opponents of Atatürk and who were not included within the First Group. It became active after the First Group had become a legal entity, making itself felt for the first time in the Assembly at the beginning of 1922. This group announced that it had been founded to avert the formation of a repressive regime, a personal dictatorship and to ensure the rule of law. Moreover, it announced that it was opposed to partisanship, autocracy and repression within Assembly. It is clear from this that the Second Group was directly opposed to Mustafa Kemal. Members of the group engaged in a staunch battle within the Assembly to have the system whereby the Chairman of the Assembly (Mustafa Kemal) nominated members to the Council of Ministers abolished. Some of the members of the Second Group succeeded in getting chosen as ministers. The internal strife and confusion promoted in the Assembly by the Second Group reached such proportions at times that some Deputies left the First Group and joined the Second Group. Notably, among the leading Deputies in the Second Group were the Unionists of the Assembly in Istanbul who had come from Malta. Principle spokesmen for the Second Group included Erzurum Deputy Hüseyin Avni, Mersin Deputy Colonel Selâhattin, Trabzon Deputy Ali Şükrü, Kırşehir Deputy Müfit Hoca, Afyonkarahisar Deputy Mehmet Şükrü, and Erzurum Deputy Celalettin Arif. The group had 123 members, but because it did not nominate candidates for the elections held in August 1923, no one from this Group was elected and it thus ceased to exist.

4. Challenges and Drawbacks

The radical reforms undertaken by the Atatürk Revolution as it attempted to shape the direction of modernization, met with adversity that stemmed from both domestic and foreign factors.

As have been discussed in various sections thus far, domestic factors were related to the social, economic, political, cultural, religious and ethnic structure and conditions of the country and society. The goal of the Revolution was to change this structure - to make the transition from a traditional society based on religious communities to a society that was modern, laïc and national. This transformation was to bring about a number of hardships - including resistance - along the way. Political structure would be changed so as to encourage modern political institutionalization and political socialization. This, however, necessitated a clash with traditional and religious authorities and other foci of authority within society. National unity would be ensured such that a consciousness of national identity within individuals would be created. This would be a consciousness that would give them a feeling of pride and pleasure from being able to say, "I'm a Turk." The development of this sense of nation, one in which individuals espousing nationalist sentiment coexisted within a society having national dimensions, was an inevitable and obligatory prerequisite. However, throughout history, nearly every segment of society had lived as Moslems belonging to the "community of Islam" and thus identified themselves accordingly. Moslems make up nearly 98' of the population, and being of Turkish origin, it would only be a matter of time before they would acquire a national identity and a consciousness of being Turkish. In contrast, the existence in society of different *millets*, comprising religious and linguistic groups who did not speak Turkish, was quite a different matter. They constituted sources of resistance to the movement and struggle toward nation-building. While the vast majority of the population was Moslem, there were also many different sects. Throughout history, Turkish society has experienced the ill-fated struggle and conflicts brought on by sectarian provocation and the encouragement of ethnic division. The economy of the country remained backward and its people poor. At the same time, it remained under the control and influence of traditional wealthy families, clans, tribes, sect leaders and large landowners. Attempting to ensure an equitable distribution of income, a just system of taxation and land reform could give rise to the formation of political camps within traditional foci of power in their opposition to the Revolution, spawning the creation of a political party that would present itself as a political alternative.

This is the fate of all movements of radical reform, including that of modernization. The way that radical reformers and progressive leaders can avoid being enslaved by this fate is to aim at and reach their goals by determining strategies and tactics through which these hardships can be overcome.

The Atatürk Revolution had aimed at a pluralist, liberal and democratic political system. But during its initial phase, creating the wherewithal through which this could be achieved and recognizing the rights of other political parties - including that of opposition - could open the door to all traditional sources of authority forming the bases for counter-revolution.

Considering the incremental approach to change Atatürk adopted, we can conclude that he was well aware of the potential hardships and dangers that faced him - including the criticism that he would receive for his approach. Not wanting to deviate from the tangible goals of the movement for radical reform, he simply forged ahead. This incremental course of action was also deemed necessary in order to avoid a possible "reign of terror."

Among the foreign threats to the Atatürk Revolution were those that stemmed from Turkey's geographical location and the policies of powerful Western states and close neighbors. Historically, both Western powers and Turkey's close neighbor, Russia, had designs on Anatolia and had hoped to partition it. The Western states had suffered defeat at the hands of the very Turkish nation they now wanted to carve up. There was the likelihood that they would look for another opportunity in the future to control the country. It is also known that ever since the Czars, it had been Russian national policy to obtain access to warm seas through the Straits. Something else that could not be overlooked was the fact that nearly every powerful state makes it a policy to encourage the use of its own political system as a model for modernization, which has the effect of creating allies.

Despite all these hardships and potential threats confronting Atatürk while putting together his own model of revolution, he took great pains not to swerve from the fundamental principles of state policy or to fail under the influence or control of others. He had chosen a national model of modernization and he was determined to carry it out.

IV

THE ATATÜRK PARADIGM
OF
MODERNIZATION

The movement of radical reform carried out in Turkey under Atatürk's leadership was, from its very inception, both pragmatic and dynamic - becoming the determining factor behind Turkish modernization. However, it was the particular vigor with which it was conducted during the Atatürk period that was particularily decisive in delineating its function, authority and responsibility. When the Atatürk Revolution is examined in detail from this perspective, what emerges is a general paradigm for nation-building and modernization - especially for developing countries. The Atatürk paradigm of modernization, a replica of neither the Capitalist nor the Marxist models of development, did not look beyond the borders of Turkey for inspiration. It derived its applicability and viability from the fact that it was both national *and* pragmatic in orientation. National solutions would be found to national problems within the Turkish context.

In the many studies of modernization that have been done, it has come to light that success is more likely in countries that use modes of development that are based on the particular structural characteristics and dynamics of the countries in question rather than on simple imitation. This has the added advantage of reducing the likelihood of excessive foreign influence - thus diminishing the prospect of independence being compromised.

The revolutionary leaders of so-called developing societies are uniquely positioned to assess the needs of these societies. By taking into consideration their structural characteristics, an appropriate model of modernization and development can be chosen. Socio-political reforms based on pragmatic consideration of particular national needs - this is the basis for success, one that was first expounded by the Atatürk paradigm of modernization. Its validity becomes even more evident when the problem of effective leadership and administration - an important problem encountered during modernization/development - is taken into account. An effective leadership is one that acts in the interest of the nation, determines the means available to that nation and then finds ways of taking appropriate action. Through energetic, deliberate and dynamic leadership, modernization will be successful.

As the Ottoman Empire was on the decline, it became increasingly overwhelmed by the, both direct and indirect, pressures of foreign powers. It took the leadership of Atatürk to dramatically transform the politico-economic climate. For the first time in ages, it became possible for Turkey and its people to not feel downtrodden vis-à-vis foreign powers.

The importance of national independence and of creating a politico-cultural entity that was unique unto itself became evident during the discussion in the Assembly over the responsibilities and powers of the Council of Ministers. In response to critics who had opposed the body, Mustafa Kemal declared, "you object that our proposal resembles neither democracy nor socialism, or anything else for that matter. Well, gentlemen, we ought to be proud of not resembling or making ourselves resemble anything else! Because we resemble ourselves."[40] This was a clear indication of his commitment to the development of a unique national identity. Atatürk's faith in the Turkish people provided him with the courage to stand up and proclaim, "This is what we are!" The Atatürk Revolution was the vehicle through which Turkish society came to acquire and express its own inimitable character. It created the milieu in which self-awareness, far removed from foreign pressure and influence, could emerge.

The Atatürk Revolution was a *national* movement of radical reform and was in no way class-based. Atatürk created a struggle for liberation that encompassed all classes within a single nation. Independence cannot be achieved through the efforts or in the name of a single class. A nation requires the solidarity of all classes in order to achieve independence. Pragmatism rules. The recognition of the need to create institutions that encompassed all classes was manifested in the founding in 1923 of the Republican People's Party (R.P.P.), the chief civilian agency, guiding and leading the reform movement. Civilian supremacy over political affairs became a distinct characteristic of the Republican era. The R.P.P. is a concrete example of a non-totalitarian single-party in a socio-political system undergoing modernization.

Another important function assumed by the party was the creation of a civilian-based political cadre. As Rustow pointed out, at the beginning, the upper echelons of the party had been occupied by military elites, but in time, this party came to be made up of civilians.[41] By establishing a single-party system, Turkey had overcome militarism.[42] But at the same time, Atatürk was certain that the officer corps had become strongly imbued with the spirit of the reforms. Moreover, Atatürk stated on a number of occasions his deep confidence in the army's dedication to the defense of the principles of the Revolution and also Turkish territory from any internal or external threat. Therefore, Atatürk looked to the army officers to safeguard the Revolution. Subsequent Turkish political developments since then have vindicated his judgment. However, the Atatürk paradigm of modernization was not based on the support of the military; neither did it aim at creating a permanent single-party regime. The single-party system was seen in pragmatic terms as transitional. Pluralism was the ultimate objective of the paradigm. Moreover, although a pluralist multi-party regime was not obtained during Atatürk's time, some degree of pluralism was tolerated even within the single-party regime - reflected in some rather liberal debates on a variety of issues being conducted in the Assembly.

Two significant attempts at transition to multi-party politics were undertaken. One of these was the establishing of the Republican Progressive Party in 1924. This party had tried to bring a two-party system to the country and to end the absolute control of the Republican People's Party over the Grand National Assembly. The leaders of the Republican Progressive Party were most emphatic that the President of Turkey not act in the capacity of the Chairman of a party. The Republican Progressive Party also stated that it was in favor of respecting religious convictions and dogmas.

In 1925, a rebellion [led by Sheik Sait] broke out in Eastern Turkey. The Republican Progressive Party was subsequently accused of political and religious reaction, and some of its members were charged with abetting the uprising. It was claimed that the Republican Progressive Party wanted to bring back the institutions of traditional Ottoman society. As a consequence of this sequence of events, the Republican Progressive Party was dissolved in 1925 by the Grand National Assembly.

Another effort to establish a two-party system took place in August 1930. Atatürk himself helped in the setting up of this opposition party, which was called the Free Republican Party. Not only did he provide guarantees that it would not be closed down as the first opposition party had been, he personally selected the founding administrative cadre of the party. It came to be seen by some as a party that would be supervised by Mustafa Kemal's own Republican People's Party. To found the Free Republican Party, Mustafa Kemal had recalled Ali Fehti (Okyar) Bey - a close associate of Atatürk and a former Prime Minister - from his post in Paris. A number of Deputies, who had up until then been members of the R.P.P., were assigned as party officials. Mustafa Kemal's sister, Makbule Atadan, was among those who held positions of administrative responsibility in the party.

While Mustafa Kemal had promised his support of the Free Republican Party, this support had been conditional. So long as the reforms undertaken in the name of the Revolution were not compromised, the party could exist. Turkey was faced with a number of difficulties during this period. The crisis that had become endemic in the world economy had had a great impact on the Turkish economy, which had emerged from war impoverished and almost in ruins. The country was struggling to rebuild what was left of the economy. Combined with the global crisis, the impoverishment the Turkish people was growing. The General Chairman òf the new party, Ali Fehti (Okyar) Bey, believed in the role of private initiative in the economy and wanted commerce, industry, and the economy as a whole to be far removed from state control. He thought that this was the way through which development could be accomplished. The party, however, was not completely free to exercise its influence in setting the agenda. The R.P.P. had acquired overwhelming ascendancy in the political arena. The chairmanship of the R.P.P., while having been handed over to the Deputy Chairman İsmet (İnönü) Pasha when Mustafa Kemal was elected President, the real leader of the party -the person held the actual reigns of responsibility and authority- was still Mustafa Kemal and everyone knew this. Thus the Free Republican Party had limited impact on agenda setting. This made the General Chairman and leaders of the party cynical about their role. Even though Mustafa Kemal had assured them that he would remain neutral in his role as President, provided the party did nothing to challenge the basic principles of the Revolution.

The new party announced in its programme that it supported laïcism, was committed to the Republic in no uncertain terms and that it would work accordingly. However, given the rather liberal political atmosphere of the time, elements challenging the laïc bases of the Republic began to appear. The Free Republican Party took this opportunity to regroup. Conservatives opposed to the Republic and laïcism, persons with political grievances or a desire for a return to the Empire, as well as members of different denominations and sects began emerging on the political scene - obtaining positions in the local party branches of the Free Republican Party. Despite the efforts of the General Chairman and party officials, it became impossible to thwart conservative and reactionary challenges. The most serious conflict that arose between the Free Republican Party and the Republican People's Party occurred in the Assembly when the former made a call for general debate over the issue of the municipal elections that had been held in 1930. The two sides incriminated one another in the debates that ensued. These debates had the effect of encouraging reactionaries; in some places, photographs of President Mustafa Kemal were torn up and counter-revolutionary activities ensued. In some places, most conspicuously in Izmir, attacks were made on the R.P.P. Provincial Headquarters and on a journalist who supported this party. This resulted in a rebuke by Mustafa Kemal. The President made it perfectly clear in a speech he delivered just what his position and response was. Indicating that he was "historically bound to [the R.P.P.]" ... and that ... "there was no reason to severe ties with it," he announced that the aggressors and those who encouraged them would not escape prosecution.[43]

Following these events, President Mustafa Kemal embarked on a tour of the country and once more, assumed personal responsibility for investigating the situation. Once the disposition of the Free Republican Party had become clear with respect to the Revolution and the implementation of its radical reforms, the leadership of the party decided to close the party – thus bringing this second attempt at [multi-party politics] to an inconclusive end.

The inexperience of the Turkish people in multi-party politics, the counter-revolutionary activities on the part of some members of these opposition parties proved to be among the most important reasons for the failure of attempts to establish other political parties. In reality, it must be said that the Revolution was still too new. Such concerted attack on traditional society by Kemal Atatürk and the revolutionary elites could not take place without opposition from those whose interests were threatened, or appeared to be threatened, by the changes. Old tribal, feudal, and ecclesiastical privileged classes rarely submit docilely to change that threatens their power, their wealth, their ways of living and ways of thinking. Nor do the masses, as represented by peasants and nomads, submit eagerly to change in the pattern of their way of life.[44]

During the embryonic years of the Republic, the two initial attempts at transition to a multi-party regime had given rise to great altercation, most of which was fuelled by the rebellion of certain fanatic elements that were opposed to the Republic and Atatürk's radical reforms. The atmosphere in 1924 created by the Progressive Republican Party had paved the way for the armed rebellion by Sheik Sait in the East, which was successfully crushed militarily. The subsequent closing of the Progressive Republican Party ushered in a period of political restrictions. With the founding of the Free Republican Party, which was the second attempt at creating a multi-party regime, conservative, fanatic, and counter-revolutionary people coalesced under its umbrella. When they began to espouse positions contrary to party leadership, the party leadership responded by closing the party on 23 December 1930. This prompted another bloody event this time in Menemen, near Izmir. Sect leader Derviş Mehmet, together with a band of supporters, created an incident when they began shouting in unison, "We demand Shariat," joined in by a number of other people in the community. Second Lieutenant Kubilay, who commanded the small army unit that confronted them, was shot. As if this were not enough, the crowd slowly decapitated him with a blunt knife. Demanding Shariat, these rebels placed Kubilay's severed head on top of a pole from which a green flag was hung. As they roamed through the streets of Menemen, they attempted to incite all the people to rebel.

Mustafa Kemal's response to this bloody action undertaken by enemies of the Revolution was severe and categorical. Capturing the provocateurs, they were executed *en masse*. This definitive response - this rapid reprisal - silenced reactionaries and enemies of the Revolution for a long time. Apart from the attempt of some to recite the call to prayer in Arabic in Bursa 1933, no other reactionary event was witnessed during Mustafa Kemal's lifetime.

A second party was founded in 1930. Requests made to set up a third party were rejected on the basis that it advocated communism. The "People's Republican Party," which was founded in Adana on 29 September 1930 by Abdülkadir Kemali (Öğütçü) Bey, failed to become no more than regional in scope. After four months, it was closed by a decision of the Government. Attempts were made to set up still another party, this time in Edirne, under the name of the "Turkish Republican Workers and Farmers Party." The published bylaws of the party called for a socialist regime in the interests of Workers and farmers. Given the emphasis that the Revolution placed on the solidarity of all classes, this appeal was not favorably regarded. After these attempts, it was not until 1945 that another party was given permission to be founded.

The single-party regime that had been established was conceived of as transitional. It was to serve to guide the modernization and the political development of Turkey. Such a period of transition was essential as the country moved away from a highly repressive, religion-based regime headed by the Caliph-Sultan to a liberal democratic regime, based on the supremacy of the Republic, National Will, and the unconditional sovereignty of the people. Historically, the political party as an institution is not a by-product of traditional society but of modern society. Parties founded upon traditional social structure tend to impede modernization. They are predisposed to reinforcing the status quo, thus contributing to stagnation - and even degeneration. They do not create the conditions through which the kind of social change characteristic of modernization is possible. This is clearly illustrated in the many counter-revolutionary activities witnessed during the multi-party period that began after World War II.

As Huntington points out, the basic condition for political modernization is the replacement of religious, traditional, familial and ethnic authority by a laïc, national, unitary one.[45] This was one of the many achievements of the Atatürk Revolution. What accelerates modernization and imbues it with meaning is not simply a change in form of authority or solving such macro-level problems as increasing prosperity in economic and social life. Modernization is a holistic phenomenon. Its coherence is derived from changes occurring also at the micro level. An important component of modernization at this level is the behavior of individuals, their value judgments and how they interact with other people, organizations, and the state. In other words, their "roles" and how they perceive those roles within society.

Atatürk recognized what modernization entailed and formulated his paradigm of radical reform accordingly. Problems associated with modernization at both the micro and macro levels were identified. Because nation-building and laïcism were concerned with problems at many levels, the Revolution enlisted the participation of both society and state. The kind of nationalism embodied by laïcism and its rejection of fatalism, had a direct influence on personal values and behavior. The revolutionary reforms undertaken in the area of education had the effect of shaping to a great extent the Turkish modernization movement on both the micro and macro levels.

The Atatürk Revolution was a dynamic movement of radical reform designed to modernize the country. Not only was it national in scope but also it was pragmatic in thrust. Its principles evolved as the Revolution unfolded. The ultimate ideological direction of the Revolution was a result of revolutionary pragmatism.

According to Berkes, until Atatürk, "previous attempts at reform had failed to understand that reform entailed a complete transformation of society. The attempt, for example, by the Ottoman State in the 18th century to borrow from the West did not entail a transition from a medieval order to a new social order. On the contrary, it was seen as a way of strengthening the state so that the former order, which was still seen as ideal, could be salvaged."[46]

Moreover, according to Eisenstadt, the Kemalist Revolution was markedly different from other "reforms" that had been attempted in the past in that it included a shift in the foundations of political "legitimacy" and the symbols of political community. Together, they redefined politico-cultural space. The redefinition of political community occurred in a very interesting and unique manner. The political community was no longer based on Islam but rather was redefined in terms of the Turkish nation.

The Turkish Revolution thus rejected the religious basis of legitimacy, striving instead to place legitimacy on a laïc and national foundation, thereby laying the philosophical basis for a new "collectivity."[47]

The Atatürk Revolution was not simply a set of superficial reforms; its objective was to bring about radical structural change.

There are two important aspects of the Atatürk Revolution that need to be emphasized. The first is related to the creation of the institutions and structures designed to ensure the establishment of a new modern nation-state. The other aspect concerns economic development and social and cultural change. During Atatürk's time, fundamental changes were made in social and political institutions that enabled the complete transformation of the Turkish political system. The reforms carried out during this period - chiefly through the spread of educational opportunities - rocked the foundations of the Turkish political system. The birth of the multi-party era, a pluralist regime and a more complex form of society was the result of the radical changes within the Turkish political system that took place during this era.

Top-down "models" have generally been used in developing countries to create national unity. These types of models frequently turn to traditions as avenues of coherence.[48] This is where the paradigm embodied in the Atatürk Revolution diverges, taking an entirely distinct, radical path.

The contentment or dissatisfaction of the people is expressed through social organizations. The most important of these organizations are political parties, followed by other institutions that assume different responsibilities, such as unions. Parties maintain a regular flow of information to the government, form a pool of human resources for the government and serve as means of governmental coordination.[49]

Political parties within the Atatürk model had these functions (which will be explained in more detail below).

1. The Objectives of the Paradigm

Models of change have certain objectives and the Atatürk paradigm was no different. But while formulated with certain general objectives in mind, it also relied on pragmatism in etching out specific reforms. The first of its general objectives was modernization and the second, development. Together they were to lead to a level of "contemporary civilization," which was the ultimate goal of the Revolution. Development and modernization are often collapsed into a single conceptual category. However, while development is inherent within the notion of modernization, because development can occur in some sense without modernization, e.g., as illustrated by certain practices under totalitarian regimes, the two phenomena need to be considered separately. The fundamental objective of contemporary democratic society is ensuring the freedom of the individual in all areas of life. Freedom does not only entail economic and social security, educational opportunities or material prosperity. At the same time, it encompasses the need for political freedoms, and the right to choose among political alternatives. It is for this reason that modernization cannot be seen as simply a form of economic development. Historically, even Marxist regimes have demonstrated a degree of economic development sufficient enough to provide for the material well-being of its citizens. However, in such countries, the individual has generally been deprived of political freedoms or the right to choose among alternatives. Thus, while these countries may be developed in an *economic* sense, they cannot be thought of as having achieved modernization. Similarly, an individual may have a plethora of political rights - such as is the case in many of the so-called developed capitalist countries. But if the rights granted to him by law are void of any kind of economic content and fail to ensure his material well-being, it is impossible to speak of genuine freedom.

These two phenomena - development and modernization - form the backbone of the Atatürk paradigm. Given their relative autonomy, it is imperative that they be examined separately. While modernization generally encompasses development, the reverse is not always true. By distinguishing between them, it is possible to determine the aspects of the Atatürk paradigm of revolutionary reform that sets it off from either the Capitalist or Marxist paradigms.

a) Modernization

As a result of the systematic analysis of modernization that began with the breakdown of the colonial system after the Second World War, a variety of academic studies of the status of new countries were conducted.

The economic, social and political changes of newly independent countries came to be addressed in terms of modernization. Modernization can be defined in a number of ways, one being the rational use of resources to establish a modern society. In turn, modern society can be characterized as a society in which such elements as technology, social solidarity, urbanization, literacy, social mobility and a consciousness of national identity are well entrenched. The move toward modernization tends to be inexorable, ensuring, to the extent possible, the demise of traditional society.

While it may not be entirely clear how modernization is to be carried out, it nonetheless remains an ideal embraced by all countries. The political elites of newly established states want their societies to acquire the characteristics of "being modern." These include dynamism, change, industrialization, autonomy, effectiveness, power and national unity. During the breakdown of colonialism, the desire for change and transformation spread to every corner of the globe. This was the stimulus for the wave of modernizing revolutions seen. Atatürk once remarked, "opposing the raging tide of civilization is of no use; societies that refuse to change and continue to preserve medieval law, ideas and behavior are doomed either to extinction or servitude."

The belief upon which the phenomenon of modernization is based is *rationalism* and *scientific management*. Modernization can also be thought of as the spread of a "global culture" consisting of the following factors: the presence of advanced technology and science, a rational perspective on life, the predominance of a laïc basis for social relations, and above all, the widespread adoption of a nation-state regime.

The modernization entails a greater dynamism of both state and society. Not simply entailing industrialization, it encompasses social, psychological and political change as well.

Thus, modernization can be examined in three main ways:

1. In terms of a basic economic movement that gives priority to industrialization;

2. In terms of the social and psychological changes that give rise to change from the point of view of traditional behavior and individual perspectives;

3. In terms of a variety of changes that ensures differentiation in political structure and institutions; the broadening of political participation; and the inculcation and expansion of nationalism.

Nevertheless, an authentic modernizing revolution cannot - or at least should not - be broken down into such distinct groupings. Economic, political, social and psychological changes are intimately linked to one another. They reinforce and strengthen each other. Once these changes are wrought, a modern society can be created.

However, the government has a function in all these changes that is perhaps far more important than all others actors. Such political institutions ought to be created and such a regime ought to be established that the government is flexible enough to meet the demands made on it and strong enough to do something about them. By finding the political means through which political receptivity is broadened and made more effective, the government can ensure that the appropriate changes are made. Political modernization is correlated with economic growth, and social and psychological transformation. This is because the receptivity of government in the face of demands and the effectiveness of the political system are influenced by economic and cultural factors.

Thus political modernization consists of three basic characteristics:

1. The increased concentration of power in the state and the weakening of traditional sources of authority,

2. The emergence of differentiation and specialization in political institutions,

3. The political participation of people on a grander scale and in a more effective manner, and the concomitant integration of individu-

als with a growing political system and the attainment of a consciousness of national identity.[50]

On the other hand, in order to bring about a complete and successful modernization of a traditional society, traditional forces in
four areas need to be met head-on: 1) the behavior of individuals, 2)
policy, 3) the economy and 4) social structure.[51]

The Atatürk Revolution had to struggle with traditional forces
and centers of power wanting to obstruct the modernization of society in these areas. Therefore, its radical reform movement had to either eliminate these obstacles completely or, at the very least, minimize them. This struggle continues even today. Accordingly, duty of the
Revolution and its revolutionary cadre was to make revolution, e.g.,
revolutionary reform, a permanent feature of society. Tunaya sees this
duty as a "vital obligation" and says the following:

> Once the Turkish Revolution has become a principle of existence, it is essen-
> tial that counter-revolutionary forces be eliminated.
>
> It is necessary to conclude that Atatürk's power did not constitute dictatorship
> but rather a means of wiping out backward institutions and rising to a civilized le-
> vel. He did not become an instrument through which civilized values would be eli-
> minated. Atatürkism was a movement that adopted as its goal the establishment
> of a democratic system at a civilized level within the conditions that existed in the
> 20th century. But above all, Atatürk acted from the belief that residual medieval
> powers would always undermine a civilized society. It is our duty today to inves-
> tigate the extent to which a regime based on these residues and the political po-
> wers representing them can be democratic and then to demonstrate that they can
> have nothing to do with democracy.[52]

In this way, the Atatürk Revolution became a movement able to
oppose traditional forces and counterrevolutionary centers of power.
And while attempts at modernization may not be uniformly successful in all areas, Turkish society of that period had undergone a remarkable transformation vis-à-vis Ottoman society. As Tunaya has pointed out, in a country undertaking such revolutionary reform, progressive action has come to mean the implementation of a specific policy,
liberation from the coercive influence of reactionary forces, and the

emergence of a conflict between progressive and reactionary powers.[53] While these conflicts could not be avoided in the Turkish case, the "price" paid for modernization was kept to a minimum compared to other radical reform movements. This has been substantia-
ted by the research conducted by foreign scholars as well. For example, as Rustow has pointed out, considering Mustafa Kemal's successes, it must be remembered that political reforms on this scale resulting in such a minimal loss of life is rare.[54]

The Atatürk paradigm for revolutionary reform encompasses both
modernization and development. The essence of all this is an independent nation-state, a modern developed society, and within this society
emancipated men and women. All radical reforms are undertaken
with this ultimate goal in mind.

b) Development

The concept of development intrinsic to modernization is concerned less with short-term improvements within the economy and increases in national income and more with long-term ones involving
an expansion of national productivity, production, income (gross national product) and profits. Furthermore, along with these increases,
the concept implies a more equitable distribution of income and a reduction of poverty, whereby individuals lead more abundant and
prosperous lives. The kind of development preferred in the economy
is that which is constant, rapid and "sufficient unto itself." Such
dynamic development increasingly sets the stage for the transformation of the economic and social structure of society, the rise of new value judgments, and new relations of production, which make possible new forms of social organization and social dynamics.

After World War II, there was great scholarly attention paid to the
developmental problems experienced by the increasing numbers of
countries acquiring independence. Scholars in different countries, as
well as international organizations, use the terms "less developed,"
"backward," "underdeveloped" and "developing" to refer to those
countries. While three-quarters of the world's total population live in
developing countries, they receive only one-quarter of the income generated worldwide. The less developed countries, which have to sup-

port the vast majority of the population of the world, have much in common with respect to their social structures and economies. Poverty is the common denominator of most of them. Per capita annual income is low. Low national income has the effect of keeping investment and savings at negligible levels. Naturally, this results in the failure to make the investments that are necessary for development. Thus supply is limited. Low per capita national income also negatively affects demand. Inadequate purchasing power brings about a contraction of markets. Market inadequacies deter entrepreneurs from making investments, which means that the economy has to suffice with a low rate of extraction. This leads to both a decline in productivity and a failure to increase production. Because of this vicious circle created by the dynamics of the liberal economic system, poverty continues unabated.

Another factor that has a. negative impact on the economies of less developed countries is population. Under conditions of low population growth and low national income, poverty naturally continues at a constant level. On the other hand, where population growth is relatively greater than the rise in national income, poverty inevitable increases.

These were among the reasons why new models of economic development were sought by the less developed countries. Following World War II, economic planning, such as that exemplified by the industrial planning carried out within the context of étatism in Turkey between 1933-1938, became an indispensable tool of development policy. This was the case not only for backward countries but also in some developed countries having rather divergent economic systems. While the Soviet Union had been the contemporary pioneer in state planning as a means of stimulating economic development, its highly centralized approach was considered by many as too dogmatic and restrictive. It was the Turkish étatist model, with its more pragmatic and flexible approach, that came to be preferred.

Today, most societies undergoing modernization and development are attempting to do so outside the parameters of the liberal capitalist economic system. But at the same time, it must be emphasized that, for the most part, the paradigm being used is not Marxist, either.

The intermediate systems that have come to be developed throughout the world use a mixed bag of methods derived from both liberal and socialist economies, which have been adapted to the particular problems and conditions present in the country employing them. Thus there has been an effort to make private initiative, private property, state intervention, public and state property - and all the institutions associated with each one of them - work together at the same time. Depending on social conditions and policy orientation, direction is provided to the economy through either prescriptive or advisory plans. In this way, the state becomes integral to the economy as advisor, entrepreneur, supervisor, and industrialist.

The Atatürk model of development and modernization was the first instance of a mixed system of planned national development being used by a modernizing society. *But it was much more than merely an intermediate system lying between the Capitalist and the Marxist development paradigms; it was a prototype of development and modernization in and of itself.*

The principle of étatism in the Atatürkist model of revolutionary reform became operational after 1930. Atatürk had called this the principle of "guided economy"[55] and assigned to the state the role of entrepreneur, industrialist and administrator in economic development.

2. The Problematical Stages of the Paradigm

Movements for independence, modernization, or other forms of radical reform do not materialize from thin air; they need something that ignites, propels and directs them. Rebellions may be initiated by the masses and may even become full-fledged revolutions. But without leadership, they are doomed to fail, something that has been documented historically.[56] In the case of struggles of national liberation, the masses need to be rallied to fight against colonial powers and forces of occupation. Suffering from poverty, oppressed by the presence of foreigners and receiving low wages, the masses are aware of their predicament. Combined with the nearly non-existence of medical doctors and hospitals, inadequate productivity of the soil they farm, and extensive illiteracy, it is not difficult to persuade people to join forces to fight for independence. However, once independent, it is the traditional elements of society that become impediments to nation-building and the acquisition of national identity. Thus, what may have served to unite and coalesce the masses to fight for independence becomes ineffectual once that independence has been achieved. Nevertheless, it is this very national unity and identity that must be attained before complete modernization is possible.

Another important problem for these societies is that they have not yet been transformed into political communities, and thus lack the established institutions of such entities. Society is fragmented - or perhaps more accurately, fragmentalized. Groups having different tribal, clan, religious, and ethnic roots form distinct traditional sources of power. In conjunction with these distinctions, in most societies there is a plurality of languages spoken. Brought together under the notion of "liberation," these fragmented communities find it rather difficult to realize "unity" and to embark upon the process of nation-building once independent. Yet, without accomplishing this, modernization is impossible. There is need for a power or legitimate "authority" that will be instrumental in nation-building. While this ought to be the government, not every government possesses adequate "authority." In order for a government - for the leader of a revolution - to be able to exercise genuine authority and to ensure that its decisions are carried out, it is imperative that the state apparatus and all of the power sources in society be placed under its control. If a government is unable to establish an effective administration and a functioning state order, other forces and sources of authority will appear. To illustrate, in recent history - in the late 1960s and 1970s, Turkey experienced a period characterized by continual chaos, turbulence and armed conflict. This was despite the fact that the government was fully intact and functioning. Society had reached a point where it could no longer put up with what it felt to be the intolerable state of affairs faced by the individual. Because people no longer felt secure and had lost their confidence in the future, they lived in a state of perpetual apprehension. During Atatürk's era, society had not been beset by this "apprehension" or "vacuum" with respect to social well-being. But contemporary society is quite different from the society of that period. Its expectations, demands, and needs have both changed and multiplied. Opportunities have similarly changed and expanded. So what caused this malaise in society? This question is particularly relevant to developing countries and actually constitutes their main problem, its answer is the same for every country: When a society embarks upon rapid change, the political regime, its institutions, and all personnel within them have roles to play and must keep up with the pace of change. Social and economic change requires new relations of production, new political institutions, new organizations, and new solutions. When the opportunities for them are not provided, conflict within society arises. The phenomenon of change is a sound step forward for all societies - however, it is on one condition: that this change does not give rise to armed conflict.

Economic development is a goal of developing societies; but so is political stability. Unfortunately, the two goals are not always compatible. Generally, the growth accompanying economic development brings instability rather than stability. If the distribution of national income among individuals is not equitable prior to the realization of economic growth; if the resources and opportunities of society are not used for the benefit of all members of society; if the injustices piquing social conscience cannot be eliminated through existing possibilities; if new institutions and organizations are not allowed to fill the voids created by changing relations of production, then the result of economic growth will be instability. In that case, if economic development and social stability is desired, social and political reforms need to be carried out in conjunction with development. This generates a new stage of modernization, which is the concern for "equality." It is a long, uphill battle, but if in spite of national unity and authority, a political system is unable to ensure equality, or at the very least, to instill confidence that its policies are being carried out with an egalitarian spirit, national unity in that society will weaken, authority will be shaken and will become ineffectual. The result will be a return to social fragmentation.

Every political system committed to modernization and radical reform must solve these three fundamental questions and successfully surmount the obstacles addressed by them.

The Atatürk paradigm of revolutionary reform embodies a regime type and consists of methods through which the model is executed. The Atatürk system of thought has been framed according to the principles of Republicanism, Nationalism, Populism, Etatism, Laïcism and Revolutionism-Reformism. However, it should be borne in mind that the paradigm was formulated, to a large extent, also through the exercise of pragmatism. Thus, ideological purity was never an issue. An archetype model of modernization, the Atatürk Revolution was confronted with the problems of "Unity," "Authority," and "Equality" – successfully overcoming the first two while making inroads into achieving the third.

The Atatürk Revolution is distinct from colonial liberation movements and other wars of independence in that Turkish society has had a well-entrenched state tradition, experience and consciousness. It is a society that has never had the expérience of being under the total control of a foreign power. The Turkish War of Independence began when foreign forces occupied a significant portion of territory of the 600-year Empire, including its state capital, and when mini-satellite states wanted to divide and share between themselves still other territory. Land was occupied, the capital and government were placed under control and the Ottoman Parliament was dissolved. Nevertheless, the Caliph-Sultan - was the head of government and state by virtue of being the traditional, legal and religious head of the 600-year-old Ottoman state. While one of the factors that made Mustafa Kemal's job of establishing a nation-state easier was the existence in Turkish society of this long state tradition, having to create a new authority in Anatolia in the face of that very same 600-year traditional, religious and legal authority of the "Caliph-Sultan" made his job difficult. It was not at all easy to establish a new authority and create a national unity in opposition to the Caliph-Sultan.

The question remains as to how the National Struggle and the subsequent program of modernization, the goals of which were the establishment of a new nation-state, were able to overcome these obstacles. Without understanding their constituent principles, it is impossible to adequately answer this question. For example, it would be entirely inaccurate to analyze the Atatürk Revolution in terms of a simple sequential relationship between "unity" and "authority." This is because at no time did Mustafa Kemal intend for "unity" to be established, and then followed by "authority" or vice versa, when he went about setting up his regime. It also must be realized that at that time, the variety of books and academic studies dealing with such issues as "stages" or "problems" of modernization that exist today were not yet available. Even so, there is no doubt that as Mustafa Kemal went forward, he did so using reason and logic. Considering the conditions and exigencies of society, he determined what would be done, as well as how and when. By ascertaining what could not be accomplished under those conditions, he proceeded, and once having made up his mind, he went about carrying out his reforms. That is why the problems of unity and authority were considered - sometimes with one taking priority, sometimes the other - with both of them being transcended almost at the same time.

a) Ensuring Unity

In the days following the signing of the Mudros ceasefire on 30 October 1918, foreigners began occupying the territories of the Ottoman Empire - including first and foremost the capital Istanbul, as well as much of Anatolia - and making plans to partition the lands among themselves. This was clearly an attempt at colonialization, the goal of which was opening up Anatolia to the unequivocal control by the Western imperialist powers. Included within this was the extension of the borders of Greece into Anatolia. The Caliph-Sultan, in his capacity as head of the imperial Government, had signed this ceasefire, which laid the groundwork for this partition, and had sought refuge in the mercy of the occupiers. Society was without an effective leader and had become completely fragmentalized by organizations set up in different places to protect rights and to liberate regions. Other activity that served to strengthen and contributed to the partition of territory got underway in parts of the Empire. In particular, Greek and Armenian minorities had been provoked into organizing to further intensify the fragmentation.

It was under these conditions that Mustafa Kemal landed in Samsun on 19 May 1919. As Military Inspector, a post he retained until he resigned from the military just prior to the Erzurum Congress, he had access to all the means of the state to establish communication with both civilian and military authorities. Mustafa Kemal had also been able to take advantage of the reputation he had acquired from his triumph at Gallipoli and success in other battles. This won him the respect of a broad cross-section of the military and civilian population in society. The first contact he made after having landed in Samsun was with the commanders of the war-weary armies. He suggested that local defense units in Anatolia and Roumelia be integrated; a national-level Congress be held in Sivas; and a "central institution" or "central organ" be formed by the Congress in a place far from the control and influence of the occupying forces. Once this proposal was accepted, he was able to proceed with his regional operations. This was the first clear step taken to ensure "unity" and to create an "authority."

The second step was talking to both civilian and military administrators, the public and the traditional powers of society everywhere he went, calling for them to come together and work in unison. Another public-oriented initiative he undertook was to send notices from Havza to all governors, provincial administrators and military commanders calling for the organization of large, enthusiastic rallies and demonstrations, with the hope that public opinion critical of the occupation taking place all over the country would be generated. He also participated in the meeting held in Havza, where an oath was taken to oppose all forms of assault through armed resistance.

Mustafa Kemal's groundbreaking initiative with respect to ensuring unity and establishing authority having national proportions was the "Amasya Declaration." This Declaration was concerned with the establishment of a "National Congress" and "National Committee," something that had previously been decided on in conjunction with army commanders.[57] Its intent was to reach out to and mobilize the public. Issued on 22 June 1919, the Declaration was sent to all civilian and military authorities. Three persons were to be chosen from each *sancak* (an administrative unit between a province and county) and sent to Sivas.

The Amasya Declaration went a long way toward ensuring "unity" and the establishment of "authority." Mustafa Kemal had been summoned to return to Istanbul but he did not heed the call. This was a clear defiance of legal, traditional and religious "authority." Mustafa Kemal's post of Military inspector was intended to cover the Northeast region of the country, where the units of the 3rd Army Corps had spread. Nonetheless, with this Declaration, he had extended his authority to include the whole of Anatolia and Thrace. The Declaration announced that because the government in Istanbul was under siege and had come under foreign control and influence - and therefore "was unable to carry out its obligations," the independence of the "nation" was to be obtained through the resistance and resolve of the nation itself. The three people to be sent from each *sancak* would be chosen irrespective of party affiliation, being careful to choose influential persons who had gained the trust of the nation. Those selected would constitute a "National Committee" at this "National Congress" held in Sivas. Members of the Erzurum Congress meeting in the name of the Eastern provinces would also participate in the National Congress in Sivas.

Through the Amasya Declaration, Mustafa Kemal had sent a message to the outside world. Aggressor states and others who wanted to partition Anatolia and to send troops to the various cities and regions of the country were expected to behave in accordance with the pronouncements of the Declaration. The Sultan and his government in Istanbul, which were under the direction of the commanders of belligerent states, no longer represented the Turkish nation. These commanders were told that, from then on, if there were any matter concerning the Turkish nation that had to be discussed or about which a decision had to be reached, it was to be discussed and agreed upon not with the Sultan and his government but rather with the elected representatives of the National Congress that was to meet in Sivas, it was in this way that the Amasya Declaration moved the Anatolian National Struggle into the limelight of international relations.

At this stage, the Anatolian National Struggle did not yet have an executive or legislative body and Mustafa Kemal was the only one working to bring this about. Nevertheless, it was through his leadership and skill as a commander that he garnered the support from both the military and the public. Once military commanders understood the nature of the situation and had confidence in the leader, the army became supportive.

Mustafa Kemal had been careful at this point not to refer to a "Parliament," a new "government," or a new "form" of government and organization. Even so, every step he took was toward this as yet tacit new order, new regime, new "state" and new "authority." When the time was ripe. he would reveal his intentions. His down-to-earth understanding of the importance of timing is reflected in his statement, "I have to gradually implement this within the whole of our society."

Since the representatives attending the National Congress to be held in Sivas were elected from all the *sancak*s in the country, the Congress would also be a symbol of "national unity."

After the Amasya Declaration, Mustafa Kemal went to Erzurum via Sivas and Erzincan. While in Erzincan, he was once again summoned to Istanbul. When he refused to go, he was stripped of his position as Military Inspector. Subsequently, the leader of the National Struggle resigned from the military and announced to Istanbul and all countries that he was going to work as a private person "without rank." The Erzurum Congress, meeting on 23 July, ending its sessions on 5 August and announcing its decisions in a declaration on 7 August 1919, contributed to enhancing the power of Mustafa Kemal. He had been made "Congress Chairman" and head of the "Council of Representatives" that had been chosen. Finally, Army Commander Kazım Karabekir placed himself under Mustafa Kemal's command after having chosen not to enforce an arrest warrant for Mustafa Kemal that had arrived from Istanbul.

Despite the fact that the makeup of the Erzurum Congress was regional in terms of participants, its decisions were to have national ramifications.[58] The Congressional Declaration reaffirmed that the government in Istanbul "had no national administrative basis" and that this was why the "Society for the Defense of Rights of Eastern Anatolian" had been established and would be extended to all provinces, counties and villages. It stated that the region was to be considered as a "whole" and that those living there shared a sense of amity, were full of mutual feelings of self-sacrifice, and were bound together by their origins. Moreover, it avowed that it would resist the attempts by

movements founded on Greek and Armenian [national] consciousness to confiscate land. Most importantly, it announced that effective
national power and sovereign "national will" would be the guiding
principle in such matters as "ensuring the unity of the country and
national independence, and the preservation of the Sultanate and position of Caliph" in addition, a call was made for "unity" to ensure
both the unity of the country and national independence. Through
the concepts of "national power" and "national will," the entire nation could decide its own destiny. Thus the Congress wanted to create a new basis for "authority" and "unity."

Legally and formally, the Erzurum Congress possessed an executive council that only encompassed the East. It had a "Council of Representatives" and it was in the name of this council that Mustafa Kemal carried out all of his duties. In practice, this Council and its executive head had contact with the rest of the country beyond the East.
Other regions - in fact, the whole country - were being taken under
control and led toward "unity of the country" and "national independence." In this way, an "executive organ" having a new "authority" based on *national will* was formed in opposition to the government in Istanbul. Among the general aims of the movement, in addition to unity of the country and national independence, was the formation of an "authority" based on the people rather than on the institutions of the Sultan and Caliph - despite having specified the preservation of each as one of its goals - because they were based on something other than "national will." Taking into consideration that
the government in Istanbul might forfeit Eastern Anatolia, it was decided at the Congress to take over regional administration through a
provisional government- as the need for a new "authority" arose. It
was decided to place the entire state apparatus in the region under its
jurisdiction, which was a precursor to the establishment of "a new
government." This new power regarded as criminal every form of behavior that contradicted the National Struggle and by announcing
that such behavior would be punished, it consolidated its "authority"
through "judicial" means.

In short, the "Council of Representatives" set up in Erzurum in
Eastern Anatolia, would make decisions and implement them, and

even if their contents were not yet disclosed, adjudicate its conventions and punish transgressors.

The attempt to bring about "unity" in the country and society resulted in making this unity even stronger and more effective. It was with this unity that national independence would be achieved and a new "executive" body, in the form of a "government," would be established.

The second stage in the achievement of national unity and the creation of authority after Erzurum was the Sivas Congress. At the Sivas Congress, organization within Eastern Anatolia reached national proportions. The "Society for the Defense of Rights of Anatolian and Roumelia" was set up. Its 16-person Council of Representatives was given executive responsibilities for the National Struggle. Mustafa Kemal was once again acting executive of the Council. All of the decisions made at the Erzurum Congress were adopted as national criteria. Two decisions made and implemented during the Sivas Congress demonstrate that it acted very realistically with respect to the attainment of unity and the establishment of authority. One of these was the newspaper, *National Will,* which was published due to the importance placed on mass communication by the national organization and movement. The other was the appointment of the 20th Army Corps Commander[59] in Ankara to the Western Anatolia National Forces Command. The newspaper would be the propaganda organ of the National Struggle and would contribute to national unity. It would disseminate the ideas, decisions and policies of this new national organization and authority - this Council of Representatives - to the people and to the world. It is noteworthy that the importance of mass communication in political development, something that has been demonstrated in our own time, was understood during the first days of the National Struggle and put into action.

The appointment of an Army Corps Commander to a different position having even greater responsibility by the Council of Representatives acting independently of the legal appointment apparatus of the government in Istanbul was an important development. This shows that the new authority had begun to carry out the duties of state and government. Nevertheless, there was as yet no "Parliament" as such and decisions were being made by congresses, with the Council of Representatives having been given the job of seeing to it that they were implemented. The possibility of the Erzurum Congress setting up a Provisional Government in the Eastern provinces was transformed at the Sivas Congress into a Provisional Government for the entire country. At the Sivas Congress, the call for the formerly dissolved Istanbul [Ottoman] Assembly to be reconvened was renewed. Since the National Struggle had not yet formed its own "National Parliament," until such a time that it did, the Council of Representatives, headed by Mustafa Kemal, would lead the struggle for independence.

The power of every authority is relative to the effectiveness with which its decisions are implemented. Following the Congress, there still remained a legal, traditional and religious authority in Istanbul in the form of the Caliph-Sultan and his government. The head of this government, which tried every means at its disposal to get rid of Mustafa Kemal and the Anatolian National Struggle, was Damat Ferit. On the other hand, the new authority was established in Anatolia and derived its authority from the Council of Representatives of the "Society for the Defense of Rights of Anatolia and Roumelia," led by Mustafa Kemal, it is impossible for two authorities to exist in a country or society. One of them will become increasingly weaker and eventually disappear. Events and the effectiveness of the implementation of policies will demonstrate which one is strong and which one is weak and who will ultimately lose power.

Despite the fact that the members of the Council of Representatives and commanders had not endorsed it, Mustafa Kemal, the leader of the National Struggle, attempted to "test out" or "determine" the strength of their "authority" and to "prove" it inside the country and abroad. The "target" chosen by this initiative was the Prime Minister Damat Ferit: it was requested that he be removed from office. The method adopted in the name of the National Struggle was to carry out non-mediated discussions with the Caliph-Sultan Vahdettin and to directly explain the situation to him. When this was not secured and Mustafa Kemal, who was to do the speaking, was not granted the opportunity to do so, the "sanctioning" of the initiative was characterized as a "last ultimatum": all of the channels of communication between the Sultan and his government in Istanbul and the state-government apparatus in Anatolia would be severed.

This testing out of the power of the new authority was actually a rather risky step to take. In any case, it was taken and, apart from a few state officials in Anatolia, the decision was implemented countrywide: on 12 September 1919, lines of communication between Istanbul and Anatolia were severed and the nucleus of the communications network became Mustafa Kemal, the leader of the National Struggle in Sivas. Moreover, the additional step was taken to announce to Istanbul that so long as Damat Ferit was not removed from office, communications would not be restored. During this 21-day show of force - this contest in determining and proving authority - the leader of the National Struggle, Mustafa Kemal, remained at the helm day and night. He conducted lengthy meetings with people who had been assigned as agents of Istanbul and with commanders that he had formerly worked with - resorting to reciprocal propaganda tactics. At the same time, the leader of the Revolution kept Anatolia abreast of all meetings, decisions and situations. Dictating each line of the texts of protest telegraphs that would be sent by the rank and file of the National Struggle to the Sultan and the head of government, he saw to it that they reached Istanbul.

The face off concluded in favor of the National Struggle and its leader - the cabinet led by Damat Ferit fell. This was the first big clear test of the new authority exercised by Mustafa Kemal, one that was to determine the fate of the movement. It was from this point on that the foreign occupiers began to acknowledge this new authority. According to British Admiral Robeck in Istanbul, it was a development "progressing toward an independent Republic" and "government dictates are not being heeded; the policies and the views of the new organization (the "Society for the Defense of Rights of Anatolia and Roumelia") are more representative of public opinion."[60]

During the transitional period prior to the establishment of a National Assembly, the national regime formed in opposition to Istanbul undertook measures designed to create and strengthen authority. For example, the Ali Rıza Pasha government, set up after Damat Ferit, was forced to recognize the executive arm of the Anatolian National Struggle - the Council of Representatives - and to discuss with it various problems concerning the state and country. To this end, the Ali Rıza Pasha government sent an emissary to Amasya, where such matters as the 1) "refusal to give up the territory where Turks lived under any condition," 2) "rejection of the mandate system," 3) "assurance of the unity and independence of the country," 4) "acceptance of the "Society for the Defense of Rights of Anatolia and Roumelia" as a legal entity by the Istanbul Government," and 5) "the convening of an Assembly in Anatolia" were discussed. These discussions led to the acceptance of the Amasya meetings and minutes by the Sultan and his government and their agreeing to the immediate convening of the Parliament and the holding of elections for this purpose. Through the endeavors of the Society for the Defense of the Rights of Anatolia and Roumelia, it was able to get some of its members elected to the Ottoman Parliament meeting in Istanbul, which convened for the last time on 12 January 1920. Nevertheless, while most Deputies who were elected to this Parliament had committed themselves to Mustafa Kemal, they were unable to create a "Defense of Rights Group" in the Parliament. In spite of this failure, in the end, the Ottoman Parliament accepted the "National Pact," which had been prepared in accordance with the ideas laid out at the Erzurum and Sivas Congresses. The National Pact was a programme that had been prepared by Mustafa Kemal and developed at the Erzurum and Sivas Congresses. After being accepted by the Ottoman Parliament, the contents of the National Pact were announced to the world. The first article of the National Pact established a national boundary that was reasonable, rational, realistic, and all encompassing. This border included the territories of Anatolia and Thrace, which had not been occupied by the enemy, as of the signing of the "ceasefire" on 30 October 1918. The Anatolian National Struggle and its leader considered the country and society enclosed within these boundaries as "an inalienable whole" and proclaimed this to the whole world through a decision of the last Ottoman Parliament. Another important decision appeared in article 6 of the "National Pact": "Just as every other state, we (Turks) have need for complete independence and freedom. This is fundamental to the existence of Turks. Therefore, all attempts to restrict political, judicial, and monetary development will be opposed." This was an appeal to national "unity" and a proclamation of the ideas of unity and independence. Moreover, the "authority" that proclaimed all this to society and world public opinion was the Anatolian National Struggle and its leader, Mustafa Kemal.

This appeal for unity as well as the call for independence led to the official occupation of Istanbul on 16 March 1920, the dissolution of the Parliament and the return of Damat Ferit Pasha to the position of Prime Minister. The new government made a concerted effort to shake and weaken the "authority" in Anatolia - in the end resorting to tactics based on religious authority. According to a *fetva* (a general religious judicial decree) issued by the Sheik-ul-Islam, Mustafa Kemal and his colleagues were "insurgents" and it was a religious duty to kill them. What was wanted was the destruction of the effort to create a unity based on territorial integrity along with language and ancestry, as well as the new "authority" that had emerged from the attempt by national will to transform this effort into action. Given the traditions and beliefs of the people at that point in time, this assault was pursued through the use of religious weapons. However, the new authority and its leader engaged in a counterassault employing an identical strategy. Feeling the need to support the creation of "unity" and the establishment of "authority" by relying on religious elements, it orchestrated the issuing by 153 muftis in Anatolia of a joint counter-*fet-va*, which did just this.

At this stage, the Caliph-Sultan, his government, and the Sheik-ul-Islam, who provided the religio-judicial legitimacy for the will of this government, and also the forces of occupation opposed the Revolution. Their aim was to undermine the unity that was part of the progressive momentum toward independence and worked at dispersing the new authority that was to bring about this unity.

In addition to the religious counter-assault by the National Struggle in the form of issuing *fetva*s, a second offensive in the creation of unity and authority, was the establishment of a new National Parliament that would be constituted through new elections. The dissolving of the Ottoman Parliament by the occupiers provided the opportunity for the revolutionary cadre to create a legislative and executive body that was national in scope.

For the duration of the War of Independence, particularly until the Republic had been proclaimed, the Atatürk Revolution took great pains to continually call for the emancipation of the "Exalted Sultan" and the "Exalted Caliph" in addition to its reiteration of such concepts as "liberation," "independence," "national will," and "national sovereignty." This was a natural consequence of the fact that an indisputable new authority had not yet been established and of the belief that undertaking a multidimensional war would not be in the best interests of the Revolution. This was because circumstances were such that liberation of the country from enemies and foreign occupiers and independence served as the basis of the mobilization of all segments of society and at the same time contributed to unity. Nevertheless, while *national will* and *national sovereignty* were in their own right goals, they were not yet concepts recognized by the majority of society as something that was longed for and whose realization was worth fighting for. The notions of "Exalted Sultan" and "Exalted Caliph" contributed much more to the attainment of unity. Even so, they were not goals as such but rather used as *means to an end* - that of unity and modernity.

Another important issue in the realization of unity in the pre-Republic period concerned the question of *with whom* and *for whom* the movement for national independence would be carried out. The leader of the Revolution had established at the very beginning the expectation that all *segments of society,* in other words, *all the individuals making up the nation,* would participate as a whole in this movement. This was not to be wrought in the narrow interest of a particular class or segment of society but rather for the universal benefit of the entire nation. Thus both during the period when congresses were convened and in parliamentary elections, people from all classes, professions and sects were guaranteed the right to participate in the congresses and Assembly, hence making participation possible irrespective of class, political, cultural, sectarian, or ethnic distinctions. This is one of the greatest factors contributing to unity and the War of Independence becoming national in scope.

At the beginning of the Revolution, especially during the pre-Republican era, mention was not made of political and social reforms.

Instead, integration was achieved by continually emphasizing national independence, the totality of nation and country, national consciousness, national sovereignty, and national will. The only document having social content during that period which gave some clue as to what was in store was the "Populist Programme." The adopted programme became the basis for the Constitution of 1921.[61] The aims specified at the beginning of the draft constitution, signed by Mustafa Kemal, leader of the radical reform movement, and presented to the Assembly, included eliminating people's poverty, bringing about contentment and prosperity. Among the responsibilities designated to the government of the Turkish Grand National Assembly were the establishment of institutions and reforms that met the real needs of people as they conducted their daily affairs in the areas of agriculture, education, justice, economy, as well as in the performance of all other social functions.[62] Moreover, in his speech to the Assembly, Mustafa Kemal stated, "our existence today attests to the general inclination of the nation, which is toward populism and popular government,"[63] confirming that the issue at hand was a Revolution that was people-oriented in all respects.

The responsibilities listed in the Populist Programme and in the preamble of the Draft Constitution of 1921 were social in content and were designed to ease the suffering of the poor, who made up a majority of the nation. Bringing the people economic and social well-being would contribute to the reinforcement of allegiance to the Revolution and the system under development as well as to consolidation of unity. It was in this way that a popular government based on the principle of national sovereignty and a unity having political, economic and social dimensions could be established.

In view of the fact that the Populist Program demonstrated early on the socio-economic dimension of both that of Atatürkism and the Atatürk paradigm of modernization, it is necessary to study this document further.

On 24 April 1920, one day after the opening of the Grand National Assembly, Mustafa Kemal delivered a speech to the Assembly on the necessity of establishing a government. This speech contained the following Proposal, which was adopted by the Assembly:

1. The founding of a government is absolutely necessary.

2. It is not permissible to recognize a provisional chief of state nor to establish a regency.

3. It is fundamental to recognize that the real authority in the country is the national will as represented by the Assembly. There is no power superior to the Grand National Assembly.

4. The Grand National Assembly of Turkey embraces both the executive and legislative functions. A Council of State, chosen from the membership of the Assembly and responsible to it, conducts the affairs of the state. The president of the Assembly is ex-officio president of the Council. Note: The Sultan-Caliph, as soon as he is free from the coercion to which he submits, shall take [his] place within the constitutional system in the manner to be determined by the Assembly.[64]

The resolution accepted by the Assembly went beyond the necessity of establishing a new government. It was in fact the acceptance of a new regime based on popular sovereignty. This was also the First Proposal included in the pamphlet entitled "Populist Program," published with the express orders of Mustafa Kemal in September 1920.[65]

According to Mustafa Kemal, the acceptance of his Proposal by the Assembly was "in reality a question of acknowledging the collapse of the Ottoman State and the abolition of the Caliphate. It meant the creation of a new State standing on new foundations. But to speak openly of the position as it revealed itself might eventually jeopardize the goal we were aiming at. For the general opinion inclined to the idea that the attitude of the Sultan-Caliph was excusable. Even in the Assembly during the first months there was a tendency to seek communion with the seat of the Caliphate, a union with the Central Government."[66] Commenting upon each of the principles in the Proposal, Mustafa Kemal stated, "it is not difficult to appreciate the character of a government standing upon such foundations. Such a Government is a People's Government, based on the principle of the sovereignty of the people. Such is the Republic."[67] According to İlhan Arsel, "by acceptance of this Proposal and the principles embodied in it, the Grand National Assembly, perhaps without full awareness, had accepted a system of people's government based on national sovereignty, but even truer, had accepted the Republican regime."[68] In Turkish constitutional history, the period from the time of the establishment of the Nationalist Government in Ankara up to the proclamation of the Turkish Republic on 29 October 1923 is referred to also as the Period of the Government of the Grand National Assembly.

During the War of Independence, although military activities were the overriding concern of Mustafa Kemal, he was also busy continuing his work, further elaborating upon the ideological platform of the Turkish National Liberation Movement. He said to the Assembly on 12 July 1920, "Let us concern ourselves with the question of what principle we shall lay down. I believe that the essential reason for our existence now has proven the general tendency of our nation, and it is Populism and People's Government. It is the taking over of the government by the people ... let us work toward giving the administration to the people. I am convinced that then many difficulties will be overcome. I am personally working on this. I shall soon inform your Supreme Assembly of my deliberations on this subject."[69]

The Draft Constitutional Law dated 13 September 1920 and read in the Assembly on 18 September 1920 is the result of Atatürk's deliberations on this subject. Thus, this is the Second Proposal included in the Populist Program of Mustafa Kemal. The Constitution of 1921, accepted by the Assembly on 20 January 1921, was based on this Draft Constitutional Law, which was in fact the second document contained in Atatürk's Populist Program. The Draft Constitutional Law contained statements about the fact that the Government of the Grand National Assembly considered the saving of the people from the oppression and cruelty of imperialism and capitalism to be its fundamental goal; that the Government of the Grand National Assembly believed it also to be its basic aim to find solutions to the poor and wretched conditions of the life of the people and to bring happiness and welfare to them by taking all the necessary measures, making all the necessary changes, and by establishing all the necessary organizations in the fields of education, justice, land, and economics and in all the other social areas, in accordance with the needs of the people and the requirements of the modern age; and that sovereignty belonged unconditionally to the people; that executive and legislative powers were united in the Grand National Assembly which was the only real representative of the people; and that the People's Government of Turkey would be administered by the Grand National Assembly and had the title of the Government of the Grand National Assembly:[70] Thus the Kemalist idea was that legitimacy of a government would be proven if it existed by right of the people's sovereignty.

Not only the necessity of establishing a new regime based on popular sovereignty, but also that of socio-economic transformation was openly declared by this Draft Constitutional Law, which was prepared principally by Mustafa Kemal. As this Draft Law constituted the essential portion of Mustafa Kemal's Populist Program, and was in fact presented to the Assembly under that title, it remains one of the key documents explaining the Kemalist principle of populism.

The speaker of the special commission that studied the Draft Constitutional Law, İsmail Suphi (Soysallıoğlu), made the following statement on 18 November 1920, when the Assembly debates on this Draft Law started:

> We gathered here in this Assembly not essentially for the purpose of making reforms but for organizing the legitimate right to self-defense of theTurkish people against aggression. But after being here for sometime, we realized that the cause of our weakness did not lie only in external reasons. Although we are still assembled here for the purpose of the defense of the country, we are also determined to search for all means and principles to keep this nation alive, we are prepared to reform everythmg; we are prepared to do anything. Thus the program that the Government presented to your Supreme Assembly under the title, the Populist Program, is the product of such ideas.[71]

The term populism was not used by Kemal to simply hide his intention of proclaiming a republic. By using this term, he also meant the establishing of a new economic and social order in Turkey.[72] However, what was to be the method for this socio-economic transformation? This question plagued the Kemalists throughout the early years of the Republic. Finding, in those years, no example of a country that has successfully developed by using methods other than those employed by the capitalist countries, and lacking know-how and trained personnel, the Kemalists desisted from their attack on capitalism, but only to embrace étatism as their economic policy in the 1930s. However, throughout the Period of National Struggle, one could come across several statements on the part of the Nationalists expressing anti-capitalist sentiments. However, this was not all. In spite of the close rapprochement between the Government of the Grand National Assembly and the Soviet Government, in view of the latter's aid to the Turkish Liberation Movement, the Nationalists were careful to *remain ideologically independent.*

Belief in "ideological independence" seems to have been a basic characteristic of the Kemalists. Even at a time when the Government of the Grand National Assembly was just in the initial stage of the National Liberation Movement and was in dire need of all the aid it could get from the Soviet Government, Mustafa Kemal spoke boldly on the subject of Bolshevism. Thus commenting on the Baku Congress, sponsored by the Soviet Government, to the Assembly on 14 August 1920, he stated:

> In recent days, an international congress is being organized in Baku. They are inviting representatives from among us as well. These invitations are being made directly to our people. Some invitations are coming and being sent to Erzurum, Trabzon and elsewhere. According to the information we have received from some places, especially from the border regions, some individuals have gone to this Congress. Gentlemen: as I have expressed whenever an opportunity arises, I would now like to repeat and reconfirm that when we decided to work toward maintaining the existence and independence of our country and nation, we depended only on our own point of view and own strength. No one gave us lessons; we never learned anything through the deceptive promises made by others. Everyone knows that our perspective and principles are not Bolshevik ones. Moreover, we have never considered or attempted imposing Bolshevik principles on our people. We believe that the existence and development of our nation can be possible only through principles that are compatible with our national life. When we analyze our basic principles - which, in fact, are populist - we see that they give all strength, power, sovereignty and administration directly to the people. It is the people who actually maintain those principles. This constitutes the world's strongest principle.

Such a principle does not contradict Bolshevik ones - in fact, they call us nationalist. Even so, our nationalism is such that we respect all the nations with which we have relations. We recognize all the particular requirements of their national existence. In any case, ours is not a selfish or arrogant nationalism.[73]

Again, in January 1921, Mustafa Kemal stated:

I did not study the social sciences in depth. Even so, I know that Communism naturally does not recognize boundaries whereas we accept national boundaries. Moreover, we talk about complete independence.

In our relations with the Russians, in principle, we have not even touched upon the subject of anti-Capitalism or anti-Communism. No one has ever told us that we had to become Communists in order to negotiate with the Russians so we have never made it a point of saying that we were just to be friends with them. There is no such basis to our friendship.[74]

This ideological independence was not demanded only vis-à-vis the Soviet Government. It was not only affirmed by rejections of Communism or by denunciations of Western imperialism or capitalism. Such independence also involved the rejection of Pan-Turanism, Ottomanism, and Pan-Islamism. The latter were more boldly rejected by Mustafa Kemal as victory became more assured. Historical experience with foreign intervention under such guises as Pan-Slavism or through the insidious Capitulations prompted the rejection of the former. Moreover, the particular content of Kemalist nationalism was an important factor in these rejections as well as in the rejection of Ottomanism, Pan-Islamism and Pan-Turanism. The rejection of the latter was prompted by the knowledge born of the difficulties encountered in the Ottoman reform movements; by the realistic assessment of Turkey's capacities; and by conviction that only through their rejection could Turkey hope to become a modern state. When it was yet too early to reject the religious basis of the Turkish state, Mustafa Kemal, as early as 1921, was clearly rejecting the cosmopolitan implications of Ottomanism and embracing nationalism.

In a speech he gave in Eskişehir during the latter part of the Period of National Struggle, Mustafa Kemal stated:

The policy that will be followed by the new Turkey... will be absolutely commensurate with the capacities and needs of the country. Neither Islamic Union
nor Turanism can form a doctrine or legal policy for us. Henceforth, the governmental policy of the new Turkey is to consist of living in- dependently, relying on
her sovereignty within her national frontiers.[75]

The Constitution of the Government of the Grand National Assembly, which was adopted on 20 January 1921, affirmed that sovereignty belonged unconditionally to the nation. It also stated that the
system of administration was based on the principle that the people
personally and effectively direct their own destinies. This Constitution established a system of government that was very different from
that of the Ottoman government. The adoption of this Constitution
was made possible principally by the activities of the modernist group
in the Assembly that was headed by Mustafa Kemal. With a very
new document adopted by the Grand National Assembly, the break
not only with the Ottoman government but also with the Ottoman regime and concepts became more and more certain. This was the Constitution of a new regime. As a matter of fact, the transition from the
Period of the Government of the Grand National Assembly to the Republican regime was brought about without writing a new Constitution: only a few articles of the 1921 Constitution were amended on
29 October 1923. And even though a new Constitution was adopted
by the Turkish government early in 1924,[76] that Constitution retained
the basic philosophy of the 1921 Constitution - hence the continuity
of the Republican regime with the Period of National Struggle.

A crucial reform, designed to create and strengthen unity during
the pre-Republican period, was the abolition of the institution of the
Sultanate. Up until then, the existence of two identical institutions of
traditional and religious unity, the "Exalted Sultanate" and "Exalted
Caliphate," had been emphasized. But after the success of the War of
Independence, the use of the "Exalted Sultanate" as a means to unity
was no longer seen as necessary, with the result being that the Sultanate and Caliphate were separated from one another and the former
dispensed with. *From then on, "unity" would be realized in conjunction with a nationalist, populist, egalitarian and laïc republic based*

on national will and sovereignty. Nonetheless, at the time when the Republic was proclaimed, the symbol of religious unity, the "Caliphate," had not yet been abolished. It was for this reason that the condemnation of and conflict over the "Caliphate," whether in the Assembly or in society, gave rise to an undermining of unity. There emerged alarming anomalies and political alignments among traditional, social and religious groups and individuals who had not approved of the spirit and goals of the Revolution. As has been observed in all independence movements, the main problem encountered by the Atatürk Revolution in the period following political independence was ensuring and reinforcing "national unity." Regardless of form of government, language, country, culture, belief, the desires and expectations shaping the future, in short, all the elements constituting national consciousness, "national unity" is the fundamental issue. While there is no doubt that struggles for independence and attempts at radical reform are difficult to carry out initially under the conditions of war, the most serious difficulties and obstacles are encountered after independence has been achieved. This is, as mentioned earlier, because prior to independence, fighting against a specific enemy or enemies is a unifying factor. However, after the enemy has withdrawn or been forced f rom the country, the unity that was derived from the presence of a colonial power, enemy or occupier no longer exists. The real issues that need to be resolved and overcome before national unity can be maintained are those concerned with social change. Success of the radical reform movement depends on the extent to which social change is accomplished; unity will be achieved through the formation of new value judgments and policies that serve to unify.

To summarize, compared to the societies in the post-World War II era that have attained independence upon the conclusion of their colonial status, the problem of "unity" in the Atatürk Revolution was more easily overcome. If one reason for this was undertaking social change as part of the creation of efficacious authority, another was the rather homogenous state of Turkish society with respect to ancestry, language, religion and history compared to other societies. Within the borders determined by the "National Pact" and fixed by the Lausanne and other subsequent treaties, it was no longer possible for a variety of different nations to exist as they had in Ottoman society. Arabs, Serbs, Albanians, Greek and Armenians mostly remained outside borders of the country.

At the beginning of 1919, according to figures given to the great powers by the Imperial Government, Eastern Thrace had a population of 331.346 while Anatolia had a population of 11 million. The population of Anatolia consisted of 9.291.346 Moslems. The remainder included 1.014.312 Greeks, 572.272 Armenians, 93.364 Jews and a total of 1.679.948 other religious minorities. This meant that 85% of the population of Anatolia was Moslem. In Eastern Thrace, compared to 360.417 Turks, there were 224.680 Greeks, 19.888 Armenians, and 26.109 Jews. Around that time, 59.7% and 25% of the population of Istanbul consisted of Turks and Greeks, respectively, with the rest consisting of Armenians and Jews.[77] According to the 1897 census, among the Turks in the territories of Anatolia, there were 1.061.000 speakers of Kurdish and 238.000 speakers of Arabic.[78]

Following the War of Independence, a great number of Greek and Armenian minorities left Anatolia – either as a consequence of treaties or socio-economic conditions.

As illustrated by these figures, Turkish society had a homogenous and integrated structure with respect to religion, language, ancestry and culture. Those living within its borders had experienced the same traditions and history and were bound together socially, culturally and religiously. From the point of view of religion, the only distinction that was present in society was sectarianism. In this regard, unity and the creation of authority on the basis of nation, was not a serious problem for the Atatürk Revolution - unlike other independence movements, such as those in Black Africa of more recent times.

b) Establishing Authority

Just as important as bringing about national unity in the struggle for independence and any subsequent modernization movement is the problem of establishing "authority" - particularly if there already exists a strong traditional authority. Still, if there is no authority in a society that is considered by the whole of society as "legitimate," it is impossible to obtain independence and create the social change necessary for modernization. The conflict and regime changes seen time and again in many of the countries that acquired independence in the previous century can be attributed to the inability to have established a sound, acceptable, legitimate and efficacious authority. Of course, it goes without saying that an appropriate authority is one not based on fear, violence, repression or armed force. On the contrary, this authority ought to exist by virtue of a constitution that has been adopted by society; conventions having social, economic, political and cultural content, as provided for on basis of this constitution; and the social acceptance of these practices. If these principles are not oriented toward the creation of a more independent, freer society in which the welfare of the individual is of concern; if the practices of the political cadre and government making these regulations do not create the impression or inspire the belief that the desires and expectations of society for the future will be met and if they are unable to harness the trust of that society, it will be impossible to hold the system together by force. During the War of Independence, the greatest difficulty faced by Mustafa Kemal, stemmed from the issue of authority. Reasons for this include the following:

1. While the Prime Minister and the government that backed him had cooperated with the occupation forces and fell under their control, they still represented a 600-year-old Empire and its 400-year Caliph tradition. In this regard, one could still speak of the continuity of a legitimate, traditional, political and religious authority.

2. The Sultan's government, though its access to state resources, was in a position to exercise influence over the administrative apparatus.

3. The idea of a new authority distinct from that derived from the social, religious and traditional authority of the Caliph-Sultan remained farfetched. Even the advocates of Westernization were guided in their efforts by the goal of maintaining and strengthening the Empire, and subsequently, the Sultanate and Caliphate. Furthermore, the aim of the supporters of Islamist movement was the unification of all Moslems under the Caliph-Sultan, thereby making his authority even more powerful. Turkists active ve within the struggle to create a nation had not envisaged a modern head of state whose authority was based on laïc foundations and which was distinct from the institution of Caliphate-Sultanate.

4. Some members of the civilian and military bureaucracy, despite having emerged tired and worn out from years of war and economic deadlocks, generally maintained their allegiance to the Caliph-Sultan and desired protecting him.

5. The vast majority of society - about 90' of the population of Anatolia - was Moslem and, by virtue of their religious beliefs, saw the Caliph-Sultan as the only "legitimate," unassailable religious authority. Every Friday, they would listen to the prayer read in his name and beseech God to maintain the success and strength of the Caliph-Sultan and safeguard the Sultanate.

For these and other reasons, the question of "authority" emerged as the most important problem that had to be overcome by the Atatürk Revolution and, from the very first days of the War of Independence, it continued to be of the greatest concern to Mustafa Kemal.

Creating a new authority to replace an existing one that derives its power from a number of factors, strengthening it, and bringing it to a position where it is the only real authority of the country is not an easy task – nor was it. Therefore, until the leader of the Revolution successfully concluded the War of Independence, he preferred taking every opportunity to say that he thought that it was his sacred duty to rescue, protect and honor the "Exalted Institution of the Sultanate" and the "Exalted Institution of the Caliphate." Seeing value in this, he repeatedly emphasized it before the public – so much so that even as he abolished the Sultanate, he separated the office of the "Exalted Caliph," preferring to keep it for a period of time.

It can be said that as far as the Turkish attempts at modernization and radical reform are concerned, creating authority was as difficult as creating national unity was easy.

The three problems that must be overcome by every independence and modernization movement are the attainment of unity, the creation of authority and the realization of equality, all of which are very important issues. Trying to give priority to one or the other flies in the face of social realities. The reasoning of the leader and his tactics and strategies, along with the structure and conditions of society, will determine this order or composition.

Mustafa Kemal recognized that it was important to solve the problems of unity and authority concurrently. Pragmatically conside-

ring the existing structure and conditions of society, it would sometimes be necessary to place more importance on one than the other, as
the need arose.

It is certain that the army played an important role in providing
support and assistance in solving such problems as unity and authority in the aftermath of Mustafa Kemal's victory in the War of Independence. It can be said that in addition to this military factor, the difficulties and adversities created by the penetration of occupiers into
Anatolia and their desire to partition and share the territory contributed to coming up with solutions to the problems of unity and authority. Other factors also helped make Mustafa Kemal's job of establishing a new authority, and with it, a new regime, easier. These included the signing of the Treaty of Sevres, which partitioned Anatolia
by using the government of the Caliph-Sultan; the formation during
the War of Independence of a new authority and organization that
was based on the nation and its people and which was apart from and
opposed to the Caliph-Sultan and his government; the cooperation
entered into by the Caliph-Sultan and his government with the occupiers; and the joining of forces of this traditional authority with the
enemy to crush the Anatolian National Struggle.

It is useful to use a two-pronged approach in examining the problem that the national independence movement and the Atatürk Revolution had in establishing authority. In the course of carrying out radical reforms, what is at issue is the creation of a new system of government built upon the requisite modern political structure and institutions. The political structure and political institutionalization entailed by the Atatürk paradigm of modernization was that of the
West. It aimed at the creation of a Republican, Democratic and Liberal order within a laïc society. The issue of authority appears as a special case of authority within this general framework. A modern political structure would be established and political institutionalization
would be accomplished; however, the question remained as to who
was to do this. At the heart of the concern over who would execute
and steer the Revolution lay the problematique of the personality of
the leader and the basis upon which his leadership authority was derived. When analyzing the matter of authority in the Atatürk Revolu-

tion, as in all revolutions, a two-pronged method ought to be considered. As has already been seen, in a movement of radical reform, the leader who is to carry it out is just as important as the goals of the revolution and the social, political and economic structure of the society in which it is going to be realized. Regardless of how modern or beneficial to society the intended goals of a proposed model are, the success or failure in reaching them to a large extent depends on the personality, character and qualities of its leader. When looking at the problem of authority within the context of the Atatürk Revolution, along with the establishment of a new authority, personal authority will have to be considered.

From the point of view of the Atatürk Revolution, the beginning of the National War of Independence began on 19 May 1919. It is appropriate to regard the date on which Mustafa Kemal landed in Samsun in the capacity of Military Inspector as the commencement of the Revolution. This was because the most significant headways in the course of the Revolution were made after this date. Mustafa Kemal had gone to Samsun with the permission of the Caliph-Sultan, who had appointed him as Military Inspector of the Third Army. His assignment was to establish relations with all state authorities and organizations - civilian and military alike - and was empowered to give orders.

His task was to ensure internal security in the region, bring about order, establish the causes for disorder, and to eliminate conditions that give rise to it . All of the army units in the region had been placed under the command of Mustafa Kemal. Except for personnel matters and documents concerning the number of troops, units were to communicate directly with Mustafa Kemal on matters concerning operations and security and they were to receive instructions from him. In all areas under the purview of the office of Military Inspector, all provinces, townships, administrative units, aside from the military units, were bound to carry out the orders of Mustafa Kemal. Moreover, army corps commanders of provinces along the perimeter of the region -Diyarbakır, Elazığ, Bitlis, Ankara, and Kastamonu - were to heed appeals made by officials from the Inspector's office.[79] This authority clearly empowered Mustafa Kemal vis-à-vis the civilian-military state apparatus both in the region and its surrounding areas. As

Inspector of the Third Army Corps, he was not only able to communicate and to establish relations with both military and civilian organizations, but also give orders. This extensive scope of authority had been carefully fashioned through his personal connections, influence and power within the Ministry of War and the Joint Chiefs of Staff prior to his arrival in Samsun, taking pains to ensure that this authority had legitimate underpinnings.

Mustafa Kemal's position as Military Inspector and the authority that went with it continued until 8 July 1919, when preparations for the Erzurum Congress got underway. It was on this date that Mustafa Kemal was dismissed from this position and he resigned from the army. He had decided to continue working on these preparations as a private citizen and announced this to the nation. Within the short period of 50 days, the Amasya Declaration was announced; plans for the holding of the Erzurum and Sivas Congresses, which were to ensure the organizational integration of the independence movement, were completed; election of representatives in most provinces had been carried out; the idea that a body based on national will, far removed from the control and influence of occupiers, was needed to insure the unity of the country and national independence was accepted by the civilian-military sectors of society. The belief that the War of Independence had been undertaken nationally and that this war could be won only by uniting at the national level all forces was spread to those struggling for independence locally or regionally.

Revolutionary movements, including those directed at independence, must inculcate society with the belief that independence is possible. Similarly, they must appeal for uniting society in the name of independence, and create the authority and organization that will work toward bringing this independence about. An independence movement will be successful only to the extent that it is able to assume national proportions, set up an extensive organizational structure, and establish effective authority under its control.

Mustafa Kemal was not a social scientist. Moreover, such notions as backwardness, independence, and modernization were not yet in vogue at that point in history. Nevertheless, even at that time, what Mustafa Kemal had was a strong sense of social realities and requirements.

He understood that the establishment of a new basis for authority was the only way that independence could be achieved. Accordingly, he resigned from the military. As a general who had experienced the vindictiveness of the Caliph-Sultan and his government, Mustafa Kemal's acquisition of power was not easy. Being chosen as the Chairman of the Council of Representatives by the various Congresses, and working toward the creation of a new authority through the Society for the Defense of Rights of Anatolia and Roumelia required enormous skill. During this period, a formal government in Anatolia, set up in opposition to the one in Istanbul, and thus a "head of government" had not yet been established. Nevertheless, there existed a "Council of Representatives" that consisted of national representatives elected by congresses and a "Council Chairman" who made and implemented decisions in the name of this Council. So even if not entirely pronounced, this Council was, in a modern sense, a political executive council. Similarly, the chairman who carried out functions under the authority of Council was some kind of de facto head of state or Prime Minister. While not originally a political party, the Society for the Defense of Rights of Anatolia and Roumelia was clearly an institution having political objectives. It later became transformed into a political party. As it stood then, apart from its bylaws, issued declarations, and decisions, this institution had no other legal basis for its authority. What sustained it the most was the authority it received from the representatives of the nation. This budding new authority and the leader symbolizing it, was in a position to enforce resolutions aimed at bringing about an independence that was based on the conditions and structural characteristics peculiar to society. Progression was made in an astute, consistent, painstaking, and deliberate manner. The Revolution evolved within the context of existing circumstances and the unfolding of events.

These national congresses paved the way for the political institutionalization that was to occur during the succeeding period. The first step in this transformation was the establishment of Turkish Grand National Assembly in Ankara, in 1920, and the proclamation of the 1921 Constitution. They were actually the legitimation of the "Council of Representatives" that had earlier formed the nucleus for their foundation.

Beginning on 23 April 1923 with the convening of the Ankara Assembly - the Turkish Grand National Assembly - and the establishment of its government on 5 May 1920, until the abolition of the Sultanate on 1 November 1922, there were two governments in Turkey. One was in Istanbul, representing the will of the Caliph-Sultan and the other in Ankara, which, in the form of the Grand National Assembly, represented the National Will. Before the 1921 Constitution, the Assembly had made and implemented decisions for nine months and had been instrumental in forming a government. Not only did this demonstrate its effectiveness, but also that its authority had been derived from the people.

Consequently, its legitimacy was recognized by the nation. Possessing both judicial and executive powers, the Ankara Assembly and its government were the first steps taken along the path of political institutionalization in the modern sense.

The government had been formed upon the endorsement by the Assembly of a proposal submitted by Mustafa Kemal. The proposal emphasized that there was no power superior to that of the Turkish Grand National Assembly. This was despite the fact that the Caliph-Sultan continued to exist and that the 1876 Constitution was still in force. The Assembly had assumed both legislative and executive authority. Ministers were chosen from among members of Assembly. These Ministers would constitute a representative committee or cabinet. The Chairman of this committee would also be the Chairman of Assembly, e.g., Mustafa Kemal. Carefully mentioning the situation of the Sultan-Caliph, the proposal stated, "When the time comes for the Sultan-Caliph to be free from oppression and repression, his position will be determined by legislation drawn up by the Assembly."

Hence, the National Struggle for independence and the Revolution created a political authority to which no other authority was recognized as superior. This political authority was a confirmation of the National Will in the Assembly," thus having the legitimate right to commandeer the destiny of the nation. This Assembly would pass legislation that would then be executed by the Chairman of the Assembly, Mustafa Kemal, who was also Chairman of the Council of Ministers. And because the latter body operated semi-autonomously, despite functioning in the name of the Assembly, a second political authority came into being in the form of the Government and the institution of head of state.

Both this political authority, and the institutions of "Assembly," "Government," "Chairmanship of the Assembly," and "Prime Ministry" that had emerged spontaneously throughout the course of the Revolution were institutionalized in a Constitution nine months later. With its ratification, the 1921 Constitution provided the legitimate basis for political power. However, there was still the question of the Sultan-Caliph. The new Constitution had not mentioned or touched this traditional religious authority. Even so, the fact that it had been clearly stated that there was and would be no power above that of the Turkish Grand National Assembly was an unequivocal indication that the existence of the Caliph-Sultan was to be brought to an end. But time was needed before this could be announced. In any case, the 1921 Constitution had naturally entailed an abolition of the Sultanate. Nevertheless, it was only as of 1 November 1922 that the Sultanate could be abolished through a law passed by the Assembly. In this law, the Assembly emphasized that the Ottoman Empire had come to an end. The institution of the Sultanate had been rendered to the backwaters of history. Moreover, with this law, it was documented that the Sultan and his government no longer remained in Istanbul, and that the administration of Istanbul had been relegated to the personnel of the Assembly in Ankara.

The problem of the "Caliph," the only remaining traditional religious authority during this time, would not immediately be overcome. It was not until 3 March 1924, after the proclamation of the Republic, that the institution was abolished, again, through a law passed by the Assembly. With that, the Caliph and all the members of his family were exiled.

With the signing of the Lausanne Peace Treaty on 24 July 1923, the new independent Turkish State was legally recognized internationally. On 29 October 1923, the Republic was proclaimed and Mustafa Kemal was elected as President. The abolition of the Caliphate meant that reactionary, traditional, religious authorities and institutions would no longer be a part of the political structure of the state.

From then on, the problems dealt with by modernization would be those of a social, economic, and cultural nature. The new Republic would work toward nation-building, political socialization, the creation of new political structures and institutions and the abolishment of sources of traditional religious authority in society.

c) Ensuring Equality

Modernization can proceed in a sound fashion, without being smothered by counter-revolution, only if the political system achieves success on a number of fronts. For example, the conditions whereby economic growth and development can flourish have to be created. An equitable distribution of the national income derived from this growth must be guaranteed. Moreover, the conditions enabling people to live decent, prosperous and free lives must be created. Of course, solving the problem of "equality" demands a long-term effort. It necessarily entails the mobilization of as much of the country's resources as possible for economic growth. As such, it constitutes one of the most important issues to be addressed by modernizing societies.

Before equality can be achieved, there first has to be a nation-state with clearly defined boundaries. In addition, the reality of national unity, and effective, powerful political authority and political institutionalization facilitate the move toward equality.

Failure to deal adequately with the issue of equality is one of the major reasons for the unrest experienced by countries undergoing modernization. For example, the regime changes, military coups, strife, division and disintegration frequently seen in the past as well as today in those countries are for the most part due to 1) the failure of regimes in those countries to implement policies that maximize equality and 2) their inability to create the conditions and opportunities for a free and confident nation. Nevertheless, because question of equality is the most difficult to come to terms with, in nearly all modernization movements it is the problem that is dealt with last.

It is entirely too easy to make laws providing for equality and then, without actually making an effort to implement the changes that are needed for their success, to point to them as evidence that political, social and economic rights have been obtained by individuals in society. Needless to say, it is difficult. Nonetheless, without breathing life into these rights through socio-economic reforms and giving them both content and functionality, they will fail to have a genuine impact on society and the lives of people. In backward countries, the economy is generally based on agriculture; and at the heart of agriculture is the problem of land. This problem takes many forms, including: the question of land ownership; the distribution of land among individuals and families; the problem of villagers – those who have no land, those who have some land, and those who have an abundance of land; the administration of land; and mechanization and other productivity-raising techniques.

Economic growth, and the equality achieved through it, demands an increase in production in all areas; and this increase in production requires new investments. Investments, on the other hand, depend on savings that can be used for economic growth and are subject to taxation. However, the vast majority of people in poor countries do not have the possibility of saving. In these countries, wide tracts of land, small-scale industry and commerce are in the hands of a relatively small segment of society. The tax and land reforms targeted at them create a new group of opponents to the Revolution. Forming alliances with centers of social, religious, and traditional authority, they engage in activities designed to hinder and weaken the attempts at radical reform.

During the inception of the Atatürk Revolution, prior to the proclamation of the Republic, "equality" was not a major issue on the agenda. To have some idea of the way in which it was dealt, the documents of this period dealing with the problem of equality must be examined. These are the "Nine Principles," the "Ereğli District Miners' Statute," the "Populist Programme," and the speech made by Mustafa Kemal at the Turkish Economic Congress.

The "Defense of Rights Group" in the Assembly used the "Nine Principles" as the Group's manifesto in the elections that were to be held anew. The Preamble of this Declaration, which was published on 8 April 1923, stated that it was the duty of the state to ensure that a "people's government" based on national sovereignty be set up and that the peacetime responsibility of this government was assuring economic development and bringing prosperity to the nation and its people. It also listed a number of issues related to economic development. The proposed measures and actions to be undertaken are as follows:

• Complaints made by people concerning tithes would be addressed and the injustices they incurred because of them will be corrected.

• Appropriate measures will be taken in the national interest with regard to the cultivation and trade of tobacco.

• The number of monetary institutions, and banks will be increased and organized in such a way as to provide credit on easy terms to farmers, industrialists, merchants and all workers.

• The existing capital of Ziraat Bankası (the Bank of Agriculture) will be raised and greater assistance will be made available to farmers more easily.

• In order to develop the agriculture of the country, agricultural machinery will be imported and be made available to farmers on easy terms.

• The necessary measures will be taken to manufacture goods whose raw materials are found in the country, protect manufacturers and support them through incentives.

• Immediate steps will be taken to begin building railroads, which are needed urgently.

• The attempt will be made to create schools according to national needs and based on modern principles. With them and through other means, an effort will be made to enlighten and educate the people.

• Institutions providing general health services and social assistance will be set up, increased in number and worker protection laws will be enacted.

• Measures will be taken to make use of forests through modern management techniques; to operate mines efficiently; and to develop and expand animal husbandry.

In addition to these measures that needed to be taken by government, mention is made of private sector initiative. In the ninth principle it states, "in order to rapidly rebuild the public infrastructure of our crumbling country, apart from those measures to be taken by the state, laws will be enacted that l) provide the incentives for the founding of companies to take care of structure and repairs, and that 2) ensure the protection of private initiative."[80]

The principle indicating that labor protection laws would be enacted demonstrates that even at that time, there was the desire to regulate working conditions. In fact, during some of the most trying days of the War of Independence - during the Battle of Sakarya - the Turkish Grand National Assembly enacted a law - on 10 September 1921 - that was able to protect the miners working in the district of Ereğli by specifying their rights and regulating their working conditions. The law provided for the building of communal dormitories for workers by employers; the limiting of the workday to eight hours; in the event that more than eight hours were worked, wages would be doubled; daily wages would be determined by a three-party commission consisting of worker, employer and state representatives; and the banning of the employment of workers under the age of 18.[81] It was maintained in the Assembly that this legislation was to encompass all workers but that given the special needs of coal miners that this particular piece of legislation addressed, it could not possibly be extended to all workers. Another law would have to be enacted for them. This, however, was not to happen until 1936 - years after the proclamation of the Republic.

From available documents, it is clear that the Populist Programme - the proposal concerning the draft 1921 Constitution read at the 18 September 1920 session of the Assembly, which we discussed earlier, was a reflection of how the issue of equality, one of the main problems of modernization, was viewed.

In this proposal, signed by Mustafa Kemal, Chairman of the Turkish Grand National Assembly, it was stated, "The government believes that it will acquire regime legitimacy and sovereignty through the liberation of its people from the repression and destructiveness of capitalism." The fundamental principle underlying this view was: "Eliminating the poverty in which the people lived, ensuring their well-being, and creating appropriate reforms and institutions to meet the genuine needs of the people while assuring that the modern needs of agriculture, education, justice, the economy, as well as all other areas of society, are attended to. While doing this, pains should be taken to avoid undermining the unity of the nation/country, and weakening its ability to defend itself. While determining political and social principles, care should be taken to do so on the basis of national spirit. And finally, in the application of these principles, the orientation and genuine needs of the nation should be taken into consideration."[82]

In a speech given at the Turkish Economy Congress held in Izmir on 17 February 1923, the leader of the Revolution, Mustafa Kemal, clarified his views concerning socio-economic matters and pointed out what needed to be done to make sure that appropriate measures were taken:

> While searching for the reasons for the advance and regression of nations, several political, military and social factors are found in history. While there is no doubt that they are influential in social events, what directly affects the life of a nation - whether or not it progresses or regresses - is its economy. This has become more than apparent in what has transpired in the life and history of our nation. In fact, when Turkish history is examined, it becomes clear that there are no other reasons for any of the progress or regression experienced than economic ones. The plethora of successes and triumphs as well as defeats, decay and collapse that fill our history are directly related to our economic situation during those times. In order to raise our New Turkey to new heights, we have to do whatever we can and place the utmost importance on our economy. This is because our time is none other than an economic era.
>
> ....
>
> Regardless of how great political or military victories are, without crowning them with economic ones, the victories that are achieved are not permanent and will wane in time. It is for this reason that in order to be able to take advantage of and build upon the victories that we have attained, it is necessary to ensure and reinforce our economic independence.
>
> ....
>
> Our greatest weapon will be economic development, stability, and success. The era of the people and nation that we have entered will provide the wherewithal through which our national history can be written. I believe that the people's era should be christened the era of the economy. Let it be such an era that our country develops and becomes prosperous.
>
> ....
>
> Let us recall a proverb: "To be happy with what one has is an inexhaustible treasure." The time where doing with little is valued and where poverty is thought of as virtuous should no longer be an acceptable philosophy in the era of the economy.
>
> ....

As we are addressing economic issues, let it not be thought that we are enemies of foreign capital. On the contrary; our country is extensive and we therefore have great need for labor and capital. Therefore, provided due respect is paid to our laws, we are always ready to provide the necessary guarantees to foreign capital and welcome its contribution to our toil and our own stagnant pool of capital. We wish for beneficial outcomes for both them and us- but not the way it was previously. In the past, particularly during the post-Tanzimat period, foreign capital had attained a privileged position in the country and it can be said that the state and government had no other responsibility than to serve as the gendarme of foreign capital. Just as any other civilized state and nation, the New Turkey will not put up with this any longer. We refuse to be captives to foreign capital.

....

In order for this extensive and productive soil to be worked - to have it worked - it is imperative that we complement insufficient manual techniques with scientific methods and tools. We must create a system of railroads and highways since there is no possibility of competing with the West with donkeys and oxcarts on rough roads.

....

We also have to expand and develop our industry. Keeping an open-mind in this matter, our industries will be respected abroad. We need commerce for the exchange of goods and the income it brings. When our commerce remains the monopoly of foreigners, we are unable to take full advantage of the wealth our country has to offer. In order to be successful in this regard, it is crucial for the entire nation to work collectively and in harmony in following a program that is consistent and harmonious with the real needs of our country and nation.

....

All of the principles and programs of our new state and government ought to be derived from the economic program since everything originates there. Because of that, we should educate our children in such a way and provide them such scientific information that they will be productive, effective and industrious in the areas of commerce, agriculture and industry - working together as one body. Therefore, whatever is provided in either primary or secondary schools should be done so bearing in mind this perspective. Programs designed for state affairs must inevitably be based on the economic program, it is necessary to propel the entire nation to work in harmony on implementing a comprehensive program.

....

Our people are not divided into competing classes having different interests. On the contrary, they consist of classes whose existence and actions are mutually beneficial. At his moment, my audience is made up of farmers and artisans, merchants and workers. Which one of these can oppose the other? Who can deny that the farmer needs the artisan, the artisan the farmer and the farmer the merchant - and that they all have need of the worker?

In all of our existing factories and in all of the factories we hope to have, our own workers should be employed. They ought to work prosperously and with pride and all of the classes that we have mentioned should also be wealthy. They should be able to get so much out of life that they are able to find the drive and strength to work. Therefore, when mention is made of a "program," this program, it should be thought of as a "National Labor Oath." in addition, it is necessary that the political system that is to emerge from within the framework of such a program should not be designed just as an ordinary political party. I firmly and wholeheartedly believe that we will be successful . All that is required is the determination and conviction of the nation, its unity, solidarity and mutual assistance - as has been the case of a political system emerging with the advent of peace.[83]

Thus it can be seen that for Mustafa Kemal, the success of an independence or modernization movement, in the true sense of the term, depended on economic progress, economic development and growth. He considers historical and social events predominantly in terms of economics and wants to base the Revolution on radical economic reforms. It is in this way, he thinks, that the political system will acquire continuity and functionality.

In the organization of relations of production, Mustafa Kemal, taking into consideration the needs of the country and nation, emphasizes inter-class harmony and balance and mutual assistance instead of class conflict. While he does not reject the existence of classes, he refuses to grant to any single class a position of supremacy. He aims at eliminating poverty, encouraging the participation of people in the production process and an increase in their productivity, and creating a standard of living that is befitting human dignity.

Under this regime, the state, society and individuals are imbued with entrepreneurial obligation. Moreover, foreign capitalists are granted the right to make investments within the framework of legislation that prevents the country from being exploited. Nevertheless, it is unacceptable in terms of the interests of the country for commerce to remain in the hands of foreigners.

In the period following the proclamation of the Republic, to the extent possible and to the degree to which they were adopted by Government and the Assembly, the attempt was made to put into practice the views appearing in the above-mentioned document. However, despite the fact that great strides were taken, the question of equality in the Atatürk Revolution was not yet fully resolved. An explanation that accounts for this can be made. In reality, the desires and expectations of societies are continually increasing along with new developments and transformations. And to be modern or progressive means having to ensure that these expectations, desires and new needs are met and kept in step with the flow of this continuity.

3. The Strategy and Tactics of the Paradigm

Mustafa Kemal was not a theoretician or an academic. However, he wanted to transform Turkish society from one that was downtrodden and poor to one that could stand firmly on its own and determine its own fate. He was determined to keep the country from being partitioned and shared among the Western powers. Ever since he was a young man, he had thought about how this could be done. He had been following and examining the rise of nationalism and independence movements in the Balkan countries that were located within the borders of the Ottoman Empire. He was a well-trained, well-read commander who knew the political history of the world and understood the reasons behind the strife and wars that occurred among states within this political history. He was fully aware of the place and influence of Turks in history and in previous civilizations. He also understood the changes that Islam brought to the structure, culture and economy of Turkish society. He was well versed in the advantages and disadvantages of the Ottoman Empire's policy of expansion and the political, economic and technological factors that gave rise to its collapse. Finally, he understood the role of the nation-state, national unity and political authority in the development of Europe. Moreover, he knew about the French Revolution and its significance and its consequences. He was not satisfied with learning only what was necessary for a soldier. On the contrary, he took great pains to learn, to the extent conditions permitted, about the ideological currents in his own country and the world. Because he was commander, he had the chance to see and get acquainted with the places, people, traditions, customs, beliefs, life styles, desires and expectations of countries ranging from those in North Africa to the Middle East, from the Caucasus to the Balkans, all the way to central Anatolia. He was born and raised in Thessalonica. As a young commander, he had lived in this town, which was a lively center of intellectual discourse during the Ottoman Empire of that period. He thus had the opportunity to participate in discussions there, which had great importance to the political future of the Empire. In addition, he had vast experience, a capacity for astute observation and correct judgment, and the ability to analyze and reach conclusions. He was successful in the battles in which he participated, winning respect from his superiors. He possessed superior strategic and tactical ability to apply what he had learned during his military education and as a professional officer. He constantly saw himself as a leader who would save the state in the future and provide direction to society and nation. This is what he had been preparing himself for, ever since he was a young man. Living together with the people at all times during the waging of battle, at the front and in the barracks, speaking with them and fighting along side them, he knew them intimately. He knew the human structure of society, its conditions, opportunities, economy, agriculture, commerce, traditions and beliefs. He was familiar with the makeup of the people and their altruistic feelings and just how inconsumable their resistance, and determination and power to fight and succeed were. He believed that with this strength, success could be attained. His accumulated experience, consciousness and passion were what enabled Mustafa Kemal to be instrumental in getting the Turkish struggle for independence and modernization off the ground. From the time he launched his Revolution on 19 May 1919, he gradually shaped and developed it, giving it form and content, until a national paradigm of modernization -one that was peculiar to the Turkish nation- was wrought for Anatolia. A paradigm that he had formed in his mind envisioned a revolution realized through the support and participation of the nation. It would first be introduced to the people, after which they would be encouraged to adopt it. Finally, the consent of the whole nation would be obtained. While neither an advocate of the use of force nor a mere dictator, he did not shy from using intimidation when the need arose. What, how, when, for whom, with whom and how much is to be done determine as well as the conditions of the country and society determine the material and moral opportunities of the progressive reformer. This undoubtedly demands a strategy and a set of tactics.

To be successful, a program of modernization requires a theoretical edifice, along with a practical strategy of reform and particular tactics tailored to the demands placed on it by the existing social structure and conditions of the country.

The political scientist Huntington outlines two strategies for reformers:

1. Specify at the beginning the real goals in their entirety and then attempt to obtain them all at once through the use of force.

2. Open the door a crack and then, by keeping a foot in the crack, gradually realize goals on the basis of applicability, degree of acceptance, and ability.

Huntington calls the first method the "root" or "Blitzkrieg" approach and the second one, the "branch" or "Fabian" approach.[84]

There are many examples of the practical application of both of these strategies. While some reformers will be rather "purist" in their approach and use strategy to the exclusion of the other, many other reformers will attempt to combine them. Such a combined approach has the advantage of enabling the reformer, upon assessing the conditions of his country and society and calculating the future advantages and disadvantages of each, to choose just the appropriate mix of strategies and tactics. Being able to select a method and prepare a plan of action is a matter of skill, sense and the ability to project into the future.

Forcibly imposing oneself at lightening speed and rapidly laying foundations may seem like a shortcut method. There are even illustrations of where it has been used, but this approach carries with it a number of disadvantages. Mustafa Kemal did not opt for this method, which is the fundamental reason for his success. Mustafa Kemal is the leader who did away with the Sultanate and the Caliphate and established the Republic. However, after Samsun, if he had immediately said in the Amasya Declaration that he was going to do this, he probably would not have been able to participate in the Congress at Erzurum. He would have been arrested and sent to Istanbul upon the orders of the Sultan. While abolishing the Sultanate, he preferred keeping the political and religious questions apart from one another and saw merit in holding on to the Caliphate for a while longer. If he had wanted to abolish both of them at the same time, he would have perhaps encountered much greater opposition in the Assembly, perhaps even not being able to find the opportunity to get rid of the Sultanate. As it was, opposition did emerge in the Assembly during the debate held regarding the proposal to abolish the Sultanate, to which Mustafa Kemal responded by threatening that "a few heads would roll" if agreement was not reached. Still, though, it ought to be born in mind that Atatürk's approach was essentially incremental; everything he did at the right time and right place. Sometimes this meant pausing after taking a particular action to assess the situation before moving on. At other times, sudden and unexpected moves were called for, as was the case with the proposal for the Republic: prepared on the eve of 29 October, the proposal was ratified the following day, followed by the proclamation of the Republic on the same day.

It summary, it can be said that in Atatürk's paradigm of modernization, the establishment of a society that was national in scope, and the creation of a political order that was modern and laïc were of the utmost importance. Socio-cultural reform and measures ensuring economic development, known to be requisites of modernization, were prioritized and put into effect according to their applicability. Those that will receive the most attention, provide the most support and be the most readily accepted are given top priority while those that will create difficulty or create impasses are postponed to an appropriate time. As opportunity and feasibility materialize, they are put on the agenda.

This is a useful, rational, realistle, and sound set of strategies and tactics. These strategic and tactical methods are determined by the structure of the country and society as well as the aptitude and skill of the leader.

4. The Function of Leadership and the Party System

A modernization movement without a leader can hardly be fathomed. Similarly, it would be impossible to imagine how such a movement could oversee the transformation of society without relying on some sort of organization. Therefore, in societies undergoing modernization, leadership and a party system have important functions. In order to come to political power, organization is a prerequisite. Moreover, political organization requires the political party. Coming to power demands a political party with which to provide direction to society. But what kind of political system should a modernizing revolution envision? Atatürk's Revolution aimed at a pluralist, liberal and democratic political system. Nevertheless, in order to reach this goal and real ize all the other goals, a powerful single-party system had to be adopted at the beginning.

From the moment he arrived in Samsun, Mustafa Kemal began organizational work. The unification of the local Defense of Rights associations in Anatolia and Roumelia under the umbrella of the Society for the Defense of Rights of Anatolia and Roumelia and its transformation into an organization having national dimensions contributed to both the success of the movement and its leader. At the same time, it kept society from being affected by counter-revolutionary groupings. After independence, this association became a political party. As the "Republican People's Party," it assumed the responsibility for the modernization of society, something that can clearly be seen from its programme.

In modernizing countries, authority vacuums are initially filled by leaders and military power. But it is impossible to maintain this authority simply on the basis of the charisma of leaders or the strength of the army. Hence, in addition to a leader, there is need for a political apparatus and organization. This is because in the contemporary world, only leaders who are able to devise, manage and influence policy can control the future. Rustow emphasizes Atatürk's characteristics as a powerful organizational man in the following way: Mustafa Kemal is not entirely a charismatic leader ... we can say that he found himself within a charismatic role but that he was basically an organizational man. Moreover, because he was an organizational man, he was successful. A leader who suffices with only "charisma" is rather limited when it comes to administrative matters. Throughout his life, Atatürk was a man firmly committed to the importance of sound administrative structure. He believed that relying on charisma was unsound and thus tried to minimize it in the exercise of his authority, pushing it into the background. For example, during the critical years for the country, 1919-1922, he took important strides on the road to organization. Instead of local administration, he pushed for one having national dimensions. Thus, by unifying and integrating national administration with the military apparatus, he took the most important step toward independence.[85]

Much continues to be said about Mustafa Kemal, with many books having already been written and analyses carried out.

Atatürk was unquestionably a great commander, a powerful state founder, a committed revolutionary, and a profound lover of peace - not only for his own nation, but also for nations all over the world. Underlying these characteristics were his rational pursuit of politics and his stature as a powerful and influential politician.

People have to be enthusiastic and committed when involved in politics. At the same time, however, they have to curb this enthusiasm and commitment so as to avoid excesses and the turmoil that can result from them.

Politics is an art; it is having the ability to recognize the extent to which beliefs and ideas can be transformed into action, and to determine the soundest and most direct route to achieving positive results of that action. This can be called skill, reasoning, the art of transforming into action what has been determined to be rational, and competent.

The skilled politician is one who is successful and can reduce error to a minimum. He is able to assess the political, cultural and social conditions of his society. This allows him to make decisions regarding the content, method, timing, and extent of policies to be implemented and take action accordingly.

Leaders of revolutions are successful to the extent that their policies are rational. Policies based on vague possibilities are doomed to failure.

In this respect, politicians have to consider the value judgments, traditions and customs -as well as their prevalence and validity- of the societies in which they want to carry out their policies. Elites who are in a position of shaping public opinion and influencing society have to take into account, from a social scientific and psychological perspective, the disposition of society to change in light of these value judgements.

Regimes in which policies are formulated on the basis of an electoral system whereby the votes are the medium through which the preferences of society are made known, tend to be more socially and politically efficacious. Policies thus formulated tend to have greater applicability and acceptability in both the state and society. They also tend to be more rational since they are more reflective of the true needs of society.

Mustafa Kemal was guided by rational policy as he launched the War of Independence, mobilized the people, large landowners, gentry, sheiks, leaders of sects, heads of clans, officers, civil servants, and the rich and poor of Anatolia, and unified all the various local liberation and defense organizations of the nation under a single umbrella for the purpose of national liberation. He had an unshakable belief that the Turkish people would realize and maintain their independence, as well as attain modernity.

There are certain prerequisites to achieving complete independence and becoming modern. Not completely or immediately realizable, they consist of offensives on a number of fronts. The limits of political, social, cultural, material and moral structure and all powers of resistance must be stretched without jeopardizing the success of the attempt. These offensives are carried out within the framework of a particular programme. A real revolutionary is one that can prioritize the issues, problems, and reforms of the development programme not only from a political, social, cultural, material and moral point of view,

but also perhaps most importantly, by using the criterion of the possibility of success. Mustafa Kemal Atatürk was a leader who knew
this and put this rational policy into practice.

Mustafa Kemal was opposed to the institutions of the Sultanate
and Caliphate, the sharing of society and its control by large landowners, gentry, clan heads, and sheiks; and the rule of the country through
traditions, beliefs and codes left over from a pre-modern era. However, he did not express these beliefs immediately. Not when he set
foot in Samsun, nor in Amasya, Erzurum, and Sivas or in Ankara,
when he opened the Grand National Assembly. His close associate
Fevzi Çakmak admired this characteristic or skill of Atatürk: "Mustafa Kemal Atatürk always knew when and where he would have to
stop to reconsider a situation. This is one of his superior traits that I
admire the most. Thinking ahead and always attentive is what made
him supreme in the affairs concerning the country."[86]

Breaking the control of the enemy over the Caliphate and Sultanate
in Istanbul was among the first goals of the National Struggle. His
preserving the Caliphate even as he decided to abolish the Sultanate,
only to do away with it too some 15 months later is a consequence of
this rational, realistic policy.

The reforms implemented after the Republic had been set up, e.g.,
the unification and laïcization of education, the abolition of the Arabic alphabet, changes in the calendar and days of rest during the we-
ek, the ratification of the citizenship law and the modifications brought about in dress, were not pre-planned but rather the consequence of pragmatic evaluation of conditions in society. While Mustafa
Kemal had had certain broad notions of what he wanted to accomplish, and how to go about doing so prior to the War of Independence, it was only by having a sense of timing and appropriateness that
he was able to accomplish these reforms. Rather then formulated and
then implemented in one monolithic package, the reforms were carried out in stages that built upon one another.

Mustafa Kemal also took pains to place his policies and actions on
sound, legal footing. Thus, he sought the support of the majority of
the nation and the participation of the people in all policies and actions he undertook.

Some have erroneously concluded that Mustafa Kemal Atatürk was a "dictator." This is largely the result of hasty and inadequate assessments of the intentions and action of Atatürk and the Atatürk Revolution, leading to gross misinterpretations. It must be emphasized that after having successfully rallied and led the entire nation, including all of its ethnic groups and religious sects, in a National Struggle during the War of Independence, Mustafa Kemal rose to become a person who was trusted, loved, respected and exalted by the nation. It was evident that he wanted what was best for the nation. Moreover, if he had been a dictator, he would not have found it necessary to abolish the institution of Sultanate or the Caliphate. Instead, he would have assumed one of those positions himself. Contrary to what some thought, Atatürk had no intentions of becoming either Sultan or Caliph. Quite to the contrary, he had a rather different form of government in mind, one based on consent of the people, and not a single individual. Nevertheless, for a progressive leader, such a regime was one of the most challenging and difficult to endure. There was significant opposition in the Assembly to the radical reform movement and its pronouncements. Society was ridden with centuries-old traditions, customs and beliefs that kept it from becoming modern. This was the case even though the general consensus in the country, especially after the great victory, was that whatever Mustafa Kemal said or recommended was correct and in the best interest of the nation. Given the widespread opposition among Deputies and groups in the Assembly that were openly opposed to Mustafa Kemal, decisions and laws that were to be made in the Assembly by virtue of majority vote would have to be reached through means of persuasion. The way in which Atatürk worked with the Assembly in the face of such antagonism, as well as his espousal of a democratic regime, demonstrates that he had democratic leadership qualities right from the start.

Consent-based radical reform movements can be realized under a democratic regime only by adroit, talented and powerful leaders following rational policies. Under such regimes, it is the policies and beliefs of leaders that determine their fate. If leaders can pursue a rational policy, not only can they realize the goals of radical reform without undermining the extensive love, trust and respect of their nations but also become immortalized. Atatürk was just this sort of leader. However, leaders who, after having attained their initial successes and ensured victory, allow themselves to get caught up with the obsession that they and their word is law, are not only soon deposed, but incur the wrath of their nations. Self-actualized leaders are those who are widely and sincerely loved and venerated by their nations. Mustafa Kemal was a leader who attained this self-actualization.

It behooves all radical reformers to carefully examine, understand, and assess Mustafa Kemal's approach toward policy-making. By doing so, they will go a long way toward ensuring the viability of their own policies, which will be enormously beneficial to themselves, their societies and their countries. In short, the general welfare of all concerned will be enhanced.

The role of the leader in the Atatürk paradigm of modernization is thus at once both considerable and powerful. It is the kind of leadership that is essential in any reform movement that is to be undertaken.

With his ability to perceive reality and his foresight, Atatürk was a person of both action and ideals. Without a doubt, his practicality and organizational ability were major components of his personality. It was he who best understood, explained and critiqued the Revolutionism-Reformism that he created; in other words, there was no better proponent of that Revolution. His speeches and statements are concrete documentation of his philosophical orientation. Realism and idealism are nestled together within Atatürk. His realism limited his idealism, making it pragmatic. His idealism was expressed through his emphasis on the importance of the state and society being independent, civilized and modern. Both were to exist within the framework of national boundaries. Remaining modern and open to reforms were the quintessential characteristics of state and society. While he had compassion for fellow Turks living in other countries under different states and would not want to see them exploited, his idealism was restricted to Turkey. But neither was he a racial supremist or an exclusionist. Atatürk was opposed to expansionism. His dream was to create a greater, more advanced Turkey within *national boundaries*. He did not base his nationalism on racial discrimination, Ottomanism or Islamism. At no time did he resort to despotic or a per-

sonal Sultanate regime. He relied on the supreme legislative authority
of the 1921 and 1924 Constitutions. Atatürk employed the methods
of speech and debate to achieve what he wanted. His success was due
to his persuasiveness. Nevertheless, particularly during the years of
his Presidency, it certainly helped to have an Assembly that shared the
same basic beliefs and views. This helped facilitate the passage of laws
required by the reform movement. It is clear that "modernization requires the creation and maintenance of an effective, progressive, and
reasonably consolidated governing elite."[87] Atatürk addressed the importance of this unity in the following way:

> The War of Independence and the Turkish Revolution achieved success in all
> that it attempted by relying on the conscious unity of Turkey in its ideological prin-
> ciples and its lofty political and civilized outlook.
>
> Success of our Republican government depends on the confidence and coura-
> ge of the nation. Consensus with respect to the principles of the Revolution and the
> Republic that has been established and cooperation in carrying them out are the
> bases for the good fortune, prosperity, and strength of our country and nation.[88]

A nation derives its strength from both its material and moral elements. Material components can be divided into the broad categories
of political, military, economic, and technological power. Subcate-
gories include population, geopolitical situation, and natural resources. Moral strength is formed by the characteristics of the nation and
its people, the state of their morale, their behavior when confronted
with difficulties and their resistance, foreign policy, and the administrative quality of government. In developed - and especially developing - countries, the people's support of the government, the existence and diffusion of belief that the political regime protects the interests of nation and state are the basic factors in the resolution of
problems between the nation and government.

This is one of the most important factors creating a milieu for modernization and contributing to increasing its momentum. Atatürk
and his political regime instilled this conviction within the nation.
Through it, the Turkish political order obtained a sound structure
that accelerated modernization efforts.

Morgenthau stresses that national morale is very important in the existence of a society and in measuring its strength: "One can say, in general, that the more closely identified a people are with the actions and objectives of their government, the better are the chances for national morale to be high, and vice versa."[89] Atatürk touched upon the meaning and importance of a sound and close relationship between the nation and government in this way:

> National ideals manifest themselves over time in the nation working together in confidence, insisting on progress and in the formation of national unity and will. This is extremely important for us since, unequivocally, we see the basis of our national existence in national conscience and national unity.
>
> The extent of the affinity between the people and government and their attempt to work together is also gratifying.
>
> The people's desire to help and support the government in its carrying out of administrative and economic measures, and their subsequent acceptance of the consequences of those measures, is to be extolled. This mood was a very important, constructive factor having a far-reaching effect on the advancement of the Turkish nation and the restoration of the Turkish country.
>
> It is a great boon and distinction for a nation to recognize the state as its own and as its protector. The Turkish nation experienced this for the first time with the founding of the Republic. This recognition has continued to manifest itself, intensifying from one year to the next. It is clear that the paramount importance we have placed on the material and spiritual well-being of our nation has not been misplaced.[90]

Politics during Atatürk's time was both progressive and stable. This was due in large part to the dynamism, nationalism, courageousness, decisiveness, consistency and superior quality of the leadership cadre. The existence of political stability undoubtedly depended on other reasons as well. In those days, a modern class structure of society had not yet formed in Turkey. The government was not besieged by the demands or ardent desires of the people. The fact that broad-based mass demands had not yet appeared meant that the government could take the initiative without much difficulty. The demands people made on the government were limited. Political consciousness was not widespread.

During Atatürk's Presidency, the country had achieved a remarkable degree of unity and stability. This situation led Ward to comment "The reason why the Turks can preserve their freedom under a single-party system is because they enjoy a fundamental unity of social purpose. It is generally admitted that where, in the West, a party split represents a fundamental cleavage in the social life of the community (for example, the unbridgeable division between Communist Left and Conservative Right in France), a party system tends to become unworkable. Does it follow that the Turks offered a new experiment in democracy: the creation of freedom via a single party that functions to unify the nation? It is worth considering, but, obviously, it is not as simple as that. Turkish unity comes in part from the common social purpose of the community - that of creating a prosperous, modernized, national Republic. But it equally comes from the fact that most of the problems of the more highly industrialized states of the West still lie before the Turks."[91]

Even though the social structure of Turkey during those years was a major factor contributing to the stability, the first-rate qualities of its political leadership are not to be discounted. They served to enhance the functional capacity of the political system. The ideological unity among the governing elites and social accord were factors that accelerated modernization. This administrative group had consensus with respect to both "means" and "ends." The goal was becoming modern since, as Atatürk had pointed out, nations that are not or are unable to become modern cannot be free and independent.[92] The means to this was working according to the principles of Republicanism, Nationalism, Populism, Etatism, Laïcism and Revolutionism-Reformism within the context of national unity, relying on national strength, national wealth, reason, and science. The sense of the leadership's responsibility toward the nation and its "giving account" of itself was expressed by Atatürk in his speech which he gave on the occasion of the 10th Anniversary of the Republic: "I have made many promises to the Great Turkish Nation over the last 15 years and I am pleased to say that in the keeping and implementation of these promises, I have not failed my nation."[93]

The progressive segment of the Ottoman political elite dominated the government during the War of Independence and founded the Republic. They formed a group that knew what was required to be a "state" and assumed the responsibility for seeing to it that these requirements were met. They provided leadership in the movement to establish a new state for a long-standing nation. However, great changes occurred in the values on which they depended and in their understanding of regime type. These changes were oriented toward modernization and nation-building. These changes in the values of political elites are of particular interest to social scientists.

When an evaluation of political elites in Atatürk's Turkey is performed, it is possible to arrive at a number of conclusions as to why these elites had these characteristics. There are many differences between the elites of various countries due to a number of historical, social and cultural factors. These differences appear in the structure of these groups, in their function, and in their effectiveness. In his study of the elites in several African, Asian and Latin American countries, Eisenstadt has reached certain significant conclusions about the reasons for the success of modernizing elites in Mexico, Kemalist Turkey, Meiji Japan and Soviet Russia. He states that in these four countries:

> The elites were able not only to impose their policies on the wider social groups and strata, but also to draw these groups into the more differentiated institutional framework, at the same time regulating, at least to some extent, their integration within the framework.[94]

> The problem of why in Turkey, Japan, Mexico, and Russia there emerged in the initial stages of modernization elites with orientations to change and ability to implement relatively effective policies, while they did not develop in these initial phases in Indonesia, Pakistan or Burma, or why elites with similar differences tended to develop also in later stages of modernization, is an extremely difficult one and constitutes one of the most baffling problems in comparative sociological analysis. There are but few available indications to deal with this problem. Very tentatively, it may perhaps be suggested that to some extent it has to do with the placement of these elites in the preceding social structure, with the extent of their internal cohesiveness, of the internal transformation of their own value orientation.[95]

Looking specifically at the Turkish case, we see that all throughout the Ottoman reform movements, the Turkish War of Independence, and the Republican era, military officers constituted a leading and
power force in the modernization of the country. On the other hand,
during the Ottoman Empire, the allegiance of this officer cadre was
to the Empire and it was through reform movements that they worked to save it. However, beginning in the early years of the Republic,
the officers were excluded from participation in politics and the great military leaders in the National Struggle served Turkey as civilians.
These leaders sought the support of the civilian groups, especially the
bureaucracy. A laïc reformist-oriented educational system increased
the number of civilians dedicated to the reform movement. However,
several army officers, after retirement or resignation from the army,
were drawn into Parliament and other important civilian organizations. As a consequence of this and the fact that these officers were
open to innovation, their value judgments and the form of state to
which they gave their allegiance changed. Together with the War of
Independence and the Republic, this allegiance was transferred to the
nation-state and to full modernization.[96]

Turkish political elites can be examined from yet another angle. In general, they consist of a group of "open elites."[97] In contrast to a group
of "closed elites," which is restricted to a limited few. A group of "open
elites" is comprised of persons from a variety of different groups who
have an opportunity to exercise an active role in political life.

During the Ottoman period and the first years of the Republic,
Turkish political elites were derived predominantly from the military-
intellectual-bureaucrat segments of society and represented the "center." As a consequence of the change and development occurring in
the country, different groups and social strata became part of the Turkish political elite. Furthermore, these were largely those who came
from the "periphery" and had different professions.[98] Some of these
new groups brought with them new value judgments and worked to
influence political life accordingly and continue to do so. However,
modernization not only depends on the existence of an effective government and successful elites. It hinges on the participation of the
people, which is what imbues it with meaning.

Even as early as the year the War of Independence began, in a speech made on 28 December 1919 in Ankara, Atatürk believed that true success came with the participation of people and society. Accordingly, he felt that demand and direction originating from below were the most sound. Stressing that "top-down" direction was only temporary, he asserted that "bottom-up" effectiveness and direction was a goal:

> Gentlemen! If a nation does not use what strength it has - all of the ideological and material power at its disposal – for perpetuating its own existence and rights; if it is unable to determine its existence and independence by relying on its own strength, it is destined to be manipulated by others. Our national existence, past, as well as our most recent form of government are all evidence of this. Therefore, we have agreed upon the efficacy of national power and national sovereignty as organizing principles of our national system. There is only one kind of sovereignty recognized in today's world of nations: national sovereignty... This organization can be looked at in more detail, starting with the village, moving on to the neighborhood and then to the people of the neighborhood; in other words, we begin with the individual. Failing to take the individual into consideration means that the masses can be pulled in one direction or another -good or bad- by anyone. In order to be able for the individual to become liberated, the future must be of relevance to him. Naturally, institutions that are built from the ground up are relatively sounder. Without a doubt, all endeavors must begin at the bottom moving upwards, rather than from the top, moving downwards.
>
> In the former, mankind as a whole is used to obtain objectives. But because a practical and concrete way for this to happen has not yet been found, it has remained for a few nations to provide leadership -thus giving rise to a "top down" approach to achieve objectives. In our travels throughout the country, we have seen that our national organization, which naturally began using the first type, owes its existence to the fact that it started with the individual and worked its way up from there. Nevertheless, we cannot assume that we have reached maturity in this matter. It is for this reason that we must consider it our national and civic duty to strive to once again create a "bottom-up" form of organization.[99]

Being able to exercise restraint, using power in pursuit of justice and freedom, abandoning expansionistic aims, and creating a more

powerful Turkish State and Turkish nation within narrower boundaries were all characteristics of Atatürk's leadership. Atatürk was a leader who wanted his accomplishments to not only survive him but hoped others would be able to surpass him.

The Atatürk reform movement stressed the importance of a rational and national leader and leadership cadre that provided reassuran-
ce and instilled trust. The sense of oppression and degradation vis-à-
vis the West that intensified during the Tanzimat period was no longer present among the Turkish people. The West had been defeated in
the War of Independence. In its place, a new, rational policy was embarked upon. This policy did not foresee the resurrection of an Empire but rather the foundation of a Turkish state that was to be guided by national policy within national borders. This new state would
contend with the requirements and objectives of modernization and
development.

Modern political parties arose as a consequence of great political
upheavals experienced in Western countries and have only less than
a 300-year history. "The political party is an element of modern and
modernizing political systems."[100] Therefore, political parties and
modernization are issues that are closely related and mutually interact.

Political parties arise from and are to some extent shaped by the
political, cultural, social and economic transformations that are peculiar to each society. On the other hand, political parties in modern or
modernizing societies attempt to provide direction to these societies
and struggles undertaken to change their political and social structures. Political parties perform several important functions. They include participating in the political system within the context of modernization movements, ensuring the legitimacy of the existing political
system, providing opportunities for conflict resolution, and assisting
in national unification. Thus, political parties are also a means of political socialization.[101] In effect, political parties are well-organized
institutions whose function it is to assume the reigns of power in government -or at least a position whereby they can be influential-
through popular support. It is in this way that they attempt to get their
programs implemented.

The party system of a country to a large degree influences the political regime of that country. Political parties are an important component of both democratic and totalitarian systems. On the other hand, it is also true that some political parties lead to the division of the country. By defending the traditional interests and groups, they adversely influence modernization efforts.

Modernization began in the West before nationalist ideologies had acquired a mass appeal to all segments of society. This is true for Turkey as well. However, in the majority of Asian and African countries, modernization emerged with the founding of an independent state.

In the West, modernization, nationalism, and the development of political parties are parallel phenomena. To the extent that the political system modernized, e.g., responded to the legitimate demands of the people, provided the means through which they would effectively participate in politics, granted political freedoms to the people, and met the socio-economic and cultural exigencies of the people, the people were able to acquire political consciousness. Political parties are one of the driving forces behind the modernization of the political system.

Political parties and modernization movements are directly intertwined. Nevertheless, there are many examples in the modern world of countries that have acceded legitimacy and a leadership role to a single political party and with it have undertaken modernization, being able to meet many of the requirements thereof. In these countries, the political party is an institution that creates a "closed regime" and within that "closed regime" provides leadership to the modernization movement.

In the case of Turkey, political parties have a history that extends back to the 19th century. The developments of Turkish political parties have not always been successful. Political parties have not always contributed to liberal democracy and efforts made on behalf of modernization. However, in spite of the problems encountered by the country at times with respect to disruptions and vacillations with respect to the creation of an "open regime," Turkey has been able to acquire an increase of "practice" and "knowledge" regarding political parties. This accumulated experience led Turkey to carry out modernization within the context of an "open regime."

Many theorists have identified the intimate relationship between political parties and democracy. For example, according to E.E. Schattschneider, "political parties created democracy, and modern democracy is unthinkable save in terms of the parties."[102]

Under a democratic regime, in order for "ruling party-opposition party" relations to function, above all consensus needs to be reached between the ruling party and the opposition on the basis of the principle, "agreeing not to agree."

Research conducted on political parties can be categorized into three main groups. Along with those studies in which political parties are investigated in both general and comparative terms, there are others that examine a specific political party or the political parties in a particular country, or consider political parties from a certain perspective.

Studies recently carried out on political parties have confirmed the view that political parties constitute the most influential factor in the formation of social mobilization and political integration. However, with respect to how and the degree to which political parties contribute to modernization efforts, it is not possible to arrive at definite conclusions that can be applied globally to all countries. The historical, cultural and political developments of individual countries influence the role and activities of parties in modernization movements.

A society in the transitional phase of modernization, or even one that is already modernized, may not be one that provides political freedoms or functions as an "open society." In other words, however much modernization may afford the opportunity for "individual" and "society" to move away f rom a static state of affairs to a more dynamic, "participatory" one, it is not a foregone conclusion that political choice, freedom of thought and the freedom to organize on the basis of political ideology will automatically be afforded. There have been cases of both developed and developing countries that have not adopted liberal democracy, a constitutional system or an open society. In such countries, the political systems generally consist of a single party or other smaller parties formed under the subjugation of the dominant party, and based on the legitimacy of a single doctrine or ideology. This is a system that obstructs the open discussion of opposing views and the competition of political parties. The state only accepts the legitimacy of a single party, authority and ideology. Accordingly, it uses its power to prevent the emergence of ideologies or organizations and, in the case where this looks likely, suppress or eliminate them. In such closed societies, political choice is not recognized. "Participation" comes in the form of support for a single legitimate ideology and single political party. Political socialization is carried out to ensure this type of participation. This does not mean that societies that are closed and do not allow political choice are traditional ones. Nevertheless, even if, in spite of being closed, a modernized society creates opportunities for "participation," it does not mean that it is a society that offers political choice or political freedoms.

According to Rustow, broad-based political parties in societies undergoing nation-building, within the context of nationalism they have embraced, usually fight on two fronts. One is external and has as its focus the threat posed to their autonomy by foreign powers. The other is the internal and consists of the struggle with supporters of the traditional political regime. By having obtained the support of nearly all strata of society, the party acquires a broad-based structure. Another reason for its broad-based structure is its recognition of the need for radical transformation of the social order. The socio-economic goal of such a single party is usually mass education, economic development and the realization of laïcism; in other words, the acceleration of the modernization. An important aspect of modernization is the inculcation of national consciousness.[103]

The Republican People's Party, the oldest party of Republican Turkey, was active and influential in Atatürk's modernization movement. An offshoot of the National Struggle, this party had an undeniably important function in the transformation of traditional Ottoman society into a Turkish nation-state. In order for political institutions to maintain their functionality and effectiveness during a process of radical reform, they must continually adapt to changing conditions. If a political party, for instance, is unsuccessful in coming up with viable solutions to the problems created by the challenges of a society undergoing modernization, and therefore begins to lose its status as a legitimate institution in the eyes of the people, it will flounder and eventually disappear.

The political party of the Atatürk paradigm of modernization is the Republican People's Party (R.P.P.). This broad-based party is the outcome of the Period of National Struggle. Mustafa Kemal announced for the first time to journalists on 6 December 1922 the creation of a party that he thought was needed and which he considered as the political, civilian apparatus of the Revolution. At the same time, he outlined its basic principles and the role it was to play in the programme of revolutionary reform. According to the leader of the Revolution, the political party assuming responsibility in the modernization movement is fully independent and it must embrace unconditional national sovereignty. This party should defend the rights of all classes in society. It should work toward the improvement and development of society, one that is happy, prosperous and free. In addition, the party should be based on populism. Mustafa Kemal made it perfectly clear what he meant by the "complete independence" that he wanted this party to adopt, defend and work toward. For him, complete independence meant independence and freedom in a variety of areas, including political, monetary, economic, judicial, military, and cultural. Lack of freedom in any of these areas meant the absence of complete independence, in the full sense of the term, of the nation and country.

Atatürk also saw this political party as laying the foundations for the pluralist, liberal democratic system that he wanted to create. He framed his ideas and system of thought within the programme of this party. The means through which modernization was to be carried out - Republicanism, Nationalism, Populism, Laïcism, Etatism and Revolutionism-Reformism – were transformed into principles. In 1937, the six principles of the party and the Atatürkist system of thought were inserted into Article 2 of the Turkish Constitution of 1924.

V

USING THE PARADIGM
TO TRANSFORM
THE STRUCTURE OF
SOCIETY AND STATE

Within the context of modernization, revolutionary reform is the transformation of thought into action. It is taking thought and using it to transform the structure of the state and society. The success or failure of a reform movement becomes apparent with the positive or negative consequences of its policies. This is why it is crucial to examine the impact of the Atatürk Revolution on the life of society and the state. In doing so, three main phases of his radical reform movement will be assessed: the provision of national unity, the formation of authority and the realization of equality. By describing the revolutionary reforms undertaken to address these problems, the extent to which the goals of the Revolution were actually reached will become more evident.

The contents of the six principles of the Atatürk Revolution -Republicanism, Nationalism, Populism, Laïcism, Etatism, and Revolutionism-Reformism- were not clearly delineated during the first years of the Revolution. Rather, they were the product of discussion and debate conducted at the many Congresses held during that period. They became part of the bylaws and program of the political party of the revolutionary reform movement in 1927 and 1931. Becoming known as "Kemalism" in 1935, these principles formed the "official ideology" of the political regime when they became part of the Constitution of the Republic in 1937. All of the reforms carried out during both the War of Independence and the years following the proclamation of the Republic were based on these principles. In all of his speeches, the leader of the reform movement continually emphasized the contents and objectives of these principles.

Ever since 29 October 1923, an assortment of revolutionary reforms has been undertaken - during and immediately after Atatürk's Presidency. Nonetheless, after the beginning of the multi-party era, several courses of action contrary to modernization were inaugurated. Without going into detail, it will be useful to examine them in terms of the phases of modernization.

1. Reforms Designed to Bring About Unity

Prior to the proclamation of the Republic, there existed in society a state of affairs where the Sultanate had been abolished while the Caliphate, which had been an inseparable part of the Empire, continued. Considering that it symbolized religious unity based not on the nation but on religious community, the Caliphate could not be permitted to continue indefinitely. To keep this institution as part of the structure of the state and allow it to continue its influence over society would be contrary to and impede the course of nation-state building. Thus, four months after the Republic was proclaimed, the Caliphate was also abolished. The Administration of Religious Affairs became a part of the structure of the state and placed under its supervision. This reform had as much to do with the problem of authority as it did to that of unity.

The educational system in the pre-Republican period was essentially an incoherent array of institutions, each operating independently from one another. Various types of schools offering religious instruction dominated the system and sectarianism was rampant among them. In addition, their curricula were void of national or secular content, for the most part. The only non-religious schools were those run by the minorities of the Empire and those operated by foreigners. While more secular in orientation, these schools provided instruction in a foreign language and, particularly those run by foreigners, tended to instill within its students a foreign culture that was alien to Turkish society. This was the state of affairs with which Republican Turkey was confronted as it began to determine the kind of educational system that would be needed to enable the Turkish Revolution to succeed. Pragmatism was a leading determinant. Given that the religious schools were contrary to the principle of laïcism and, due to their sectarianism, were a centrifugal force working against national unity, they needed to be replaced with schools that were both laïc and national. The presence of culturally alienating foreign schools was also a source of national disunity. Thus, on 3 March 1924, the Ministry of Religious Affairs and Foundations was abolished and all educational institutions were brought under the authority of the Ministry of Education.

Shortly thereafter, the cornerstone of the Republic and what appears in constitutional law as the "1924 Constitution," was ratified on 20 April 1924. It formed the framework within which the entire contents of the [new] system were formulated. The New Constitution stipulated that the state was a Republic and that its sovereignty unconditionally belonged to the nation. It emphasized that it was the Turkish nation that formed the basis for unity. The 1924 Constitution initially had one contradictory feature. In addition to stating, "The official language of the state is Turkish," it also indicated that its religion was Islam. For a state that has abolished the Caliphate and the Ministry of Religious Affairs and Foundations and created a system of unified education with the goal of creating a laïc society to mention religion in its constitution was paradoxical. This inconsistency was removed four years later on 10 April 1928, when the Constitution was completely laïcized by removing the world "Islam" from the text. The "fez," which had become a symbol of the "sick man" of Europe, was banned on 25 November 1925. In place of it, the "hat" was to be worn. This reform may appear to be a rather superficial one but considering the vast array of headgear that existed in society, it was a very pragmatic move. Ranging from the fez to the conical cap and from fur caps to turbans, this headgear symbolized membership in various sects. The "hat," on the other hand, was a symbol of the rejection of out-dated traditions.

In addition to the social forces of traditional societies, there are sources of religious authority and power. The dervish lodges of traditional Ottoman society were places of religious ceremony, congregation and education. With these characteristics, they had a centrifugal effect on national unity. Moreover, it is known that lodges were leading actors in the past in various bloody conflicts, uprisings and activities contributing to the emasculation of the state by resorting to opportunistic, subversive, profiteering behavior having nothing to do with religion. It was necessary to remove these obstacles from both the point of view of national unity and the creation of authority. Therefore, on 30 November 1925, all *tekkes* and *zaviyes* were closed down. The goal was to prevent practices that were incompatible with science such as superstitions and sorcery.

A modern society needs modern laws. Change in society entails a transformation of its traditional elements, relations of production and its order of religious and customary law. Every radical transformation of society has to be accompanied by a new modern legal order. The needs of a society desiring modernization cannot be met through traditional, religious laws. The legal order that was bequeathed to the Republican regime by the Ottoman era, despite having gone through several reforms, beginning with Mahmut II, was for the most part based on religious conventions. The main sources for this religious jurisprudence were the *Kuran, Hadis* (traditions of the prophet), comparative ecclesiastical law, and *İcmai Ümmet* (legal consensus among religious scholars and jurors). Among these was included the *Örfi Hukuk,* customary law that was not contrary to religious conventions. Just as these regulations were incompatible with meeting the needs of a modernization-oriented society, because they created sectarian distinctions between people, they fomented separatism. Another privilege granted by the Ottoman judicial order was the special judicial rights given to foreigners and non-Moslems. These, too, were abolished and replaced by modern laws.

In order to prevent this chaos, to ensure jurisprudential unity, laïcism and equality before the law throughout society, and to meet the needs of society through modern laws, between 17 February 1926 and 24 April 1929, a number of modern laws were enacted. These included the Turkish Civil Code, the Turkish Liabilities Code, the Commercial Code, the Bankruptcy Code, and the Civil and Criminal Courts Statute. They were liberal copies of Swiss, French, German and Italian legal codes. In addition, with the opening of the Ankara School of Law (today's Ankara Faculty of Law), a new generation of lawyers was trained.

Among the other unity-promoting measures taken during the initial years of the Revolution were the changes made in assorted measurement systems (e.g., the calendar, weights, lengths and time). One of these changes was abolition of the various calendars based on the Islamic, Orthodox, Gregorian and International/Christian "year" and replaced it with the international calendar and the 24-hour day. The dualism in keeping time, between the "à la Turca" and "à la Franga" hours, was also eliminated. A sundry of measurement units had been in use prior to the reforms. For example, the yard (t.n.: about 28 inches), *endaze* (t.n.: about 26 inches) and fathom were used to measure length while such dissimilar units as the *dirhem* (t.n.: "drachma": 400th part of an *okka), okka* (t.n.: roughly 2.8 pounds) and *kile* (t.n.: "bushel") were curtailed and substituted with the meter and kilo, respectively. These changes not only brought about uniformity in units, they laid basis for nation-wide equivalence with respect to their use.

The radical reforms made during the first nine years of the Republic in the areas of nation-building and "laïcization" contributed to the strengthening of national unity. Following these, the Atatürk Revolution pressed forward with implementing a new Turkish alphabet and the opening of the Turkish History and Turkish Language Associations, National Schools, and People's Houses.

In the course of transition from a traditional to a modern society, nation-building, establishing a nation-state, pursuing a national policy, creating a national culture and disseminating it among the population has been among the primary objectives of the Republic. This fundamental phase of modernization, encompassing as it does renovation and transformation, was kept in mind with each step taken by the Atatürk Revolution by virtue of its Nationalist, Populist, Laïc, and Republican content.

Reform movements in new states are necessarily faced with a unique configuration of politico-cultural variables. Through appropriate reforms, they can be reshaped and then transformed into the basis of a new national culture by means of political and cultural socialization. By inculcating a new political culture in every strata of society, the conditions are created whereby commitment to the Revolution and legitimacy of the new order established by it is ensured.

The reforms carried out by the revolutionary reform movment, which lent it "legitimacy" and secured the formation of a nation-state included: 1) the adoption of an easily learned new Turkish alphabet, 2) the opening of national schools, 3) compulsory primary school education for all Turkish children, 4) the intensification and spread of the efforts to make Turkish a language that is more easily written, spoken and understood by everyone, 5) researching Turkish history, and thereby clarifying it, through the use of national historical sources, 6) the establishment of People's Houses to ensure the education and cultural development of the people and realize cultural development, and 7) through the founding of a "History of the Turkish Revolution institute," making History of the Turkish Revolution classes mandatory at all institutions of higher learning.

Linguistic unity is one of the most important factors contributing to national unity. When the same language is spoken and understood by everyone living within the same national boundaries, there is less chance for socio-cultural alienation. Over the course of history, a nation or cultural community may find its members estranged, torn asunder, dispersed from one end of the world to the other for one reason or another. It is only natural that this dispersion, disintegration, and fragmentation may rise to great difference in languages due to a variety of influences. Nevertheless, if people living together within the same politico-cultural space of a nation-state are unable to understand one another because they do not speak the same language, and if nothing is done to remedy the situation, it is difficult to characterize such a society as modern.

After Turks converted to Islam in the 9th century and particularly after the founding of the Ottoman Empire, Turkish increasingly came under the influence of Arabic and Persian in the carrying out of the affairs of state. In state correspondence, schools, the palace, medreses, among the literate strata of society having relations with the palace and state, the language used was almost entirely made up of Arabic and Persian vocabulary. This "language" was called Ottoman. The stratum of society that was unable to keep up with this development was the masses. Because of this anarchy, confusion and unconcern for the language, it became riddled with degenerate vocabulary in different regions. Nevertheless, the language spoken and understood by the vast majority of the masses was Turkish. Every language needs an alphabet that suits the features of that particular language. The Arabic alphabet was derived from the sounds that were unique to the structure of the Arabic language. This alphabet would reflect these sounds in such a way as to be understood by Arabs. The structure of the Turkish language is essentially polyphonic and its vowels are short. In contrast, Arabic has fewer vowels but has both long and short forms. This lack of vowels in Arabic compared to Turkish makes the Arabic alphabet unsuitable for Turkish, which is a Ural-Altaic language. Writing or teaching Turkish using Arabic letters is extremely difficult. Another characteristic of Arabic is that the written form of many letters changes depending on whether the letter appears at the beginning, middle or end of a word. Yet another difficulty with the use of the Arabic alphabet is determining when to use the different consonants representing similar but different sounds in Arabic to represent a single sound in Turkish. Thus a completely mixed up written language - one that only a small group of people could learn - developed. This confusion stemmed from the assertion that since Arabic was the language of the Kuran, the use of scripts or alphabets other than the Arabic alphabet was considered sacrilegious. It is apparent that this linguistic chaos and confusion in Writing was the natural consequence of language falling under the influence of religion. In 1928, as part of its efforts at laïcization, the Atatürk Revolution addressed this previously debated subject with firm determination. Accordingly, it made possible a new, Latin-based alphabet that was compatible with the structure of Turkish, Turkish being a Ural-Altaic language.

Initially, on 28 May 1928, the system of international numbers were adopted, but then, on 3 November 1928, the "Law Pertaining to Turkish Letters" was enacted and put into effect. In addition, Arabic and Persian would no longer be taught in high schools. On 1 January 1929, "National Schools" were opened to teach the new alphabet. Everyone, first and foremost Mustafa Kemal himself as "Head Teacher," who had learned the new alphabet, was mobilized using every resource available to teach reading and writing to men, women, young and old alike - to all citizens - in these schools. Newspapers began publishing in the new alphabet. A result of the determination, insistence and drive, literacy rose within a very short time.

Throughout the Ottoman era, Turks had been deprived of national history. What was called "history" consisted of *Islamic* history. It was this history that was to be studied and memorized. For all intents and purposes, Turkish history had been forgotten. Beginning with the inception of the Ottoman Empire and continuing until the establishment of the Republic, there were essentially three approaches followed to the study of history. The first concentrated on Islamic history from the founding of the Ottoman Empire until the Tanzimat. Taught in detail, it was expected that it be memorized. The literate segment of society was thus conditioned by the dictates of Islam and Islamic history. The second approach was used between the inauguration of the Tanzimat and the First Constitutional Period. At this time, new schools had been established alongside the existing medresses. It was in the curriculum of these new schools that Turkish history was included. However, this history was not completely *Turkish* history, but rather that of the Ottoman State, e.g., the Ottoman Dynasty. To compound matters, it was taught employing the unscientific "Chronicles" conception of history. History had been deprived of the requisite scientific understanding and content. The third approach resulted from a need that arose during the First Constitutional Period to know, teach and research Turkish history from its early origins. What was emphasized during this period were the claims made by certain Western-educated thinkers, in light of developing nationalist movements, that the Turkish people also had their own history. They went about researching this subject and publish their assessments. Inspired by books on Turkish history written by foreign authors, they began the preparation of their own history books. Even so, because they did not have an in-depth understanding of national history, these studies were extremely shallow.

One of the most important references a nation has for its present and future is its past. In an era characterized by pre-national societies searching for attempting to create their own histories, for a people such as the Turks, one of the oldest and established nations of the world, a people who created civilizations in Anatolia, to not know their own authentic history and to leave it to foreigners to define this history was a situation that the Republican regime could not accept. Therefore, the "Turkish History Research Committee," later known as the "Turkish History Society," was set up on 15 April 1931 for the purpose of carrying out regular research and academic studies and publishing its findings in the form of books and articles. Atatürk bequeathed fifty percent of his shares in İş Bank to the Turkish History

Society. This institution has made a major contribution to uncovering Turkish history and making it more widely available, something that even international institutions have acknowledged. The other fifty percent of Atatürk's shares in the bank went to the Turkish Language Society, also set up by him, the purpose of which is to carry out research on the Turkish language and to help create a sense of linguistic identity among Turks.

The "People's Houses, founded on 19 February 1932, were agencies through which the struggle engaged in by the Atatürk's reform movement to create a national culture and the spread of that culture reached the people. They were centers for the acculturation of the masses, where men and women, young and old, in short, all citizens were responsible for participating in its activities and cultural programs and initiatives. By establishing "People's Houses" in the cities and "People's Rooms" in the towns and villages, research into history, language, all the fine arts, ethnography, and village studies were sustained and magazines were published. In the various regions, people's houses were transformed into individual cultural action centers. Nearly all of People's Houses opened libraries, which enabled the education and training of youth and provided for the acquisition of knowledge.

The work of People's Houses and Rooms continued up until 8 August 1951, when they were closed down under Law no. 5830, which had been proposed by the Democrat Party and ratified by the Turkish Grand National Assembly. It was put into effect on 11 August 1951. There were 478 People's houses and 4322 People's Rooms closed by this law.

Attempts were made during the final years of the Ottoman era by a number of intellectuals to create a "pure Turkish." However, the real move to purify the Turkish language by removing foreign elements, particularly Arabic and Persian, from it and to have state communications and the education provided in schools carried out in a Turkish that was comprehensible to the people became possible only after the establishment of the Republic. In place of Ottoman, which was a composite of Arabic and Persian, what had been called "crude Turkish" -the genuine Turkish- was enhanced, becoming state policy.

The Turkish Language Society was founded on 12 July 1932. Holding its first Language Congress on 26 September 1932, the studies to be carried out on language were stipulated in a programme.

The return to Turkish, its development and advances made to create a sense of self-identity were required by the nationalist, populist, laïc and progressive principles of the Turkish Revolution.

As a natural consequence of the return to Turkish, *ezan* (the call to prayer) and the *hutbe* (Friday sermon) were conducted in Turkish for years. In 1950, *ezan* began to be read once again in Arabic, upon the instigation of the Democrat Party (D.P. - *Demokrat Parti*).

2. Reforms Designed to Establish Authority

Some of the reforms implemented by the Atatürk Revolution to ensure unity are also related to the problem of authority encountered by the modernization movement. The abolition of the Caliphate, the imposition of educational uniformity, the ratification of the 1924 Constitution, the banning of the dervish lodges, the enactment of modern laïc laws, the laïcization of the Constitution, and the creation of national unity that were examined in previous sections were reforms related to the creation of the nation-state. These advances contributed equally to the formation of national unity and solving the problem of authority. The Caliph was a religious authority; however, a laïc, modern society rejects dualism in the basis for authority. Religious authority cannot exist alongside, and compete with, political authority. A religious authority, whose legitimacy is based on religion and power is exercised within a religious community, and whose influence within the Islamic faith extends beyond the borders of the country, will only weaken political authority, reduce its effectiveness and invites a conflict in authority. This discord has the effect of bringing modernization, which needs a powerful political authority, to a standstill. Furthermore, it opens the door to either a degeneration of the Revolution or its repression through a counter-revolution. It can not be denied that one of the reasons for the conflicts such as those seen in Iran or Pakistan is the presence of religious authority and/or undue influence of religion in the affairs of the state.

In addition to the Caliph, there were the less influential religious leaders such as the *çelebis,* sheiks, *post-nişes,* dervishes, *dedes, nakips, emirs,* Caliphs of individual sects, and mollas. They performed a number of duties, which included providing guidance to, and training co-religionists, co-members of sects, and the "sectarian community," and leading them in ceremonies. They also applied customary law, issued punishments and rewards, and collected money and goods. Furthermore, they were the people who cooked and distributed food in the lodges and received "offerings" in exchange for assuming the role of "protector" of tombs and shrines. In the periphery, the political authority of these people, who exercised influence among those who shared their beliefs, constituted a source of counter-revolutionary power. It was derived from not only faith and supporters but from the economic opportunities it engendered. Therefore, in order to create a laïc political authority and sustain political institutionalization while at the same time preventing the exploitation of the beliefs of the poor, dervish lodges and shrines had to be abolished.

A natural consequence of the populist principle of the Atatürk Revolution was that people no longer would be granted special rights or privileges based on family or clan or titles such as *bey,* pasha (a high official), pashazade (son of a pasha), hadji, mullah, or *hazret* (exalted). As much as this is an issue of equality and populism, it is a matter of the problem of authority. There is no place in a modern political system for these titles of respect that serve as sources of authority within immediate circles. Therefore, the "surname" law, which made it mandatory for everyone to be known and addressed by both a personal and surname, was enacted in 1934. This practice also made possible the elimination of confusion.

3. Reforms Designed to Realize Equality

The greatest problem to be overcome by any revolution, or for that matter by any progressive regime, is that concerning equality. The Sultanate, Caliphate, lodges, shrines and sources of traditional authority can be abolished and outlawed. Rights can be assured for people through laws. Everyone can be said to be equal before the law.

However, in spite of all these modern practices, if the individual in a society has not acquired economic independence; if rights are not reinforced with economic content, then it will not be possible in that system to completely overcome either the problem of unity or that of authority. In every traditional society there are as many sources of economic authority as there are social and religious authority - and they are perhaps even more influential. Taking advantage of the poverty of the individual, they create dependence on them and their sphere of influence.

In modern societies, the prosperity and well-being of people are as important as the wealth of the state. Moreover, countries making the transition from a traditional to a modern society have generally been poor. They lack the resources for economic growth and development. Consequently, the most important problem of all countries undergoing modernization is economic growth and equality. Equality can be ensured by tax regulations and wage and price policies that guarantee that the revenue derived from economic growth is shared equitably. What makes this one of the most difficult problems is that in nearly all cases of countries trying to overcome backwardness, the issue of equality is left to be resolved only after political problems have been addressed. To achieve this, and overcome this problem, demands long-term, effective effort.

The Atatürk reform movement dealt with this problem of equality after the problems of unity and authority were overcome. While it is true that the 1924 Constitution and other modern laws, such as those concerning the changes in the measurement system, the abolition of titles, lodges and shrines were at the same time matters related to the problem of equality, practically none of the changes contributed to the economic life of the individual.

The first of the reforms taken by the Revolution that were economic in content was the elimination of the repressive tithe for the poor villager, which had remained from the Ottoman period. In the following years, tuition-free education in national schools was initiated. The ownership rights of foreigners in the operation of railroads, ports, mines, electricity, water and tramway companies and tobacco factories were purchased. Coast trading rights were reclaimed. Laws promoting industry, as well as the "Labor Law" dated 1936, which regulated working conditions, were enacted. Health institutions designed to counter such diseases as malaria and syphilis, which were rampant in Ottoman society, were set up all over the country. Agricultural sales and credit cooperatives that provided credit opportunities to farmers were established. Equipment and tools to be used for the construction of highways and bridges and the productivity of irrigation systems and agriculture was increased . All of the afore-mentioned constitute reforms that were economic in content and directed toward the impoverished people. All the same, the greatest and most important step forward was taken after the Great World Depression of 1929. This was the first five-year plan, which was begun in 1933 and concluded in 1938. This was the first successful, concrete, significant example of the implementation of the Revolution's principle of étatism. It characterizes the economic policy that grew out of the model of the Turkish Revolution.

Without a doubt, economic development, which is fundamental to the question of equality, is a matter of capital and investment. In addition to this, however, development also requires a technical cadre and modern technology. Backward societies lack these as much as they do opportunities for income and savings. The inadequacy of technical cadre and technology during the early years of the Republic of Turkey was one of the reasons for delays in efforts to development.

The issue that Atatürk, the leader of the Revolution, continually stressed but was unable to accomplish - and which is still unresolved today - is the question of land reform.

Apart from these problems experienced during Atatürk's time, the national modernization movement was faced with four other ones. The first of these was the founding in 1924 of the Progressive Republican Party, which resulted in a counter-revolutionary movement. In reaction to this, the party was closed and a law restricting freedoms (the "Law Establishing Public Order") was enacted. The second was the Sheik Sait rebellion, which was supported from abroad and threatened national unity in the East. The uprising was crushed but the Revolution encountered its third problem in 1930 with the resurgence of the Free Republican Party and its eventual closing down by its founders because it had unleashed counter-revolutionary activity. This resurgence gave rise to the Menemen incident, which was the fourth problem. This affair was crushed but these cases resulted in the postponement of a transition to a multi-party system.

4. Characteristics of the Post-Atatürk Era

The first seven years following the death of Atatürk on 10 November 1938 were ones of turmoil and the uncertainties created by the advent of the Second World War. While it is true that the state had remained out of the war, it had affected the country's economy and delayed the implementation of the Second Industrial Plan. Investments for the most part dried up. The national modernization program thus began to flounder.

But this does not mean that it stopped altogether. All throughout this period, which lasted until 1950, there were both successful and abortive attempts made in this regard. For example, Village Institutes, which provided production-oriented education for the peasants, were established during these years. Advances were made with respect to the spread of primary school education. An important step in the area of land reform was enactment of the "Farmer Land Provision Act" in 1945. Transition to a multi-party regime, which was to have a major impact on modernization, was probably one of the most important political developments of the era. Perhaps equally important, was the framing, ratification and implementation of 1961 Constitution. A product of the 27 May 1960 military intervention, the Constitution contained provisions for a pluralist political regime and gave primacy to human rights.

These developments must be assessed not only within the context of synchronous events, but in terms of the impact - both positive and negative some of them continue to have on contemporary Turkish society.

Through the establishment of Village Institutes, transition to a production-oriented education for peasants and the spread of primary education was inaugurated, However, this radical reform lost its efficacy during the multi-party political setting. The Farmer Land Provision Act was enacted to eliminate an inequitable distribution of land, but this law was not implemented in its entirety. Nor was any meaningful land reform realized. People's Houses had been set up by the Revolution to assist in nation-building and cultural development. They were intended to function autonomously from any particular political party and were thought of as important institutional components of the nation-state but they were closed by the Democrat Party in the 1950s. They were not given the opportunity to evolve into functional actors within a pluralist regime.

The economy lost its national autonomy and became externally dependent. Western capitalism had amassed such power that it was impossible to avoid coming under its influence and control. This was intensified with the establishment of industry, which increasingly came under the control of the Western capitalist order, thus opening the door to new exploitation of the country's economy. The Atatürkist principle of "complete independence" was dealt a severe blow.

The reforms undertaken to lay the basis for laïc education and the creation of a laïc society were also largely disregarded. The influence of religion on laïc educational institutions and society grew as institutions providing religious education were established all over the country.

The transition to a pluralist political regime produced a revitalization of conservative and traditional elements in society. People sympathetic to or allied with this newly emerging conservatism subsequently replaced the progressive leadership cadre of the past.

The étatism that had formed the basis for economic development and industrialization had to be suspended during the Second World War. It was replaced by a state-subsidized mode of development, which led to the growth of economic powers and interests within society that eventually contributed to the debilitation of state economic reforms.

Atatürk's concept of a "people's state" and his principle of "Populism" had been largely abandoned, which paved the way for the intensification of capitalist forces within society. The notions of the "social state" and "equality" were also one of the victims of this phenomenon.

Yet, the question of equality is one that must be addressed by modernization. It is second in importance only to the creation of national unity and authority. In fact, without it, the continuity of neither unity nor authority is possible.

Equality contains several important elements: a) political participation; the transition of the individual from subject to effective citizen status; b) equality before the law; the law applies to everyone,
using the same criteria of justice; c) appointment or assignment of people based on ability.

There are several issues regarding the capacity of a political system
that must be addressed. These are a) the extent to which the political
system is able to meet demands, offer solutions and obtain results is
an issue that needs to be stressed; b) moreover, when speaking of capacity, there is need to take into account the degree to which this
system affects society and the economy; c) efficacy, and successful
implementation is an important gauge to be used in the evaluation of
capacity. In addition to all these aspects, rationalism, the presence of
laïc views, and the predominance of laïc decisions within the policy
regime are all issues that have a positive impact on the capacity of the
political system. Getting to the crux of the matter, the scope of the
tasks assumed by government, how much it can accomplish, and how
efficaciously and successfully it executes and implements these tasks
on the whole are important criteria in the evaluation of the capacity
of the political system.

Institutional differentiation and specialization carried out in a holistic fashion is a criterion of being a modern society. Even so, it is not
enough to consider this in isolation; it is also necessary to taken into
consideration the following characteristics that are related to the other issues pertinent to modernization. Most of the time, regardless of
how much effort is exerted, given the complexity of issues that need
to be resolved and historical, social, cultural and structural differences, results are late in coming. A number of institutional changes may
be observed in a modernizing society; however, no matter how carefully social change is planned, some institutional changes will occur
more quickly while others will lag behind.[104]

One of the fundamental reasons for the unrest witnessed in modern Turkey has been the inability to adequately meet the demands
placed on the political system with respect to equality. While it may
be true that Atatürk's time was largely unperturbed by this issue, it is
also important to realize that the demands for equality had not reac-

hed sufficient proportions to even become part of the political agenda. Moreover, in practice, the need for specialization, talent and accumulation of knowledge may be contradictory to the principle of equality as it places a premium on those who possess it. Perhaps, however, this ought to be seen as a natural consequence of the dynamics of modernization, one that must be addressed in a pragmatic way.

As the modernization reforms undertaken during the Atatürk period proceeded, demands from society, the people or the masses for organization were not yet prominent or widespread. The people had not yet attained adequate political consciousness. For these reasons, the leadership cadre had not encountered extensive demands from the people while radical reforms were being undertaken. What's more, so many reforms had been undertaken in the interest of the people that for the afore-mentioned reasons, this cadre had a lot of leeway for independent action. Nonetheless, it is also true that Atatürk and his cadre of revolutionary reformers undertook the implementation of an economic plan that would not create new sources of dependence and took many significant steps toward ensuring equality.

These developments in the post-Atatürk era led to the weakening of [Atatürkist] revolutionary consciousness. Many of the radical reforms that had previously been implemented were soon abandoned, with many of them undergoing a complete about-face.

According to Atatürk, his Revolution - the system of thought that gave rise to it and its set of practical reforms - would serve as a model for the awakening of subjugated countries of the East. Through it, not only would they be able to achieve independence from their colonial status but also successfully undertake a program of modernization. Atatürk strongly believed in the importance of the *national* component of modernization. However, Turkish foreign policy in the 1950's tended largely to discount the many independence movements in the world. The basis for the estrangement of Turkey from so-called "Third World" countries, which continued for a few decades, lays in the rupture with Atatürkist foreign policy and the accommodation to the policies of the Western states.

VI

ATATÜRKISM
AND
THE ATATÜRK PRINCIPLES

Commitment to ideals, nationalism and technology are dynamic elements that influence and direct both domestic and international relations. Emerging with the War of Independence and developed during the Republican era, Atatürkism is a system of thought that strengthened and reinforced the Turkish national political system.

The success of the War of Independence led to the rise of a new, independent Turkish state. One of the pillars of this new national political system was the unconditional sovereignty of the nation.

Important radical reforms were taken in a variety of areas. These included abolishing the Sultanate, making Ankara the capital, proclaiming the Republic, preparing a new constitution, and the establishment of the Turkish Grand National Assembly as the sole official representative of national sovereignty. They are all steps that contributed to the reinforcement of state "authority." The fact that repression was not employed in the realization of these radical measures is a subject that needs further examination.

The Atatürk paradigm of modernization was particularly sensitive to avoid authoritarian practices. It also denies the validity of an elitist system that functions in the interests of a certain few. The Atatürk Revolution and Atatürkism, the system of thought that supported it, are not divisive or separatist but rather unifying and integrating. They call for the supremacy of a National Will founded on a unification of all classes.

According to Apter, there are two basic functions of ideology. One is social and the other is individual. The former is directed toward the integration of society while the latter contributes to the formation of role identification in the maturing and modernizing individual. Legitimacy for "authority" is achieved through the two. The importance of ideology is derived from the relationship it has with "authority."[105]

At the initial stages of development, nearly all societies encounter tension created by an assortment of cultural idiosyncrasies. "Ideology consciously employed toward the establishment of authority can simultaneously lessen the negative impact of such tensions. In this way, it serves as a means of ensuring solidarity. At the same time, while the former and new competing socialization tendencies create confusion with respect to "identity," ideology is used to create greater "unity" and consensus.[106] Ideology can be a fundamental means through which a new political culture is created.

Particularly between the years 1917-1990, it was common in the countries throughout the world to openly espouse particular ideologies. Interpreted in terms of the interests of the person or groups in power, they were often used to repress the individual and limit his freedom. Moreover, they assumed the form of "commodities" as they were "exported'" to other countries, both directly, through force, or indirectly, through serving as example. Their export allowed for the control, or at the very minimum, influence of domestic policies of the importing countries by the exporting country, the latter often a single hegemonic state. Thus, ideology came to serve as a vehicle for domestic repression and international expansion that acted as an impediment to the emancipation of man and society. The state of affairs gradually began to change during the last decades of the 20th century. The system whereby ideology and influence were dominated by one, or at most two states, came to an end. Indigenous currents of thought and movements began to intensify. Opposition grew to the manipulative use of ideologies. The desire for personal freedom, the right to life and well-being, and humane living conditions had been misused by individuals and groups to impose a preconceived order on their societies.

Modeling themselves after one or more Western ideologies, countries in the world had experienced destabilizing crises of identity and faltering attempts at autonomy, nation-building, democratization and modernization. But a new era had begun. Instead of standardized, "conventional" ideological approaches and "models," brand-new ones reflective of novel relations, perspectives and forms of solidarity began to emerge. Developing countries had reached a point where they could say "enough already" to a world-order based on exploitation, an inequitable distribution of economic resources, and repressive hegemonic political relations. In today's world, the establishment of hegemony and the desire to maintain it via radical and neo-radical means and instrumental ideologies has for the most part been rendered illegitimate. The "sun has begun to rise" over the sleeping "oppressed countries." The primary struggle these countries have been waging is that of modernization. In addition, they must succeed so that they can effectively maintain their independence and create an order that will provide them with a greater sense of well-being. Perhaps equally important, modernization is a phenomenon having a profound impact on the entire world. The historical source of inspiration, one which has served as a catalyst and which has created the unrelenting determination to succeed is the modernizing experience of the Turkish nation.

1. The Atatürkist Commitment to Modernization

The Atatürk paradigm of modernization rejects Islamic perspectives or foreign ideologies. Both pragmatic and functional, Atatürkism alone is what is needed to see to it that Turkey is successful in its use of its future-oriented, paradigm of *national* modernization.

Atatürkism originated in the struggle to liberate the land of the Turkish people. It developed by effecting reforms undertaken to solve such domestic problems as an archaic social structure, value system and lifestyle, as well as issues having to do with foreign relations. The fundamental notions of the Atatürk system of thought were rationalism, nationalism and laïcism. Only by relying on modern criteria rather than traditional ones could decisions that were both appropriate and effective be made.

Western positivism and solidarism had an impact on Atatürkism. But at the same time, Atatürk believed that the independence and freedom of nations, societies and people to be indispensable to the life of modern man, society and state. What he proposed was the creation of a new national model that would provide functionality to his belief. This model was to be based on a form of development, progress and modernization in which national interest and benefit would be paramount - superseding that of the individual and class. In this respect, it was rather unique. It adopted neither the Western capitalist model of development nor the Soviet Russian one in its entirety. Nevertheless, Atatürkism very much embraced the ideology of the "social state," which was reflected in the importance it placed on the role of the state in development. At the same time, the "state" did not become a fetish. It was the "nation" that was to serve as the basis for the *national* model of development and modernization. This was what was to serve as a prototype, not only for Turkey, but also for other "subjugated" countries in the world.

Somewhat of the "flavor" of this paradigm of *national* modernization can be gotten from the words spoken by Atatürk: "The starting point of our journey is the very realm in which we live. We draw our strength to persevere from the Turkish nation, and the lessons we have learned from the innumerable tragic events and sorrowful chapters of our history."[107] Such experiential and national factors as the history of the Turkish nation, its social structure, culture, internal and external developments, accumulated experience, problems encountered and how these problems will be solved form both the essence and the pragmatic basis for Atatürkism.

The aim of the Atatürk Revolution was to transform the Turkish nation into a modern, civilized one without creating a closed society. To reach this goal, it was necessary to create a society and government that was both rational and laïc, populist, progressive, liberal, nationalist, and republican.

Atatürk's dream was to completely modernize traditional Turkish society in all areas. He expressed his determination when he said, "Glossing over problems arising within our social structure with partial measures is not what distinguishes the Republic."[108] Atatürkism is the expression of the belief that modernization and "nation-building" are of the utmost importance to countries. It was by undertaking and implementing radical reforms that this was to be brought about. The Atatürk Revolution combined thought with action and was courageously and without hesitation or compromise committed to the modernization of Turkish society. While benefiting from the previous experiences of countries that have successfully reached a contemporary level of civilization, his was still a unique paradigm. Driven by national will and what was in the national interest, Atatürk led the reforms that were to form the basis of the modernization of Turkey. In short, Atatürk believed in the realization of Turkey's modernization through the pursuit of a national policy:

> Our great problem is to raise our nation to the highest levels of civilization and prosperity.
>
> ....
>
> This is the dynamic ideal of the great Turkish nation that has carried out a revolution not only with respect to institutions but ideas as well. In order to be successful in reaching this ideal in the shortest amount of time, we have to combine thought with action. Success depends on working in a planned and rational manner. Therefore, seeing to it that such important ideals as ensuring that not a single citizen remains illiterate; training technicians required by the development efforts and all that it entails; and creating individuals and institutions capable of understanding and explaining the problems of the country from one generation to the next are attained are the vital responsibitities of the Ministry of Culture.
>
> ....
>
> Keeping the principles that I have indicated perpetually fresh in the minds of Turkish youth and in the consciousness of the Turkish nation is the major responsibility of our universities and institutions of higher education.[109]

2. Atatürkism - The Ideology of the Anatolian Revolution

Atatürkism provides the *ideational* foundations of the liberation of Anatolia. This system of thought encompasses both the Turkish War of Independence and the rapid and radical transformation of Turkish society entailed by the Atatürk Revolution. Under Atatürk's leadership, Turkish political elites actively participated in this National Struggle and were committed to its principles. This combined effort contributed to an extraordinary unity. Even though Atatürkism had not become sufficiently systematized during Atatürk's lifetime, the development of its principles during Atatürk's term as President provides us with enough information to be able to reach important and definite conclusions concerning this system of thought. Moreover, the increasing interest in Atatürkism in recent decades, as reflected in the growing number of research and publications continues to shed even further light on it.

Atatürkism is not an ideology that existed prior to the Turkish War of Independence of 1919-1922. This system of thought was developed under Atatürk's leadership, for the most part, after the establishment of the Turkish Republic. Nevertheless, much of its content was derived from some of the basic ideas appearing in the documents of the Period of National Struggle. It is an ideology that grew out of action - out of the period of the Turkish National Struggle and out of the Atatürk reform movement. At times, it was the ideas that prompted action and at other times, it was the political and historical events that gave birth to an idea. Therefore, Atatürkism is a composite of ideas, of action, and of Turkish national aspirations - it is an ideology that combines elements of realism and idealism.

In order to fully assess Atatürkism, the following factors have to be kept in mind. As stated earlier, in the formative period of this ideology, action rather than theorizing gave it its particular bent. The War of Independence; the reforms of Atatürk; struggles with counter-revolutionaries - all these events and activities were instrumental in the formative development of this system of thought. Nevertheless, there are certain philosophical and political convictions, a frame of reference to which Atatürk and his closest associates subscribed, by which they judged events and according to which they acted. These were an interest in complete independence, total commitment to change the identity of the Turkish state from that of the Ottoman Empire to the Republic of Turkey, and to base the new regime on popular sovereignty. In fact, popular sovereignty, nationalism, populism, and republicanism were among the earliest developed principles of this system of thought.

Atatürkism underwent a dynamic course of development. Between the years 1919 and 1938, due to the special efforts made by Atatürk, the opportunities for the analysis, formation and implementation of this system of thought were made possible. National struggle, radical reforms, Atatürk's ideas, beliefs, and the R.P.P. Congresses all contributed to the development of Atatürk's principles. In the programme of the R.P.P. in 1935, Atatürkism was defined as "Kemalism" and the principles of Atatürkism were laid out: Republicanism, Nationalism, Populism, Etatism, Laïcism and Revolutionism-Reformism.

Some of the basic precepts and principles that would later become part of the more developed Atatürkist system of thought were present in incipient form in the documents, congresses, decisions made by the Turkish Grand National Assembly, and the speeches and talks given by Atatürk during the period of National Struggle. Specifically, these are: the people, populism, national sovereignty, national will, the nation, nationalism, national unity, equality of countries, national independence, national solidarity, the right of all nations to be independent, human rights, technology, world civilization; the rejection of expansionism, the Sultanate, the Caliphate, Pan-Islamism, Pan-Turkism; and *complete independence*. It is this principle of complete independence that is the focal point for Atatürkist thought as it pertains to national liberation and nation-building.

The Atatürkist understanding of independence is more than simply political, economic, monetary, or judicial independence. As discussed earlier, it also includes "ideological" independence.

In the Amasya Declaration and the work carried out by the Erzurum and Sivas Congresses; in the Resolution of the Turkish Grand National Assembly on 24 April 1920 to form the Government; in the Populism Programme published in 1920; in the debates held in the Turkish Grand National Assembly over the Constitution; and in the conflicts that occurred in the Second Group, is it clear that Mustafa Kemal was not simply interested in realizing the political, economic, monetary, judicial and ideological independence of Turkey. He was, at the same time, striving for a new and modern order, a new state, and a new political regime. The principle of complete independence - the determination to generate a system of thought that was national in orientation - provided the direction and momentum to the attempts made for independence in other areas. In a speech made during the years of the War of Independence, Atatürk had this to say:

> ... Retaining friends, protecting our complete independence, and assessing everything from the Turkish point of view: these are what are realistic [for Turkey]. They are a reaction to the ideology that destroyed the Ottoman Empire.[110]

National Struggle was not entered into for the purpose of rescuing the Empire. On the contrary, it was carried out so as to create an independent Turkish state within the borders of its genuine homeland. The National Struggle resulted in the foundation of the Republic and the implementation of radical reforms. By eliminating the precepts and institutions that were incompatible with modernization, and in their place introducing the institutions, precepts and system of values that were essential for modernization, these reforms were instrumental in establishing a modern Turkish nation-state and ensuring its development. The Ottoman Empire and the notion of religious community were replaced by the Turkish nation-state and nation, respectively, and instead of a system based on religious principles, one based on laïcism was adopted.

The essence and goal of the Atatürk Revolution were different from the Ottoman attempts at reform of the past: The reforms undertaken by the Atatürk Revolution were designed not to sustain a traditional Empire but rather to establish a Turkish nation-state and to modernize it. The goal of the Atatürk Revolution was the complete modernization of the Turkish state and Turkish society. Ottoman attempts at reform were not committed to total modernization. Moreover, they were characterized by an array of conflicting and contradictory precepts and perspectives that included, for example, Ottomanism, Islamism and Turkism. In contrast, Atatürkism was for the most part free of such contradictions. Its commitment was to the Turkish nation-state and its aim was the complete modernization of this state. Atatürkism understood the importance and necessity of realizing the modernization of society by means of a national "ideology," e.g., a system of thought grounded in both an idealistic as well as a pragmatic concern for what was right for the nation, and implemented it accordingly.

The basis of the new [Turkish] nation-state was the Republic, with the 1924 Constitution as its fundamental source of legitimacy. This Constitution was tailored to the political reforms and was open to new ones as well. In fact, the 1921 Constitution was based on the principle of "unconditional sovereignty," which placed representation of the national will in the Turkish Grand National Assembly alone. Indicating that there was no power superior to this Assembly, the Constitution had the effect of distancing the new Republic rom the Ottoman regime, which had been bound to the Sultanate and the Caliphate. During the discussions held in the Assembly on the 1924 Constitution, Celâl Nuri (İleri) had this to say about the basic constitutional distinction between Republican Turkey and the Ottoman Empire: "The previous Ottoman Sultanate was a Sultanate that was a semi-international, supra-national institution. To the extent that it did not allow for the development of the Turkish nation, it restricted our nationality and existence. It was also the basis for the Constitution of the Ottoman Empire. This [the 1924 Constitution under consideration] is the Constitution of the Turkish Republic and, because of that, it is the Turkish nation that forms the basis for that Republic."[111]

The main factor that brought the Turkish nation face-to-face with the collapse of the Ottoman Empire and with it the danger of losing complete independence was the continuation of a form of state that had become obsolete and archaic. Moreover, the Ottoman Empire, which had maintained its traditional structure, had become subject to the excessive influence and direction of the modernized powers of the West.

The success of Mustafa Kemal's movement lay in its bringing this manipulative order to an end and initiating the modernization of Turkish society. Accordingly, its first step was the preparation of the conditions for establishing a nation-state and then actively working toward its development. Consequently, both stagnation and expansionism were rejected.

During the R.P.P. Congresses held in 1927, 1931, and especially 1935, a good deal of work was done on the development of Atatürkism as a system of thought.[112] In the programme adopted by the R.P.P.'s Fourth Grand Congress in 1935, Atatürkism was specified as "Kemalism" and it was announced that it consisted of four "cardinals" and six principles. The four "cardinals" are: "Fatherland," "Nation," "Government," and "Political and Public Rights of the Citizen." The six principles are: Republicanism, Nationalism, Populism, Etatism, Laïcism, and Revolutionism-Reformism. As a result of changes made in 1937, these principles were adopted in Article 2 of the 1924 Constitution as forming the basis for the characteristics of the Turkish state.[113]

In short, it can be said that during those years, Atatürkism had become the national system of thought of the new Turkish Republic, which reflected the national will and the aspirations of the people.

Despite the single-party regime of the Atatürk period, the Atatürk Revolution aimed at the development of a national policy that was above the customary "party policies." To assist in the realization of this goal, Atatürk set up a variety of institutions outside the party such as the History of the Turkish Revolution institute, the Turkish History and Language Societies, and the People's Houses. His hope was for the greater systematization of the Atatürkist system of thought through activities conducted by them.

The one-party system was used to speed up the process of modernization and to protect the Revolution. As Walter Livingston Wright states: "The one-party system that was set up gave such fair representation to all influential elements of the population, however, and balanced so expertly the interests of classes and localities, that it was able to carry out a fundamental reorganization of Turkish society.[114]

Emil Lengyel points out that Kemalist Turkey did not have an organization as that of the N.K.V.D. of Soviet Russia and the O.V.P.A. of Fascist Italy.[115]

Analyzing the nature of the dictatorship of Kemal Atatürk, Hans Kohn says that his dictatorship was based on liberal principles. Kohn points out that the achievement of democracy was the aim of Turkish education. He emphasizes that the goal of Atatürk's dictatorship was to prepare the Turks for a democratic system. Kohn also stresses the fact that the policies of the R.P.P. did not support mysticism, but were secular and rational in content.[116]

Lewis V. Thomas states:

> At the start, the total eligible electorate was by no means ready to exercise the franchise. Let alone the peasants, not even did the ruling group have traditions wholly preparing them for this; but in any case, forms of an election were carried out. Mustafa Kemal organized his own party, ran it, picked its candidates, had them campaign (on a one-party ticket, for they ran unopposed), and was unquestioned party boss after his candidates were in. Certainly, this made him a dictator. But in the first half of the twentieth century, there were dictators and dictators.

Since you grant that Mustafa Kemal and his associates had the long-term idea-lism to see in Turkey of 1923 the makings of what could eventually be a functio-ning Republic, what other course was open? And is there any serious question of their not having this vision? Atatürk himself worked to undermine his own dicta-torship. He died a relatively poor man, poverty-stricken for a chief of state in the Eastern Mediterranean.[117]

Atatürk's Revolution was a movement of radical reform designed to overcome backwardness and the six principles were the guiding principles of this movement.

3. The Atatürk Principles

In Atatürkism, action and thought are intertwined; they support and complete one another. The ideological aspects of the problems of "unity," "authority," and "equality" in Atatürk's model of revolutio-nary reform are particularly evident in the six principles. The resolu-tion of the problem of national identity was undoubtedly a prerequi-site to the formation of the nation, the reinforcement of national existence, and the attainment of national "unity." Moreover, solving the problem of "authority" was necessary for the existence and strengthening of the state. "Equality," on the other hand, was a sig-nificant factor in ensuring that modernization and the condition of the citizen were placed on sound footing.

An adequate evaluation of the Atatürk model of revolutionary re-form depends on an examination of these six principles upon which its ideological component is based.

There is an intimate relationship between Atatürk's principles and "unity," "authority," and "equality," which form the basis for the stages of implementation of the Atatürkist movement of radical re-form. These principles served to facilitate and strengthen the imple-mentation of the phases of the model.

The connection between the principles and the stages of the Ata-türk national model of revolutionary reform - which principles were used or were of assistance at which stage - has been outlined in the table below:

Unity	Authority	Equality
Nationalism	Republicanism	Republicanism
Populism	Nationalism	Nationalism
Laïcism	Laïcism	Populism
Etatism		Etatism
		Laïcism
		Revolutionism-Reformism

As it can be seen, the six principles are oriented toward providing "unity," "authority," and "equality;" rendering the state powerful and seeing to it that society becomes modern.

a) Republicanism

Atatürkism accepts the Republic as the only legitimate regime. Through the Republic, political "authority" is obtained, its legitimacy being derived from the unconditional sovereignty of the people. The source of political authority is the nation and its people. On 13 August 1923 - even before the Republic was proclaimed, Atatürk had this to say with respect to this matter: "The New Turkish State is a people's state; it is the state of the people. In the past, it was the state of a single person or only a few people."[118]

The Republic also brought about change with respect to "equality." Since the Republic is the zenith reached by the "nationalization" and "popularization" of the political regime and given the overriding concerns of Atatürkism, there was no other alternative but to adopt the Republican form of government. Furthermore, combined with the establishment of a laïc order based on the principles of science and reason, both society and state were able to acquire a more modern structure. The radical reforms taken toward laïcism, especially when changes were made in the 1924 Constitution in 1928 to make it laïc by removing the term "Islam" giving the Republic its modern attribute. Political "authority" became grounded completely on laïcism, e.g., legitimacy was no longer derived from God.

Under Republicanism, the will of the Turkish nation had ascendancy in the formulation of policies. Governing the nation, state and society could not be left in the hands of certain classes, families or social groups. All the individuals of society had the right to participate efficaciously in government. Society must be open and participatory.

In terms of the features we have already laid out, Republicanism is a principle that is at once rational, democratic, liberal, equality-oriented and open to pluralism. The basic qualities forming the backbone for "Authority" in the Atatürkist model of revolutionary reform is laïcism, nationalism and republicanism.

The proclamation of the Republic on 29 October 1923 has a special place and meaning within the unfolding of the Atatürk Revolution.

On 1 November 1922, the Sultanate was abolished and on 29 October 1923, the Republic was proclaimed. With the elimination of the Sultanate, a 600-year form of government, based on the tradition of *personal will* had legally come to an end. The declaration of the Republic, on the other hand, legitimized the notion that the new government was to be based on *national will, on the sovereignty of the people.*

The unfolding of the Anatolian National Struggle that began on 19 May 1919 went through many stages, all the while guided by the national will. The development of national will was preferred to that of personal will. The strength, effectiveness and continuity of the National Struggle and the War of Independence was obtained as the National Struggle became truly *national* in scope, and as the national will was expressed. From its very beginning, the goal of the National Struggle, even if not explicitly expressed, was to lay the foundations and create the ideological and organizational structure for a new and modern Turkish state. Nevertheless, the whole of society and many of the members of the leadership cadre of the Revolution were unaware of this. In the announcements, statements and speeches made in the name of the National Struggle, in addition to saving the nation from the enemy, the saving of the Sultan was always mentioned, too. The truth - the path that was to be taken, the form of government that was to be adopted and implemented, and the details of what the new order would bring - was known by the leader of the Revolution, Mustafa Kemal, and a few of his close associates. However, Atatürk was careful not to move too quickly in carrying out some reforms. He waited for the most expedient time to announce them. Even so, for those who understood what modernization entailed, there was no need for advanced knowledge to be able to see where the Atatürk Revolution was headed and the kind of government that would result. The statement "Rendering sovereign the national will" can have no other interpretation. This was the definition of a form of government based on the will of the people and their votes, e.g. a Republic, which had simply not been stated explicitly. Nonetheless, many people believed that the National Struggle would lead to saving both the Sultanate and the Caliphate and thus result in their perpetuation. But at the same time, there was a sense that a change in the status of the Sultan could lead to a change in that of the Sultanate.

During the Ottoman era, the institutions of the Sultanate and the Caliphate had seemed entrenched, having a kind permanency about them; these institutions represented an unalterable stratum of "command." Society was accustomed to Sultans being removed from their positions and şehzades (Princes) and sadrazams (Grand Viziers) being assassinated. These were seen as normal ways in which transition occurred in the "Sultan form of government." What was continuous was the institution of the Sultanate and the Caliphate. Ottoman society was not used to a "change in dynasty."

It was within this historical context that the National Struggle was launched, a National Assembly was convened in Ankara in opposition to the Sultan and Caliph and their government in Istanbul, a Speaker of the Assembly was elected and the Government founded. It was in no uncertain terms, the beginning of a completely new political regime.

After the Sultanate was abolished on 1 November 1922, all that was left of the old political order was the "Caliph," who had come from the Ottoman Dynasty. The conflict intensified at this point. Attempts to block the establishment of the "Republic" grew as it became increasingly evident that this was the intention. The defenders of the Sultan and Caliph in the Assembly as well as most of the newspapers in Istanbul, who backed them, began to raise the issue of the problem of head of state. They supported the creation of a new position that would be held by the "Caliph," which would be able to wield power over and above the National Assembly, the Speaker of the Assembly and the Government.

In the midst of this controversy, Mustafa Kemal announced on the evening of 28 October 1928 that the Republic was to be proclaimed the following day. By doing so, he had hoped to get to the root of the problem.

The Balkan wars and the First World War that followed them led to the defeat of the Ottoman Empire and to the further decline of its state power. The Capitulations, which granted special privileges to foreigners, as well as foreign debt, had made the state powerless and subservient vis-à-vis foreigners. The state had reached a point where it was unable to carry out even the very rudiments of what was required of a state. In spite of its entrenched and powerful state tradition, because of the resistance and apathy of its government leaders and social forces to modern [Western] development, Turkish society had remained traditional in scope. The state became known as the "Sick Man" of Europe. Apart from the superficiality of the reform efforts begun during the period of decline of the Empire, there were no attempts at radical change. The result of this was the misfortunate attempt by Western powers to wipe the Empire off the face of the map and then to partition Anatolia and share it amongst themselves, which the government leaders of the Empire agreed to at Sevres. Opposition to this attempt appeared in the form of Mustafa Kemal and the national movement of resistance, the National Struggle, through which he mobilized the people for action, resistance and war. There was potential for both good fortune and misfortune for the Turkish Revolution. To the extent that the National Struggle was successful, the Revolution would pave the way for its leader, accelerate modernization, and initiate a movement of radical reform oriented toward sweeping change. On the other hand, if the National Struggle ended in failure, the country would be carved up. Turkish society would then begin a dismal period, the end of which would be unknown. Nonetheless, there was no middle path for the progressives. This was symbolized by Mustafa Kemal's statement, "either independence or death."

The concept of independence included not only the independence of the state, but of society and the individual as well. The form of government within the country that would express this and which was based on the sovereignty of the people and their will was the "Republic."

After the establishment of the Republic, Kemal Atatürk aimed at creating in the minds of the people a sense of identity with the new Turkish Republic. In all the reforms of Atatürk and in his speeches and statements, his efforts in this direction were apparent. The symbols as well as the values of the Republic replaced those of the Empire. The Sultan's collaboration with the forces of occupation during the Period of National Struggle was an important factor that facilitated this change of identity from Empire to the nation-state of Turkey. One of the remarkable consequences of the ideology of Kemalism and the reforms of Atatürk could be observed in the high degree of, self-confidence they created in the minds of the Turkish people as to their new national identity. This was particularly true in the case of the Turkish political elite. As Lewis Thomas states, "What was dead was the Ottoman Empire. The Turks remained. Turkish nationalism, in fact, was only now being born, for it was only now freed of those Ottoman style imperial responsibilities that had hitherto encased it."[119]

As previously stated, Mustafa Kemal did not aspire to becoming a "Sultan" or "Caliph." He did not want to begin yet another dynasty. Mustafa Kemal was a leader who knew political history well and had a good sense of what modern development entailed. For him, this entailed, first and foremost, the establishment of a "Republic." The proclamation of the Republic was to be the most efficacious, trail-blazing reform undertaken by the Turkish Revolution. In spite of the resistance and many dead ends that have cropped up from time to time in the implementation of the pluralist democratic regime in today's modern Turkey, development and modernization have continued apace.

The dynamism of society is based upon the fact that the new Turkish state is firmly established as a Republic.

b) Nationalism

At the beginning of the 20th century, the concept of nationalism in Turkey was still a novel one. That it was adopted by all the strata of Turkish society, is an accomplishment of the Atatürk Revolution.[120]

The impact of nationalism on the Turkish people was late compared to the impact of nationalism on the subject nationalities of the Ottoman Empire. Ottomanism rather than Turkish nationalism had been embraced by the Ottoman ruling elite. Ottomanism was a cosmopolitan concept which included all the nationalities that were subjects of the Ottoman Empire. Turkish nationalism began to emerge only toward the end of the 19th century. Early in the 20th century, Turkish nationalism was distinctly embraced by the Union and Progress Party. The foremost theoretician of Turkish nationalism during the Second Constitutional Period was Ziya Gökalp. Although the Union and Progress Party was principally responsible for the decline of attachment to the idea of Ottoman brotherhood, this Party did not entirely give up its allegiance to Ottomanism. In addition, there was a Pan-Turanist trait of Turkish nationalism as embraced by the Union and Progress Party; in contrast, Kemalist nationalism rejected Pan-Turanism as a viable policy for Turkey.

Turkey had emerged defeated from World War I. The War of Independence won back for the Turks their own land, and the Lausanne Conference sanctioned this victory.

Kemal Atatürk, in a speech he gave on 20 March 1923 at the Turkish Hearth Organization to the Youth of Konya, expressed his views on the damages the Turkish people had suffered because of their late awakening to the idea of nationalism:

> We have been negligent as a nation in applying the notion of nationality. We must make up for the resulting shortcomings by being more active in this field. The theories that have attempted to abolish the ideas of nationalism and the national ideal cannot be applied in the world. This is because history, events, phenomena and observations have shown that nationalism is prevalent among the people and nations of the world. Moreover, it can be observed that in spite of large-scale attempts to abolish the principle of nationalism, it has not been possible to kill feelings of nationalism. Nationalism has continued to flourish.
>
> Our nation, in particular, has suffered because her nationality was ignored. Various nationalities within the Ottoman Empire saved themselves by embracing the nationalist faith and by the force of their nationalist ideal. We understand what we were, that we were a nation that was different and foreign to them after we

were forced from among them. They insulted and humiliated us when our power declined. We understood that our fault was to have forgotten what we are. If we want the world to show us respect, first let us show respect toward our own character and nationality through our feelings, ideas, and actions and with our own activities and deeds; let us be aware that a nation which has not found her national identity is prey to other nations.[121]

Atatürkist nationalism placed a high value on Turkish citizenship. Nevertheless, at the same time, it was not racist or persecuting nationalism. According to Kemalist ideology, Turkishness was not necessarily determined by one's race or religion but by the degree to which a person associated himself with the ideas, ideals and goals of the Turkish nation and by determination to protect all that had been won as a result of great hardships; and also by commitment to Turkish modernization. For this reason it was not surprising that one of the outstanding works on Kemalism was written by Moiz Tekinalp, a Turkish citizen of Jewish faith.[122] Another such example was Agop Dilaçar, a Turkish citizen of Armenian descent. Agop Dilaçar, who was one of the foremost experts of the Turkish language, was invited by Atatürk to participate in all aspects of the Turkish language reform movement. Until his death in 1979, Agop Dilaçar remained an active member of the Turkish Language Society, publishing several important books on the Turkish language. As Clair Price states, "Nationalism in Turkey today welds and does not divide. Its cry strikes a sound and healthy note."[123] And Bernard Lewis remarks that Kemal Atatürk's "nationalism was healthy and reasonable; there was no arrogant trampling on the rights or aspirations of other nations, no neurotic rejection of responsibility for the past."[124]

Atatürkist nationalism was secular - a trait that is markedly different from contemporary Arab nationalism, which is intertwined with Islamism. Atatürkist nationalism is a rejection of Islamic nationalism. Through its rejection of the right of an individual, a group, an organization or dynasty to rule over others, Atatürkist nationalism expresses its populist nature as well.

One of the outstanding characteristics of Atatürkist nationalism was its anti-imperialism. Atatürkist nationalism respected and recognized the right to independence of all nations. It viewed with sympathy the national liberation movements in the oppressed countries of the world. In this, the essentially humanitarian trait of Atatürkist nationalism could be observed. Kemal Atatürk believed in the essential unity of mankind and of the world. As Lord Kinross states:

> Kemal was a nationalist; but there was nothing parochial in his nationalism. He saw that the day of empires was done and that the day of nations had arrived. But with his global sense he saw beyond this conception toward that of a federation of nations, an amalgamation of sovereignties such as Wells had envisioned in his United States of the World. He was attracted by the idea that a number of individual federations might precede something of the kind. He was too much of a realist to believe that such an apotheosis could really be achieved. But he saw that Russia would seek to achieve it in terms of the Communist ideology, and that the principle of internationalism would animate the second half of the twentieth century as that of nationalism was animating its first half. Meanwhile, the welfare of nations was interdependent.[125]

The characteristic ideas associated with Atatürkist nationalism could be found in such statements as "If we work hard, we can accomplish a great deal and become a modern state," "Our goal is the goal of civilization." Atatürkist nationalism was not based on hatred of other nations. School textbooks did not contain propaganda against other nations or nationalities. In fact, one of the fundamental tasks of Atatürkist nationalism was to eliminate the inferiority complex created in the Turkish nation by the decline of the Ottoman Empire and by the several wars she had lost in the last couple of centuries. In short, to give the Turkish nation the needed confidence that, if she worked hard enough, she too could become a modern nation.

Atatürkist nationalism did not make Turkey a closed society. The Atatürkist emphasis on Turkish culture did not culminate in the denial of the achievements of other countries. On the contrary, the Atatürkist reform movement was characterized by its Turkishness as well as by its receptivity to ideas, methods, and legal codes from the modern states of the world. The qualifying element of the open character of Atatürkist nationalism was that this reception of ideas, of methods, of legal codes should not be used by these states to subject Turkey to the status of a vassal state nor prevent her from determining freely the nature of her own institutions. Atatürkist nationalism was basically dedicated to a vigilant protection of Turkish independence. The nature of Atatürkist nationalism did not impede the growth of democratic ideas and institutions in Turkey.

Implicit in the idea of Atatürkist nationalism was the idea of modernization. Kemal Atatürk believed that only a modern Turkish state could truly maintain her independence. As Bernard Lewis states, "The two dominant beliefs of his (Atatürk's) life were in the Turkish nation and in progress."[126] Atatürkist nationalism accompanied Kemalist attempts at modernization of Turkey. This accompaniment of modernization by nationalism is a process discernable in other contemporary developing societies.

It is generally recognized that an important aspect of political development is related to the phenomenon of nationalism. As Lucian W. Pye states:

> With the emergence of the modern nation-state, a specific set of requirements about politics came into existence. Thus, if a society is to perform as a modern state, its political institutions and practices must adjust to these requirements of state performance. The politics of historic empires, of tribe and ethnic community, or of colony must give way to the politics necessary to produce an effective nation-state which can operate successfully in a system of other nation-states.
>
> Political development thus becomes the process by which communities that are nation-states only in form and by international courtesy become nation-states in reality. Specifically, this involves the development of a capacity to maintain certain kinds of public order to mobilize resources for a specific range of collective enterprises and to make and uphold effectively types of international commitments. The test of political development would thus involve, first, the establishment of a particular set of public institutions which constitute the necessary infrastructure of a nation-state, and second, the controlled expression in political life of the phenomenon of nationalism. That is to say, political development is the politics of nationalism within the context of state institutions.
>
> It is important to stress that from this point of view, nationalism is only a necessary but far from sufficient condition to ensure political development. Develop-

ment entails the translation of diffuse and unorganized sentiments of nationalism into a spirit of citizenship, and equally, the creation of state institutions which can translate into policy and programs the aspirations of nationalism and citizenship. In brief, political development is nation-building.[127]

The Atatürkist principle of nationalism viewed within the broad context of all of Kemal Atatürk's reforms included the above-mentioned activities that were necessary in the process of Turkish nation-building. The Atatürkist principle of nationalism was dedicated to Turkish political development. Atatürkist nationalism played an important role in bringing about an accelerated pace of Turkish political development during his Presidency.

In the transition from traditional to modern society, the orientation toward national culture is a fundamental stage. Mustafa Kemal recognized the importance of such a stage as early as the first years of the War of Independence.

> I believe that the mistakes made in the areas of education and training is one of the most important reasons for the backwardness of our nation. So when I speak of a national training program, what I am proposing is a culture that is commensurate to our national and historical character - a culture that is completely far removed from the unjustified accommodation of former ages, alien ideas that are not compatible with our temperament, and influences coming from the East and West. This is because the development of Turkish government is possible only through such a culture. The indiscriminant acceptance of just any foreign culture has had no other effect up to now than promoting on-going destruction. The efficacy of this culture is only as great as its compatibility with the place where it has been introduced. This place is the unique makeup of a nation. In raising our children and youth, we should instill within them the need to staunchly oppose all foreign elements that are incongruous with their own existence, rights and solidarity, as well as to the exuberance of their national beliefs. The preservation of these feelings and behavior in the internal world of the new generation is of great importance. The full intensity of these feelings and behavior is obligatory for nations whose existential philosophy was established during an interminable, horrible war and for every nation that wants to remain independent and content.[128]

Every new state that has begun to modernize brings its own peculiar political culture to the task and works toward developing that culture. At the same time, every new state attempts to have this culture assimilated by all strata of society through political socialization. The Turkish language reform and the creation of a new conception of history were important steps taken by the Turkish nation-state toward this end. In addition, the establishment of the People's Houses in 1932 was instrumental in getting the new political culture accepted and spread. Political consciousness was further strengthened and extended through organized efforts. The Turkish Historical Society, the Turkish Language Society and the People's Houses were important contributions in this regard.

Türkçülük (Turkism) is a movement that denotes the cultural activities of Turkish nationalism. Under its impact, two important reforms were made in the early 1930s. One was in the field of history and history teaching and the other was in the field of Turkish language. As Donald E. Webster states:

> *Türkçülük* is a movement compensatory to the national inferiority complex incurred in the declining years of the Osmanlı Empire. But it is more than that; especially in its linguistic phases, it is a practical program for democratizing the vernacular by freeing it of its slavery to the Arabic terms and grammatical forms. In general, Türkçülük is an attempt to separate the principle stream of Turkish culture from the waters in which it became diluted and muddied as it flowed from Central Asia and settled in the sea of Anatolian civilizations.[129]

Sigmund enumerates the objectives of a modernizing nationalism as: national independence, rapid economic development, the creation of a nation-state, imbuing the administrative regime of this state with a populist identity, and non-alignment in international affairs. There is no mention of liberal, pluralistic democracy. The theory and practice of constitutional democracy as it is known in Europe or North America is not much in evidence. What has emerged in the developing nations is a reasonably coherent set of ideas about society and government that constitutes the ideology of modernizing nationalism.[130]

The commitment to the Turkish nation, Turkish state and to innovation; the openness to change; and the attainment of national unity
-in short, a modernizing nationalism- are the means through which
the Atatürk Revolution could unfold.

The answer provided by the Atatürk Revolution to the question,
"How is this state to be saved?" was "within national borders and
guided by a national, modernizing policy." The Atatürkist movement
of revolutionary reform was nationalist and modernizing. Atatürk
was not interested in *world* revolution, but rather his own *national*
revolution. The belief and position that a nationally based policy was
one of the most important factors in the preservation of a country's
existence was expressed by Atatürk:

> Gentlemen, what is of the greatest concern to foreign policy and upon which
> it is based, is the internal organization of the state. The foreign policy of a state
> wnose internal organization consists of communities that are incompatible with
> one another in terms of internal makeup and ideals drawn together within a sing-
> le border is undoubtedly witnout foundation and unsound. In this case, foreign po-
> licy cannot be stable or sound either. Just as the internal organization of such a
> state is far from being national, so is its political administration. Accordingly, the
> policy of the Ottoman State was not national, but rather personal, unclear and un-
> certain.
>
> Gathering together under a common and general name various nations and
> establishing a powerful state so as to be able to provide them with equal rights
> and conditions is a brilliant and attractive political position; but at the same time it
> is deceptive. Likewise, the unification of all Turks in the world under a state re-
> cognizing no borders is an unattainable goal. This is a reality that has come to
> light through the bitter and bloody events of the centuries and of the people living
> these hundreds of years.
>
> At no time in history has the policy of Islamism or Turanism been successful.
> The consequences of aspirations to found a single world-state irrespective of ra-
> cial distinction have been shown to be ill fated historically. We have no desire of
> being "repressive or expansionist." The theory of creating a humanistic state ba-
> sed on getting people to forget all forms of special feelings and ties and uniting
> them under the principles of brotherhood and full equality has its own unique
> constellation of conditions.

The political means that we see as feasible is "national policy." Given the general conditions existing in the world today and the realities that have been ingrained within the minds and hearts of the centuries, there can be no greater error than that of being a visionary. This is what history has made clear and it is what science, reason and logic has demonstrated.

In order for our nation to be able to live within a powerful, content and sound order, it necessary that the whole state be guided by a national policy and that this policy be completely compatible and based on our internal organization. What I want to make clear when I say "national policy" is this: it is working toward the preservation of our existence and the genuine contentment and development of our nation and country by relying more than anything else on our own power within our national boundaries; avoiding the pursuit of indiscriminate and unattainable goals; and expecting civilized and benevolent behavior from the civilized world and mutual friendship.[131]

In attempting to spread the consciousness of national identity, mass communication, educational institutions, the Turkish Historical institute, the activities of People's Houses, and especially the radical reforms taken in the area of culture were used. In these efforts, a nationalism that reinforced the consciousness of national identity, national security and the raising of national pride was embraced. The burden and responsibility of modernization was born not through foreign assistance but rather on national decisiveness, diligence and on the nation itself. In fact, giving to the nation the responsibility for solving problems, looking for the answers to problems within the nation itself and making the nation work toward this end is a fundamental position of Atatürkism. For example, the notion that the country can achieve independence only through national will and the determination and self-sacrifice of the nation was a dominant view during the era of the national struggle.

The maintenance of the continuity of every political system demands the acceptance by the nation -particularly its youth- of the basic values and beliefs upon which that form of political administration is based. Moreover, how these values and beliefs are adopted by the nation and the people influences the way in which political life operates and the form of operation it assumes.

According to Greenberg, political socialization in general is related to the beliefs and values of the political system of which a person is a member and the citizenship role that person plays in that political system.[132]

The basic principles of cultural modernization are nationalism and laïcism. Educational unity was achieved through the Atatürk Revolution and was erected upon a national, laïc foundation. Furthermore, education was used as a means of socialization in the acceptance and spread of the new political regime. Educational institutions, People's Houses, the Turkish Historical Society and the Turkish Language Society were employed for this purpose.

Atatürk believed that by creating a national, laïc and progressive educational system committed to the identity of the new Turkish state, the Republic and its continual renewal would be enhanced. Atatürk knew very well the importance of the spread of a national and modern education[133] throughout the entire country in bringing intellectuals, the broad masses, villagers and city-dwellers closer together; and in the realization of social change and economic development. Therefore, he continually stressed the issue of education and paid particular attention to it. The establishment of Village Institutes was also a by-product of such a populist educational policy. By carrying out educational reform in the village, the village would be integrated with the nation. All of these radical reforms were important stages in nation-building.

c) Populism

Since its decline, the Ottoman Empire struggled to overcome its backwardness. Attempts at reform were a by-product of this. Their goal was the "salvation of the Ottoman state." The element of "the people" had no place in these attempts at reform. Together with the War of Independence, people and populism were placed on the agenda as part of the Atatürkist movement.

Atatürk had been inspired by the concepts of freedom, equality and security of the French and American Revolutions but he gave them a populist dimension. Atatürkism is not an elitist ideology. Populism and nationalism were among the leading concepts during the

War of Independence and the years of the Republic during Atatürk's Presidency. The Republic was based on a regime that was national in scope and had a popular base of support. Populism and nationalism had important functions in the attainment of "unity" in the country. Many of the radical reforms were carried out under the direction of the principles of populism, nationalism and laïcism. For example, the Turkish language reform was influenced by all these three principles. The profound mark and influence of Arabic and Persian on Turkish was due to dominance of Islamic culture on Turkish culture. The carrying out of laïcism paved the way for a Turkish language reform. On the other hand, in the words of Atatürk, "the liberation of the Turkish language from its subjugation to foreign languages" and his stress on the need for this language to develop in its own independent way was a reflection of the nationalist aspect of this reform. Ottoman was not a language of the people; it was a language of the upper classes. By ridding the Turkish language of foreign vocabulary and simplifying it, the people and the intellectuals could understand one another better. It would also contribute to the elimination of the estrangement and distance between the governing and the governed. The populist orientation of the Turkish language reform can readily be seen.

Kemal Atatürk himself was of a humble social origin. His social background, his experiences, his temperament, and his convictions prevented him from being aloof to conditions of poverty in his own country as well as elsewhere. His experiences before the War of Independence had led him to believe that something had to be done to eradicate poverty in general and to improve the lot of the peasants in particular. All his experiences led him to admire the Turkish peasant and the Turkish soldier. By temperament and conviction, he loathed palace life, its intrigues and its aloofness to the common people of Turkey. His assumption of command of the Turkish forces at the age of thirty-four at a critical moment of Turkish history, in the battle at the Dardanelles in 1915, and his success in defeating the enemy could not be explained only in terms of his superior military strategy. He was a man who had confidence in the Turkish soldier, and in return, he inspired confidence in the minds of the soldier as to his own ability, capacity and quality of leadership. As Barbara Ward states, "The

behavior, the dogged endurance, the patience, the heroism of the ordinary soldiers did more for the democratic temper of Kemal's mind
than years of reading in the scholarly source books of French liberalism. It filled him with an angry devotion to the rough sons of Anatolia who for centuries had borne, either the taxes on their fields or
the guns on their shoulders, the full burden of the imperialist follies
of the Sultanate."[134]

In the Populist Program of 13 September 1920, which was discussed in relation to the Period of National Struggle, we had a chance to
analyze some of Mustafa Kemal's ideas pertaining to populism. However, in order to get a broader perspective of this principle, we should keep in mind the various reforms which were discussed before
and which outlined the Atatürkist principle of populism. In addition,
we should not forget the content of many of Atatürk's speeches and
statements in which he clarified further the principle of populism. The
following are several excerpts from Kemal Atatürk's speeches dealing
with populism.

In his speech to the Grand National Assembly on 1 March 1921,
he said, "Our domestic policy can be characterized by the principle of
populism; that is to say, this principle which makes the people master
of their destiny has been established by our own Constitution."[135]

In a speech he gave to the Assembly, on the occasion of discussions
on the duties and rights of the Cabinet, on 1 December 1921, he said,

... Our government is a... 'people's government'... When we think in terms of
our social life, one fact definitely emerges, which is that we are a working people, we are a poor people who work and who have to work in order to live and in
order to achieve our independence! Let us know ourselves. Therefore, all of us
have rights. All of us have authority. But we acquire a right only through working.
In a society, a person does not have a place or a right if he wants to lie back and
does not want to work ... Populism is a social system that aims to base the social order on work.[136]

In the speech he delivered to the Grand National Assembly on 1
March 1922, he reiterated the fact that the Constitution of the Government of the Grand National Assembly was based on the princip-

le that sovereignty belonged unconditionally to the people. Although he talked about the necessity of unity between the people who constitute the Turkish society, he paid a particular tribute to the Turkish peasant who, in his estimation, was the most exploited segment of the Turkish population:

> The real Lord of Turkey is the peasant, who is the real producer. Hence, the peasant, more than anyone else, is entitled to wealth, riches and well-being and is deserving of them. Consequently, the economic policy of New Turkey is aimed at the attainment of this principle objective. I may say that the sole course of our present misfortunes is the fact that we had not been aware of this truth. Therefore, from now on, we will pay, with the greatest modesty, respect to this principle owner of the country, the blood of whom has been shed and whose bones we have left in the soil through the centuries. We have squandered this resource and have deprived him of all opportunities for over seven centuries. We have repaid him for this with condemnation, insults and humiliation. We have wished to keep the lord of the land in subjugation by ingratitude, force and aggression in recompense for all his sacrifices and all his good will.[137]

In his speech at the Izmir Economic Congress on 17 February 1923, Mustafa Kemal expressed his opinion that the present era was a people's era and that he would best describe the people's era with the concept of the economic era.[138]

On 16 March 1923, Mustafa Kemal told the farmers in Adana, "The government has two goals: One is the safeguarding of the nation, and the other is securing the welfare of the people."[139]

In his opening speech to the Second Grand National Assembly on 13 August 1923, he stated, "The new Turkish State is a people's state. The institutions of the past established a personal state; it was a state which belonged to individuals."[140]

On the second anniversary of the final, decisive battle of the War of Independence, he gave a speech at Dumlupınar, on 30 August 1924, in which he stated:

> These who ruled over Turkey for centuries thought of everything, but they did not think of one thing: Turkey. All the hardships Turkey had to endure because of

the absence of consideration for her can be compensated for only in one way: by thinking only about Turkey in Turkey. Only by acting in accordance with this idea can we reach all the goals of security and happiness.[141]

He further stated in this speech that the national ideal of Turkey was to become a modern society and that nations that were not capable of becoming modern could not hope to be free and independent.[142] In these two above-mentioned statements, we have a chance to observe Mustafa Kemal's effort to create a sense of identity in the minds of the Turkish people with the new frontiers of Turkey and with the new Turkish regime. At the same time, he brings out clearly the idea of the Anatolian Revolution - that the War of Independence was unlike the military activities of the Ottoman Empire. The goal of the Anatolian, of the Atatürk Revolution, had been to achieve the independence of the Turkish homeland. And now only through complete modernization could this independence be truly maintained. Again, in this same speech, he addressed Turkish youth with these words, "The future is yours. We established the Republic; it is you who will exalt and continue it."[143]

There are many controversies over what Atatürk really meant by populism. But within the context of various speeches he gave and in terms of his reforms and discussions at the R.P.P. Congresses, it is possible to understand that Kemal Atatürk meant by the term populism the entire nation and not a specific class. For example, the closing words of his speech to the Grand National Assembly on 1 November 1937 substantiate this point of view: "The essence of the Program in our hands prevent us from being interested only in certain sections of the citizen body. We are servants of all... We do not recognize differences between classes..."[144]

Yet, throughout the speeches and statements of Atatürk, we encounter that an essential characteristic of his principle of populism was its intimate relationship with his principle of nationalism. In other words, Kemal Atatürk gave special importance to national unity and believed that one of the important reasons for the successful termination of the National Liberation Movement could be found in the unified efforts of the Turkish nation to achieve her independence. There-

fore, his intention was to establish a political party and a program
that would emphasize the essential unity of the Turkish nation. As
was stated in the 1935 Program of the R.P.P., the Kemalist principle
of populism rejected the idea of class conflict and believed in the necessity of establishing social order and harmony and solidarity betwe-
en the different occupational groups in Turkish society. But at the same time, the Party Program pointed out that the benefits a person was
to receive was to be proportional to his aptitude and to the amount
of work done.

Atatürkism opposed both dynasty and Sultanate. It respected the
rule of law rather than of a person. The concept of sovereignty of the
people was one of the earliest concepts of Atatürkism. This concept
had political as well as social connotations. Politically it meant the establishment of the Republican regime, of a representative government, and of the equality of all before the law. Socially it meant the
rejection of the rule of an individual, of a group, of an organization,
or a dynasty over others. Atatürkist ideology was particularly emphatic on the question of the rights of peasants and women. Several Atatürkist reforms aimed at changing the status of these individuals with
the specific intention of bringing them to a status of equality with other groups in Turkish society.

The Turkish War of Independence was anti-imperialist. However,
it was won through the cooperation between classes and was not based on the idea of class conflict. Kemal Atatürk talked of unity between groups and not of the proletariat and the capitalists. The anti-
capitalist stand of the revolutionary elite during the period of National Struggle was particularly due to the existence of the Capitulations and to the imperialist policies of several capitalist countries toward Turkey.

This special emphasis on national unity could also be observed in
Republican Turkey. Atatürkism looked at the Grand National Assembly and the Turkish government as the trustees of the people because they represented the sovereignty of the people. The Atatürkist
view of the state was not Marxist. It held that the state could be an
impartial agency in reconciling differences of interest between groups in Turkish society. In short, Atatatürkism, through its principle

of populism, showed its rejection of the force theory of the state and embraced the idea of the impartiality of the state. However, a qualifying element must be brought into the Atatürkist concept of the state. Certainly, Atatürkism did not believe in the impartiality of the Sultanate or the upholders of traditional society in Turkey. It believed in the impartiality of the revolutionary elite; that is to say, of the modernist elite.

The principle of populism, as well as the various reforms of Atatürk in the legal, economic, and cultural fields, showed his desire to base both his system of thought and the regime on the people. It was a pro-mass, pro-nation ideology. Nevertheless, the solution to the problems of the masses had been solved from above. The masses had not yet reached political consciousness and did not press for a change of the traditional order. Through its principle of populism and through the particular form of application of this principle, the revolutionary elite led by Kemal Atatürk tried to shake the masses out of their centuries of lethargic existence and acceptance of the traditional order. The Atatürkist principle of populism aimed at involving the people in the political processes of the country. In the achievement of all this, Kemal Atatürk believed two factors would play the most important role: economic development and education. Kemal Atatürk believed that a modernist-secularist educational system and the availability of it to all would play a fundamental role in bringing about social reorganization.

The social outlook represented by the principle of populism was largely egalitarian in nature. It can be generally suggested here that certain strong elements of egalitarianism in Ottoman society, the absence of hereditary classes except for the Ottoman dynasty, facilitated the adoption of such an outlook during the Presidency of Atatürk.

Lewis Thomas states that from the point of view of a social scientist "on every significant level of her fundamental class structure, Turkey's is an essentially open class society in which both upward and downward mobility are common features."[145] Although Atatürkism was dedicated in principle to the idea of social mobility, the complete realization of this depended on major socio-economic changes and substantial educational reforms that had to take place. To some extent, these did take place. However, they were not sufficient enough to transform the entire traditional structure. Sabahattin Selek attributes the lack of adequate success in the socio-economic field mainly to what he believes to be a confused interpretation that was given to the concept of populism. He says that the concepts of people and nation, and of populism and nationalism, were intermingled. Furthermore, that populism was given predominantly a political interpretation and its socio-economic aspects were largely neglected. He believes also that the insistence on the belief that class interests could be completely reconciled was unrealistic. The emphasis should have been more on ways and means of decreasing the tensions resulting from class interests or on attempts to hold some kind of a balance between these interests.[146]

One can state with a fair degree of accuracy that one of the fundamental reasons for this lack of success in the socio-economic field was due to the lack of knowledge of the revolutionary elite in these matters and the lack of resources and technical know-how. The necessity of socio-economic transformation was expressed on many occasions by certain leading members of this elite. The fact that this reformist elite, which had effected such major reforms in many fields, should not have been able to bring about a major change in the socio-economic structure of Turkey was unfortunate. At that time, such a socio-economic structural change would have met with less opposition than now, basically for two reasons: this revolutionary elite had complete control of the Turkish government and Turkish state while the social structure was more attuned to a traditional class structure. New class interests had as yet not patently emerged.

Ali Mazrui offers an interesting observation about Atatürkist populism by making a comparison between the Atatürk Revolution and the Meiji Period in Japan:

"Mustafa Kemal was too egalitarian and not elitist enough. His reforms sought to narrow the gap between the city and the countryside, between the upper and lower classes, between Turkish and ethnic minorities, between men and women, between the rulers and the ruled. Kemalist populism was too egalitarian to serve the purposes of Meiji transformation."[147]

Mazrui continues his analysis with the following words: "Mustafa Kemal was a moralist prematurely. He sought moral perfection simultaneously with material modernized achievement. This was his undoing - at least if the material perspective is deemed more important... There are many reasons why Turkey has not matched Japan industrially. But one of those reasons might well be that Turkey outstripped Japan morally in the Atatürk period."[148]

The Atatürkist interpretation of populism rejected class differences, class conflicts, and recognized no special privileges for any individual family, class, or organization. It rejected currents of thought that could disrupt national unity. Kemal Atatürk talked about solidarity between classes. He said that Turkish society was composed of a united group of people with no classes and no special privileges. Atatürkist attempts at modernization of Turkish society involved also attempts at socio-economic transformation. Ideologically, Atatürkism was committed to this from the time of the Period of National Struggle and this was evidenced in one of the early documents of this Period, namely, the Populist Program of 13 September 1920. The question that plagued the Atatürkists was one of method and implementation. The revolutionary elite, for the most part, did not have an adequate knowledge of the socio-economic questions. Therefore, particular difficulties were encountered with regard to implementation. At times, the revolutionary elite simply took action in this field through trial and error.

The Turkish revolutionary elite embraced the idea of solidarism. The principle of populism emphasized *tesanüt* (solidarity) between classes. The principle of populism was interpreted to mean that Turkish society was not composed of classes but of individuals who belonged to different occupational groups. On the other hand, the principle of populism as interpreted by Kemal Atatürk did not mean upholding a socio-economic order that was based on the wealth of a few and the poverty of the many. Solidarism did not mean the maintenance of the *status quo*. But two questions remained of the most importance for Kemal Atatürk in his attempts at the modernization of Turkey: First, Kemal Atatürk did not wish to achieve modernization through the total abandonment of political liberty. The question of how to reconcile the necessities of rapid development with political liberty retained its importance for him throughout his life. Although there was a one-party system, the nature, goal and operation of this one-party system had not made Turkey a closed society. Second, Kemal Atatürk and the revolutionary elite wanted the number of "victims" of the modernization to be very few, and if possible, for there to be none. Atatürkism did not subscribe to a method of modernization that believed in the destruction of one class or classes by another. Atatürkist attempts af modernization also involved an attempt to keep at a minimum level the number of people who would suffer physically by these changes. In short, the Atatürkist principle of populism, which was based on solidarism, aimed at keeping the price to be paid for modernization, in terms of human suffering, as low as possible. Atatürkism rejected the method of modernization as employed in the Soviet Union where mass killings took place, such as those of the kulaks. The Atatürkist attitude was one of commitment to radical and, whenever necessary, to revolutionary changes, but Atatürkism did not believe in the killing of groups of people or destruction of certain classes for the attainment of modernization. Atatürkism clearly rejected the Soviet-Marxist method of modernization. Nevertheless, populism retained its leftist nature by insisting on the necessity of socio-economic transformation. A capitalistic type of economic development was also rejected in the early 1930s. Atatürkism retained its attachment to the realization of Turkish political development through the possibility of solidarity between classes. In this, an impartial state,would play a very important role. However, as suggested earlier, implicit in this idea of impartiality was the fact that a modernist elite should be in control of the government.

As William Yale states:

> The vitality of the new Turkey will depend, in the long run, upon the awakening and the modernization of the Turkish peasantry. The liberal intellectuals of Turkey created during the past thirty years the framework within which the isolation, ignorance, and intense conservatism of the peasants could be eliminated if the process continues uninterrupted, the future of Turkey would seem assured.[149]

The realization of equality is dependent upon ensuring the transition of the individual from subject to citizen status and the achievement of an order in which the citizen and the society in which he lives can participate in resolving the problems of the country. Sovereignty based on the notion that it belongs unconditionally to the nation was a source of legitimacy for the new political regime. In 1924, the election law was changed, reducing age of franchise to 18. Women won the right to run in municipal elections in 1930 and in general elections in 1934. These progressive reforms were important steps taken toward "participation" and populism, an important stage in modernization.

Bose sees participation as a crucial element in the carrying out of development. In his opinion, development policy is a basic problem of both developed and developing countries. The common experience of these countries demonstrates that both in the formation of relevant policy and in its implementation, the participation and contribution of the people are necessary for the success of this development program.[150] The issue of participation that is present in both the contents and objective of the principle of populism was not entirely resolved during Atatürk's era. Nonetheless, it must not be forgotten that some very significant reforms were taken in this direction during this period. In this way, the Atatürk Revolution was able to raise the level of participation to a meaningful level and practice. It lay the foundations for an environment in which the transition to a multi-party regime and pluralist order that strengthened and reinforced participation. It should not be forgotten that a despotic, single-party, closed regime was never an aspiration in the system of thought or movement of Atatürkism. In spite of all these developments, populism was not adequately imbued with a social content. Undoubtediy, there was an acceleration of vertical mobilization in Turkish society. The spread of educational opportunities contributed to bringing about this mobilization and continues to do so. It is also a reality that this was dependent upon the power of the government and the capacity to accelerate the pace at which social mobilization was achieved.[151]

During the 1930s, the R.P.P., the sole party of the Revolution, was given the job of putting things in order and, in fact, several organizational changes were made. Attempts were made to make the party more sensitive to the demands of the people and both the party and government more open to criticism. Steps taken to popularize the culture can be seen as part of the efforts to ensure this equality. The Sun Language Theory and the Turkish History Thesis were part of this struggle to be free but because the thesis proposed by the former was scientifically invalid, it was deprecated and soon became a topic to which emphasis was no longer given. Even so, during that time, they had served to hasten nation-building efforts and raise confidence in the nation and its history. In particular, the principles of Nationalism and Populism and the radical reforms taken in this regard functioned to bring about "unity."

The concept of "people" in Atatürkism belonged to no discrete class. It was used to refer to all Turkish citizens. The War of Independence was against capitalism and exploitation and had been won through the cooperation of all the people and classes. Populism was construed as being opposed to class supremacy and class distinction. No single individual, family, class or community was above another. Mention was made not of social classes but rather the existence of a variety of occupational groups and the alliance between them. Radical reforms were based on the understanding of a society free of classes and privileges. But it was not a perspective adopted to preserve the fixity of "national solidarity." The need for "national unity" for the prosperity and development of the nation was promoted. What was important was not only unity but also the attainment of an order whose rationale was modernization and the fact that it was one of the principle proposals of Atatürkism.

The solidarity movement that developed in Europe in the 19th century as a reaction to classical liberalism and Marxism had a significant impact on the principle of populism. However, because solidarism was insufficiently developed as a social concept, it failed to have much of an impact on socio-economic change. Atatürk and his administrative cadre embraced solidarism and held that there was solidarity between communities. Selek, critical of the denial of classes, which was an erroneous consequence of the limited class differentiation and inadequate development of class-consciousness in Turkish society, submits the view that it was not realistic to expect complete reconciliation of class interests. He suggests that perhaps it would have been more valid or appropriate to attempt to reduce the conflict resulting from class interests or establish a balance between them.[152]

Nevertheless, there is another important point that should not be forgotten, which is that during the early years of the Republic, Turkish society was devoid of a modern class structure. Moreover, putting aside the existence of a sector of workers having reached class-consciousness, at that time the overall number of workers employed in places of employment was about 50-60 thousand. Even the publishers of *Risaleler* (pamphlets), in support of those attempting to form a political party of workers, put the figure of workers at 20 thousand in transportation, such as train, boat, and tramway; 20 thousand in mines, such as those in Zonguldak and Balya; and 20 thousand female factory workers in such cities as Adana, Bursa, Izmir and Istanbul - totaling some 80-100 thousand workers.[153]

The administration, the economy, the policy of Atatürkist populism and its state and social regimes were for the weak, those who toiled to survive, in short, the people. It was not for social powers or entities that had acquired importance by virtue of traditional assets and vestiges from the past. Rejecting class supremacy, populism intends to safeguard the interest of the people in government, policy, development, income distribution, and in the utilization of state and national resources. Toward this end, it assigns to the state the responsibility for seeing to it that measures are taken, laws are enacted, regulations are created and obstacles eliminated.

d) Etatism

The activity of the state in the economy had been a reality since the beginning of the Republic but étatism became a major principle of state policy only as of 1931. Provisions were made for private initiative between 1923-1930. However, private initiative was not in a powerful enough position to be able to exercise much influence in economic development. Such factors as the scarcity of private capital, inadequacy of technical information, and the lack of experienced Turkish businessmen were some of the reasons why private initiative was not a major factor in economic development. In contrast, according to the official definition of étatism, the state would organize the general needs of economic activity, directly taking economic initiative itself in areas where private initiative shows no interest or has not been successful, as well as those areas of public interest. Thus it was entirely pragmatic.

The bankruptcy of the economic policy, "laissez-faire, laissez-passé" reached its pinnacle with the outbreak of global depression in 1929-1930. This situation was instrumental in strengthening the principle of étatism. That economic independence would be achieved more quickly and more easily by following an étatist policy became evident. A scheme for economic development under the supervision of the bureaucracy was launched. This was a conception of an interventionist, guided economy. In the application of the principle of étatism, the state assumes a leading role in the economy.

In the new Turkey, rationalism reigned supreme in all areas. The notion that the "raiding, military state should become the economic state" became more influential. Because it would be a primary factor in getting the country to use its own resources and in establishing a national economy, a planned economy was adopted. Atatürk made his views concerning industrialization and planned economy known in a speech he made to the Assembly on 1 November 1937:

> Industrialization is among our most important national causes. In order for it to work and to survive, we shall establish all kinds of industry, whether it be large or small scale, for which the requisite economic inputs exist in our own country. It is paramount that we make national defence our primary concern, increase the value of our national products, and reach the ideal of the most progressive and prosperous Turkey by the shortest route.[154]

In the same speech, Atatürk made the following remarks on economic development:

> Economic development is the backbone of the ideal of a free and independent, always stronger, and always more prosperous Turkey. In her development, Turkey depends on two pillars of strength:

The climate of the land, its wealth and its valuable geographic setting; and also the strong hand of the Turkish nation, which is as capable of holding a machine as it is a gun, and her high sense of national identity, which manifests itself in a sturdiness to change the course of history in affairs and at times which she believes to be of national importance.[155]

Atatürk adopted planning in order to hasten economic development. He hoped that in this way a more prosperous Turkey would be created, leading to a higher standard of living for all and adequate compensation for labor based on an equitable distribution of national income. And while the socio-economic change was not accomplished with an "iron fist," certain symbolic aspects of socio-economic existence did undergo rapid, radical transformation. For example, the international calendar, hour and numbers were adopted and, abolishing traditional names and titles, the surname law was enacted. On the other hand, progressive reforms taken in the area of law such as enacting new laws - predominantly in the areas of civil, criminal and commercial law, extending to women the right to vote, basing the educational system on laïc and modern principles, and establishing Village Institutes in rural areas so as to enable their development ensured changes in the economic infrastructure that enabled the raising of new generations.

A more gradual method was used to make more radical economic changes. The principle of étatism was one such principle of gradual change, which was manifested in the first five-year plan. Broad-based, extraordinarily rapid and radical socio-economic change requires the force and intensity characteristic of a totalitarian method. Neither Atatürk nor his cadre preferred such a method, stressing instead, the "cost" of development. Without a doubt, the judiciousness inherent in Turkish political culture was an influential element here.

A gradual, peaceful method of economic development was sought; the system of large rural landlords could not be destroyed. Even within the framework of such a gradual approach, more positive results vis-à-vis the village could have been attained. For example, an effective program of road development, which plays an important function in village development, by facilitating transportation between town and village and thereby enhancing the "dialogue" between them was not established. Nevertheless, through the measures initiated by the Atatürk Revolution, because of developments in later years, the village was not cut off from the life of the nation.

Etatism is a product of the search for and a belief in the necessity of an economic development model different from pure capitalism or pure Marxism. It arose out of an emphasis on pragmatism as a basis for finding unique national solutions to problems of national interest. On the one hand, one of the deepest economic depressions of the capitalist world began to be experienced in 1929. On the other hand, there were the Soviet model and its rejection of nationalism and opposition to the principle of populism, along with the extremely excessive methods it employed. Both of these led Turkey to making an effort to create its own national economic development model through the principle of étatism. The theorists[156] of the journal *Kadro* contributed to the formation of this model of development. They worked toward systematizing Atatürkism (Kemalism). Their aim was to build an infrastructure upon which the Revolution in all of its dimensions could be realized. These theorists did this through their studies and the articles they wrote. By creating an independent society and economy, the *kadrocular*[157] (staff members of the journal) aimed at the formation of a concrete example of development for all nations that have fought for their liberation from colonialism, which was distinct from the Soviet and capitalist models. However, some circles criticized proposals made in this direction as being excessively socialist. The *Kadro* journal stopped publication in 1934 and the *Kadro* movement was suspended. In spite of all these negative reactions, the principle of étatism and the influence and contribution of the ideas of this movement led to the first period of economic planning. The foundation of modern industry began during this time. The economic cooperation established with Soviet Russia was of support at this stage. But Atatürk had not embraced a development path that depended on either the pure Capitalist or the pure Marxist system. Atatürkism strived to establish a national model of economic development that consisted in both theory and practice of the concept of the "social state" and attempted to implement this as étatist policy.

Those who emerged victorious from the War of Independence, those that met success in the Anatolian National Struggle, saw economic independence as the fundamental principle through which a genuine independence could be achieved and maintained. The economic independence of a country or nation is acquired once it reaches a state where it is sufficient unto itself. It is the way in which it can exist and develop free from the control of others. After a long period of Capitulations, where all of the resources of the country -both below and above ground- were exploited and siphoned abroad, for Turkey to have an honorable existence, the move toward a national economy was inevitable and necessary. Even before the Republic had been proclaimed, because of this understanding, the "Turkish Economic Congress" meeting in Izmir on 17 February 1923 determined what needed to be done by getting the views of representatives from all walks of life and professions. Mustafa Kemal attended this Congress as well and, making a long speech, explained why and how the nation had become impoverished and what was necessary to be able to live an honorable existence upon Anatolian soil.

Mustafa Kemal emphasized the point of view that one of the major reasons why the Ottoman Empire declined was its neglect of economic affairs:

> Those who make conquests with the sword necessarily must succumb to those who make conquests with the plough and, in the end, must relinquish their positions. And that was the very thing that happened with the Ottoman Empire. The Bulgarians, the Serbians, the Hungarians, and the Romanians held on to their ploughs and so preserved their existence; these became strengtnened. But our nation, following the plans of her conquering leaders, set out on adventures and one day succumbed because the nation had not worked within their own Fatherland. This is a truth, verified in the same manner in each epoch of history and in every place in the world. While the French in Canada brandished the sword, the Englishmen entered there as farmers. In the struggle between plough and sword, the plough is victorious in the end. And as a result, the English have become the masters of Canada. The arm which wields the sword tires and finally sheaths the sword; and probably that sword is condemned to rust in the sheath. However, the arm which uses the plough becomes stronger every day. The stronger it gets, the

more soil is taken into possession. It was the Ottoman conquerors and their satellites, through their utter neglect of the plough, who sowed the seeds of the
greatest of their disasters.[158]

In the early years of the Republic, the Turkish government experi-
mented with the idea of bringing about industrial development through a liberal economic policy. A number of laws were passed both to
encourage private enterprise and to accord certain privileges to private industry, especially in its initial years of operation. The *İş Bank*
(Bank of Business) and the *Sanayi ve Maden Bank* (Bank of Industry
and Mining), which were established in the mid-twenties, were to finance Turkish economic development. The result of attempts to bring
about economic development through the support and encouragement of private enterprise was largely unsuccessful. There were a
number of reasons for this. These were the lack of private capital,
lack of technical know-how, and the lack of experienced Turkish businessmen. Another factor of importance was that the Turks preferred
official careers or professions such medicine, law, and engineering rather than the field of private enterprise. In this attitude of the Turks,
historical factors as well as cultural values played an important role.
Traditionally, the Turks had left or, at times because of the existence
of the Capitulations, they were forced to leave, commercial affairs to
either the minority groups or the foreigners.

It must be noted, however, that in the early years of the Turkish
Republic, Mustafa Kemal was concerned primarily with the question
of making sweeping political, social, cultural and legal reforms. Having abolished the concepts and institutions that would impede economic development, Mustafa Kemal and the Kemalist elite began to
focus their attention on the economic field - in particular, on the question of industrialization. This concentration on economic affairs
and in particular on the problem of industrialization was prompted
by the conviction that Turkey could not be a truly modern state and
could not also safeguard her independence easily if she were not industrialized.

The lack of capital, both foreign and domestic; the lack of skilled
workers; the inexperience of the Turks in economic matters; the dis-

couraging results of the experiment with a liberal economic policy; and the Depression of the late 1920s caused Mustafa Kemal and the revolutionary elite to seek a new policy for economic development. *Etatism* was embraced by Kemal Atatürk and the Kemalist elite as the new economic policy of the Turkish government. Thus, the Kemalist elite rejected the idea of bringing about industrial development through a liberal economic policy. This rejection did not involve the depreciation of the liberal political institutions of the West as was in the case of the Marxists and the Fascists. As William Yales states:

> The revolutionary leaders in Turkey as in most of the Near East during the past hundred years had concerned themselves largely with political and social studies rather than economics. They had shown very little interest in the complexities of the Western economic system although they were keenly conscious of the fact that European domination of the Ottoman Empire had been based on economic controls. The Kemalists were determined that the Turkish Republic should not be controlled by European governments and Western capitalists. With little knowledge of Marxian philosophy and no inclination toward Soviet Communism, they turned toward what is commonly spoken of as state socialism, but more correctly called étatism, which is a modernized form of seventeenth and eighteenth-century European mercantilism.[159]

The National Struggle was waged against the Western imperialist states and it concluded in victory. Throughout the War of Independence, both in Mustafa Kemal's speeches and talks and in conversations that he had with his colleagues, he had a word to say about repulsing and defeating imperialism and colonialism. For example, he stated, "Colonialism and expansionism will be eliminated from the face of the earth and replaced by a new epoch where nations will live in harmony and cooperation devoid of distinctions in color, religion, and ancestry;" "when complete independence is referred to, naturally what is meant is complete independence and freedom in all areas, including political, judicial, monetary, military, cultural, economic and other similar matters. If in any of these independence is missing, in the true meaning of the term, the nation and country are devoid of independence as well."

During the early years of the Republic, to some extent due to the inadequacy of state revenue, Atatürk had to take a pragmatic stand with respect to the relative roles of private initiative and state participation in economic development. While initially rather supportive of the latter, as a result of the impact of the world economic depression of 1929 on Turkey and the subsequent increase in the suffering of the people, the state announced in 1932 the necessity of state involvement in the economy. This was followed by the initiation and implementation of a five-year plan. During this period, a directed economy, one that called for state entrepreneurial activity became the main approach used to stimulate the economy. In fact, the first large industrial investments were made during the period of this first five-year plan. These investments proved to be very productive. The populist and progressive components of the Atatürk Revolution were conducive to the development of an étatist economy. Nonetheless, throughout the Republican era, Mustafa Kemal and his close colleagues did not repel private initiative or preclude private entrepreneurs from benefiting from the resources of the state and the national economy. Thus, a new commercial/capitalist sector -a sector of businessmen- began to develop through all kinds of resources provided by the state. Becoming ever more wealthy, their influence on the multi-party system grew.

Lewis Thomas has this to say on étatism:

> The Republic's program of installing modern plants is summed up in the general term of "Etatism." it is an ambiguous but amorphous program for state-owned and for state-operated industrialization, having for its goal the concept of a Turkey self-contained and self-sufficient in terms of a twentieth-century industrial state.[160]

In relation to the question of economic development, we once again have a chance to observe Atatürkist nationalism and Atatürkist dedication to independence, as well as Atatürkist readiness to experiment with new ideas and new policies. Turkey was one of the first countries to engage in economic planning. In this and in other aspects at modernization, Kemal Atatürk and the revolutionary elite studied the experiences of other countries. Moreover, at times, they adopted some of the same institutions, ideas, and methods. However, all this was not imposed on Turkey. Whatever was adopted was done so through the free will and decision of this revolutionary elite. Hence, Kemal Atatürk wanted to achieve economic development through ideological independence. As was discussed in relation to other issues, a predominant characteristic of Atatürkism is its insistence on ideological independence in the seeking of solutions to Turkey's problems and in the realization of Turkish modernization. It is interesting to note that there was not much reaction in Turkey against economic planning. The opposing interests to economic planning were not so well organized or articulate. In addition, the masses in particular did not understand the full implications of such an economic undertaking. The question of laïcism had brought forth much more discussion and dissension.

A number of progressive economic reforms were made during the early years of the Republic and while Atatürk was still in good health. These included 1) the support of agriculture through cooperatives, bank credit, and agricultural tools and equipment; 2) the establishment of such state industrial and mining institutions as Sümerbank and Etibank, paper, concrete, sugar, iron and steel factories, the glass industry and the purchase of railroads from foreigners; and 3) the nationalization of maritime lines. During the initial years of the Republic, there had been, a shortage of trained, educated, highly skilled technical personnel. The traming of such people in schools that were opened and their assuming positions in the work force was another factor contributing to the economy during this period. It enabled both state and private sector enterprises to operate productively. During this period, there was a two-pronged need. One was for initiating economic development while the other was training the requisite personnel. In both cases, this was largely accomplished.

Etatism was the principle of Atatürkism that provided direction to the use and management of national resources by the state and was particularly instrumental as a development and modernization policy. All societies having a state tradition -including Turkish society- tend to look to the state for guidance. This is only natural. The raison d'être for the rise of the state is just this. People, the individuals of a nation, have a responsibility toward the country and society in which they live. However, it is the primary duty of the state to provide guidance to individuals; use and develop the nation's resources and the country's wealth for the benefit of the nation and its people; to carry out development; to provide for the well-being of people in society; and to build up the public infrastructure of the country. As is the case within the country, the state is also responsible for rendering the nation independent, powerful and modern, as well as protecting itself from being subjugated, exploited, and dependent vis-à-vis other states.

The principle of Republicanism demands the transformation of society into a democratic, liberal, plural and participatory one. The principle of populism calls for people to be fully active. But how is this to be realized? When the people are basically poor and are subsisting on their toil, how will they be able to confront the powerful, those who govern them so that the rights given to them by law will be adequately taken advantage of and acquire efficacy? How are they to benefit from the fruits of development, the distribution of the national income and the interregional distribution of state resources? Given the conditions in Turkey at that time, the answers to these questions could be found in the reasons for the adoption of étatism. Turkish society had a structure that was backward in all respects. During the Empire, the economy had gotten increasingly weaker and externally dependent: debts, the Capitulations, railroads, ports, transportation, communication networks, mines, energy sources, and taxes - in short, everything- was in the hands of the colonial, expansionistic states and their industrialists, bankers and merchants. As a result of this, the Empire languished and eventually collapsed. This collapse was followed by a War of Independence, from which a new Turkish state had emerged triumphant. With an impoverished nation - a country that had been razed and brought to ruin and burdened with a large debt that it had inherited from the Empire, the new Turkish state started along a new trajectory. Not only was the country to be reconstituted and reclaimed, the nation rescued from poverty, debts paid, and businesses purchased from foreigners and nationalized, but also the level of modern civilization desired was to be reached. Furthermore, there did not even exist a private entrepreneurial, capitalist sector in the country. It was within this state of affairs and after the global economic depression in 1929 that étatism actively and out of necessity was initiated and began to be implemented.

Etatism, e.g., where the state assumes a role in the economy, industry and business in the interest of nation and society, would activate and manage the main resources of the national economy and the main sectors required by independence, and use the assets thereby generated in activities that again are in the interest of the nation and people.

The principle of étatism does not reject private entrepreneurship. Neither does it call for all of the means of production to be concentrated in the hands of the state. It respects the right of private property but it does not permit its use in a way that is contrary to the interests of the nation. Etatism sees the state's role in the economy as one of organizing, planning and guiding, as well as manager and entrepreneur. It should be emphasized once again that the choice of étatism in Turkey was entirely a pragmatic one. Not at all ideological, it simply suited the conditions at the time.

The allegation that the Atatürk Revolution was unable to solve economic problems or bring about economic development is a rather frequently encountered criticism. However, while examining the issue of economic development in Atatürk's period, certain considerations have to be made: 1) Western countries were able to achieve economic development at the end of a long process. One must be more realistic than to expect a comprehensive and profound transformation in infrastructure to occur in such a short period as between 1923-1938; 2) The Atatürkist model of radical reform did not use an "iron fist" approach to socio-economic change but rather stressed the "cost" of development; 3) The economic "inheritance" Turkey got from the Ottoman State was a partially colonial economy; 4) The private sector at that time was weak; 5) On the other hand, the position of the world "conjuncture" at that time was not at all promising either.

Production Indices for Turkey and the World[161]
(1929=100)

Year	Turkey	World
1929	100	100
1930	106	86
1931	112	76
1932	118	65
1933	131	75
1934	141	80
1935	141	92
1936	149	102
1937	165	110
1938	174	96
1939	196	119

Despite these limitations, as can be seen in the table below, Atatürk's Turkey was able to carry out a successful policy of industrialization by relying on its own efforts.

During those years, only Soviet Russian, after 1933, and Japan, after 1934, had higher rates of industrial growth than Turkey. It can be seen that the rate of industrial growth in the world between 1929-1939 was much lower than it was for Turkey. Compared to the 19% rate of increase in global industrial production, that in Turkey was 96%.

Moreover, when the contribution of the total rate of Turkish industrial growth to global production is examined, it can be seen that compared to other Balkan countries, a very rapid development process had begun in Turkey.[162]

Year	Turkey	Greece	Bulgaria	Romania
1929	0.14	0.11	0.08	0.4
1939	0.23	0.16	0.11	0.5

From the table, it is clear that after industrialization was initiated, per capita income rapidly increased in Turkey.[163]

The restrictions brought by the Lausanne Treaty (the inability to dominate customs) and the "inheritance" of the debts passed down from the Ottoman era necessitated this economic policy.

The foremost characteristics illustrative of the 1929-1938 era are the following:

Year (TL)	National Income (Million TL)	Population (Million)	Per capita National Income
1927	1000	13.6	73
1929	1147	14.2	80
1935	1315	16.2	82
1938	1589	17.2	92 (about. $75)
1939	1625	17.5	95

Despite the fact that it was a country where domestic capitalist accumulation was extremely meager and whose economic structure was very backward, and the global economy was in the throes of a major depression, Turkey was able to implement a sound policy of industrialization without receiving any significant foreign aid or incurring domestic debt. The main reason why the industrialization policy can be qualified as sound is that investments in both heavy industry and consumer-oriented industry, particularly given the time, were begun with modern technology. In addition, in the industrialization in question, whether from the point of view of energy sources or raw materials, resources found within the country were relied on, resulting in a reinforcement of independent economic development. If this policy of industrialization was continued in later years, it is safe to say that the economic situation in Turkey today would have been much better.

e) Laïcism

Laïcism: One of the fundamental principles of Atatürkism is laïcism. In terms of Turkish history and of the requirements of modern civilization, it was not surprising that in Atatürkism and the reforms of Atatürk, which represented the most concerted and fullest commitment to modernization in Turkish history, laïcism should play such a predominant role.

As laïcism is an indispensable component of modernization, many of Atatürk's reforms involved the laïcization of the Turkish state and society. Atatürkist laïcism did not merely mean separation of state and religion, but also the separation of religion from educational, cultural, and legal affairs. It meant the realization of independence of thought and institutions from the dominance of religious thinking and religious institutions.

The principle of laïcism under Atatürkism is also the recognition of religious freedom to the individual and the safeguarding of this freedom. Individuals are equal before the law irrespective of religious differences. In this respect, laïcism as the freedom of the individual in religious matters is recognized and respected by other persons, society and the state and is protected through sanctions.

Being modern, basing the existence of society and state on reason and science, can only be realized through the thorough implementation of the principle of laïcism in education, policy, and in the organization and administration of the state and society. The fundamental characteristics of the Republican administration that Atatürk established are its laïc and national components. Many radical reforms were undertaken to create a laïc society. Others could be executed thanks to the opportunities that arose due to the adoption of such a principle.

Beginning in 1517, when Yavuz Sultan Selim assumed the title of Caliph, in addition to their authority on earthly matters within the borders of the Empire, the Ottoman Sultans acquired the opportunity to become the religious leader of all Moslems. In the Ottoman Empire, which had a theocratic state, religion became an integral part of the state. It assumed a position through which it was to be able to play a leading role or, at the very least, an influential one, in all areas.

In the West, rapid and intense opposition had grown within circles supporting the king. This was commensurate with the desire and efforts on the part of clergy to expand their range of influence. In contrast, leadership in state and religious affairs in the Ottoman Empire had been united under the Sultanate, which meant that the occasion for such a struggle did not appear for a long time.

During the Ottoman era, the authority to determine whether "customary" practices were contrary to religious codes belonged to the *ilmiye* (Ulema) class, who also had the right to intervene. In contrast to the West, which had rapidly developed since the Renaissance, the Ulema class, with such broad authority and static grasp of the world, was attempting to solve the problems of society. The Ulema saw the continuity of their own authority and interests in the preservation of an "absolutist" regime. As of the 18th century, progressive Sultans, statesmen and intellectuals began reforms in opposition to the class of Ulema. If influence and authority of this powerful class, which had had Sultans murdered and many rebellions prepared in the name of maintaining the status quo, had been used to bring about reforms, it is certain that these reform movements would have been much more comprehensive. Mahmut II, who was an enlightened Sultan, is a clear example of what collaboration with this class could achieve, when through an agreement made with this class, the Janissaries were abolished. This class had all-encompassing authority, had not encountered a power strong enough to curb it for many long years, and held within itself the only force that could restrict them. Therefore, it did not feel the need to keep up with the changing world, to carry out reforms of its own ideas or to progress. It resisted attempts at innovation within Ottoman society. In brief, it wanted to interpret a changing world with an unchanging understanding of it. It became a prime example of how an unlimited power could become decadent. The entrenched understanding of the world of this class gave rise to degeneration and deterioration in such areas as education and justice. The Ulema class was not tolerant of groups that supported reform and refused to live together with them. This class was not satisfied to simply concern itself with religious matters; it did not abandon its desire to be the final word in all areas. Supporters of reform continually met with opposition from the Ulema class. The reforms could only be carried out against them and not with them. Consequently, in no area in which reforms were conducted up until the Republican era except for the replacement of the Janissaries with a new army, reforms were complete. Meeting with the antagonism of the Ulema class, reforms could only be realized through bitter struggle.

The principle of laïcism has a much more comprehensive meaning than the separation of state and religion. As Lord Acton indicated in an essay entitled, "Freedom," the modern democratic state did not emerge from the medieval church or state but rather from the conflicts between the two. Western society, which had successfully countered the claim of absolute sovereignty of the Pope -whether over state or society- was prepared to oppose similar claims made by rulers who later had become powerful through their unbounded authority. This successful conclusion reached by the West not only separated state and religion but also led to the development of a legal order and system that kept society from coming under the control of any one person or group.

The resistance of the religious powers to the reforms of the Ottoman Empire, the assassination of Selim III, the reactionary movement of 1909, and the opposition of the official religious apparatus of the Sultan-Caliph and especially the Sheikhulislam to the War of Independence and its leaders during the period of National Struggle led the national progressives to see the religious forces as the most important obstacle to modernization. It is for this reason that laïcism was not seen as only a division between state and religion but rather as a way in which the state monitored religion.[164]

Such reforms as measures as the termination of the Ottoman dynasty, the abolition of the Sultanate, Caliphate and the fez, the integration of education, the closing of the *tekkes,* and the laïcization of the Constitution were significant changes made toward the realization of laïcism.

The Atatürkist principle of laïcism did not advocate atheism. It was not an anti-God principle. There was no liquidation of religion in Atatürk's Turkey. Rather, religion and clergy were removed from areas that they had traditionally controlled. The latter were asked to confine themselves to specifically religious affairs. In short, it can be stated that the Atatürkist principle of laïcism did not involve abolition but de-emphasis of Islam. The Atatürkist principle of laïcism was not against an enlightened Islam but rather against an Islam that was opposed to modernization.

The Ottoman Empire had been a theocratic state. The Sultan was the political ruler over the Empire; but he was also the Caliph and as such, he was the spiritual head of the Moslem world. As Halide Edip Adıvar states, "The Caliphate, apart from its futility as a political institution, was proving to be a source of political complication with the Western powers who had Moslem subjects. They either suspected Turkey constantly of scheming against their sovereignty, or else they themselves were involved in intrigue in Turkey in order to get control of the Caliphate and use it on behalf of their own ambitions."[165] in reality, at the end of World War I and with the subsequent Treaty of Sevres, the Ottoman Empire came to an end. As Karl Krüger states, "But the moment the Holy Places of Arabia were lost to Turkey, the external emblem of the Khalif at Stamboul became illusory, and this was immediately demonstrated by the attempts of the Grand Shereef of Mecca, as well as of the Senussi Community, to reestablish the Khalifate."[166] Furthermore, although *cihad* (Holy War) was proclaimed by the Turkish Sultan-Caliph in 1915, the Arabs for the most part supported the Allied Powers and fought the Turks. In World War I, many Moslem soldiers from French and English colonies also fought against the Turks. Particularly the Arab collaboration with the British during World War I, in spite of the existence of the seat of the Caliphate in Istanbul, proved once and for all to the Turkish revolutionary elite that the goals of nationalism and independence were far more important than the existence of a common religious bond. Kemal Atatürk and the revolutionary elite realized that neither Pan-Islamic sentiment nor the Caliphate could be realistically considered as unifying elements. The experiences of the Turkish nation in World War I could be cited among the important factors which led Kemal Atatürk to reject Pan-Islamism as a viable policy for Turkey.

In as much as the Arab attitude toward the Turks during World War I had been a contributing factor to the decline of the prestige of the Caliphate and the religious group in Turkey, there were far more important reasons which could explain the concerted drive of Kemal Atatürk to achieve laïcism.

One of the fundamental factors that moved Atatürk to insist on laïcism was born from a knowledge of Ottoman attempts at modernization. Since the eighteenth century, the struggle with the religious group throughout all the different periods of reform in the Ottoman

Empire had been a source of great tension between the modernist elite and the conservative-religious group. The latter group was interested in the maintenance of the *status quo* of Islamic institutions and
way of life. Moreover, it had acquired complete control over Ottoman
state and society. It was also among the most influential and enthusiastic supporters of traditional society. The attempts of the Turkish
modernist elite at reform of the Empire met with the resistance and reaction of the religious-conservative group. At times, attempts at modernization were sabotaged by revolts instigated by this group. Therefore, the antagonism of the religious-conservatives to modernization could be cited among the important factors that explain the less
than successful attempts of the Ottoman Empire at modernization.

The final decisive blow to the prestige of the religious group and
in particular to the religious hierarchy in Turkey was, as explained
earlier, due to the *fetva* of the Sheik-ul-Islam in April 1920. In it, the
Nationalist forces in Anatolia were declared as rebels and in which
the Turkish people were ordered to kill them. The Nationalist forces
were then involved in a struggle not to maintain an Empire but to maintain the Turkish homeland. This *fetva* and the collaboration of the
Sultan-Caliph with the forces of occupation were among the fundamental factors which facilitated the abolition of the Sultanate in 1922
and then the abolition of the Caliphate in 1924.

The Ottoman Empire was gone. The Republic was established in
its place. The fundamental goal of Kemal Atatürk was total modernization of the Turkish state and society. He believed that laïcism would play a decisive role in the attainment of this goal.

Those Atatürkist reforms, which were made to realize laïcism or
which had connections with laïcism were principally aimed at bringing Turkey to the status of the advanced states of the world. To understand the underlying philosophy of the Atatürkist principle of
laïcism as well as its application, the following factors should be kept
in mind: In Atatürk's Turkey, in accordance with the requirements of
modernization, religion and religious institutions were removed from
areas, such as education and law, which did not fall within the proper sphere of their activity. And in their place, laïc concepts and institutions were substituted. Historical experience with the religious

groups' opposition to modernization had a profound impact on the formulation of the Atatürkist principle of laïcism. The application of this principle not only involved separation of state and religion and the severance of traditional ties between religion and education and law. In addition, the Directorate of Religious Affairs was attached to the office of the Prime Minister. Atatürk's government assumed the right of interference, whenever necessary, for the purpose of controlling religion and in order to prevent the religious-conservative group from making any attempts on its part to play its traditional role in Turkish society. Nevertheless, there was no persecution of the religious group. Parents were free to bring their children up as Moslems. The mosques were not closed. The government recognized the right to freedom of conscience of all Turkish citizens; secularized the Turkish Constitution and took upon itself the major responsibility of controlling religion. This included preventing any pressures that might be brought upon citizens because of their religious convictions. On the other hand, the government limited itself by recognizing the right to freedom of conscience of all the citizens. The prerogative of seeing to it that all citizens were free in the enjoyment of their right to freedom of conscience tell within the domain of Atatürk's government. In short, the government took upon itself the major responsibility to control and to limit actions that could violate freedom of conscience. Some people have described the above-mentioned application of laïcism in Atatürkist Turkey as the "one-sided character of Turkish secularism." Writing about Turkey in the mid-thirties, Henry Elisha Allen states that the Atatürkist attitude "is favorable to whatever in Islam is consistent with the Republican ideas, relentlessly opposed to anything which might endanger Atatürkist success, and, for the rest, more or less neutral."[167]

The supreme commitment of the ideology of Atatürkism was to the Turkish Republic and its modernization. Absence of laïcism would have disrupted the basis of that commitment. The nature and the source of reaction to the ideology of Atatürkism and the reforms of Atatürk were not very different from those encountered by the modernist elite in the Ottoman Empire. The basic opposition to the reforms and ideology came from the religious group and other conservatives who used the shield of religion to try to continue their hold over Turkish society. In a few cases, these reactions reached serious proportions in Atatürkist Turkey. However, they were quickly brought under control and quelled. The effectiveness of the revolutionary elite to deal with reaction could be attributed to the firmness of its convictions; its commitment to modernization; its essential unity; and its control over the political apparatus of the Turkish state. Moreover, the reforms were supported in the main by the Turkish military, the civil servants, the intellectuals, and the Youth.

Atatürk founded the first laïc state in the Islamic world. He wanted the Turkish Republic to be a laïc state since he believed that the theocratic basis for the previous state had been an important reason for Turkey not having been able to attain a modern level of civilization. The progressive reforms undertaken in the fields of law and education were products of a national rather than religious orientation. At no time did Atatürk understand laïcism to mean atheism. By saying, "We respect religion," he wanted to refer to a genuine religion present in the conscience of people. Atatürkist laïcism does not reject religion or encourage atheism; it calls for religion to deal with its own peculiar problems in a modern social context. It proposes that religion distance itself from the functions it had in traditional society and find its true place in modern Turkish society. Finally, it opposes those who wish to bring about the domination of society by religion, those who want to impose reactionary thought on society under the cloak of religion, and those who want to maintain traditional society.

Efforts to realize laïcism enabled the comprehensive rise of ideas oriented toward making Turkish society an open society. Therefore, it provided for the strengthening of views and behavior of an open Turkish society that would bring about a pluralist and constitutional regime. It also recreated the conditions whereby expansionist institutions and ideological movements could be countered. It was in this way that the Atatürkist principle of laïcism brought a rational and humanistic thought system, which is a prerequisite for the establishment and maintenance of a modern, democratic society in Turkey.

While Atatürk's progressive reforms were designed to bring society up to a modern level of civilization, they were opposed by advocates of the old order who sought to impose their reactionary views on society under the guise of religion. Because the same groups had opposed reform movements under the Ottoman Empire, Atatürk had the advantage of experience in implementing laïcism in Turkey. Thus, during the Atatürk era, state and religion were separated but religion remained under the supervision of the state. The individual was free with respect to faith and worshipping God. However, certain measures were taken through the Turkish Criminal Code to prevent the interference of religion in the affairs of state and society.

What Atatürk had to say about development based on reason and science, and divesting Islam of meaningless beliefs and fanaticism, clarifies the society-oriented understanding of the Revolution.

> The aim of the revolution that we have carried out and are continuing to carry out is to make the people of the Turkish Republic completely modern and accordingly, to create a civilized society having both form and content. The underlying principle of our revolution is this. It is essential that ideas that do not accept this reality be wiped out. Up till now, there have been those espousing these ideas who have eaten away at and numbed the brain of the nation. No doubt the meaningless beliefs making up these ideas will be completely thrown out. As long as they are not removed, it will be impossible for the light of reality to illuminate the brain.
>
> ....
>
> To beseech the dead for assistance is disgraceful for a civilized society.
>
> Gentlemen and O nation, know that the Republic of Turkey cannot be the country of sheiks, dervishes, disciples and members of sects. The most correct -the most genuine- sect is the sect of civilization.
>
> ....
>
> We take our strength from knowledge and science and walk along their path. We recognize nothing else. The aim of tekkes is to make people lose rational balance and become stupid. Nonetheless, the people have decided to not lose their rational balance and not become stupid.[168]

Hence, the leader of the Revolution is attempting to direct society to embrace reason and laïcism.

Through laïcism, the positions deemed necessary in administration, policy, education and the life of society and the state are freed from the influence and monopoly of religion and religious codes. The functions of the state and those of religion are kept distinct from one another. Reason and science occupy a supreme position in the state and society. People have religious freedom; the state cannot discriminate on the basis of religious belief. No matter what their beliefs are, people have to respect one another. Religion is a social institution; it is the idea of spiritual faith. But it has no legitimate role to play in shaping the life of the state or society. Contrary to what some would want to be believed, laïcism is not antagonistic toward religion. The history books everywhere are replete with accounts of the misery suffered by societies, the wars and conflicts during eras dominated by religious worldview and religious institutions. In contrast to the religious reform accomplished in the West, it is impossible to ignore the stubborn fanatical opposition of the Ulema and predominantly religious sectors to reforms in the area of technology during the period of increasing decline of the Ottoman Empire. The society, nation and state will be administered and guided through reason. The absolutely essential principle of the Turkish Revolution was laïcism. Mustafa Kemal touched upon the importance of laïcism when he said, "the truest guide in life is science." At the same time, the principle of laïcism necessitated the dominance of reason and science for the implementation of the other principles.

The Atatürkist system of thought embraces the nation-state and works toward the legitimization of its goals. It rejects a political structure in which Islam is superior to the state and is beyond its control. The Atatürkist perspective, which holds that sovereignty belongs to the people and the nation, and the Islamic one, which considers genuine legitimate authority to be the authority that reflects the will of God, are contradictory. In Atatürkism, the authority of the laïc Republic is legitimate while Islam sees authority as being derived from the "religious congregation" or "religious community." The Atatürkist view is based on the nation and its sovereignty. On the other hand, Islamic thought demands subordination to a religious state authority. Atatürkism considers the authority of the laïc Republic, which is founded on the sovereignty of the nation, as legitimate. Islamic thought stresses religious "unity." In contrast, it is national "unity" that is emphasized by the Atatürkist perspective.

When examining the subject of laïcism, it is necessary to make a distinction between traditions and traditionalism. Traditions are the building blocks of the culture of a nation. They can be constructive in bringing about change from place to place and from time to time in various societies. Atatürk wanted to stress his aspiration of revitalizing "Turkish traditions" and "Turkish culture" when he spoke of Turkism as "a great forgotten civilization." Traditionalism, on the other hand, performs a function of being closed to innovation and constructiveness. Because of the contradiction between the Atatürkist laïc perspective and the politically motivated Islamic one, while laïcism was being implemented, the Islamic institutions giving rise to this contradiction were abolished. In fact, within the principle of laïcism, there was an appeal for the "nationalization" of religion. Laïcism once again brought to the agenda the issue of tolerance, which had for centuries been a component of Ottoman society, and which is an important requirement for the functioning of a democratic order.

The Atatürkist principle of laïcism has been a fundamental factor of Turkish modernization. Through its principle of laïcism, Kemalist Turkey sought to substitute rational calculation in place of traditional calculation in the making of decisions.

In view of all the above-mentioned facts, the Atatürkist principle of laïcism gives us an important insight into the nature of Atatürkism and its commitment to full modernization. Kemal Atatürk's description of the Turkish Revolution, which is given below, provides us with more information about the relationship between the Kemalist principles of laïcism, nationalism and the Turkish Revolution:

> What is the Turkish Revolution? This Turkish Revolution, an expression that includes the reversal of the system of Government, means a fundamental transformation. Our present Constitution has become the most perfect, abolishing those old forms that have lasted for centuries. The common bond that the nation has now found between individuals and communities for its general welfare and existence has changed the old forms and nature, which for centuries had existed. This means that the nation has united as individuals instead of being united by religion and as adherents of sects; now they are held together only by the bond of Turkish nationality. The nation has accepted as a principle an irrefutable fact that science and means are the source of life and strength in the field of international competition and only in modern civilization can these be found.[169]

f) Revolutionism-Reformism

Modernization is consciously oriented toward innovation and reform. As a modernizing "ideology," Atatürkism is receptive to innovation and assumes the ongoing movement toward it as its principle. This is the principle of Revolutionism-Reformism.

In order to maintain the validity and efficacy of, and preserve and develop the efforts to achieve a modern level of civilization through the principle of Revolutionism-Reformism, Atatürkism demanded the assumption of responsibility for progressive reforms. Additionally, it called for the formulation of new radical reforms and solutions when confronted by new exigencies.

Revolutionism-Reformism was instituted so as to engender and maintain a dynamic progressive worldview and to prevent the reification, stagnation, obsolescence, loss of function and the backwardness of society. Just as Toynbee emphasized, it was not interest with the "old" but rather the "new" or the "future" that characterized the essence of the Atatürk movement.[170]

Atatürk believed that it was not only the expansionist powers that were responsible for the backwardness of Turkey. He also attributed it to poor Ottoman administration and the failure of the Turkish nation to keep up with Western developments. Dodd, stressing the same view, had this to say: Concerning the principle of Revolutionism-Reformism, it can be said that Atatürk held Turks themselves, and not the expansionist powers, responsible in great measure for the backward state of Turkey.[171]

It is not just to ensure modernization that the society, political system and political culture have to be receptive and committed to change but also to sustain the continuity of the modern existence. It is the Atatürk movement and especially its principle of Revolutionism-Reformism that were able to bring this about.

There is yet another characteristic of the principle of Revolutionism-Reformism that needs to be emphasized. Atatürkist Revolutionism-Reformism rejects oppression and tyranny. Within Atatürkism is the aspiration for and belief in a peaceful and democratic Revolutionism-Reformism.

The principle of Revolutionism-Reformism carries with it an understanding that new institutions and systems of thought, through the realization of progressive reforms in Turkey, would replace the old ones that served to undermine the development of the country. Moreover, that the progress of Turkey would be maintained consciously and with determination. The aim of the Atatürk Revolution was not simply the transformation of Turkey into a modern, democratic society. At the same time, it was the on-going preservation of this development. Atatürkism is not a stagnant system of thought. The principle of Revolutionism-Reformism provided Atatürkism the flexibility it needed to ensure the independence and modernization of Turkey and to create the indivisible unity of the country and nation over time, without undermining the foundations of open society.

Atatürkist Revolutionism-Reformism is the principle through which the Turkish Revolution and its principles of revolutionary reform are protected from dogmatism and manage to survive in the face of new developments - both present and in the future. The greatest obstacle to modernization is the increasing dogmatism of revolutions - the growing inability of its principles to meet the challenges of new developments. Dynamic revolutions are those that will have the wherewithal to survive by maintaining continuity along with change. Society is a living, breathing phenomenon. By its very nature, it is subject to change and development. Stagnation is an anathema to modern ways of thinking and viewing the world. Atatürkism is at once both dynamic and national in orientation. What protects it from dogmatism, maintains its vitality and keeps it from falling by the wayside is its principle of Revolutionism-Reformism.

Revolutionism-Reformism is preservation of the accomplished reforms while at the same time being committed to new reforms whenever possible. Nevertheless, since the measures taken to realize this radical reform may not be sufficient, this principle is also dedicated to the carrying out of other changes required to achieve a modern level of civilization. These developments are ones that ensure that the society remains modern amid other societies in an era undergoing transformation and development. Specifically, the attainment and maintenance of "equality" in a developing and changing society is buttressed by the dynamic content and goals of the principle of Revolutionism-Reformism.

The principle of Reformism-Revolutionism of the ideology of Atatürkism was committed to Turkish modernization then and in the future. Reformism-Revolutionism was in reality a commitment to the necessity of self-renewal of Turkish society. This was because a society that was capable of self-renewal would not be stagnant and would be able to maintain its modern character. The history of the Ottoman Empire showed how a powerful state would decline if it did not keep abreast with new developments. Writing about Turkey in the late thirties, August Ritter von Kral states, "The new domestic policy includes a healthy revolutionism as regards Turkish life... This conception of revolutionism, which is simply a form of natural evolution, implies that man - knowing well the transitory nature of things half achieved - must continually strive after improvement and progress in his national and social life."[172] In short, the principle of Reformism-Revolutionism meant first, the protection of the principles of the 1920 Revolution and second, the realization of a modern Turkish state. Third, it meant a continuing employment of reformist, radical, and revolutionary policies to maintain the modern character of the Turkish state.

Atatürkism has retained its reformist-radical nature through its principles of Reformism-Revolutionism. This has prevented the freezing of this system of thought and it has enabled it to grow with the times.

In summary, it can be stated that among the six principles of Atatürkism, two stand out as having been of particular importance in the retention of the dynamic quality of this system of thought. These two are the principles of Reformism-Revolutionism and laïcism. This is because it is they that give the other four principles not only a chance for development but also a definite commitment to development. Moreover, it is they that help to maintain the open character of this system of thought. Finally, it is they that prevent this system of thought from being an ideology of the *status quo* by keeping it committed to a continuing process of modernization.

4. Atatürkism and the Atatürk Paradigm of Modernization

The fundamental principles and characteristics of the Atatürk paradigm of modernization began to emerge during the War of Independence. Atatürk's Great Speech, which provides an account of the War of Independence and the reasons for it, begins with the sentence "In the year 1919, on the 19th day of May, I arrived in Samsun." "Even before leaving Istanbul, we had decided to implement what we had thought about as soon as we set foot on Anatolian soil in Samsun."[173] The goal that he had set was "to establish an independent Turkish nation-state based on national sovereignty."[174] "The most powerful idea upon which this decision was based was the existence of the Turkish nation as a respectable and honorable nation." "And this could only be achieved through complete independence." "Complete independence is complete independence and freedom in monetary, judicial, economic and military matters, as well as all other ones." "If in any one of these areas, independence is absent, this means that in the true sense of the term, both the nation and the country are devoid of independence."[175]

With this decision and idea, Atatürk, would have to cultivate, little-by-little, step-by-step, the "great faculty for development inherent within the nation, carried in its sub-conscience like a national secret."[176]

Atatürkism grew out of the Turkish War of Independence. While on the one hand, it was opposed to the expansionist, imperialist foreign powers, it was also against the administrative leaders of the Empire who had collaborated with these foreign powers. It began to take shape with the victorious conclusion of the War of Independence.

Thus, there was opposition to expansionism in Atatürkism right from the beginning. The Atatürk Revolution rejects personal sovereignty in society. Sovereignty in Ottoman society resided in the Sultan, which had become reinforced, entrenched and legitimized by a 600-year-long Empire. Moreover, the Sultan was not simply an administrative sovereign but also a religious leader. He was the leading representative of all Moslems in the world of God. This religious leadership made the Sultan even more powerful.

From the very beginning of the Turkish War of Independence, national sovereignty had been adopted in place of personal sovereignty. A movement in which the nation participated emerged; the people of Anatolia were organized politically for the War of Independence. Under the administration of the Society for the Defense of Rights of Anatolia and Roumelia, it became a national movement, one based on national will. This movement was not religiously oriented. It was as much a laïc movement as the Turkish War of Independence was a national one.

The goal of the Turkish War of Independence was two-fold: one was to expel the enemy beyond the delineated national borders. The other was to create a state and society that was completely independent in every way, economically, culturally, politically, administratively, commercially, judicially and militarily - in effect, in everything.

Thus, Atatürkism is a system of thought that aims at a nationalist, laïc and completely independent state. Just as it rejects exploitative economic and commercial relations, it rejects ideologies that are contrary to national independence and national sovereignty.

The Atatürkist system of thought has its origins in the conditions that presented themselves during the Turkish War of Independence. However, it must be emphasized that the goal of that War was not simply to repel the Western imperial powers. It was, at the same time, the first step taken toward a restructuration of society and state based on Western positivism, as well as Western pluralist, liberal democracy.

Reaching a modern level of civilization would be possible through changing the structure of Turkish society. The components and objectives of the principles laid out by Atatürkism designed to transform the structure of society and create a modern society and state can be summarized as follows:

The form of government sought after for society was that of Western democracy. This was specified as "Republicanism." it contains within it the notion of the sovereignty of the people. According to this administrative perspective, there is no room for the sovereignty of class, group, family, or person. The first principle is this.

The second principle is nationalism. Atatürkism considers everyone Turkish who lives within the same national borders, who believes in the same destiny, and who shares the ideals and the same national consciousness. This nationalism is not racist, aggressive or expansionist. It is laïc. Moreover, it respects the existence of other nations. It sees all nations in the world as belonging to a community that has rights and responsibilities simply by virtue of their being human and a nation. Because of this, they all have dignity and respectability. It opposes the exploitation and domination by nations of other nations whose states are weak and whose societies have not yet gone through nation-building. It is in this way that nationalism acquired humanistic and universal dimensions in Atatürkism.

Through these two main ideas, e.g., Republicanism and Nationalism, a thorough transition to a modern state and society would be accomplished. What was, and would be, the means with which this would happen? Atatürkist thought produced the other principles that needed to be implemented in order for development and modernization to occur. What would be put into effect were "Populism," "Etatism," "Laïcism," and Revolutionism-Reformism." What are these principles and what are their objectives?

Just as nationalism was opposed to the exploitation, oppression and domination of the powerless by the powerful within the community of nations, so too was the principle of populism against the oppression of the weak by the strong in society. Atatürkism is against the domination of a class, group or family over other classes, groups and families within a country. In every society, those living through their labor are in the majority. All they have is work. This cannot be used without proper compensation. Initiatives and privileges that are not in the interest of the majority of the people cannot be allowed. Laws and policies of the state must be people-oriented. Administratively and economically, populism gives priority to those who earn a living through their own labor.

Atatürkism believes that reaching the goal of being modern is the prime responsibility of the state. Without making fundamental changes in society, rights created on paper cannot effectively be used by the masses. By getting involved in the economy in the capacity of both as organizer and operator, the state will direct the economy in the interests of the entire country and its people and bring about fundamental changes in the infrastructure of society.

There is no opposition in Atatürkism to private enterprise. Nevertheless, the state is opposed to development based on the exploitation of the people and the material resources of the country that results from capitalist demands of private enterprise that have foreign support. Through its role as organizer and operator, the state will prevent the exploitation of both the people and the country. It will also work in the interests of the great mass of people in the distribution of income and in the sharing of the wealth created in the country.

Atatürkism is laïc in orientation. In every practice, in every area of the life of society and state, the criterion will be reason and science. There is no place for religious codes and atavistic traditions in the administration of the state. The affairs of the world and those of religion are separate matters. Everyone has freedom of religious belief. No one can be censured on account of his religious belief. Nevertheless, in addition to this, the state does not recognize religious privileges or the acquisition of influence in the life of society and the state of religious or sectarian powers.

Atatürkism is not a dogmatic system of thought. Society is seen as a living entity that undergoes change, develops, and encounters new demands in light of new conditions and feels the need for solutions, accordingly. Atatürkism refers to the innovation that comes with this change as "Revolutionism-Reformism." This is the principle that keeps Atatürkism from becoming obsolete and dogmatic. Rigid, unchanging rules that are thought of being correct and valid for all time cannot possibly keep up with the new developments, new demands and requirements that crop up with social development and change. Therefore, ideology must shy away from restrictions that will make it obsolete. Through the principle of "Revolutionism-Reformism," the Atatürk Revolution acquired the characteristic of an on-going, progressive transformation. However, it ought to be kept in mind that although the principle of Revolutionism-Reformism commits Atatürkism to continuing change, Atatürkism will not compromise on the laïc basis of political authority nor on the fact that the Turkish state is an indivisible whole comprising its territory and people.

Given the conditions and exigencies of the era, Atatürkism is a system of thought and action that emphasizes Revolutionism-Reformism. And while Atatürkism has not been able to attain all of the goals that it has laid out for Turkey, it has created a milieu in which its principles continue to play a constructive and guiding role in Turkish society. Its emphasis on progressive reforms based on pragmatic solutions to national problems acts to maintain the dynamism of Revolutionism-Reformism now and in the future.

Atatürkism was born out of the Turkish National Liberation Movement. It guided the radical Turkish Reform Movement of the 1920s and 1930s. Through its ideal of an advanced Turkey, it made continual Reformism-Revolutionism a predominant aspect of Turkish political culture, especially as subscribed to by the modernists in Turkish society.

A summary of the major reforms for which Atatürk was responsible shows how large and varied were the fields they covered: abolition of the Sultanate; abolition of the Caliphate; secularization of education and reforms in the field of education; abolition of the fez; adoption of Western numbers; secularization of the legal system; adoption of European codes of law; laïcization of the Turkish Constitution and thereby of the Turkish State; emancipation of women and the realization of their political and social rights under the law and by the amendments to the Constitution; adoption of the international calendar; adoption of the Latin alphabet; a fuller analysis of Turkish history; reform of the Turkish language; abolition of the titles of Pasha, Bey, Efendi, and others; change of the weekly holiday from Friday to Sunday; adoption of family names; reforms in the economic and agricultural fields; and changes in the basic tenets of Turkish foreign policy as compared to the foreign policy of the Ottoman Empire.

The reforms of Atatürk and Atatürkism aimed at the establishment of a modern Turkish state and society. Atatürkism constituted the ideological basis of this commitment to modernity and the reforms involved the practical application of the principles of this ideology.

The speech which Kemal Atatürk gave in Ankara on the occasion of the tenth anniversary of the Turkish Republic on 29 October 1933 also indicated the intimate relation between Atatürkism and the radical reforms.

> Citizens! We did great things in a short period of time; the greatest of these is the Turkish Republic, which is based on Turkish heroism and on our great Tur-

kish culture. We owe this success to the determined forward march of the Turkish nation, together with the worthy army. We never think that what we have done is enough. We are determined and obliged to accomplish more and greater things. We are going to advance our country to the level of the most prosperous and the most civilized countries of the world. We shall make it possible for our nation to acquire the necessary resources and means for her to live in uniform prosperity. We shall attempt to raise our national culture above the level of contemporary civilization. Therefore, we think and shall continue to think not according to the lethargic mentality of past centuries, but rather according to the concepts of speed and action of our country. As compared to the past, we shall work harder. We shall accomplish greater things in a shorter time. We have no doubt that we shall succeed in them as well. This is because the character of the Turkish nation is worthy and noble; the Turkish nation is industrious; and the Turkish nation is intelligent. It is also because the Turkish nation has been successful in overcoming hardships through national unity and togetherness. Moreover, we will succeed because the torch of the Turkish nation holds in her hand and in her mind while marching on the road of progress and civilization is positive science. I would like to point out with special emphasis that one of the historical characteristics of the Turkish nation, which is a society composed of worthy people, is to appreciate the fine arts and to advance in them as well. Therefore, it is our national ideal to support and to develop the worthy and noble character of the Turkish nation, her industrious quality, her intelligence, her dedication to science, her love of fine arts, and her feeling of national unity always and with every available means and measures.[177]

VII

THE ATATÜRK REVOLUTION: THE INTERPLAY BETWEEN PRINCIPLES AND POLITICAL EXIGENCIES
May 1919 – January 2007

After the defeat of the Ottoman Empire in the First World War, Western powers had sought to divide and control its vast former territory. Turkey was in the position of having to defend its very right to live as an independent country. During the ensuing period of National Struggle (1919-1922), the question for the Turks was no longer the maintenance of the Empire, but the retention of their very homeland. This supreme national crisis rallied people form all social strata to its defense. The National Struggle made patent the political and legal boundaries of the Turkish homeland. The establishment of the Republic and the reforms of Atatürk followed . All these events were instrumental in the defining of the national identity of Turkey. The question, however, of how to achieve this sense of national identity in the minds of the rural masses was to be an important task that largely lay in the future.

The course of modernization undertaken by the Atatürk Revolution in its about 84 years of existence has not been without its difficulties. Based on the principles of creating national unity, establishing authority, and ensuring equality, the Atatürk Revolution has frequently encountered serious obstacles -both political and economic. Particularly after the death of Atatürk, due to the strengthening of institutions and value judgments of traditional society, which were counter-revolutionary, the Revolution at times had to implement policies that were at odds with modernization, thus losing momentum and even at times coming to a standstill. The failure of the political system to adequately address the issue of equality not only contributed to an undermining of national unity, but also resulted in a weakening of authority. Nevertheless, compared to other societies attempting to modernize, the Atatürk Revolution clearly has had greater longevity, has experienced fewer difficulties, and has been much more effective and successful.

The so-called "developing" countries of today have experienced a similar phenomenon. They, too, have had to overcome a number of impediments to modernization, not the least of which is economic development. Naturally, this involves the issue of equality. However, if transition is made to a pluralist political system without first eliminating the political, social, religious, and cultural elements of traditional society, the solution of problems associated with modernization becomes even more challenging. A liberal democratic parliamentary regime necessarily demands the lifting of restrictions on political freedoms. Yet, those restrictions are the very ones needed to keep traditional forces in check. This dilemma is one shared by both Turkey and other developing countries.

Turkey's attempt to break with an archaic socio-political regime came in the form of the 1920 Revolution. Its leadership in the hands of the modernists, the Revolution undertook the establishment of the Republic, which it accomplished in 1923. Under the guidance of Kemal Atatürk, the revolutionary elite was able to achieve complete control of the political apparatus of the state. Fully committed to modernization, they embarked upon a program of reforms that would come to form the basis for all future conflict between the powers supporting the Revolution and reactionary ones intent on turning back the clock.

Setting the stage for the Atatürk Revolution had been the defeat of the Ottoman Empire and the Sultan's collaboration with the forces of occupation. While the Sultan's government had attempted to undermine and discredit the Independence movement, the National Struggle was successful in discrediting allegiance to Empire, Ottomanism, and Sultanate - thus reversing the tables. A series of events served to seal the coffin of the dispossessed Empire: The Republic of Turkey was proclaimed in 1923. The Caliphate was abolished in 1924, and in 1928, an amendment to the Constitution separated religion and state. As a result, the allegiance to Islam was no longer an official policy of the Turkish state. Turkey had become a laïc state, and laïcism has been and still is one of the most fiercely defended principles of the modernists in the Turkish Republic.

Following the establishment of the Republic, the all-embracing program of reforms initiated by Kemal Atatürk in the 1920s involved a change in values and accordingly, a change in basic institutions. The values of Ottomanism and Islamism, were replaced by those of nationalism and laïcism.

Kemal Atatürk's reforms and the ideology of the 1920 Revolution, as expressed by the principles of Atatürkism (Republicanism, Nationalism, Populism, Laïcism, Etatism, and Revolutionism-Reformism), aimed at the rapid and radical change of Turkish society and state in all fields.

The reforms of Atatürk represent a political revolution: a change from the multi-national Empire to the establishment of the nation-state of Turkey and the realization of the national identity of modern Turkey.

The reforms also brought about a cultural revolution through the adoption of a new alphabet, reform of the Turkish language, an emphasis on pre-Islamic Turkish history, as well as a complete laïcization of the Turkish educational system. Atatürk's reforms brought new institutions and new attitudes and values to Turkish nation-building. On a number of occasions, Atatürk stated his belief that Turkey's political development was very much dependent upon the solution of her educational problems. During his Presidency, the Turkish educational system became completely rationalist and laïcist, and it made a significant contribution to Turkey's political development.

The revolutionary elite believed that education would be one of the most important bridges for linking the peasant masses with the urban educated groups. In addition to increasing the number of public schools, Village Institutes were set up in 1940 *in situ* for the training of peasant boys and giriş. However, especially during the Menderes period in the 1950s, the Village Institutes came under attack by the conservative groups as centers of radical or revolutionary ideas and they were abolished. The modernist group, on the other hand, believed that the Institutes were the best centers for training the peasants in the modern skills needed for agricultural development as well as being the best means of integrating the peasant masses into national life. The intra-elite controversy on the pros and cons of the Village Institutes would reach enormous proportions during the early days of the multi-party regime and, in fact, remains a source of contention.

The Atatürk Revolution was also a *nationalist* revolution but Atatürkist nationalism was not based on racist exclusionism. Rather, it was dedicated to the preservation of the independence of the Republic of Turkey as well as to the Republic's political development. It was a nationalism with a social content. It was not only anti-imperialist, but it was also opposed to the rule of a dynasty and of any particular social class over Turkish society. The spirit of nationalism as evidenced in the various documents of the period of the National Struggle was intensified during the Republican era and reached its most articulate definition in article 3 of the 1961 Constitution, which stated "The Turkish state is an indivisible whole comprising its territory and people."

The Atatürk Revolution was also intrinsically a *social* revolution in terms of its content and goals. This was a Revolution led by an elite that was oriented toward the needs and well-being of the people at large. Much of the social and political conflict that were to appear in later decades was the result of attempts to compromise the social content of the Revolution and undermine social justice.

The Atatürk Revolution is often referred to as the Anatolian Revolution. But this has much more than a geographical connotation. The period of National Struggle had rallied people from all social strata round the defense of their homeland. The military battles were fought on Anatolian soil; victory was sealed on Anatolian soil. The political institutions of the Nationalists were established in Ankara, Istanbul was the capital of a dead Empire; Ankara would be the capital of a new state. Ankara, being in the center of Anatolia, was closer to the life of the average person than a cosmopolitan city like Istanbul. Anatolia had revolted against both the Sultan and the forces of occupation. The Istanbul government had become a tool in the hands of the occupation forces. The decision to retain Ankara as the capital of the new Turkish Republic had, therefore, reasons that went far beyond strategic considerations.

Atatürk's reforms brought about a revolutionary change in the status of women through the reception of Western codes of law in Turkey, particularly the Swiss Civil Code.

Although the leadership of the 1920 Revolution had come from the revolutionary elite, peasants had rallied round the cause of independence. Atatürk stated on a number of occasions that the true rulers of Turkey are the peasants. This was actually a goal rather than a reality in Turkey. Although Atatürk aimed at principally broadening the elite cadres that would protect and carry on the reform program, he was convinced that these reforms would bring about a radical change in the social and economic life of the peasant masses. While this was not realized completely in his lifetime, it does not deter from the fact that this was his ultimate goal. In fact, in the official explanation given to the principle of Populism, it was stated that Kemalism was against class privileges and class distinctions and that it recognized no individual, no family, no class and no organization as being above the others. Kemal Atatürk's reform program tried to bring a sense of *dignity* to all citizens through recognition of their importance to the polity. Kemalist ideology was in fact based on the supreme value of Turkish citizenship. A sense of pride associated with this citizenship could give the needed psychological spur to the people to make them work harder and to achieve a sense of unity and national identity.

The Atatürk Revolution is also a *laïcist* revolution. Many of Atatürk's reforms were made to bring about laïcism and still others were realized because laïcism had been achieved. Therefore, Atatürk's reforms basically consisted of a laïcization of the Turkish state and society. Atatürkist laïcism is rationalist and anti-clericist. In fact, laïcism and nationalism are the basic tenets of Kemalism. Over the years, as with social justice, political conflict has emerged repeatedly over the principle of laïcism. The reemergence of political parties, for instance, attempting to repudiate the laïc basis of modern Turkish political institutions and ultimately the laïc basis of the Republic, have been a continual source of political contention.

While social, cultural and political reform was top on the list of priorities for the Atatürkist Revolution, economic considerations were not completely excluded. Atatürk had recognized and indicated early in the life of the Republic that Turkey's complete modernization was very much dependent on economic and technological development.

Thus, the adoption of étatism in the 1930s as a principle for economic development did not result from any basic ideological preparation, but was derived from pragmatic considerations given the existence of certain conditions. Some of the factors that the Revolution had to deal with include: the effect of the Great Depression in the capitalist countries, lack of private capital, lack of technological knowhow, and lack of experienced Turkish businessmen. In addition, historically, Turks favored official careers and looked down upon people engaged in commerce. Even in the Republican period, it took some time before this negative attitude declined. The principle of étatism was interpreted to mean that the state was to regulate the general run of economic activity, and that the state was to engage in areas where private enterprise was not willing to do so, or where private enterprise had proved to be inadequate, or if national interest required it. In the application of the principle of étatism, however, the government emerged not only as the principle source of economic activity but also as the owner of the major industries of the country. Later, étatism was to be abandoned, for the most part, due to the rise of strong economic groups in society who were successful in getting their interests placed on the agenda of political parties, thus complicating even further the political complexion of the country.

One of the most important principles that Atatürk formulated was the principle of Revolutionism-Reformism. This principle meant that Turkey made reforms and that she replaced traditional institutions with modern ones. In other words, traditional concepts and institutions were eliminated and modern ones were adopted. The principle of Revolutionism-Reformism went beyond the recognition of the reforms that were made. Atatürkism is not an ideology of the *status quo*. It is a radical ideology capable of growth with the times. Its principle of Revolutionism-Reformism is what gives it the needed flexibility and power of growth without sacrificing its basic tenets, namely, a dedication to Turkey's independence and modernization.

Throughout the reforms, there had been extensive cultural borrowing from the West. Although the political and economic independence of the Ottoman Empire was grossly violated because of the Capitulations, especially during the nineteenth and the early years of the twentieth centuries, the fact that Turkey was never reduced to colonial status and that she was successful against the West during her National Struggle (1919-1922) had been important psychological preparation for this wholesale cultural borrowing from the West. Added to this were two other important factors. Throughout all the reform periods, Western institutions had been copied. Moreover, it was an indigenous elite, with freedom to decide what to borrow or leave, which made this wholesale cultural borrowing by the revolutionary elite not only acceptable to a growing number of Turkish people, but fiercely defended by this elite as their own. Lewis Thomas says:

> Of course, the factor of imitation is always in the westernizing individual's mind, but it is seldom itself dominant. Instead, the real and complex motivation is frequently so preponderantly patriotic or idealistle or crusading that the Western ideas which the westerner strives to introduce into his own milieu and thereby become important to him simply as 'his own' and certainly are his own in fundamental senses.[178]

The Atatürk Revolution was an attack on the old order. Turkish political development during the Presidency of Atatürk was determined by the modernist group's complete control of the Turkish government and elimination from political life of the upholders of traditional society. The reforms of the Ottoman Empire had reduced the status, but had not eliminated the role of the religious group as a factor in Turkish social and political life. Atatürk's purging of the religious group from active political life was the result of his historical knowledge of the role of this group as an anti-reformist force.

Atatürk aimed at the establishment of those institutions, methods, concepts, and attitudes that would bring Turkey up to the level of the most advanced states of the world in the shortest possible time. Barbara Ward points out:

> It is important to understand from the start what Mustafa Kemal (Atatürk) meant by westernization and modernization. His training and mental formation belonged to the period of Liberal enlightenment. He believed in the inalienable right of the nation to lead a completely independent and sovereign existence. He believed in the rights of men, in the equality of citizens before the law, and in the State as an association to serve their common well-being. He believed reason

and scientific method could create an almost unlimited future of material progress for mankind, that the Western world, through science and industrialism, had discovered the key to this progress, and that if Turkey were to benefit from it, then the Turks, too, would have to apply rational and scientific methods to every sphere of their national life. He believed that 'irrational beliefs' - which virtually meant processes of thought not amenable to scientific proof- were in almost every case hostile to his ideal of progress.[179]

During Atatürk's lifetime, the internal cohesiveness of the modernist elite was made possible not only because of his personality, his fame as a successful General, but principally because of the acceptability of his reform program. Certainly, earlier reform movements had contributed to the Atatürk Revolution. But the Atatürk Revolution had its differences from past Turkish reform periods.

As evidenced in the National Struggle, Kemal Atatürk defined the territorial limits of Turkey and cast aside ideas of the re-establishment of the Empire. Atatürk's reforms, hence, were not resorted to for the maintenance of a polyglot Empire, but for the maintenance of the nation-state of Turkey. Atatürk also rejected Pan-Islamism and Pan-Turkism as totally unrealistic ambitions for Turkey, stating that from then on, Turkey's policies would be guided by purely national interests. Hence, Kemal Atatürk and his revolutionary elite demonstrated very early a degree of realism, a scaling down of ambitions and a kind of political responsibility that was not to be found in the Pan-Turkic ambitions of the Unionists. Atatürk undertook thorough reform in all areas, which put an end to the dualism of institutions and goals that characterized the earlier reform periods. It was in this way that both the reforms of Atatürk and Atatürkism were able to mobilize the Turkish modernist elite, giving it an internal cohesiveness to an extent that had not been possible before in Turkish history.

The Atatürk Revolution had made important political, social, cultural, legal, educational, and economic reforms. Although the Revolution had aimed at it, the social and economic status of the peasant masses had not drastically changed. The implementation of the reforms in terms of the peasant masses had not been very successful. For example, the reasons for the dissolution of the Free Republican Party in 1930 indicated that the reforms had not really reached the peasants. The advent of the multi-party regime made this fact even more evident. On the other hand, during Atatürk's lifetime, the modernist elite grew in numbers and influence. The principle support for Atatürk's reforms still comes from the army officers, civil servants, professors, students and other groups of intellectuals. Members of all these groups are from all social strata and from all geographical areas so that one can state that they are representative of the Turkish nation.

The Republican People's Party was the most important civilian agency of Turkish political development between the years 1923-1950. It was a mass party that aimed at representing all influential elements of the Turkish population. It also tried to assimilate new groups into its cadres - even if, as some have argued, too slowly.

The one-party system was looked upon as a temporary instrument of political modernization. Leading Republicans repeatedly stated that once the reforms had been thoroughly established, a multi-party system would be set up.

After the death of Atatürk in 1938, İsmet İnönü was unanimously elected President of the Turkish Republic. During İnönü's Presidency, there was mounting criticism of the one-party system both in and outside of the Party, especially during the last year of World War II. The Republican People's Party had within its ranks people from all social strata, though certain groups were more predominantly represented. Once the overall excitement of winning the War of Independence; of establishing a Republic; and of going through an intensive period of reforms had begun to fade, the differences of opinion among these people came out into the open. The victory of the Allied Powers over Nazi Germany also contributed to the demands for the establishing of a multi-party regime. Added to these were other important factors. Elite elements which had not been completely assimilated by the Republican People's Party and who had remained politically inactive wanted to put an end to the one-party system. So did the rising Turkish bourgeoisie and some landowners, who were opposed to the Republican People Party's principle of étatism and plans for land reform. In addition, intellectuals saw a multi-party regime as the culmination of the reforms of Atatürk. The years between 1945-1950, which had ushered in such a regime, were characterized by a bitter struggle for power between the Republican People's Party and the opposition groups, especially the Democrat Party.

The reforms of Atatürk and the principles of Atatürkism had emphasized but had not achieved the politicization of the Turkish peasant. With the advent of the multi-party regime in 1945, and the introduction of a direct electoral system based on the already existent universal suffrage, the peasants became active participants in the political life of the country, essentially in the sense of going to the polls and voting for party candidates set before them. The arrival of competitive politics suddenly brought to the peasants hope of the economic betterment of their lives. They thought that through voting for the "right" party their economic expectations would be met. For them, voting had acquired a materialistic connotation.

During the post-1945 multi-party regime, the effectiveness and steadfastness of the R.P.P. with regard to the principles of Laïcism, Etatism, Populism and Revolutionism-Reformism, principles it had so staunchly fought for during the Atatürk era, were lost. In large part, this had much to do with the tendency of the leadership cadre of the party to be concerned with "vote mongering" in the hope of gathering support from the traditional strata of society. But at the same time it was also due, if even to a lesser extent, to their not having embraced the radical reform, movement to the extent that their predecessors had.

Since the peasants constituted nearly 80% of Turkey's total population in 1950, they could largely determine the result of the elections. Although other segments of the population voted for the Democrat Party, the Democrat landslide in the 1950 national election was made possible by the rural vote.

The Republican People's Party lost the 1950 national election. After twenty-seven years, the revolutionary elite was no longer to control the government. Members of a new elite group, especially newly emerged industrialists, lawyers, engineers, landowners and private physicians won seats in the Assembly. These new elite elements were educated, but many were local figures rather than national ones. All this meant a considerable reduction in size of the elite with an official background such as civil servants, retired army officers, judges, and professors.

The new elite, having first discovered the importance of the peasant vote in winning any national election, was willing to make concessions contrary to Atatürk's reform in order to have the continual support of the tradition-oriented peasant masses.

During 1950-1960, the Democrat Party (D.P.) had a great impact on state and society. Determined to acquire seats in the Assembly, the Party maintained a more concessionary orientation than the R.P.P. toward a number of issues in the hope of mustering as many of the votes of the traditional strata of society as possible. The economic policies during this period provided the opportunity for the appearance of a new and powerful group - the commercial and industrial bourgeoisie, which would throw its support to whatever political party afforded the best opportunities for its survival and growth. Another source of backing for the D.P. were the rural village communities. While the interests of these two segments of society were fundamentally and economically contradictory to one another, they both looked to the D.P. as a vehicle through which their interests could be furthered. Peasants, living in the traditional structure of rural village communities; artisans and tradesmen living in the towns and cities, together with the commercial and industrial bourgeoisie constituted a force allied against the Revolution. Due to nepotism, the coalescence of these segments around the governing D.P. led to a reduction in the influence of the civilian and military bureaucracies and the intellectuals on power formation. Quite naturally, this gave rise to a new atmosphere of conflict in society.

New laws pertaining to petroleum and foreign capital reopened the economy to the influence and control of powerful foreign economies - undermining the principle of complete independence that had been so important during the Atatürk Period. Combined with the increasing difficulty of living conditions and economic crises due to rising prices, and the social tensions created by them, political conflict naturally grew even more intense. The enactment of laws restricting freedoms in order to quell the turmoil that inevitably resulted had the contrary effect of instigating greater opposition to the policies of the Menderes government.

As the Menderes government began to employ increasingly dictatorial policies, the Turkish intellectuals, members of the opposition parties, army officers, and the students in their disillusionment became skeptical of the possibility of a peaceful change of power. The modernist elites were alarmed by the Democrat Party's policies, seeing them as regressions from the path of development.

Lack of experience with a multi-party regime, acute tension between the Democrat Party and the Opposition, increasing economic difficulties, violation of Atatürk's reforms, dictatorial measures of the Menderes government to silence criticism of its policies by the Opposition, and attempts by the Menderes government to involve the military on behalf of its policies led to the 27th May 1960 Revolution undertaken by the military. This Revolution was an attempt to reset the course of the Atatürk Revolution from which it had been thrown off due to events developing during the multi-party regime.

Although the 1960 Revolution was not prepared by civilians, the army knew that when it acted, it would have civilian support chiefly from the Republican People's Party, the intellectuals and the students.

The Turkish officer corps is drawn from all segments of the Turkish population and from all geographical regions. In terms of its social origin, it is representative of Turkish society in general, it also represents more than any other group in Turkey, the Kemalist ideology of dedication to Turkey's independence, to Turkish nationalism, and to Turkish political development. In fact, the military has played a crucial role in Turkish modernization ever since the end of the eighteenth century.

The army was kept out of politics by Atatürk and the principle of civilian control of political life was achieved. Atatürk believed that several civilian groups would protect the reforms. But he also was aware that when it came to a showdown with any reemergent reactionary group, the army's stand would make the difference. Therefore, he relied on the army both for the defense of the country and for the protection of the reforms. Hence, the military intervened in 1960 to protect the Turkish state from policies of the Menderes government that they believed violated the reforms of Atatürk and undermined the prestige of the Turkish state.

The 1961 Constitution prepared in the aftermath of the military intervention introduced a new phase in the development of the Turkish political order.

The 1961 Constitution, the second Constitution of the Republic, was dynamic, progressive, pluralist, liberal - placing particular emphasis on both civil and human rights. It also established new political institutions through which these rights would be guaranteed – both within society and in the functioning of the state apparatus. It created new powers representative of the national will to exist alongside the political power.

The freedoms instituted by the 1961 Constitution created new forms of social organization. Together with developing industry, this environment provided the opportunities for the rise of powerful - both quantitatively and qualitatively - labor unions and associations.

Rapid population growth in rural areas and the inability to support a growing population from the income generated through agriculture led to the beginning of rural migration to the cities. The rapid urbanization that resulted from this migration and growing industrialization added new and powerful elements to the simmering political conflict.

This rapid change, along with the rights and freedoms proposed by the Constitution, created new needs and aspirations in society and in individuals. The inability of economic development to adequately address these aspirations and the failure to provide the new political and social institutions demanded by social change led to a swelling of social conflict.

This political climate acted to foment an open debate with respect to what constituted the appropriate means of modernization. While there were, of course, the supporters of the Revolutionism-Reformism proposed by the Atatürkist model, there were also staunch advocates of the Marxist model. Moreover, the establishment of new political parties provided the avenue through which such different views could be expressed. Advocates of various positions used political parties as a means of disseminating their ideas and encouraging support for them within society. The new Constitution had proposed a "mixed economy." The multitude and importance of the responsibilities the Constitution gave to the state naturally meant that there had to be an important role for state entrepreneurship in this mixed economy to guarantee public interest. However, in practice state policies were oriented toward capitalist private initiative and resulted in the external dependence of the industry of the country on foreign loans. This dependency and the foreign debts incurred through it have been growing ever since.

These circumstances compelled the R.P.P. to devise a strategy that would control Marxist schemes and the swing to the left in society. Consequently, the party chose to re-emphasize its commitment to Atatürkism. It assumed for itself a "Left of center" identity, characterized by its orientation to national independence and the Atatürk Revolution.[180]

With the advent of the closing of the D.P. by court order, the Justice Party (J.P. - *Adalet Partisi*) emerged as its heir. The J.P. proved to be a major contender for political power, enabling it to overwhelm the R.P.P. and to hold power for seven years from 1965-1971. A fierce advocate of capitalist development, it derived its electoral support from an alliance of traditional rural powers and the commercial and industrial bourgeoisie. The J.P. was not at all supportive of the 1961 Constitution and was intent on changing it. From the very first time the Constitution was submitted for public referendum, the party took every opportunity to indicate that it would, once it had a sufficient majority of votes, amend it.

In addition to the J.P., two other elements appeared on the political scene during 1961-1971. These were the Marxist, class-based Turkish Labor Party (T.L.P. - *Türkiye İşçi Partisi*) and the religious, sectarian-based National Order Party (N.O.P. - *Milli Nizam Partisi*) and Turkish Unity Party (T.U.P. - *Türkiye Birlik Partisi*).

The National Salvation Party (N.S.P. - *Milli Selamet Partisi*) was a continuation of the N.O.P., which had been closed down by the Constitutional Court. It advocated a "sheriat" regime and argued that only by adopting such a regime, refraining from "Western imitation," and returning to "Islamic principles," could society attain vitality and prosperity. Moreover, it claimed that an international alliance of Moslems could counter the power wielded by capitalism.

The T.U.P., on the other hand, was essentially socialist in terms of its proposed policies and, because of the way in which it sought solidarity with certain segments of society, it was also sectarian.

These two developments, the religious and the sectarian, became influential elements within the ensuing political conflict. Nevertheless, both parties espoused principles that were contradictory to those of modernization and the Atatürk Revolution.

The T.L.P. was a class-based, Marxist party. Receiving support particulary from among the youth and workers in society, it came to exercise influence and control over an assortment of youth and labor organizations.

The political conflict that grew in intensity and severity toward the 1970s increasingly became one of armed conflict -especially with the emergence of Marxist movements- both legal and illegal -in urban and rural areas. Confronted with insurmountable social unrest, the ruling party and Assembly were unable to find a solution, thus precipitating another military intervention -this time on 12 March 1971. This intervention resulted in the amendment of many articles of the Constitution and the instilution of restrictions on certain rights and freedoms. But it did not result in the abolition of the Assembly. What happened at this point in the history of Turkish political development is a clear case of the dilemma spoken of earlier of trying to keep political restrictions to a minimum under a liberal democratic parliamentary regime while at the same time needing to impose such restrictions in order to protect the regime.

With the elections that were held in 1973, Turkey entered yet another phase of its political development. The R.P.P. witnessed an increase in its electoral strength, which enabled it to become the majority party in Assembly. At the same time, however, since it did not have enough seats to form a government single-handedly, it had to form a coalition government. In seeking the support of the religious N.S.R, a party that openly advocated a return to "sheriat," the R.P.P. was put into the incongruous position of having to share political power in the 55th year of the Atatürk Revolution with a party that supported the very regime that that Revolution had abolished over a half century before. This was nearly the equivalent of political "heresy" since the decision to form such an alliance was contrary to the very essence of a political institution that had been the vanguard in the radical reform movement carried out to modernize the country - and to move it away from the kind of regime now advocated by its coalition partner. After this, the N.S.P. became, for some time to come, a "key party" in the formation of future governments. This was an entirely new development for Turkish democracy and the Revolution.

Adding to the on-going political conflict after 1973 were ethnic and "racial" ones. The elections of 1977 gave rise to a new "key party" - the Nationalist Action Party (N.A.P. - *Milliyetçi Hareket Partisi)* - that came to be seen as an advocate of racist ideas and a right-wing authoritarian regime. The error made by the R.P.P. by forming a coalition government with the N.S.P., was repeated by the J.P. when it agreed to form a coalition government with the N.S.P. and the N.A.P. Both coalitions contributed to the strengthening of traditional powers and advocates of a right-wing authoritarian regime since under these coalitions, they were able to get the upper hand in the state bureaucracy.

Through the kindling of religious, sectarian and ethnic divisions and the encouragement of ethnic consciousness, the issues of unity and authority, key concerns of the Atatürk Revolution, once again acquired contemporary significance.

Moreover, the attempts made on the part of Marxist movements to create a nationalist consciousness in ethnic groups were as influential in making the issue of national unity relevant as those efforts waged by religious, sectarian and racist movements.

The increasing transformation of political debate into bloody social conflict and the spread of this discord throughout the country contributed to the weakening of the national unity the Atatürk Revolution had worked so hard to achieve. When conditions reached a point where the political system was no longer able to cope, the military seized power on 12 September 1980.

This intervention is illustrative of the role the Turkish military has played since the founding of the Republic in maintaining the regime embraced by the Atatürkist paradigm of modernization. It was through the success of its army that the Turks were able to emerge triumphant from their War of Independence. Moreover, it is this army that has repeatedly appeared in times of regime crisis to defend the principles of the Atatürk Revolution. In reality it is also true that it is the genuine responsibility of the political system and its political cadre to solve problems stemming from national unity, authority and equality. After the 12th of September, the 1961 Constitution was abolished and a new one put into effect. The 1982 Constitution gave priority to the supremacy of the state and the restriction of political rights of the individual. Political parties had been closed down in 1980. Only later were new ones allowed to be set up in their place. As the re-democratization of society accelerated, the formerly outlawed parties began reappearing in the political arena under new names or with new identities. One of the new parties, which became the dominant party in the elections of 1983 and 1987, was the Motherland Party (M.P. - *Anavatan Partisi).* This conservative party managed to bring together a number of different political persuasions under one umbrella. Another development resulting from the 1982 Constitution, e.g., the imposition of mandatory religious instruction at secondary schools (as religion was thought to be a panacea against the Marxist and Maoist movements) contributed to the strengthening of rightist thought, which made possible the spread and strengthening of groups whose views were contrary to the Atatürk Revolution and the Atatürk paradigm of national modernization.

Although the Turkish military enjoys a progressive tradition, the 12th of September 1980 did not adequately represent this tradition. This intervention gave the green light to the activities of the rightist forces, delimiting the activities of the leftist forces, even those which were moderate and were of a social democratic persuasion. Although in due course of time these restrictions were lifted, the position of the liberal-progressive forces was weakened in the process. The Turkish people have great confidence in the Turkish military. But perhaps this was an important instance whereby that confidence was somewhat shaken. Especially beginning with the 1990s, the Turkish military once again embraced its progressive heritage. However, it should be pointed out that while the top echelon of the military, who actually directed the 1980 intervention, was conservative, the main body of the army retained its progressive, Atatürkist heritage.

The M.P. lost the 1991 election and because no single party emerged with a sufficient number of the votes to form a government by itself, a coalition was formed between the True Path Party (T.P.P. - *Doğru Yol Partisi*) and the Social Democrat Populist Party (S.D.P.P. - *Sosyal Demokrat Halkçı Parti*). The Republican People's Party (R.P.P. - *Cumhuriyet Halk Partisi*), after a long and difficult struggle, united with the S.D.P.P. in February 1995, retaining the R.P.P. name. It was in this way that the T.P.P.-R.P.P. coalition government was put together. The 25 December 1995 elections also failed to produce a party that had the majority of seats in Parliament and it took quite a long time to establish a new government. In March 1996, the M.P.-T.P.P. coalition government was formed, and it was called MotherPath *(AnaYol)* only to be replaced in June 1996 by a coalition between the Welfare Party (W.P. - *Refah Partisi*), which was in effect a continuation of the defunct National Salvation Party, and the T.P.P., called WelfarePath *(RefahYol)*. This coalition government received a vote of confidence on 8 July 1996. Principally because of the activities of its Welfare Party wing and the anti-laïc discourse of its official members, the national and laïc foundation of the state began to be jeopardized. However, actions countering this threat were taken by a great many civic organizations, along with the National Security Council, an institution having constitutional authority, in support of Atatürk, Atatürkism and modernity. What is crucial to emphasize in this context are what are known as the "28th of February Resolutions," which consisted of positions taken and proposals proffered by the National Security Council on 28 February 1997. Included within these resolutions was the call for compulsory eight-year education, a decision that contributed to the strengthening and spread of national laïc education, thus providing a new impetus to the Atatürkist system of thought.

With the resignation of Prime Minister Necmettin Erbakan in June 1997, the Chairman of the M.P., Mesut Yılmaz, was asked by the President to form a new government. The resulting ANASOL-D government consisted of the M.P., the Democratic Left Party (D.L.P. - *Demokratik Sol Parti*) and the Democratic Turkey Party (D.T.P. - *Demokratik Türkiye Partisi*). However, the anti-laïc politicking could not be adequately stopped. There was extensive evidence, for example, that the Welfare Party was actively working toward undermining the laïcism upon which the Republic was based. The party was subsequently closed by a decision of the Constitutional Court, which was announced in the *Resmi Gazete* on 22 February 1998. However, this was followed in a few days by the formation of a new party, the Virtue Party (V.P. - *Fazilet Partisi*), by former members of the Welfare Party. As a result of the interpellation in Parliament held on 25 November 1998, the Mesut Yılmaz-led government resigned, initiating a search for a new government. On 11 January 1999, the fourth Ecevit government was established. The general elections held on 18 April 1999 failed to produce a party with the requisite number of votes to form a government without having to enter into coalition with other parties. What resulted was a compromise: a coalition between the Democratic Left Party (D.L.P. - *Demokratik Sol Parti*), N.A.P. and M.P. formed the basis for the fifth Ecevit-led government. The R.P.P., which had played a pioneering role in the formation of the Turkish Republic, was unable to receive even the minimum number of votes to enter the Assembly. Four reasons have been given for the electoral failure of the R.P.P.: the intense factionalization within the party; the failure to appear before the electorate with a credible program; the move by the party away from the national-revolutionary course; and the presence of certain persons in the upper echelons of the party who did not accept or who did not want to accept the six principles of Atatürk and also of the party.

After the term of office of President Süleyman Demirel came to an end, Ahmet Necdet Sezer, President of the Constitutional Court, was elected as the 10th President of Turkey in May 2000.

In the course of 2001 a number of new amendments were made to the Constitution of 1982 for the purpose of its further democratization. On the 22nd of June 2001, the Virtue Party was closed down by a decision of the Constitutional Court. However, on the 20th of July, 2001, the Felicity Party (F.P. - *Saadet Partisi*) and on the 14th of August, 2001, Justice and Development Party (J.D.P. - *Adalet ve Kalkınma Partisi*) were established - both being offshoots of the Virtue Party.

Since its establishment, the 57th Government, the Government of Bülent Ecevit, confronted a number of serious economic problems. The economic policies as designated by the IMF did not help to improve the economic situation. Great many companies closed down. Unemployment mounted. A devastating earthquake in 1999 accentuated further the economic hardships. On the other hand, there was considerable friction between the parties which constituted this coalition. This friction was in particular between the N.A.P. and the M.P., especially on policies regarding the EU and the IMF. Corruption and nepotism decreased further the credibility of the coalition government. It proved to be a fragile coalition. The growing restlessness of the political scene led to the decision of the government to hold new elections.

The elections took place on 3rd of November, 2002. Except for J.D.P. and the R.P.P. none of the other parties received enough number of votes to be represented in the Grand National Assembly. The Turkish voters "voted out" all the parties which were represented in the Assembly. In a sense the people showed their protest to the policies of the coalition government which did not find a solution to their growing poverty. People wanted a change. Of the forty million voters only thirty million went to the polls. J.D.P. received 34.28% of the votes and the R.P.P. received 19.39% of the votes. Due to the terms of the Electoral Law, with such a percentage the J.D.P. was able to get sixty percent of the seats; namely, 363 seats in the Assembly. The R.P.P. received only 178 seats and the independents received 9 seats in the Assembly. Hence, the J.D.P. and the R.P.P. received altogether 55% of the votes. However, 45% of the votes are currently not represented in the Assembly.

One cannot solely blame the strict condition, a threshold, in the Electoral Law, that in order to be represented in the Assembly a party must receive at least 10% of the votes. Through their voting the voters showed their anger and disappointment regarding mounting poverty and unemployment. On the other hand, proliferation of parties of the left as well as of the right is also responsible for the outcome of this election.

The J.D.P. must be aware of the fact, that at most 10% of those who voted for this party did so because of their religious convictions. The rest of the votes this party received can be labelled as "protest" votes, protest of the policies of the 57th government.

The R.P.P. received far less than the expected votes. Some people who have traditionally voted for the R.P.P. did not do so mainly because of the following reasons: the moving away of this party from the Party's long-time commitment to the "social state" and its embracing to a large extent the policies of the IMF; and the leniency of the Party towards laïcism as shown by its endorsing the candidacy of a person who has insisted all along that the chanting of prayers must be in Arabic. In the Atatürk era, the R.P.P. had been in the forefront of the laïcization of Turkish state and society, including the move towards ensuring that the chanting of prayers would be in Turkish.

Recep Tayyip Erdoğan, Chairman of the J.D.P. could not become a candidate in the 3 November, 2002, elections due to his criminal record. Erdoğan had been convicted because of his radical Islamic statements which violated Article 312 of the Turkish Penal Code. Hence, Ahmet Necdet Sezer, the President of Turkey, appointed Abdullah Gül, the Vice-Chairman of the J.D.P., to form the new government. As a result, on 16 November, 2002, the 58th government was formed and Abdullah Gül became the new Prime Minister of Turkey.

As soon as the results of the elections were officially announced Erdoğan and his supporters initiated efforts to remove the legal barriers to Erdoğan's becoming candidate as a deputy. And amending Articles 67, 76 and 78 of the Constitution opened the way for Erdoğan's candidacy. However, a great number of people; especially those from the legal profession, including the President of Turkey, were critical of these amendments contending that you cannot amend laws, let alone a Constitution, to meet personal needs.

The Supreme Election Board cancelled the elections in the province of Siirt due to some irregularities at the time of the elections. After the resignation of the deputies from the province of Siirt, the need to hold new elections in that province arose. It was decided to hold elections in Siirt on March 9, 2003, giving Erdoğan a chance to announce his candidacy from that province. If elected as a deputy, he would then have assured his Premiership.

The controversies regarding the 3rd of November elections have continued. On the 22nd of January, 2003, the Constitutional Court ruled that although his name appeared on the ballot, for some legal reasons Erdoğan was not technically the Chairman of the J.D.P. at the time of the elections. And Erdoğan was elected to the Chairmanship of the Party on the 23rd of January 2003. On the 24th of January 2003, the Youth Party (Y.P. - *Genç Parti*) and the Turkish Labor Party (T.L.P. - *Türkiye İşçi Partisi*) appealed to the Supreme Election Board for the annulment of the 3rd of November elections claiming that the appearance of Erdoğan's name on the ballot misled the people and violated the principle of honesty so essential to the holding of just elections. On the 25th of January 2003, the Supreme Election Board rejected this appeal on the contention that the ruling of the Constitutional Court could not be retroactive. Hence, the way was opened for Erdoğan's candidacy in the March 9, 2003, election. And Erdoğan was elected as deputy from Siirt. In the days following his election Abdullah Gül's 58th government resigned. Erdoğan became Prime Minister and formed the 59th government.

The J.D.P.'s orientation is Islamic. Its becoming the ruling party is a first in the history of the Turkish Republic. Hence, this party had a great responsibility to show that it is embracing the principles and the values of a modern, laïc state. However, as the policies of the J.D.P began to unfold it became clear that such was not the case. During the course of its over 4-year performance the J.D.P. has demonstrated that it has not come to terms with the institutions, principles and values of the laïc, democratic Turkish Republic. The government has beeen and continues to be at odds with such institutions of the state such as the Universities, the judiciary, the armed forces, and the Presidency. All this has made it necessary once again to focus upon the meaning and aim of the Turkish Revolution and *Islam and Laïcism in Contemporary Turkish Society.*

Instead of trying to solve the problems related to the dire economic situation in Turkey, the J.D.P. is busying itself with minor matters such as the wearing of *"türban"*, a special way of covering the head with a scarf. *Türban* has become a symbol of political Islam. State laws, including the decisions of the Constitutional Court and the Council of State, rule that while people are free to wear the *türban* in their private life, they cannot do so at work in public institutions and at schools and universities. This decision of the Turkish Constitutional Court and the Turkish Council of State was upheld by (AİHK) the European Court of Human Rights. Leyla Şahin, a citizen of Turkey, went to the European Court of Human Rights suing Turkey on grounds that she was barred from attending the University because she was wearing a *türban*. In its decision, dated June 2004, European Court of Human Rights unanimously ruled that Turkey had made the right decision to ban the wearing of *türban* in public places; thus, safeguarding the laïc nature of political authority. In its decision, the European Court of Human Rights further pointed out that laïcism was indispensable for the preservation of the democratic system in Turkey.

It is unfortunate that in the 21st century the question of *türban* is still on the agenda of the J.D.P. The President of Turkey and the Chief of the General Staff, including the spokesmen for several civilian institutions and academics have felt the need to reiterate Turkey's commitment to laïcism, to the values and principles of Atatürkism; in short, to the Turkish Enlightenment. On various occasions President Ahmet Necdet Sezer has declared that all attempts to violate the democratic, laïc basis of the Turkish Republic shall be steadfastly and firmly resisted.

Türban is being used as a protest symbol to laïcism, to Republican values and to the Atatürk Revolution. It is a well-known fact that radical changes of political and social transformation do not necessarily follow a unilinear line. At times and occasionally there may be attempts at complete or partial reversions to the old order. Turkey's case is no exception to this general phenomenon. In contemporary Turkey radical change is still represented by the Atatürk reforms with direct implications for Turkish political life and Turkish constitutionalism in general and Turkish education in particular.

After the successful termination of the War of Independence (1919-1922), the task of the Kemalists was to transform Turkey into a modernized, industrialized, and secularized nation-state. The Kemalists did not feel the need to maintain elements of traditional culture as has been the case with most nationalist leaders of developing

countries. Religion was not used to mobilize the masses in Turkey as
has been and is still the case in such countries as Iran and Libya. The
Kemalist idea of a national community ran counter to the Islamic
conception of a community which is essentially religious. For this reason education was not looked upon by the 1920 revolutionaries, the
Kemalists, as a means of preserving traditional order but as a means
of its total transformation because the inherent characteristics of Ottoman culture were viewed as impediments to nation-building, to the
assertion and development of Turkish culture.

The Islamic establishment opposed efforts at modernity during the
Ottoman Empire and took an adverse stand to the National Liberation Movement, 1919-1922. These historical realities facilitated the
integration of the Turkish people around a laïcist, nationalist platform during the Atatürk period. Hence, during the Atatürk era Otto-
man-Islamic legacy was replaced by a national, laïc political culture
and Islamists were drawn into political inactivism. Since the advent
of multi-party politics in 1946 and especially since the 1980's Islam
has made a comeback, but it still seems not to be interested in a reconciliation with the modernizing reforms of Atatürk, in essence, Islamic idea of legitimacy negates both laïc legitimacy and laïc authority. As is widely noted and accepted, political modernization involves rationalization of authority, the replacement of a great many traditional, religious, and ethnic political authorities by a single, secular,
and national political authority.

The religious right in contemporary Turkey has not yet come to
terms with the principles, goal and the meaning of the Atatürk Revolution. Among the various Islamic groups an aversion to Kemal
Atatürk can be easily discerned; the modernizing, laïcizing policies of
the Atatürk era, and Turkey's westernization processes during his
Presidency are viewed as having been contradictory to the interests
of Islam.

It is important to remember that Atatürk's laïcist policies did not
oppose religion nor did they suppress religion. These policies simply
disestablished religion. These policies kept religion out of state affairs. One should not overlook the fact that it was through the implementation of these policies that Turkish women were enfranchised

and received equal rights with men under the law. As Bernard Lewis says: "Atatürk put political rights for women in the forefront of his program."[181]

The essence of the matter is *whether Turkey is to be the laïc Turkish Republic or the Islamic Turkish Republic?* There are now increased attempts at making dispassionate, objective analysis of the role of Islam in Turkish society. but one cannot observe a commensurate satisfactory objectivity on the part of Islam towards its role in Turkish society. To begin with Islamic groups continue to make statements and announce policies which are not compatible with the secular laïc culture of modern Turkey nor with the requirements and performance of a modern laïc, democratic state. Furthermore, they have not abandoned their commitment to a religious-oriented educational system. Islam in Turkey has to accept the reality of the Atatürk Revolution and Atatürk principles which enjoy wide-spread acceptance and which constitute the very essence of the Turkish Enlightenment.

Not for political/and or tactical purposes, but in reality Islam in Turkey needs to rethink of its values and role in a modern society. *Islam in Turkey has to decide whether it wants to be the protagonist of reaction or of enlightened conservatism.* Their choice is likely to have a great impact upon the course of constitutional and political developments in Turkey.

What is of immediate interest to us, however, is the organization and spread of political perspectives opposed to those embodied by the Atatürk Revolution. It is important not to forget that the defining characteristic of the Turkish Republic is its being a laïc, democratic, national state in which the rule of law prevails. This is what distinguishes it from the Ottoman state regime.

The Ottoman order had been a religious one based on the amalgamation of the Caliphate and the Sultanate. The Sultan was the head of state of all the *millet*s within the Empire, and in the capacity of Caliph, he was the protector and religious leader of Moslems all over the world. In complete contrast to this, the Turkish Republic has embraced the nation-state and a laïc regime – one that derived its legitimacy from the will of the nation. All the laws, regulations, organizations, policies and constitutions put into force by this state and in this social order had to be laïc, national and democratic. Beyond this, they also had to conform to the principle of the rule of law. Regardless of the source of its power - economic, political, religious, social or traditional - no class or community could be above the law.

Under the Ottomans, there had been a whole array of legitimate sources of power and control, ranging from the religious, economic, social and traditional, beginning with the Caliph and the Sultan and extending all the way down through the social hierarchy. The Turkish Republic of today and tomorrow is committed to a national, laïc regime in which the rule of law prevails.

Interest has grown in recent years, both at home and abroad, in conducting Ottoman research. However, while ostensibly academic, this research has tended to be for all intents and purposes politically and ideologically motivated. Its aim has not simply been to create respect or admiration for Ottomanism but rather to work against the very "Enlightenment" that has been achieved since the founding of the Republic in Turkey. Advocates of the so-called Turkish-Islamic synthesis that has thus emerged strive to inculcate its ideology in society and the workings of the state. They long for a regime that is no longer viable and a political Islam that would carry Turkey back into the dark ages. Consequently, this ideology is both contrary to Atatürkist thought and dangerous with respect to the future of the Turkish nation. Turkey is still trying to grapple with replacing the mentality of belonging to a religious community with that of being a citizen of a political community, where Moslem identity is subordinated to Turkish identity. Opening the door to such ideologies as the Turkish-Moslem synthesis, or to those that openly espouse a return to an Islamic regime spells disaster for the continuity of the Turkish Republic. These ideologies represent no less than a desire and attempt to transform the Turkish Republic into either an Ottoman or a Turkish-Islamic Republic, going as far as supporting a return to the conditions provided for by the Sevres Treaty. Such a regression would be more in the interests of foreigners and of foreign states than it would be of Turks. The rise in recent years of anti-modern influences would just as soon undo all that has been achieved by the Atatürk Revolution and work to thwart attempts to reach the level of civilization envisaged by it.

To a large extent, such undesirable developments in Turkey stem also from the appearance of two groups of actors in the political arena: One group consists of what are known as the "Supporters of the Second Republic." The other group is made of those who essentially back "globalization" and the policies necessitated by it. The goal of the first group is to lay aside the underpinnings of the Atatürkist system of thought and the Atatürk Revolution upon which the Republic was set up. In place of the society unified on the basis of common denominators after the War of Independence, they want to create a multi-cultural order in which special privileges are institutionalized. This group's ideological ambitions are reminiscent of the *millet* system of the Ottoman Empire - a system that contributed greatly to the collapse of the Empire. In effect, what they want is a situation that would be no different from what existed during the latter years of the Ottoman era. However, such a course will only lead to a weakening of the country, instigating instability and providing greater potential for interference in the internal affairs of Turkey by foreign countries, thus undermining its political independence.

With respect to the advocates of globalization, the problem can be better understood if it is remembered that Atatürkism rests on the *nation-state* and that it is this nation-state that presents the greatest impediment to the objectives of globalization. Nevertheless, neither in principle nor historically was Atatürk or the Atatürkist system of thought ever against international dialogue or international cooperation. A state can enter into international cooperation without completely surrendering itself. What is important is maintaining national independence within the context of international relations.

The Atatürk Revolution also has an *universal* aspect to it. While nationalism was an important component of the Atatürk Revolution, Atatürk was not content simply with Turkey emerging triumphant from its own War of Independence. He was also a strong supporter of what he referred to as "Subjugated Nations" and "Subjugated Countries" in Asia, Africa and South America. He encouraged their struggle for independence. The Atatürk Revolution became for them a source of inspiration.

Another dimension of the Atatürk Revolution's universalism is reflected in Atatürk's repeated references to "modern civilization" and "the common values of humanity." While Atatürk was a champion of *national* policy and sought the protection of *national* values, he was receptive to universal values. Nevertheless, Atatürk and his system of thought are not open to the views that see less developed countries as cheap markets and their people as cheap sources of labor.

To appreciate the context in which globalization is unfolding, it must be pointed out that while globalization is generally presented as if it were a new phenomenon or policy, it is in fact simply the adaptation of 19th-century imperialism to contemporary conditions. The arguments in support of globalization actually began in conjunction with the new technological developments of the second half of the 19th century. The leader of the globalization of that period was Great Britain. The phenomenon began to lose momentum with the advent of the First World War, when protectionism became the order of the day. Today, the policies of the globalization led by the United States -the complete liberalization of foreign exchange, goods and capital markets, the remarkable reforms in the areas of information, communication and computing- have accelerated since especially the 1970s.

The contraction of the state and its complete withdrawal from the economy, which is the goal of globalization, has meant the decline in wages of workers and civil servants in developing countries and an intensification of their impoverishment. Such a policy is in the interests of countries that have a large accumulation of capital and technology. Nonetheless, the working class and the ordinary people of those countries are also negatively affected by globalization.

In reality, it is not only the working class or less developed countries that are critical of the negative effects created by globalization. Many intellectuals and institutions in developed countries are also quick to point out the disadvantages of globalization as it is implemented nowadays. They propose the equitable sharing among countries of production and consumption, information and technology. In short, they challenge and ultimately undermine the argument that "there is no alternative to globalization." They call for the abandonment of the policies of globalization that harm the people living in both the "North" and "South" and that are in the interest of a "minority." Not only do they maintain that economic risks and problems should be shared, they also argue that doing so is a prerequisite to living together with other nations, making possible a more social, more democratic world.

Globalization is in the interests of developed economies and countries enjoying advanced technology. The system wrought through the dynamics of globalization protects the rich state; it preserves "wealth." What makes the Atatürkist system of thought distinct from the artificial worldview that underlies the policies of globalization is its opposition to wealth that benefits only the rich. His is essentially a humane, humanistic worldview that embraces the "subjugated man" and "subjugated nation."

Spheres of interest, both within and outside the country, see Atatürk and his system of thought as the greatest impediment to the imperialist goals they want to carry out in Turkey under the guise of globalization. This is because in the game that they want to play, the humanistic, modernizing nationalism created by Atatürk and the Atatürk system of thought have no place.

Both the advocates of globalization and the so-called "Second Republic" supporters want to eliminate the viability of Atatürkist system of thought. Countries intent on getting globalization accepted in its entirety are not content with simply supporting those who are hypercritical of Atatürkism. The prime reason for this is that in spite of their influence, they are somewhat few in number, which has limited their impact on the "masses." Because of their relatively mutual interests, though motivated by entirely different concerns, the so-called "moderate Islamists," supporters of globalization, and advocates ef the "Second Republic" have often been closely intertwined with one another on a number of issues.

Possibilities to reach the masses remain for those who want to use religion for political purposes. It is for this reason that such regressive groups have been supported by other political groups, even those having different objectives. This explains why both the advocates of the "Second Republic" and supporters of globalization have been known to employ some of the same misleading statements used by the Islamists to undermine the laïc, national, modern and modernizing Atatürkist system of thought. The common objective is to question the Atatürkist system of thought and the nation-state upon which it is based so that a discussion of the whole issue of "regime" can be encouraged. Both groups are motivated by the desire to undermine the Republic and the nation-state upon which it is based. Politically motivated Islam lacks a national consciousness; the notion of religious community dominates its worldview. It is exactly at this point that politically motivated Islam and the policies of globalization coincide since those guiding these policies have many common views and interests. In order to carry out their policies, the nation-state and the consciousness of national identity have to be eliminated. This is the fundamental reason why political Islamists -those who call into question the very bases of the Republic- and the advocates of uncontrolled globalization are opposed to Atatürk. The Atatürkist system of thought supports the nation-state and embraces a modernizing, rational nationalism. Atatürkism aims at the strengthening of the consciousness of national identity.

Another problem that must be addressed with respect to the consciousness of national identity is the contradictions Turkey has experienced therewith. A society that is unable to resolve the problem of the consciousness of national identity cannot modernize. During Atatürk's time, because of a coherent, national and laïc educational system, by the "consciousness of national identity" embraced modernity. For approximately 50 years, especially over the last few, the groups wanting to replace the consciousness of national identity and of being a citizen of the Turkish Republic with a Religious-Islamic consciousness, have gotten more powerful. On the other hand, supporters of globalization and those of the so-called Second Republic have been repudiating the modernizing nationalism and understanding of national identity espoused by Atatürk.

Completely contrary to what Tito did in Yugoslavia, Atatürk institutionalized "similarities" rather than differences. Atatürk's understanding of national identity is based on the common denominators of the "common history" and "common culture" of the Turks that has been and continues to be experienced. Atatürk had considered being a citizen of the State of the Turkish Republic to be an integrating factor and saw to it that it was seen as such by others. This rational, unifying, modern consciousness of national identity will continue to live regardless of all the counter-revolutionary opposition it faces.

It is for these reasons that Atatürkists must make a special effort to keep the Republic of Atatürk, the Atatürk Revolution and Atatürkism alive forever against the developments, influences and changes of course that are out to undermine the laïc, democratic, social and legal bases of the Turkish Republic. This is not only our duty as state, nation and individual but also the guarantee of our future and of our attaining a contemporary level of civilization.

Not only is Atatürkism a commitment to modernity, it is the system of thought upon which the Turkish nation-state depends for its survival. The Atatürk Revolution embraces all radical attempts to raise Turkey to a level that is on par with contemporary civilization.

Within the framework of its six principles, and under the guidance of science and reason, and fully cognizant of the ongoing changes and developments in the world, the Atatürkist system of thought has been able to provide the most progressive solutions possible to the problems of Turkey. In short, Atatürkism does not involve simply the protection of the past, but in a sense, it is guidance for the future. Both Atatürk and the Atatürkist system of thought are future-oriented and it is for this reason that Atatürk has bequeathed his Revolution, in the main, to the Turkish Youth.

Futurism is an integral part of Atatürkism. Atatürk did not focus on things that had already been accomplished. He always focused on the future - on those matters that still had yet to be accomplished. This future-orientation on Atatürk's part did not involve theretical matters; rather, they were objective ones that dealt with concrete issues. They consisted of plans, programs, and of all those matters that had to be achieved with a great degree of success. In short, "futurism" is an integral part of the Atatürkist system of thought.

To interpret the Atatürk Revolution as Westernization is an inadequate assessment of this paradigm of modernization. Turkish language, Turkish history, Turkish folklore and all those aspects of Turkish culture that had been stifled under Ottoman rule became subjects of scientific study during the Atatürk era. To use Atatürk's words: "We finally learned who we were."

The Atatürkist paradigm of modernization is a "national-revolutionary" paradigm. In this regard, it is important to emphasize once again that Atatürkism is committed to each and every one of its principles. If one or two of these principles are emphasized at the expense of the others, the "wholeness" of the Atatürkist system of thought will be violated.

The six principles of Atatürkism prescribe the methods and views that aim at reaching the level of contemporary civilization within the framework of an open society. Atatürkism is the system of thought of the Turkish Enlightenment.

To Kemal Atatürk and his reforms, there is not only an intellectual, but also an emotional component on the part of the Turkish people. This is an observation that is vindicated by developments since his death. This commitment is not just to the reforms and to the principles of Atatürk but to their continuing development as the principle of Revolutionism-Reformism ensures. Therefore, Atatürk continues to be the symbol of Turkish political development for the Turkish people.

VIII

EPILOGUE

The Atatürk Paradigm of Modernization, Turkey and The European Union, Cyprus, Globalization, Republic and Democracy

Especially since the 1980s and with a new sense of urgency since the 1990s, Turkey has had to deal, among other things, with problems related to joining the European Union (EU) and globalization. These two topics have brought into greater focus the relationship between republicanism and democracy. The Atatürk paradigm of modernization and Atatürkist system of thought are related to these topics. There is a clear, discernable Atatürkist stand on such issues as the nature of Turkey's international relations, Turkey's international commitments and the paradigm of development and modernization most suitable to the needs and realities of Turkey.

Some important issues in contemporary Turkey, including the political crisis in the summer of 2002, have to be analyzed within the cantext of all the afore-mentioned topics. As mentioned earlier, the principle of *devrimcilik* gives Atatürkism the needed flexibility to grow with the times *without abandoning its basic commitments.*

The basic commitments of the Atatürkist system of thought are to republicanism, to laïc basis of political authority; hence, to laïcism, to the unconditional sovereignty of the people, to the indivisibility of Turkey as regards its territory and its people, and to continual change, development and progress. *Atatürkism is also republicanism. Atatürkism is commitment to an "honorable state."* These attributes of Atatürkism and the Atatürk paradigm of modernization shed considerable light on the debates in contemporary Turkey between the so-called *ulusalcılar* (those who support the national interest and do not want to compromise the national interest in international relations while at the same time, for example, remaining committed to the goal of full membership in the EU) and the so-called *unconditional internationalists.*

It is necessary to discuss these challenges before Turkey within the context of the basic theme and argument of this book. The principle of *devrimcilik* enables both the Atatürkist paradigm and the Atatürkist system of thought to have relevance to the topics under discussion. Both the Atatürk paradigm and the Atatürkist system of thought should be analyzed within the context of *ulusalcılık,* in fact in contemporary Turkish political life *ulusalcı* views and commitments involve to a large extent a reassertion of Atatürkism in the 21st century.

1. Turkey And The European Union

Situated at the point where Europe, the Middle East, Russia, the Caucuses, and the Mediterranean region meet, Turkey sits strategically between East and West and North and South. The city of Istanbul is divided into two main areas by the Strait of Bosphorus. One shore of Bosphorus is Asia and the other is Europe. Because of its position on the fringe of Europe, some differences in her cultural heritage, and its economic divergence from many of the EU countries, Turkey's application for full membership in the EU poses one of the most dramatic challenges facing the EU. The complexity of this challenge is not necessarily or exclusively prompted by the present realities of Turkish society. Much of what Turkey must overcome has its roots in history, which continues to, in effect, "condition" contemporary developments.

After the conquest of Istanbul in 1453, the Ottoman Empire expanded across the Balkan Peninsula and into south and mid-Europe. Thus, the Turks established themselves as the common enemy of most European nations. In the following years the Turks conquered most of the Middle East and North Africa. The Turks besieged Vienna in 1529 and then again in 1683. Confronted by the rising strength of the Ottoman Empire, the European nations cooperated in order to stop first the Ottoman expansion and later to retrieve some of the lands they had lost to the Ottoman Turks. The decline of the Ottoman Empire commenced in the 17th century. Beginning with the first half of the 19th century relations between the Ottoman Empire and some European countries began to improve. An example of this improvement was the alliance between France, Great Britain and the Ottoman Empire, during the Crimean War of 1853-1856, against the expansionist policies of Tsarist Russia. *Moreover, the Paris Treaty of 1856 acknowledged that the Ottoman Empire was a European power by initiating her as a member of the Concert of Europe.*

In the 19th century, closer relations developed between the declining Ottoman Empire and the European states. During the Tanzimat period of 1839-1876, the Ottomans were also preoccupied with closer cultural ties with Europe. The Empire was increasingly integrated into European institutions after being accepted into the Concert of Europe in 1856. And at the end of the 19th century, the Ottoman Empire was referred to as the "sick man" of *Europe* and not of Asia.

The Industrial Revolution bypassed the Ottoman Empire. The factors that had given rise to scientific, economic, social, and political developments in Europe were absent in the Ottoman Empire. The defeat of the Ottoman Empire in several wars, increasing economic and political exploitation by European powers and the inability of the Empire to forestall effectively these threats to her security brought about a desire on the part of some Sultans and leading Ottoman officials to reform the country along Western lines. The Ottoman movement toward reform and westernization commenced in the 18th century and continued up until the end of World War I.

During the course of 19th century, the European states gave encouragement to and supported the separatist activities of the subject nationalities of the Ottoman Empire; thereby, hastening the break up of the Empire. During World War I, the Ottoman Empire was in alliance with Germany and the Austro-Hungarian Empire. Following World War I, the victorious allies concluded the Treaty of Sevres with the Ottoman government which brought about the final dismemberment of the Empire. The Treaty of Sevres aimed also to divide Anatolia, the very homeland of the Turkish nation, into several non-Turkish states.

The Turkish nationalist forces, under the leadership of Mustafa Kemal, repudiated the Treaty of Sevres. During the period of National Struggle (1919-1922), the issue was not the maintenance of the Empire, but the retention of the very Turkish homeland. The drive was to solidify national independence and assure survival as a nation. As one observer of Middle Eastern affairs, Felix Valyi stated: "During the National Struggle in Asia Minor, between 1919 and 1923 the fundamental question was whether the Turkish nation was to be made the advance guard of Islamic revolution, or whether she was to be allotted the role she aspired to play in the happiest moments of her dramatic historical career - that of the rearguard to the West on the confines of the two continents of Europe and Asia. Were the Turks to be for or against Europe."[182]

This question was ably answered by another observer of Turkish history. A.J. Toynbee who noted: "Russia... was at least as alien in the guise of a Socialist Soviet Republic as when she had been an Orthodox Christian Czardom. Not Petersburg and not Moscow, but Paris, was the spiritual home in quest of which they had cast loose from their ancient Islamic moorings, and they were not willing to be diverted to another port. While they were fighting the Western powers tooth-and-nail for their political and economic independence, they were reconstructing their national institutions from top to bottom on Western lines."[183]

Mustafa Kemal Atatürk cast aside all imperial goals whether of the Pan-Turkic, Pan-Islamic or Ottoman variety. Military and foreign policy considerations of survival propelled the Kemalists to strengthen the internal cohesion and civilian organization of the Turkish polity. The 1920 revolutionaries limited Turkish political aims, accepted the new national frontiers and decided to establish an enduring political structure. Although supreme national crisis had brought military defense and military affairs to the forefront, the Kemalist movement, in time, established the civilian institutions to which the military were increasingly subordinated. The Republican People's Party became the chief civilian agency of political development.

The successful conclusion of the nationalist movement made patent the political and legal boundaries of the Turkish homeland, the establishment of the Republic and the reforms of Atatürk followed. All these events were instrumental in the defining of the national identity of Turkey. Turkey's efforts to establish closer relations with the European states were accelerated after the proclamation of the Republic in 1923.

The major source of the present commitments of Turkey to Europe lies in the Kemalist reform movement. Kemal Atatürk employed a strong parliamentary government and expanding laïc system of education to turn Turkish national identity from its Ottoman commitments toward closer identification with Europe. Atatürk's legacy of

Europeanism flourished through the continuing rise and expansion of Turkey's westernized middle class, bureaucracy, and the military.

Despite the modernist and westernist orientation on her part, Turkey was interested in achieving good and peaceful relations with all the nations of the world. The Kemalist government demonstrated through word and deed that peace on earth could only be realized though mutual cooperation and understanding between all nations. The most important maxim of Kemalist foreign policy was "peace at home and peace abroad." Kemalist foreign policy was dedicated to peaceful co-existence between all nations.

While engaging in a vigorous program of modernization, Kemalist foreign policy did not limit Turkey's relations to the European states. Kemalist foreign policy was characterized by its rationalism and humanitarianism. Its humanitarianism could be observed by its insistence on the right to independence, to equal opportunities, and to prosperity of all nations and peoples everywhere in the world. The Turkish struggle for independence had meaning not only for the Turkish, but also for all the oppressed nations of the world.

Atatürk and his cadre were not interested in imperialistic adventures. They did their utmost to inculcate in the minds of the Turkish people a rational as well as an emotional commitment to the new frontiers of Turkey. This has proven to be one of the most remarkable accomplishments of the Kemalist era. Hence, Kemalist foreign policy was anti-irredentist and anti-imperialist.

In his attempts at modernization, Atatürk used often the terms "contemporary civilization," "the common civilization," "the civilized world." Hence, Atatürk's intellectual frame of reference encompassed the whole world, while focusing in the main on Europe. Kemalist heritage, be it in the main tenets of Turkish foreign policy or the principles guiding the restructuring of Turkish society, has brought Turkey closer to Europe than any other part of the world. However Atatürk did not hesitate to take his stand against the policies of those states that were disruptive of international peace. Atatürk was particularly bothered about Hitler's policies which disrupted peace and instigated rising tension in Europe in the thirties. As Ernest Jackh stated: "Kemal ... in the last years of his life, anticipated the world issue of today and set the definite course of tomorrow: 'Once we so-called pagan and infidel Turks, though believers in the Mohammedan version of Judeo-Christianity, seemed to threaten civilization in Central Europe; now, however, world civilization has to be defended by us against the menace of modern barbarism and paganism which is spreading from Central Europe to the four corners of a world of neighbors'."[184]

It should also be noted that many scholars principally from Austria and Germany who were of Jewish origin and/or who opposed Hitler's regime came to Turkey at the invitation of the, Turkish government to teach at Turkish Universities. Professors Ernst Hirsch, Gerhard Kessler, Alexander Rustow, Andreas Schwartz, Fritz Neumark, Wilhelm Röpke, city planner Ernst Reuter, architect Clement Holzmeister, former head of the Berlin Opera Carl Ebert and orchestra conductor Ernest Praetorius were among those who taught and worked in Turkey for many years. Both Carl Ebert and composer Paul Hindemith played important roles in the founding of the Ankara State Conservatory.

Hans Kohn sees much similarity, as do other thinkers such as A.J. Toynbee, Barbara Ward, and S.N. Eisenstadt, between the Atatürk Revolution and the processes of change in thought, life and production in Western countries that has taken place since the 17th century. Kohn summarizes these changes in Turkey as "the adoption of rationalism, individualism, and industrialism."[185]

Atatürk stated on several occasions that: "The Turks have for centuries moved in the same direction. We have always moved from the East to the West." It is true that the Turkish people have come from Central Asia, from the East, but throughout the centuries, the Turkish people have continuously moved westward. As a matter of fact, the Ottomans aimed first at the acquisition of territories in Europe. Their taking over the Balkans is much earlier than their conquest of Trabzon and some other Eastern areas. Following the establishment of the Republic in 1923, Turkey increasingly asserted her "national" as well as "western" identity under the leadership of Atatürk.

Following World War II, Turkey became a member of a variety of western institutions such as the International Bank for Reconstruction and Development, the International Monetary Fund, Council of

Europe and NATO. On 31 July 1959, Turkey first applied to become a member of the European Community. According to the Ankara Agreement signed by Turkey in 1963, Turkey became an associate member of the European Community the following year. Although the stages outlined by the Ankara Agreement had not yet been completed Turkey applied for full membership in April 1987.

Because of a number of reasons, Turkey's application for full membership in the EU has not thus far materialized. These reasons are varied and range from matters related to the so-called question of human rights, the state of the economy in Turkey, and the Aegean and Cyprus questions.

Atatürk paradigm of modernization and Atatürkism seek not merely standards of living befitting human dignity, but a more democratic regime in which the Turkish people live freely. Turkey's transition to a multi-party system and to a plural society are the natural culmination of the Atatürk reforms.

The Atatürkist paradigm has had to use the state, given existing socio-economic realities, for the betterment of the lives of the individual - both economically and politically. This is clearly a "welfare" understanding of the role of the state. Atatürkism never embraced a one-party system in principle. The ultimate aim of the Atatürk paradigm of modernization was, and is, reaching the level of contemporary civilization and, to the extent possible, rising above it.

It is important to point out at this juncture that the EU seems to employ a double standard when it comes to the matter of human rights and democracy. At the Helsinki Summit, it was decided that once a country fulfills all the Copenhagen political criteria, leaving aside the economic, the EU could initiate negotiations toward full membership with it. As a result of this decision, EU started negotiations with all these candidate countries, *excluding only Turkey*. The countries with which negotiations have begun are the former Communist countries that lived under a Soviet dominated closed regime for nearly fifty years. These candidate countries started to implement a democratic regime just a few short years ago. In contrast, Turkey has had experience with a democratic regime for about eighty years. It is hard to believe that these former communist countries are ahead of

Turkey regarding human rights and democracy. Moreover, there are some serious questions regarding the rights of minorities in some of these candidate countries. Nonetheless, EU has started negotiations with them, asking these countries to improve upon the pertinent laws in the matter of minority rights at a future date. Furthermore, EU is trying to impose a minority status on the Kurds of Turkey, who are historically, politically and culturally not a minority group in Turkey and who constitute an important segment of the population and with whom the Turkish people have lived together for a thousand years. Moreover, within the context of the European Council, an Agreement on the Rights of Minorities has been prepared. And several European states such as Germany, Austria and Sweden have registered their reservations to the document on the contention that a country has the right to designate which group or groups could be designated as minority. These states also have the right not to extend minority status to other groups even if these groups do not qualify for such a status.

Given the above-mentioned facts, it is obvious that the EU does not want and/or wants to postpone Turkey's membership by employing double standards. An attempt is made to uncover all the undesirable elements in Turkey so as to prevent Turkey's membership. Needless to say, a sufficient number of "negative" elements can be found in any of these countries if one looks closely enough at them and if one wants to go out of the way to use these elements to prevent their accession to the EU. Historically, at least some of the present EU members have resorted to adverse and unfounded propaganda against the Ottoman Empire and Turkey to justify their unjust policies toward both of these countries. In short, several of the present-day EU criticisms of Turkey are unjustifiable. It should be further noted that *among the 51 states in the world where the Moslems constitute the majority, Turkey is the only laïc state and Turkey is the only state that has been implementing a democratic regime with success.*

The double standards being employed by the EU toward Turkey in political matters extend also to the economic realm. The economic and financial aid which the EU has extended to the East European countries in the past six years is more than double the total amount of such aid given to Turkey during the past thirty-five years.

Membership in the European Customs Union was a hasty move on Turkey's part. Because of this membership, Turkey is confronted with implementing the decisions of the EU - a Union which she has not joined and in which she does not as yet have an effective voice. This situation adversely effects Turkish economy. But perhaps more importantly, Turkey is being asked to pay an important price as a condition for her membership in the EU, particularly as relates to the ongoing issues of the Aegean and Cyprus. From the Atatürkist point of view Turkey should join the EU as an "honorable" state, without having to compromise on some of the vital interests of the country. On this point the Turkish population is largely in agreement.

Turkey made a major thrust in the direction of compatibility with the Copenhagen criteria on 3 August 2002. On that date, the Turkish Grand National Assembly accepted a "reform package" which was in effect the third such a reform package since the beginning of 2002. This package included several changes in some Turkish laws so as to make Turkey's legal and political systems more compatible with the EU standards. This reform package, which in effect was a landmark move on the part of the Turkish Assembly, among other things, lifted the death penalty (though since 1984 the death penalty has not been implemented in Turkey), made possible the instruction and publishing in one's own mother tongue, and liberalized the law of associations. There was considerable discussion on the question of lifting the death penalty. The N.A.P. in particular protested the lifting of the death penalty on the contention that this was a covert amnesty for Abdullah Öcalan, the leader of the PKK terrorist organization which has been responsible for the death of 30.000 Turkish people, women and children included.

The discussions on the "reform package" and its acceptance by the Assembly came soon after the Assembly's decision on 31 July 2002 to hold new general elections on 3 November 2002. As discussed in chapter VII a number of political issues in the country has contributed to cutting short the 4-year term of the coalition government of Prime Minister Bülent Ecevit.

The EU Report issued on 10 October, 2002, and dealing with the "Expansion Strategy" in 2002, stated that in view of the fact that Turkey has not fulfilled all the necessary criteria no date was set to initiate discussions towards her membership and that if Turkey would continue her reforms she could in time meet the EU goals.

In this Report the names of ten countries were given which were expected to be admitted to the EU in 2004. And 2007 was given as the date of possible accession for Bulgaria and Romania.

EU started negotiations with such countries as Estonia and Latvia whose human rights record should not have been acceptable in view of the treatment of minorities in these two countries. Although Estonia somewhat improved upon her "record", the situation in Latvia was less than desirable. The Russian population in Latvia is larger than the Latvian population. Despite this fact, Latvian law did not grant citizenship rights to the Russians who had lived there for about fifty years. In order to qualify for citizenship rights the Russians in Latvia had to prove their proficiency in the Latvian language and their command of citizenship laws. All this was tested in special exams which the Russians had to pass in order to get citizenship rights. The EU was well aware of this negative element in the human rights record especially of Latvia. The EU simply asked Latvia to solve the matters regarding this country's treatment of minorities in the future. Nonetheless Latvia was admitted to the EU on 1st May 2004. This clearly is a case of a double standard because the package of "reform laws" passed by the Turkish Parliament during the course of 2002 brought Turkey closer to meeting the Copenhagen criteria more than some of the 10 countries which were admitted in 2004.

In December 2002, prior to the 12th of December Copenhagen Summit of the EU, The Turkish Parliament made once again a major thrust in the direction of democratizing her political life and legal system by accepting a "fourth reform package". And she began discussing a "fifth reform package" which in effect more or less completed the "standards" required for full membership in the EU. In spite of all positive efforts on her part, Turkey could not overcome EU's reluctance to admit her, let alone to even begin "negotiations". In Turkey there was much hope that such would not be the case. However, the statement by Per Stig Möller, the Danish Foreign Minister, in Brussels, on November 18, 2002, gave a clear sign of what would be the outcome for Turkey at the Copenhagen Summit. Möller gave the names of the following countries regarding the expansion plans of the EU in the future: the admission of Hungary, Poland, the Czech Republic, Slovenia, Estonia, Latvia, Lithuania, Slovakia, Malta and Cyprus into the EU shall take place on ist May, 2004 and prior to that date, in April 2003, "Accession Agreements" with these countries will be signed. Hence, instead of 15 members, Turkey would have to convince another 10 new members regarding her membership. Moreover, by stating that in 2007 the membership of Bulgaria and Romania would be considered, it became obvious that Turkey would not also be included in the next wave of enlargement of the EU.

The outcome of the Copenhagen summit for Turkey proved to be a great disappointment for the Turkish people. In spite of the fact that Turkey had fulfilled almost all the Copenhagen criteria for EU membership Turkey was not given a definite date for the initiation of negotitiations with the EU. It was simply stated that in December 2004 the EU would review the case of Turkey and in the case of Turkey's fulfilling all the criteria then negotiations would begin in 2005. What the EU gave Turkey at the Copenhagen Summit was a "conditional" and evasive calendar. The Turkish public generally believes that the EU needs Turkey for strategic considerations and economic advantages which have augmented especially after Turkey joined the Customs Union. It is claimed that the EU does not say I shall not admit Turkey, but by giving false hopes it aims at keeping Turkey at the door while maintaining the advantages of the relations with Turkey. By and large the Turkish public believes that the policies of the EU towards Turkey are procrastinating and evasive.

On May 1st, 2004, 10 new countries were admitted into the EU. These were Hungary, Poland, Czech Republic, Slovakia, Slovenia, Estonia, Latvia, Lithuania, Malta and Cyprus.

Responsible spokesmen for the EU always pointed out that no country would be admitted into the EU which had "problems" with another state. Hence, in view of the ongoing "problem" between the Greek Cypriot state, namely the Republic of Cyprus and the Northern Cyprus Turkish State, it was a major mistake on EU's part to admit the Republic of Cyprus into the EU, as the representative of the entire island of Cyprus.

During the years between 2004-2007 the Turkish Parliament accepted a series of reform laws bringing her closer to the Copenhagen criteria. But reports given by the EU during these years were full of unfair criticism, similar in content to the reports given in earlier years. Moreover these reports made quite a few unwarranted demands on Turkey. A case in point were the reports referring to minorities in Turkey, designating the Kurds, who are an integral part of the Turkish population, as a minority group. According to Lausanne Treaty of July 1923, a treaty which is still in force, only non-Muslim groups are given minority status. The double standard approach of the EU countries towards Turkey can be illustrated yet by another example: Keeping in mind that France is both a member of the EU and the Council of Europe the following response of France to ECRI (European Commission Against Racism and Intolerance) of the European Council is a very clear-cut case of this double standard. ECRI asked France to give them statistical information regarding the minorities in France. In February 2005 the French government refused to give such statistical information and pointed out that the concept of "minority" is against the indivisibility and the unity of France and that the concept of "minority" is foreign to French law.

In spite of various difficulties, on December 17, 2004, the EU Council decided to strart accession negotiations with Turkey in October, 2005. (This was a long-awaited decision. On July 31st, 1959, Turkey had applied to the European Economic Community, then the name of EU, for membership). Initially compability of the Turkish laws to EU laws, to the *"acquis communautaire"* of the EU laws was the first item on the agenda. To that end, the screening of laws listed under 35 chapters commenced on October 25, 2005. This process was completed on October 13, 2006. The negotiations on the chapters commenced on June 12, 2006. "Science and Technology" was selected as the least likely to stir controversy. Nonetheless, the negotiatons ended abruptly due to the adverse attitude of the Republic of Cyprus. However, it was pointed out that this was a temporary suspension of the negotiations on this chapter.

A new negative development in Turkey's relations with the EU involved the recommendation of the EU Commission on November 29,

2006. In December 2006, this recommendation of the Commission was endorsed by the other responsible organs of the EU. According to this recommendation, the EU decided not to open talks on 8 important chapters "covering policy areas relevant to Turkey's restrictions as regards the Republic of Cyprus until the Commission verifies Turkey has fulfilled its commitments related to the "Additional Protocol."[186] One can say that at this juncture, Turkey's relations with the EU has considerably slowed down. Taking into consideration the following points, it is quite clear that the prospects of Turkey's EU membership have become rather dim: in order to open negotiations on any of the 8 chapters, the affirmative votes of each of the 27 members of the EU is needed. Even if that were to be granted in order to achieve membership status not only the member states, but people in some member states such as France and Austria, have to give a "Yes" vote. Even if all this were realized, the EU could say "I am not able to absorb this country" or "I do not have the capacity to absorb this country."

On January 1st, 2007, Bulgaria and Romania joined the EU. From the perspective of economic strength and democratic experience, Turkey is far ahead of these two countries. It is quite likely that Croatia shall be a member of the EU either in 2009 or 2010. But Turkey has no entry date, despite talks having been officially opened on her candidacy.

All the developments so far have indicated the reluctance of the EU to admit Turkey to full membership However all these developments have also led to a noticeable decrease in the desire of the Turkish people to join the EU. Moreover, there is a growing complaint that Turkey has concentrated too much and for far too long on matters related to joining the EU.

It is contended that this has had a limiting effect on Turkey's foreign policy alternatives, and that Turkey should concentrate more on developing and implementing a "regional oriented" foreign policy. Some people go farther and claim that all this concentration on the EU has been a "waste of time" for Turkey because the EU shall never admit Turkey as a full member. Moreover, in view of the fact that countries with less economic and political potential than Turkey have been and are being admitted to the EU, quite a growing number of Turkish people find this a "humiliating" experience for the country.

Furthermore, it is emphasized that this is a one-way relationship: The EU demands and Turkey gives.

In addition to the above-mentioned developments, it ought to be noted that the EU itself is experiencing important internal problems. These problems prompt some observors to comment that there is not a single EU and that three are several EU's, that the viability of the organization is in question, and that in a few decades we may be confronted with the "demise" of this organization. One of the great blows to the viability of the organization was the negative votes the French and Dutch people gave to the EU constitution. This constitution bore heavily the values and principles of globalization which a sizeable portion of the European population find to be too individualistic, lacking an understanding of the needs of the common man. Moreover, there are and there have been profound differences of opinion regarding the EU budget. Furthermore, the demand on the unanimity of voting has prompted a serious and ongoing discussion as to how democratic the voting procedure is as employed by the EU.

In EU's relations with Turkey two elements are obvious. Firstly, The West has preconceived notions about Turkey. And secondly the West does not have adequate knowledge about Turkish history, Turkish institutions and Turkish political culture. Another case in point is EU's ongoing negative comments about the role of the military in Turkish society, showing a profound lack of knowledge on the part of EU about Turkish history and Turkey's socio-economic realities. It is therefore necessary to make some comments about the *role of the military* in Turkish society.[187]

The *Turkish military* does not have a *"militaristic"* tradition as was the case with the sons of the "Junker" class in Prussia who formed the backbone of the Prussian army. And it does not have an aristocratic heritage. Members of the Turkish officer corps do not come from rich families. During the course of 19th century, Turkish economy was in the hands of Western powers. Industrialization had bypassed the Ottoman Empire. In reality Ottoman Empire had no economy. She had become a market for the industrialized Western countries. Hence there was no Turkish bourgeoise. In particular the *military* filled this vacuum. The *Turkish military* became the chief agency pushing for modernization. And again the *Turkish military* became the guiding force during the War of Independence. Mustafa Kemal Atatürk was himself a successful general. And after the establishment of the Republic in 1923, it is him who pushed for the radical modernization of Turkish state and society. However, during Atatürk's Presidency the *military* remained in the background principally because it shared the same ideological outlook, the same commitment to total modernization and laïcization, with the Turkish political elite. During Atatürk's Presidency the Republican People's Party (R.P.P.) became the chief agency of political movement.

The Turkish *military*, by and large, has not wavered from its ideological commitment. Whereas, the transition to multi-party regime in Turkey, has once again brought reactionary religious forces into political life. And this reaction on occasion is supported by political parties for vote-getting purposes. The Turkish people, by and large, and the *Turkish military* are committed to Turkish Enlightenment as represented by the Atatürk Revolution. *The Turkish people are proud of their army for what it has represented in the past and for what it stands for today.*

In spite of some interruptions, the *Turkish Military* has retained its progressive character and it continues to be the most *"trustworthy"* organization in Turkey as almost all the public opinion polis show. *The reasons for this trustworthiness are briefly stated below:*

The *military* is not "alone". A sizeable segment of the civilian population supports its policies and are of a like-mind. Moreover many non-governmental civilian organizations are solidly behind the policies of the military. By and large, the universities and the students are supportive. At least some of the important business groups understand the role of the military. At this juncture it is worth noting that some labor unions are aware of the intent of these policies and are supportive. The egalitarian background of the military helps it to understand the problems of the needy.

It ought to be kept in mind that the *military* does play an integrative role in Turkish society. All the three military interventions in Turkey, 1960, 1971 and 1980 had this particular motive; namely, to consolidate democracy in a country which had shown tendencies of polarization and fragmentation. By and large, it has been the weakness of civilian institutions which has instigated military intervention in Turkey.

It can be stated that the *Turkish military* has risen above its narrow interests and has not opted for staying in power. The excellent education the officers are getting, their broad international contacts, and their sensitivity to the wishes of the Turkish people make them committed to a democratic way of life. If the *Turkish military* were an anti-democratic force the Turkish people would not designate them as the most trustworthy group in Turkish society.

Social scientists of a liberal or Marxist persuasion may look at the role of the military in a way which may not be applicable to some societies. The *Turkish military* is not an anti-democratic force nor is it part of a financial oligarchy. The *Turkish military* has always been interested to get back to its barracks. Ideologically the *Turkish military* is constitutionalist and laïcist.

It ought to be kept in mind that the *Turkish military* is not against religion. It is not against Islam. But the Turkish military is against religion in politics-a conviction it shares with the great majority of the Turkish people.

The role of the *Turkish military* has to be assessed also within the context of "republic" and "democracy". The *Turkish military* embraces the values of republicanism. It is committed to the preservation of the Republic. And it shares with the Turkish people the view that the ultimate goal is the further democratization of the Republic.

With the 28 February 1997 "Resolutions" of the National Security Council, the *military* stood by the Republic. In effect, it said "stop" to attempts of reactionary religious groups to infiltrate the educational system and thereby influence and if possible exercise complete control over Turkish political life. The *military* showed that it would not compromise on the laïcist basis of the Turkish Republic. And this stand of the *military* was supported and applauded by the progressive elements and organizations of Turkish society.

Some EU reports about Turkey, refer to Kemalism in a negative manner and suggest that the Turkish people should move away from commitment to it. This book has discussed at some length why *Ke-*

malism is Turkey's imperative. Such negative comments about Kemalism prompt most Turkish people to think that the members of the EU are totally ignorant of Turkey's history and Turkish realities. Yet some Turkish people believe that the main reason for the negative attitude of the EU is due to the anti-imperialist and pro nation-state message of Kemalism.

In view of all the above-mentioned developments, the Turkish people have become disillusioned about EU's policies towards Turkey. Some Turkish scholars contend the following: You (Turkey) fulfill the political criteria, then they (the EU) say let us see their implementation; you say we completed the points which were deficient, then they bring forth the question of Southeastern Turkey or the Armenian claims; you say we prepared a new package of reform laws, they then bring forth the question of Cyprus; further they question the role of the army in Turkish society. This is an "endless" List. Some claim that the West is out to get all it can from Turkey before Turkey becomes more developed and before it gets stronger. It is also claimed that behind all this is the continual desire of the West to bring Turkey under its hegemony - a policy which it has followed since the 19th century.

In spite of the above-mentioned negative developments, one should not overlook the fact that Turkey's national identity has become increasingly linked with Europe during the past century. Given the possibility of full membership, Turkey would act as a force of stability in the fairly unstable Mediterranean and Middle Eastern regions. The EU's growing interest in influencing the regions surrounding it will act – or rather, should act as a catalyst for granting full membership to Turkey. Moreover, Turkey offers the EU vast opportunities for enrichment through the incorporation of a large and dynamic society. However, as things stand both the EU and Turkey have mutual reservations about full membership. Some of the conditions the EU is demanding for full membership infringe upon the vital interests of Turkey. Some of these conditions challenge the right of Turkey to join the EU as an "honorable" state - a commitment that Atatürkists were not prepared to compromise in the past and will not compromise now or in the future. However, in spite of certain setbacks, the drive toward Europe remains a consistent element of Turkish foreign policy.

2. Cyprus

The EU is making the solution of several issues as a condition for Turkey's membership. A case in point is the *Cyprus* issue. A brief analysis of the *Cyprus* issue would shed light on the double standards the EU is employing in its relations with Turkey. The status of the *Cyprus* Island and the relations between both the Greek and Turkish communities on the island were defined and guaranteed by the Zurich and London Agreements of 1959, the Cyprus Constitution, and the Treaty of Guarantee of 1960.

Article 8 of the Zurich Agreement reads as follows:

> The President and the Vice President, separately and conjointly, shall have the right of final veto on any law or decision concerning foreign affairs, except the participation of the Republic of Cyprus in international organizations and pacts of alliance in which Greece and Turkey both participate or concerning defense and security as defined in Annex I.

The Treaty of Guarantee signed in 1960 by the *Republic of Cyprus of the one part, and Greece and Turkey and the United Kingdom of Great Britain and the Northern Ireland of the otherpart,* established the status quo of relations between the Turkish and Greek communities on the Island of Cyprus. And the nature and the limit of the relations between the two communities were elaborated in the Constitution of Cyprus. The same Treaty stated that Greece, and Turkey and the United Kingdom prohibit the union of Cyprus with any other state. Furthermore, Article 4 of the Treaty reads as follows: *In the event o f a breach of the provisions of the present Treaty, Greece, Turkey and the United Kingdom undertake to consult together with respect to the representations or measure necesary to ensure observance of those provisions. In so far as the common concerted action may not prove possible, each of the three guaranteeing Powers reserves the right to take action with the sole aim of re-establishing the state of affairs created by the present Treaty.*

The Zurich and London Agreements and the Treaty of Gurantee were violated by a series of events instigated by Makarios, who was both the religious leader of the Greek community and the President of the Republic of Cyprus. The growing tension on the island was further augmented in 1963 by a series of massacres of the innocent Turkish people living on the island. Finally the Greek military junta of the time supported the activities of a Greek terrorist, Nikos Samson, to unite *Cyprus* with Greece. All this move entailed a clear violation of the London and Zurich Agreements and the Treaty of Guarantee. As stated above, the Treaty of Guarantee gave the right to the signatories to intervene together or alone in the case of the violation of the terms of the Treaty. In view of the clear violation of the Zurich and London Agreements and the Treaty of Guarantee, in July 1974, Turkey used her right to intervene. Since 1974 *Cyprus* has remained a peaceful island. A series of events led to the proclamation of *The Turkish Republic of Northern Cyprus*. However, the Greek government has sought for years to reduce and if possible to eliminate the Turkish presence in *Cyprus*. The efforts of the Greek government in this direction began to get more support after Greece became a member of the EU. Hence, instead of leaving the solution of this question to the Greek and Turkish communities on the island, now the EU has seized of the matter. Moreover, the United Nations has become involved.

Secretary General of the United Nations, Kofi Annan released a "plan" in the Fall of 2002 for the solution of the *Cyprus* question. And a deadline of 28 February 2003 was given for both parties, Greek and Turkish, to negotiate and accept the plan. The Annan Plan was replete with conditions and principles which grossly undermined the position of the *Turkish Cypriots*. The plan did not involve a "just" settlement of the issues between the two communities. The major drawbacks of the "Plan" were such that this "Plan" could not assure a durable peace between the two communities.

Moreover, "The Annan Plan" involved the weakening of the "guarantor" position of Turkey. The weakening of Turkey's position on *Cyprus* would be tantamount to confining Turkey to Anatolia, a situation which is neither strategically tenable nor acceptable by Turkey. In spite of the above-mentioned reservations, the referendum on the Annan Plan took place on April 24, 2004. The referendum in the Turkish Republic of Northern Cyprus resulted with 64.91% of the people voting "Yes" and 35.09% of the people voting "No". The voting results were due mainly to two reasons: the younger generation had not experienced the years of Greek atrocities inflicted upon the Turkish Cypriots until the Turkish intervention of July 1974. Secondly, the fact that Cyprus would become a full member of the EU on May 1st, 2004, prompted some Turkish Cypriots to believe that they too could benefit from this membership. On the other hand, 75.83% of the Greek Cypriots voted "No" and only 24.17% voted yes. This showed that the Greek Cypriots would not be satisfied until they would have complete control of the island.

Several high-ranking and responsible members of the EU had publicly announced that if the Turkish Cypriots would vote affirmatively, the EU would end the isolation of the Turkish Republic of Northern Cyprus and resume direct trade relations with it. However, *the EU did not keep its promise*. This enhanced further the lack of confidence the Turkish people have in the EU.

Another aspect of the Cyprus problem should also be noted: In 1995 Turkey had signed the Customs Union with the EU. As noted earlier this was not a wise move on Turkey's part because she would be bound by the decisions of the Customs Union, in which she did not have an effective say or vote since she was not a member of the EU. The EU requested from Turkey an "Additional Protocol" extending the same privileges provided by the Customs Union to the newly admitted ten members of the EU. And the EU made it clear that if Turkey were not to sign the "Additional Protocol", negotiations between the EU and Turkey would not commence in the Fall of 2005. The Permanent Representative of Turkey to the EU, Ambassador Oğuz Demiralp, signed the Protocol after consultations with the Turkish government. Thereby both the "Additional Protocol" and Turkey's "Declaration" were sent to the Presidency of the Council of the EU in July 2005. The Turkish Declaration simply stated that Turkey's signing the "Additional Protocol" was not tantamount to recognition of the Republic of Cyprus. On September 21st, 2005, the EU issued a "Counter Declaration" in which it stated that Turkey's Declaration was unilateral, that it had no legal effect on Turkey's obligations under the Protocol, that the EU recognized only the Republic of Cyprus as a subject of international law, and that the EU underlined the importance it attaches to the normalization of relations between Turkey and all EU member States and as as soon as possible.

The Turkish Republic of Northern Cyprus has made a number of serious conciliatoy gestures towards the Republic of Cyprus, which includes the affirmative vote to the Annan Plan. However, the Republic of Cyprus has not reciprocated this conciliatary approach. As pointed out earlier, it was a wrong decision on the part of EU to admit Cyprus into the Union before it settled its disputes with Turkey. "Normalization of relations" which the EU demands, is a process that involves both states, not just the Turkish Republic of Northern Cyprus.

The above-mentioned claims of the "Counter Declaration" are not tenable for several reasons: First of all, the Cyprus problem was not created by the Turkish Cypriots. The Cyprus problem was instigated by the Greek Cypriots. The Greek Cypriots continued to harass the Turkish Cypriots with actual and continual threats of massacre. Furthermore, the Turkish Cypriots were virtually excluded from the administration of the island. Moreover, in July 1974, as a result of a *coup*, the island was annexed to Greece upon which the Turkish intervention took place- a right which was bestowed upon those countries which had signed the The Treaty of Guarantee of 1960. And it should also be noted that the island of Cyprus has lived its most peaceful years following the Turkish intervention in 1974. Secondly, it ought to be kept in mind that only the signing of the "Additional Protocol" by the Turkish Parliament would give it validity. And thirdly, as is generally believed in Turkey that if the economically strong members of the EU such as France and Germany, were willing to admit Turkey into the EU, they would exert the necessary pressure on the Republic of Cyprus to abandon its negative voting pattern towards Turkey.

For many years, solution of the Cyprus problem was not a condition of Turkey's membership in the EU. It is a fairly new development. And certainly it has and it continues to have a considerable effect on the slowing down of the negotiations between the EU and Turkey.

Meanwhile a new development has begun regarding EU's position towards the Turkish Republic of Northern Cyprus. On January 22, 2007, the Foreign Ministers of the EU (GAERC- General Affairs and External Relations Council), sent a recommendation to the EU Commission to prepare a "Direct Trade Regulation" so that trade with those areas of the island of Cyprus on which the Republic of Cyprus did not have effective control, could commence. GAERC shied away from a direct reference to the Turkish Republic of Northern Cyprus. It looks as if the realization of this recommendation will entail a long and arduous process. And the Greek Republic of Cyprus could and would bloc at any given time the negotiations. However, the EU continues to make the solution of the Cyprus problem a condition for Turkey's membership. With the Republic of Cyprus and Greece in the EU and the Turkish Republic of Northern Cyprus and Turkey outside of the EU, it is very difficult to solve the Cyprus problem.

In all the negotiations dealing with the solution of the Cyprus problem, the main target is the presence of the Turkish armed forces on the island. However, if the Turkish military's presence would come to an end, that would be tantamount to giving up all the legitimate claims of the Turkish Cypriots. Moreover, the safety of the Turks on the island would be irreparably jeopardized. One should not also overlook the fact all over the island of Cyprus, especially in the area of "Maraş", the Ottoman Foundations own land and other properties. These properties and "foundation lands" have been blatantly taken over by the Greeks on the island.

Cyprus is strategically a very important island both for Turkey and for the big powers of the world. Moreover, the bottom of the sea around the island is supposed to be replete with oil deposits. All this prompt both the USA and the EU to exert pressure in the direction of the solution of the Cyprus problem as soon as possible. Both Greece and the Greek state of Cyprus; namely, the Republic of Cyprus, are members of the EU. Their populatin is Christian. All this constitute important factors for EU's generally unequivocal support of the policies of these two respective states leading to the non-recognition of the Turkish Republic of Northern Cyprus and to the shoving aside of its just claims. In view of the irredentist "*Megali Idea*"[188] policies of Greece, it is quite obvious that neither Greece nor the Republic of

Cyprus shall be satisfied until they have complete control of the island; end the existence of the Turkish Republic of Northern Cyprus, and assure the withdrawal of the Turkish troops from the island. Both the Republic of Cyprus and Greece have managed to make the Cyprus problem one of the important items on the agenda of the EU.

The only workable, durable and just solution to the Cyprus problem can be achieved through the recognition of the existence of two separate states on the island and of the rights of Turkey as emanating from the international treaties and the acceptance of the presence of the Turkish troops on the island as a guarantor of peace.

3. Some Comments On Globalization

Some comments on globalization are needed to adequately assess the Atatürkist view on the subject.

Globalization encompasses North and South Relations - relations between the developed North and the underdeveloped South. But that is not all. To discuss the policies made within the context of globalization and their implementation, it is essential to examine their impact on the very rich and the very poor within societies. Moreover, the rule of law is a concept that embraces all and seeks justice for all, irrespective of race, creed, religion and economic status. Even at the outset, it seems that there is a contradiction between the prevalence of the rule of law and the results of globalization policies since the implementations of the so-called "global economic policies" seem to widen the gap between the rich and poor nations and between the rich and the poor in all societies. This state of affairs is a great challenge to and adversely affects the prevalence of the rule of law. Freedom in and of itself is not enough. There is an economic basis to freedom as well.

It should be kept in mind that a global economy has one overriding task: to create efficiency and growth, measured in economic terms only. Growth is exclusively emphasized and at the expense of equal distribution. This is potentially a dangerous situation. Globalization cannot survive in a world of poverty and exclusion. It needs an ethical framework, one which "includes" and does not "exclude." Globalization may bring many benefits if properly executed -

and if properly "inclusive." Globalization may help to create peace and development. But if millions are excluded from the potential benefits it offers; if we have what as some call a "global apartheid;" and if the poor are denied the right to determine their future, and pull themselves out of degradation, then the globalization policies will threaten and adversely affect peace, democracy and development. As things stand, the globalization policies that have been implemented so far have been exclusive, working for the good of the financial elite groups.

James N. Rosenau believes that certain aspects of the processes of globalization constitute real threats to democratic institutions. He points out that in many ways the logic of the "market" undermines the ties that bind communities as well as the non-economic values to which people might aspire. He gives the following reasons why democratic institutions face severe challenges in the years ahead: the dispersal of authority away from states, the prevalence of economics over politics, the growing role of the NGO's and various transnational collectivities which point to a diminishing relevance of the basic procedures whereby the governed have a voice in the decisions and policies that shape their lives - in short, where the governed have a chance to use the rights of citizenship. However the way things are developing in the world, elections, legislatures, courts, public bureaucracies, political parties and their functioning are likely to become peripheral in relation to the dictates of the market and/or the decisions of transnational organizations that lack mechanism for holding leaders accountable. Hence, a real threat exists to democracy when decisions are taken and implemented by huge transnational corporations which affect our lives, but which we cannot call accountable. Moreover, the operations of the corporations lack transparency, which constitute another threat to democracy and to the rights of citizenship.[189]

Theodore J. Lowi contends that over the past two decades an economic theory of democracy in which "free enterprise" is alone sufficient to accomplish all other goals has become dominant. He claims that this economic theory of democracy is not economic science and that it is not even good ideology because the free market does not make free all those who enter and that it does not prosper without the support of the state. Lowi goes on to say that the challenge to democracy, the situation we have to be on the guard of has something to do with the tyrants - whether the tyrant be repressive rule by malevolent political elites or repressive rule by benevolent market mechanisms. Lowi points out that there was emphasis on a more equitable distribution of wealth in the post-war years, which he designates as the social democratic years. Giving examples from various studies, Lowi states that the ideological debate during the 1970's and 1980's was settled by the victory of the Friedmanists over the Keynesians - hence opening the way to the new international monetary policy.[190]

If "market" determines all values, and if these values have high priority than humanity, human beings, human values are pushed to a secondary position. Under these conditions how can we talk about human rights? How can democracy and human rights and for that matter the rule of law survive?

How is the infrastructure of globalization constituted? Large private national enterprises merge with international capital and hence share the same destiny. Scientific and ideological monopoly is exercised through the hegemony of the internationally powerful enterprises. "Free market" values are imposed on students in poor countries via the curricula of the educational system, which is integrated with the interests of capital. Moreover, the integration of communications and of the media leads to a manipulation of national public opinion in the direction of international "interests," which, in effect, constitute threats to the freedom of thought.

Globalization has also adversely affected the European worker. During the meeting of the Textile Industry Labor Unions of the European-Mediterranean area in Istanbul in December 1997, the European Labor Union leaders complained that the governments were formulating and implementing policies against the interests of the working classes. It was claimed that even the socialist parties had lost touch with the working classes, and that there was need for labor to cooperate and work internationally just as international capitalists were doing.

The economy should be serving people and not dominating them. Uncontrolled globalization should come to an end. Globalization and the demands of the market economy hit worst the salaries of the workers. In order to compete on the international market, the developing economies make use of the payment of low salaries, which are generally thirty times less than those of the workers in industrialized countries.

Nobel Award winner economist Paul Krugman emphasizes the fact that a sign of a healthy economy is the prevalence of an equitable distribution of the national income. He says that protectionist policies may be required in view of rising discontent with liberal economic policies. Krugman says that perhaps a serious, shocking economic crisis may cause the United States to revert to protectionist policies. Such statements are reminiscent of Roosevelt's New Deal Policy following the great economic crash of the late 1920s.

In the past, conflicts were in the main between capital and labor. Over the past twenty years, this situation has been replaced by the reality of conflict between the developed and underdeveloped countries.

As statistics and social conditions in different countries show, globalization is making the rich, richer and the poor poorer. The rich countries have to understand that such an unjust system will eventually create conditions and situations that will ultimately be against their interests as well. In a world where there are gross inequalities and where there is so much poverty, such a system cannot sustain itself in the long run.

It should be kept in mind that while the rich and developed countries promote unrestrained globalization, free flow of goods and an end to protectionist policies, they do not always abide by what they advocate. For example, in 1999 the U.S. imposed high tariffs on some of her imports from Europe such as cheese, tobacco, handbags and scarves. In 2002 the U.S. imposed about 30% tariffs on the importation of steel from abroad for the purpose of gaining time to modernize its ailing steel industry. This decision has adversely affected several countries, including Turkey, who exports 860 tons of steel to the U.S. annually. Some of the decisions E.U. countries make are for the protection of each country's national interest. For example, the selling of the largest German telecommunications company to an

English firm was prevented by the German Prime Minister himself on the grounds that such a critical sector could not be given to the hegemony of another country.[191]

Mats Karlsson points out that: "We lack today a driving force for cohesion in multilateral policy, in norms creation as well as in actions and operations, in all different multilateral fora: the UN system, the IMF, the development banks, the WTO, etc. With the acceleration of globalization, that is going to become even more necessary. In fact, it might be said that in terms of who is to benefit, the decisions that must be made with respect to globalization are of the same kind facing the nation. It is undeniable that globalization has the potential to offer an array of benefits to the individual, groups in society and the state. But the question is whether those benefits are to be shared equitably by as many people as possible, thereby contributing to a more social and democratic world or they are to be "captured" and monopolized in the interests of the few. In short, the choice is between a "solidaric" or "captured" globalization.[192]

What in fact is needed is the recognition and implementation of mutual dependency, of interdependence between states, between nations, between peoples - sharing knowledge, technology, hardships as well as prosperity. As things stand even at the theoretical level the world has not reached a consensus as to how all this is going to be brought about.

4. Republicanism, Democracy, and Globalization

Globalization aims at overpowering that which is social and public through privatization and the market economy. As implemented now, globalization eliminates that which is social and public; hence, it clashes with the principle of republicanism.

The world is said to be one large market. This would be fine if only the over six billion people of the world had some say in the formulation of policies that affect their lives. The vast majority of the population of the world, not being active participants in the policy-making process, is simply on the "receiving end" of this process. Policies are imposed on them. They are reduced to "taking orders." This flies in the face of republicanism since the freedom that is supposed to be so important in a democracy is itself denied. In effect, what is called "freedom" is no more than the freedom of the market mechanism.

Thus, the way in which globalization is being implemented in the contemporary world necessitates a serious discussion of the core meaning both of republicanism and democracy.

The central meaning of republican government since Cicero has been legislation for the common good of the people. In Cicero's words "a republic is a people's state." A republic rests on the "sovereignty of the people." And republican liberty rests on the premise of the pursuit of the common good. Legislation for the realization of public welfare is a republican commitment. Democracy can pursue the highest ideals of humanity. But democracy can be used; it has been used, and it is continuing to be used for the pursuit of selfish interests, for personal gain, for the pursuit of policies that undermine democracy and exclude the people from participation in the formulation of policies shaping their own lives.

Globalization attacks the basic premise of republicanism, which is commitment to "public welfare." Democracy is used for the pursuit of private profit, for uncontrolled exploitation of the resources, in particular of developing countries, for upholding the private benefit against public benefit. As they are now being implemented, policies of globalization violate the basic core of republicanism, which is commitment to the common good. And democracy is used to justify these very policies that result in violating the public good.

There are ongoing debates in several countries of the world, especially in such countries as France, Turkey, and the United States, as to the question of the relative importance of democracy and the republic.

Mortimer Sellers points out that the essential elements of a republican legal system include pursuit of common good through popular sovereignty, and the rule of law under a mixed and balanced government. He goes on to say that this system secures liberty. And it is republican liberty that characterizes government in pursuit of the common good, where no citizen is subjected to the unfettered will of another. In short, the republican conception of liberty is service to the common good, under the rule of law.[193]

The republic has to consider the common good of the people and how the conditions befitting human dignity and enabling the functioning of the rule of law can be achieved. Democracy gives us the opportunities for self-expression and the use of our liberties. But a republic gives us the socio-historical and institutional context in which this use occurs. Democracy may be tolerant of the "particular," of the "private," of the "selfish," but a republic is always committed to the good of the whole. Hence, republicanism is prior to democracy. In fact, republicanism is a pre-condition of democracy. If a society loses touch with republican values, if it loses sight of the public good, if it is exclusionary and committed to particularism and particular interests, it may lose its grasp on democracy. If democracy is lost, but if the republic and republicanism remain viable, then democracy can be reborn. But if the republic is destroyed, and the republican commitments to sovereignty of the people and to public good are neglected, democracy will die. Only if the republic and republican commitments survive will it be possible to reincarnate democracy. *But the real goal is, of course, the democratization of the republic.* The republic receives its priority due to its commitment to the good of the whole, to public good. Therein lies the great contradiction between republicanism and globalization.

As stated above, republicanism is the doctrine that laws and the state should always serve the common good of a nation's people or citizens. The French thinker Régis Debray approaches this theme much in the same vein in his provocative essay: "Etes-vous démocrate ou républicain?" Debray says the following: democracy may allow the promotion of private interests and egoism; it may allow unlimited materialism, it is tolerant of appearance of religiosity. In a republic the state is free from all religious influence. In a republic, liberty is the conquest of reason; hence, a republic is committed to laïcism. A republican wants primarily an honorable state - a state which serves society.[194]

For a republican, it is not solely the individual that is important but also the citizen. Republican doctrine emphasizes equality of citizens. The doctrine is committed to public freedom in addition to that of the individual. It believes that you cannot achieve freedom for the public without realizing equality. Republicanism emphasizes social justice.

Republicanism shies away from theories and practices upholding private gain and private interests. In Seattle in December 1999 and again in Prague in September 2000, people were protesting, in the name of social justice and the public good, the hegemony of big capital, personal and private gain - very much in line with republican doctrine. Republican doctrine is essentially opposed to the kind of world envisaged by globalization. Republicans oppose globalization because it undermines public good and citizenship rights. And where public good is neglected, it is difficult to sustain rule of law.

It is often noted that globalization policies adversely affect the socio-economic and political order as well as the cultural values of the developing countries. However, the damage done, in varying degrees, to the values of Western Civilization itself is not generally considered.

It is important to note that globalization policies have done and continues to do immense damage in the realm of "values". The West has inflicted this damage also to itself, to the values of the Enlightenment which constitute the very essence of Western Civilization. Especially since the second half of the 20th century, in order to continue their technological and economic superiority and to create room for the pursuit of globalization policies, it became indispensable for the developed countries of the West, to eliminate all, including the values of Enlightenment, which could be in the way of such policies. The values of Enlightenment give priority to the individual and his rights. Enlightenment is commitment to human and humanist values. These values constituted an obstacle to the very logic of globalization. Hence, they had to be abandoned. This situation has had two important outcomes: The developed West began to move away from the values of the Enlightenment, the very values which constitute the most important source of Western civilization. And the West began to abandon policies upholding social consciousness and social justice. The West began to lose its sensitivity to social issues; hence, speeding up alienation in Western society. The Reagan era in the U. S. and the Thatcher era in Great Britain are important examples of such globalization policies.

5. The Atatürk Paradigm of Modernization, Republicanism and Globalization

The Atatürk paradigm of modernization provides an interesting case study when analyzed within the framework of republican doctrine and globalization.

Few countries in the world have undergone as thorough and as rapid a transformation of their cultural, social and political life as has Turkey, particularly between the years 1923-1945. In fact, Turkish society has been undergoing transformation for a long time. In a century and a half, Turkey has changed her political regime from absolutism to a constitutional monarchy and finally to a secular republic. Between the eighteenth century and the end of World War I, Turkish history is the history of attempts at modernization led by indigenous elites with the purpose of keeping intact the Ottoman Empire. On the other hand, Turkish history between 1919 and 1945 is characterized by the attempts of a revolutionary elite first to establish the nation-state of Turkey out of the ruins of the Ottoman Empire and then, with a singleness of purpose and complete unity, to modernize it under Mustafa Kemal Atatürk's leadership. From 1945 up to the present-day Turkish political development has been characterized by the advent of competitive politics, and by the more apparent unevenness in the various phases of her political development.

Turkey shares certain features, including low per-capita income, with other developing nations. But in several important respects, Turkey differs sharply from the pattern prevalent in other developing nations of Africa, Asia and Latin America.

Today all independent states are referred to as nations for reasons of diplomatic courtesy. However, Turkey is a nation in the strict sense, it is a country with a historical legacy of statehood, its political elite is heir to a seven-hundred year tradition of political responsibility. Furthermore, Turkey was never a colony, and the Turkish War of Independence was fought to maintain independence, not for the sake of attaining it. Moreover, Turkey has made great strides toward industrialization since the establishment of the Republic in 1923.

With very little capital and know-how, and the lack of a successful model of economic development other than the capitalist West, the Kemalists reluctantly agreed to the functioning of a market economy in the 1920s. The unsuccessful functioning of the market economy and the impact of the Great Depression were important factors leading the Kemalist government to search for other methods of economic development during the period 1928-1933. Thus, the adoption of the étatist principle was the result of pragmatic considerations rather than the result of profound ideological debate. Given the lack of capital, entrepreneurs, and skilled labor, the state emerged as the principle source of economic activity. With its assistance, Turkey was able to make great strides in economic development during that era. Nevertheless, the Atatürk paradigm of economic development was not simply interested in growth. It also emphasized welfare, the equitable distribution of the national income. The increased pace of industrialization has subsequently led to the emergence and growth of an entrepreneurial class and the labor movement. The primacy of the state in economic development has been challenged for decades now. On the other hand, both during Atatürk's Presidency and now, the commitment to a mixed economy is the Atatürkist principle of étatism taken to its bare minimum.

In recent decades, there has been a tendency in Turkey to emphasize economic growth rather than distribution. Particularly over the past two decades, a growing number of corporations and entrepreneurs and, to some extent, a succession of governments, have been pursuing globalization-oriented economic policies. With this increasing emphasis on growth rather than on distribution, various kinds of socio-economic problems have begun to emerge, thus generating growing social unrest. This has contributed to a questioning of the viability of the rule of law by the population at large - a population that at best is living under rather difficult economic conditions.

Globalization policies have an adverse effect on the lives of the common man in Turkey. For example, there has been a decrease in the amount of sources allotted to social services. The gap between Turkey and the rich countries is being paralleled by a widening of the gap between the rich and the poor in Turkey itself. Turkey has found it necessary to borrow from abroad, thus expanding foreign debt. On top of this, interest rates are a constant burden. The economic policies being dictated by the IMF and the World Bank emphasize privatization and, to a lesser extent, growth. The question of distribution is given short shrift. Privatization policies have led to job lay-offs and, subsequently, unemployment. This has been compounded by a rise in salaries for both blue-collar and white-collar workers far behind the rate of inflation. All this leads to social alienation and social discontent, which tend to feed the ultra-religious groups. Religion has begun to play a more important role in the political life of society. However, in the more developed societies of the West, social alienation and social dislocations have tended to produce fascism.

The adverse effects of other globalization policies have also been felt in Turkey. In some ways inseparable from the policies of the IMF or the World Bank, domestic policies aimed at keeping the state fully out of the economic life of the country; at freezing the pay of the working classes, at decreasing the sources allotted to health and other social services have also led to social discontent. Globalization policies see the nation-state as an enemy. Atatürkism is committed to the nation-state. It should be noted that most of the states in the world have acquired their independence only in recent decades and are still in the process of nation-building. Hence, the needs and realities of the developing nations and the demands of globalization are in contradiction with each other.

The socio-economic problems instigated by adherence to globalization and privatization have given rise to serious debate in Turkey with respect to republicanism and democracy, bringing into focus once again the Atatürk paradigm of modernization. Supporters of globalization policies as well as those who oppose the laïc ethos of the country have all jumped on the "democracy" bandwagon. Hence, democracy is currently being used by certain groups to defend a number of agendas: globalization, private interests, and rising religiosity.

The republican tradition is fairly strong in Turkey. There is by and large a broad allegiance to the "Republic." The Turkish Republic was established after a successful War of Independence. What was dead was the Ottoman Empire. The Republic signified the rebirth of the

Turkish nation. And with the implementation of the radical Atatürkist program of modernization, which included among other things a
full-scale adoption of the European Codes of Law, the term "Republic" began to be equated with modernity. So to the average Turkish
person "Republic" has many meanings: it is rebirth of the Turkish nation; it is commitment to modernity; it is commitment to public good; it is commitment to laïcism, it is commitment to social justice, it
is commitment to the rule of law, and it is commitment to an "honorable state."

NOTES

1 M. Kemal Atatürk, *Söylev, II.* Türk Dil Kurumu Yayınları, Ankara: Ankara University Press, 1978, p. 458.

2 Robert E. Ward and Dankwart A. Rustow (eds.), "Conclusion," *Political Modernization in Japan and Turkey.* Princeton: Princeton University Press, 1967, p. 467.

3 Leonard Binder et al., *Crises and Sequences in Political Development.* Princeton: Princeton University Press, 1971.

4 Samuel P. Huntington, *Political Order in Changing Societies.* New Haven: Yale University Press, 1968, p. 1.

5 C.H. Dodd, *Political Development.* London: MacMillan, 1972, p. 40.

6 Milovan Djilas, *The New Class,* 9th ed., New York: Frederick A. Praeger, 1958, p. 37-70.

7 David E. Apter, *Some Conceptual Approaches to the Study of Modernization.* Englewood Cliffs, New Jersey: Prentice-Hall, Inc., 1968, p. 193.

8 Paul E. Sigmund Jr. (ed.), *The Ideologies of the Developing Nations.* New York: Frederick A. Praeger, 1963, p. 3.

9 Ibid., p. 4.

10 Ibid., p. 5.

11 Tarık Z. Tunaya. *Türkiye'nin Siyasal Hayatında Batılılaşma Hareketleri,* Istanbul: Yedigün Matbaası, 1960, p. 228.

12 Sigmund, op. cit., p. 11.

13 Ibid, p. 12-13.

14 Ibid., p. 17.

15 Ibid., p. 22-23.

16 Ibid., p. 25.

17 Ibid., p. 31.

18 Ibid., p. 32.

19 Ibid., p. 37-40.

20 Huntington, *Political Order in Changing Societies,* op. cit., p. 8.

21 *Atatürk'ün Söylev ve Demeçleri, 1906-1938, II.* Ankara: Türk Tarih Kurumu Basımevi, 1959, p. 40.

22 Loc. cit.

23 Selâhaddin Çiller, *Atatürk İçin Diyorlar ki.* Varlık Yayınevi, Istanbul: Ekin Basımevi, 1965, p. 97.

24 Ibid., p. 283-284.

25 Ibid., p.99, 194, 282.

26 Ibid., p. 286.

27 Kemalism and Atatürkism are often used interchangeably.

28 Ibid., p. 150.

29 Bekir Sıtkı Baykal, "Atatürk Devrimlerinde Tarihin Rolü," *Atatürk Önderliğinde Kültür Devrimi,* Türk İnkılap Tarihi Enstitüsü Yayınları, Ankara: Ankara Üniversitesi Basımevi, 1972, p. 95.

30 Apart from the compact group of high administrative officials and the fighting class, the rest of the Ottoman Empire was divided into organizations called *millets.* The word *millet* has no direct equivalent in Western terminology. The term *millet* can neither be equated with nationality nor with church since the same *millet* could be spea-

king different languages in different areas. Although the head of each *millet* was a religious dignitary, a *millet* could still not be called a church since *millet*s were subordinate political parts of the Ottoman system. The *millet*s registered births, deaths, wills and marriages and even maintained courts of law for trying cases involving the people belonging to the same *millet*. They also raised taxes to pay for these functions. These functions, which were delegated to the *millets,* were at the time among the privileges exclusively enjoyed by the central governmental bodies of Western states.

31 See Tarık Z. Tunaya, *Türkiye'de Siyasi Partiler 1859-1952.* Istanbul: Doğan Kardeş Yayınları, 1952; Mete Tuncay, *Türkiye'de Sol Akımlar (1908-1925).* Bilgi Yayınevi, Ankara: Başnur Matbaası, 1967.

32 For the full text of "The National Pact" in English, see Suna Kili, *Kemalism.* Robert College Publication. Istanbul: Menteş Matbaası, 1969. Appendix B, p. 224-225.

33 For more on this subject, see: Vedat Eldem, *Osmanlı İmparatorluğu'nun İktisadi Şartları Hakkında Bir Tetkik.* Türkiye İş Bankası, Kültür Yayınları, Ankara: Tısa Matbaacılık Sanayii Tesisleri, 1970; Tevfik Çavdar et al., *Türkiye'de Toplumsal ve Ekonomik Gelişmenin 50 Yılı.* Başbakanlık Devlet İstatistik Enstitüsü Yayını, Ankara: D.İ.E. Matbaası, 1973.

34 See Vedat Eldem, ibid.; Tevfik Çavdar et al., ibid.

35 For the full text of the Declaration of the Sivas Congress in English, see Suna Kili, *Kemalism,* op. cit., Appendix A, pp. 222-223.

36 Yılmaz Altuğ, *Türk Devrim Tarihi Dersleri (1919-1938).* Istanbul: Fatih Yayınevi Matbaası, 1978, p. 270-273.

37 Mustafa Kemal Atatürk delivered his "Speech" to the second Congress of the Republican People's Party on six consecutive days. In this Speech, he explained the events leading up to the Turkish National Struggle, the Period of National Struggle (1919-1922) itself, and the early years of the Republic. This Speech, of which there are various Turkish texts, remains as one of the most important accounts of the 1920 Turkish Revolution. For an English translation of this Speech, see, A *Speech Delivered by Ghazi Mustafa Kemal: President of the Turkish Republic, October 1927.* Leipzig: K.F. Koehler, 1929.

38 Sabahattin Selek, *Anadolu İhtilâli,* Istanbul: Istanbul Matbaası, 1968, p. 219.

39 Tunaya, *Türkiye'de Siyasi Partiler,* op. cit., p. 534-539.

40 M. Kemal Atatürk, *Atatürk'ün Söylev ve Demeçleri: 1919-1938, I.* Ankara: Türk Tarih Kurumu Basımevi, 1961, p. 196-197.

41 Dankwart A. Rustow, A *World of Nations.* Washington, D. C.: The Brookings Institution, 1967, p. 213.

42 Ibid., p. 274.

43 *Cumhuriyet,* 10 September 1930.

44 William Yale, *The Near East.* Ann Arbor: University of Michigan Press, 1958, p. 297.

45 Samuel P. Huntington, "Political Modernization: America vs. Europe," *World Politics,* XVIII (3 April 1966), p. 378.

46 Niyazi Berkes, *İkiyüz Yıldır Neden Bocalıyoruz?,* Istanbul: Istanbul Matbaası, 1955, p. 91.

47 S.N. Eisenstadt, *Revolution and the Transformation of Societies.* New York: The Free Press, 1978, p. 233.

48 C.H. Dodd, *Political Development,* op. cit., p. 58.

49 David E. Apter, *Some Conceptual Approaches to the Study of Modernization.* op. cit., p. 69.

50 Claude, E. Welch Jr., "The Comparative Study of Political Modernization," *Political Modernization: A Reader in Comparative Change.* (Claude E. Welch, Jr., ed.). Belmont, California: Wadsworth Publishing Co., 1967, p. 1-7.

51 M.I.T. Study Group, "The Transitional Process," *Political Modernization: A Reader in Comparative Political Change.* (C.E. Welch, Jr., ed.), ibid., p. 31.

52 Tarık Z. Tunaya, *Atatürk ve Atatürkçülük,* Istanbul: Baha Matbaası, 1964, p. 124.

53 Tunaya, *Türkiye'nin Siyasi Hayatında Batılılaşma Hareketleri,* op. cit., p. 113.

54 Dankwart A. Rustow, "Devlet Kurucusu Olarak Atatürk," *Abadan'a Armağan.* A.Ü. Siyasal Bilgiler Fakültesi Yayını, Ankara: Sevinç Matbaası, 1969, p. 598.

55 *Söylev ve Demeçler,* I, op. cit., p. 381.

56 Niyazi Berkes, "Atatürk'ün Yöntemi ve Yönetimi," *Cumhuriyet,* 27 Ocak 1979, p. 5.

57 For the Amasya Declaration in English, see: Suna Kili, *Kemalism,* op. cit., pp. 11-12.

58 Representatives from the following provinces attended the Congress: Siirt, Van, Ağrı, Erzurum, Sivas, Tokat, Amasya, Ordu, Giresun, Gümüşhane, Rize, and Trabzon; representatives chosen from Mardin, Elazığ and Diyarbakır were kept from attending by the governors of those provinces.

59 Ali Fuat (Cebesoy) Pasha.

60 Suna Kili, *Türk Devrim Tarihi,* 10. baskı. Türkiye İş Bankası Kültür Yayınları. Istanbul: Eylül 2006, p. 54.

61 For the full text in English of the Constitution of 1921, see Suna Kili, *Turkish Constitutional Documents and Assembly Debates on the Constitutions of 1921 and 1961,* Robert College Research Center. Istanbul: Menteş Matbaası, 1971, Appendix B, p. 160-162.

62 İsmail Arar, *Atatürk'ün Halkçılık Programı,* Istanbul: Baha Matbaası, 1963. p. 34.

63 *Söylev ve Demeçler,* I, op. cit., p. 90.

64 Donal E. Webster, *The Turkey of Atatürk: Social Process in the Turkish Reformation.* Philadeiphia: The American Academy of Political and Social Science, 1939, p. 86.

65 The Populist Program of Mustafa Kemal, which was published in September 1920, and submitted to the Grand National Assembly on 13 September 1920, is no longer available in printed form. In order to analyze this Program, one has to study the *T.B.M.M. Zabıt Ceridesi (Records of the Grand National Assembly),* especially the *Records of the Assembly* on 24 April 1920 and 18 September 1920, as well as the *Records of the Assembly* between the dates of 18 November 1920 and 20 January 1921; See also *A Speech Delivered by Ghazi Mustafa Kemal in 1927,* p. 379-380 and 477-481.

66 Atatürk, *Speech,* ibid., p. 379.

67 Ibid, p. 380.

68 İlhan Arsel, *Türk Anayasa Hukuku.* Ankara: Ankara Üniversitesi, 1959, p. 56.

69 *T.B.M.M. Zabıt Ceridesi,* II, p. 255.

70 For the full text of this Draft Constitutional Law, which constitutes the Second Proposal of Kemal Atatürk's Populist Program, see İsmail Arar, *Atatürk'ün Halkçılık Programı,* op. cit, pp. 33-38.

71 *T.B.M.M. Zabıt Ceridesi,* V, p. 364.

72 Arar, *Atatürk'ün Halkçılık Programı,* op. cit., p. 12.

73 *Atatürk'ün Söylev ve Demeçleri,* I, op. cit., p. 101.

74 Karal, *Atatürk'ten Düşünceler,* op. cit., p. 125.

75 Henry Elisha Allen, *The Turkish Transformation: A Study in Social and Religious Development.* Chicago: University of Chicago Press, 1935, p. 54.

76 For the full text of the Constitution of 1924 in English, see Suna Kili, *Turkish Constitutional Developments*, op. cit., Appendix C, p. 163-171.

77 Selek, *Anadolu İhtilâli*, op. cit., p. 60-61.

78 Vedat Eldem, *Osmanlı İmparatorluğunun İktisadi Şartları Hakkında Bir Tetkik*, op. cit., p. 55.

79 For details see: Kili, *Türk Devrim Tarihi*, op. cit., p. 19-21.

80 For additional information, see: Fahir Giritlioğlu, *Türk Siyasi Tarihinde Cumhuriyet Halk Partisinin Mevkii, I*, Ankara: Ayyıldız Matbaası, 1965, p. 30-33.

81 For detailed information, see: Cahit Talas, *İçtimai iktisat*, S.B.F. Yayınları, Ankara: Ajans-Türk Matbaası, 1961, p. 91-98.

82 For detailed information, see: İsmail Arar, *Atatürk'ün Halkçılık Programı*, op. cit.

83 *Atatürk'ün Söylev ve Demeçleri, II*, op. cit., p. 99-112.

84 Huntington, *Political Order in Changing Societies*, op. cit., p. 346.

85 Dankwart, A. Rustow, "Atatürk's Political Leadership," *Near Eastern Round Table*, 1967-68 (ed. R. Bayly Winder). New York: New York University Near East Center, 1969, p. 143-144.

86 Çiller, *Atatürk için Diyorlar ki*, op. cit., p. 110.

87 Roland J. Pennock and David G. Smith, *Political Science: An Introduction*. New York: MacMillan Co., 1964, p. 603.

88 Enver Ziya Karal, *Atatürk'ten Düşünceler*, Ankara: Türk Tarih Kurumu Basımevi, 1956, p. 43.

89 Hans J. Morgenthau, *Politics Among Nations*, 3rd edition. New York: Alfred A. Knopf, 1966, p. 137.

90 *Atatürk'ün Söylev ve Demeçleri, I*, op. cit., p. 387.

91 Barbara Ward, *Turkey*, London: Oxford University Press, 1942, p. 59.

92 *Atatürk'ün Söylev ve Demeçleri, II*, op. cit., p. 181.

93 *Atatürk'ün Söylev ve Demeçleri, II*, ibid., p. 275-276.

94 S.N. Eisenstadt, "Breakdowns of Modernization," *Economic Development and Cultural Change*, XII (July 1964), p. 363.

95 Ibid., p. 365-366.

96 See, for example, Suna Kili, *Turkey: A Case Study of Political Development*, Istanbul: Robert College Publication, Menteş Matbaası, 1968, p. 13-25.

97 For more on this, see: Harold D. Laswell et al., *'The Comparative Study of Elites*, Palo Alto, Calif.: Standford University Press, 1952, p. 13.

98 For more on this, see: Suna Kili, *1960-1975 Döneminde Cumhuriyet Halk Partisinde Gelişmeler: Siyaset Bilimi Açısından Bir İnceleme*, Boğaziçi Üniversitesi Yayını, Istanbul: Çağlayan Basımevi, 1976; Suna Kili, *Turkey: A Case Study of Political Development*, op. cit.; Frederick W. Frey, *The Turkish Political Elite*. Cambridge, Mass: The M.I.T Press, 1965.

99 *Atatürk'ün Söylev ve Demeçleri, II*, op. cit., p. 11-12.

100 Joseph La Palombara and Myron Weiner, "The Origin and Development of Political Parties," *Political Parties and Political Development*. (J. La Palombara and M. Weiner, eds.). Princeton: Princeton University Press, 1966, p. 3.

101 Myron Weiner and Joseph La Palombra, "The Impact of Parties on Political Development," ibid., p. 424.

102 E.E. Schattschneider, *Party Government*, New York: Holt, Rhinehart and Winston, 1942, p. 1.

103 Dankwart A. Rustow, "The Politics of the Near East, Southwest Asia and Northern

Africa," *The Politics of the Developing Areas.* (Gabriel A. Almond and James S. Coleman, eds.), Princeton: Princeton University Press, 1960, p. 399-400.

104 Neil J. Smelser, "The Modernization of Social Relations," *Modernization: The Dynamics of Growth,* op. cit., p. 111-112.

105 David E. Apter, *Some Conceptual Approaches to the Study of Modernization,* op. cit., p. 237.

106 Ibid., p. 244. For a discussion of the connection between ideology and politics and their mutual interaction, see: Martin Seliger, *Ideology and Politics,* New York: The Free Press, 1976.

107 Mustafa Kemal Atatürk, *Atatürk'ün Söylev ve Demeçleri, II,* op. cit., p. 405.

108 See for example, the speech made by Atatürk on 20 March 1923 in Konya, "Konya Gençleriyle Konuşma": in *Atatürk'ün Söylev ve Demeçleri, II,* op. cit., p. 137-146.

109 *Atatürk'ün Söylev ve Demeçleri, I,* op. cit., p. 401.

110 Enver Ziya Karal, *Atatürk'ten Düşünceler,* op. cit., p. 122.

111 Şeref Gözübüyük ve Zekai Sezgin, *1924 Anayasası Üzerinde Meclis Görüşmeleri,* S.B.F. Yayını, Ankara: Balkanoğlu Matbaacılık Ltd. Şti., 1957, p. 30. See also Kili, *Turkish Constitutional Developments,* op. cit., p. 30-35.

112 See: Suna Kili, *1960-1975 Döneminde Cumhuriyet Halk Partisinde Gelişmeler: Siyaset Bilimi Açısından Bir İnceleme,* op. cit., p. 57-75; Kili, *Kemalism,* op. cit., p. 60-80.

113 At RPP Congresses held after 1935, several changes were made in the definitions of "Fatherland" and "Nation." "Government" and "Political and Public Rights of the Citizen" were expanded. For a discussion of the development and evolution of Atatürkism (Kemalism), see: Kili, *Kemalism,* op. cit., and Kili, *Cumhuriyet Halk Partisinde Gelişmeler,* op. cit.; and Kili, "Kemalism in Contemporary Turkey," *International Political Science Review,* I, No. 3, July 1980, p. 381-404.

114 Walter Livingston Wright Jr., "Truths about Turkey," *Foreign Affairs,* XXVI (January 1948), p. 352.

115 Emil Lengyel, *Turkey.* New York: Random House, 1941, p. 142.

116 Hans Kohn, *Revolutions and Dictatorships.* Cambridge: Harvard University Press, 1939, p. 255-256.

117 Lewis Thomas and Richard N. Frye. *The United States and Turkey and Iran.* Cambridge, Mass.: Harvard University Press, 1952, p. 76.

118 *Atatürk'ün Söylev ve Demeçleri, I,* op. cit., p. 320.

119 Lewis V. Thomas and Richard Frye, *The United States and Turkey and Iran,* op. cit., p. 57.

120 Rustow, "Devlet Kurucusu Olarak Atatürk," op. cit., p. 628.

121 *Atatürk'ün Söylev ve Demeçleri, 1906-1938, II,* op. cit., p. 142-143.

122 See (Moiz) Tekinalp, *Kemalism.* Istanbul Cumhuriyet Matbaası, 1936.

123 Clair Price, *The Rebirth of Turkey.* New York: Thomas Seltzer, 1923, p. 233.

124 Bernard Lewis, *The Emergence of Modern Turkey.* London: Oxford University Press, 1961, p. 286.

125 Lord Kinross, *Atatürk: The Rebirth of a Nation.* London: Weidenfeld and Nicholson, 1964, p. 464.

126 Lewis, *The Emergence of Modern Turkey.* op. cit., p. 286.

127 Lucian W. Pye, "The Concept of Political Development," *The Annals of the American Academy of Political and Social Science,* March 1965, p. 358.

128 *Bugün'ün Diliyle Atatürk'ün Söylevleri,* op. cit., p. 75-76.

129 Webster, *The Turkey of Atatürk: Social Process in the Turkish Reformation,* op. cit., p. 240.

130 Sigmund, *The Ideologies of the Developing Nations,* op. cit., p. 40.

131 *Atatürk'ün Söylev ve Demeçleri, II,* op. cit., p. 322-323.

132 Edward Greenberg (ed.), *Political Socialization,* New York: Atherton Press, 1970, p. 3.

133 For more on education and development, see: James S. Coleman (ed.), *Education and Political Development.* Princeton: Princeton University Press, 1965; Frederick W. Frey, "Education in Turkey," *Political Modernization in Japan and Turkey,* op. cit., p. 205-235; Andreas M. Kazamias, *Education and the Quest for Modernity in Turkey,* Chicago: University of Chicago Press, 1966; Şevket Gedikoğlu, *Kemalist Eğitim İlkeleri,* Çağdaş Yayınları, Istanbul: Erdinç Basım ve Yayınevi, 1978.

134 Barbara Ward, *Turkey, op. cit.,* p. 40.

135 *Atatürk'ün Söylev ve Demeçleri, I,* op. cit., p. 166.

136 Ibid, p. 221.

137 Herbert Melzig, *Thus Spoke Atatürk,* op. cit., p. 8.

138 *Atatürk'ün Söylev ve Demeçleri, II,* op. cit., p. 108.

139 Ibid., p. 121.

140 *Atatürk'ün Söylev ve Demeçleri, I,* op. cit., p. 320.

141 *Atatürk'ün Söylev ve Demeçleri, II,* op. cit., p. 180.

142 Ibid., p. 181.

143 Ibid., p. 182.

144 Ibid., p. 405.

145 Thomas and Fry, *The United States and Turkey and Iran,* op. cit., p. 113.

146 Selek, *Anadolu İhtilâli,* op. cit., p. 713.

147 Ali Mazrui, "Africa between the Meiji Restoration and the Legacy of Atatürk: Comparative Dilemmas of Modernization," *Papers and Discussions. Türkiye İş Bankası International Symposium on Atatürk (17-22 May 1981).* Türkiye İş Bankası Cultural Publications. Ankara: Tisa Matbaacılık, 1984, p. 410.

148 Ibid., p. 410-411.

149 William Yale, *The Near East: A Modern History.* Ann Arbor: The University of Michigan Press, 1958, p. 422.

150 Nirmal Bose, "The Politics of Development and System Change," *Participation II,* No. 3 (1978), p. 45.

151 Apter, *Some Conceptual Approaches of the Study of Modernization,* op. cit., p. 69.

152 Selek, *Anadolu İhtilâli,* op. cit, p. 173.

153 Ahmet Cevat Emre, "Amele ve Köylü Kitleleri Nasıl Fırka Teşkil Eder?," *Toplum ve Bilim* (Spring-Summer 1980), p. 116.

154 *Atatürk'ün Söylev ve Demeçleri, I,* op. cit., p. 396.

155 Ibid, p. 398.

156 They are the following: Yakup Kadri (Karaosmanoğlu), Şevket Süreyya (Aydemir), Vedat Nedim (Tör), İsmail Hüsrev (Tökin), M. Şevki (Yazman) and Burhan Asaf (Belge).

157 For the *Kadrocular* current of thought, see: *Kadro:* 1932, Cilt: I (prepared for publication by Cem Alpar), Ankara: İktisadi ve Ticari İlimler Akademsi Yayını, Ankara: Kalite Matbaası, 1978; *Kadro* - 1933, Cilt II (prepared for publication by Cem Alpar), Ankara İktisadi ve Ticari İlimler Akademisi Yayımı, Ankara, Kalite Matbaası, 1979 and *Kadro* - 1934, Cilt III (prepared for publication by Cem Alpar), Ankara İktisadi ve Ticari İlimler Akademisi Yayımı, Ankara, Kalite Matbaası, 1980.

158   Melzig, *Thus Spoke Atatürk,* op. cit., p. 10-11.

159   Yale, *The Near East,* op. cit., p. 297.

160   Thomas and Fry, *The United States and Turkey and Iran,* op. cit., p. 34.

161   Oya Köymen, A Comparative Study of the Anglo-Turkish Relations: C. 1830-1870 and 1919-1939. University of Strathclyde (Glasgow), unpublished doctoral thesis presented to the Department of Economics, 1967, p. 324.

162   Ibid., p. 324

163   Ibid., p. 325.

164   For discussions and views proposing that religion needs to be controlled by the state to some extent, see: Kili, *Turkish Constitutional Developments,* op. cit., p. 98-104.

165   Halide Edip (Adıvar), *Turkey Faces West.* New Haven: Yale University Press, 1930, p. 206.

166   Karl Krüger, *Kemalist Turkey and the Middle East.* London: George Allen and Unwin, 1932, p. 30.

167   Allen, *The Turkish Transformation,* op. cit., p. 176.

168   *Atatürk'ün Söylev ve Demeçleri,* II, op. cit., p. 214-215.

169   Melzig, *Thus Spoke Atatürk,* op. cit., p. 9-10.

170   Arnold J. Toynbee, A *Study of History, Volume VI,* London: Oxford University Press, 1947, p. 102-103.

171   C.H. Dodd, *Democracy and Development in Turkey,* Hull England: The Eathon Press, 1979, p. 86.

172   August Ritter von Kral, *Atatürk's Land: The Evolution of Modern Turkey,* translated by Kenneth Benton. Wien: Wilhelm Braumüller, 1938, p. 225.

173   *Söylev, I,* op. cit., p. 1.

174   Ibid., p. 9.

175   Ibid., p. 458.

176   Ibid., p. 12.

177   Herbert Melzig, *Thus Spoke Atatürk,* op. cit., p. 315-316.

178   Lewis V. Thomas and Richard N. Frye, *The United States and Turkey and Iran.* op. cit., p. 74.

179   Barbara Ward, *Turkey.* op. cit., p. 51.

180   See, Kili, *Cumhuriyet Halk Partisinde Gelişmeler,* op. cit., p. 211-266; Kili, *Kemalism,* op. cit., p. 190-215.

181   Bernard Lewis, "Speech Delivered by Bernard Lewis On the Occasion of his Receipt of the ASA 'Atatürk *Award' Voice of Atatürk,* year 7, No. 18. November 2002.

182   Felix Valyi, *Spiritual and Political Revolutions in Islam.* London: Kegan Paul, Trench and Trubner, 1925, p. 24.

183   Arnold J. Toynbee and Kenneth P. Kirkwood, *Turkey.* New York: Scribners, 1927, p. 288-289.

184   Ernest Jackh, *The Rising Crescent: Turkey Yesterday, Today and* Tomorrow. New York: Farrah and Rinehart, 1944, p. 260.

185   Hans Kohn, *Revolutions and Dictatorships,* op. cit., p. 249.

186   The content of the "Additional Protocol" shall be discussed under the "Cyprus" heading.

187   See the following on the Turkish Military: Suna Kili, "Role of the Military in Turkish Society: An Assessment from the Perspective of History, Sociology and Politics" in *Military Rule and Democratization: Changing Perspectives.* (Ed: Asha Gupta). New Delhi: Deep &Deep Publications PVT Ltd., 2003. pp. 145-183.

188 *Megali Idea* has been for a very long time, the underlying ideological underpinning of Greek foreign policy.*Megali Idea* aims at the taking over by Greece all lands which Greece claims belonged to the country in history. And as such *Megali Idea* constitutes the imperialistic ambitions of Greece.

189 James N. Rosenau, "Global World Order and Political Space: Changing Dimensions of Sovereignty and the Nation-State," *Seminar Report: International Solidarity and Globalization: In Search of New Strategies.* Swedish Ministry of Foreign Affairs. Stockholm: Tryckeri AB Smaland, 1998, p. 89.

190 Theodore J. Lowi, "Our Millenium: Political Science Confronts the Global Corporate Economy," Quebec, Canada. August, 2000.

191 Onur Öymen, *Cumhuriyet*, 21 July 2002.

192 Mats Karlsson, "Solidaric or Captured Globalisation," *Address at India Center for International Cooperation.* New Delhi, 10 March 1997.

193 Mortimer Sellers, "Republicanism, Liberalism, and the Law," *Kentucky Law Journal*, Vol. 86, No. l, 1997-98, p. 2-9.

194 Régis Debray, "Etes-vous démocrate ou républicain," *Le Nouvel Observateur.* 30 November-6 December, 1989.

BIBLIOGRAPHY

BOOKS

Adams, J., *A Defence of the Constitutions of Government of the United States of America*, 1987.

Adıvar, Halide Edip. *Turkey Faces West*. New Haven: Yale University Press, 1932.

————— *Türkün Ateşle İmtihanı (İstiklâl Savaşı Hatıraları)*, Istanbul: Kutulmuş Matbaası, 1962.

Ağaoğlu, Samet. *Kuvayi Milliye Ruhu*. Istanbul: Ahmet Sait Basımevi, 1944.

Ahmad, Feroz. *The Turkish Experiment in Democracy: 1950-1975*. Boulder, Colorado: Westview Press, 1977.

Akarsu, Bedia. *Atatürk Devrimi ve Yorumları*. Ankara: Ankara Üniversitesi Basımevi, 1969.

Akay, İhsan. *Atatürkçülüğün İlkeleri*, Istanbul: Ekin Basımevi, 1964.

Aksal, Sadri Maksudi. *Türk Dili İçin*. Türk Ocakları İlim ve Sanat Heyeti Neşriyatı. Milli Seri, Sayı l, 1930.

Albrow, M. *The Global Age*, Cambridge, Polity Press, 1996.

Almond, Gabriel. A *Political Development: Essays in Heuristic Theory*. Boston: Little, Brown and Company, 1970.

————— and Coleman, James, S. (eds). *The Politics of the Developing Areas*. Princeton, N.J.: Princeton University Press, 1960.

————— and Powell, G. Bingham. *Comparative Politics: A Developmental Approach*. Boston: Little, Brown and Company, 1966.

————— and Flanagan, Scott, Mundt, Robert, J. *Crisis, Choice and Change: Historical Studies of Political Development*. Boston: Little, Brown and Company, 1973.

Allen, Henry Elisha. *The Turkish Transformation: A Study in Social and Religious Development*. Chicago: University of Chicago Press, 1935.

Altuğ, Yılmaz. *Türk Devrim Tarihi Dersleri (1919-1938)*. 3. Baskı, Istanbul: Fatih Yayınevi Matbaası, 1978.

Anderson, Eugene, N. and Anderson, Pauline, R. *Political Institutions and Social Change in Continental Europe in the 19th Century*. Berkeley: University of California Press, 1967.

Apter, David E. *The Politics of Modernization*. Chicago: University of Chicago Press, 1965.

————— *Some Conceptual Approaches to the Study of Modernization*. New Jersey: Englewood Cliffs: Prentice-Hall, Inc., 1968.

————— (ed.) *Ideology and Discontent*. New York: Pree Press of Glencoe, 1964.

Aralov, S. İ. *Bir Sovyet Diplomatının Türkiye Hatıraları*, Istanbul: Istanbul. Matbaası, 1967.

Arar, İsmail. *Atatürk'ün Halkçılık Programı*, Istanbul: Baha Matbaası, 1963.

————— (editor). *Hükümet Programları 1920-1965*. Istanbul: Tipo Neşriyat ve Basımevi, 1968.

————— *Atatürk'ün İzmit Basın Toplantısı*, Istanbul: Istanbul Matbaası, 1969.

Armaoğlu, Fahir. *Siyasi Tarih 1789-1960*. 3. Baskı. Ankara: Ayyıldız Matbaası, 1975.

Aron, Raymond. *Progress and Disillusion: The Dialectics of Modern Society*. London: Pall Mall Press, 1968.

Arsel, İlhan. *Türk Anayasa Hukuku.* Ankara: Ankara Üniversitesi, 1959.

———— *Teokratik Devlet Anlayışından Demokratik Devlet Anlayışına.* Ankara Üniversitesi Hukuk Fakültesi Yayınları. Ankara: Ankara Üniversitesi Basımevi, 1975.

———— *Arap Milliyetçiliği ve Türkler,* Istanbul: Yükselen Matbaacılık Ltd. Şti., 1977.

Ashford, Douglas. *Ideology and Participation.* Beverly Hills, Calif.: Sage Publications, 1972.

Aşkun, Vehbi Cem. *Sivas Kongresi.* Sivas: Kamil Matbaası, 1945.

Atatürk, Mustafa Kemal. *Atatürk'ün Söylev ve Demeçleri (1919-1938).* I. Cilt. 2. Baskı. Ankara: Türk Tarih Kurumu Basımevi, 1961.

———— *Atatürk'ün Söylev ve Demeçleri (1906-1938).* 2. Cilt. Ankara: Türk Tarih Kurumu Basımevi, 1959.

———— *Atatürk'ün Söylev ve Demeçleri (1918-1937).* 3. Cilt. Ankara: Türk Tarih Kurumu Basımevi, 1961.

———— *Atatürk'ün Tamim, Telgraf ve Beyannameleri.* 4. Cilt. Ankara: Ankara Üniversitesi Basımevi, 1964.

———— *Zabit ve Kumandan île Hasbihal.* Türkiye İş Bankası Kültür Yayınları, Istanbul: Baha Matbaası, 1973.

———— *Söylev.* Türk Dil Kurumu Yayını. 2. Cilt. Ankara: Ankara Üniversitesi Basımevi, 1974.

———— *Söylev,* (abbreviated version prepared by Hıfzı Veldet Dedeoğlu). Çağdaş Yayınları, Istanbul: Erdini Basımevi, 1978.

———— *Nutuk.* 3. Cilt. Istanbul: Milli Eğitim Basımevi, 1962.

———— *Atatürk. (Komutan, Devrimci ve Devlet Adamı Yönleriyle).* T.C. Genelkurmay Askeri Tarih ve Stratejik Etüt Başkanlığı Yayınları. Ankara: Genelkurmay Basımevi, 1980.

Atay, Falih Rıfkı. *Çankaya. Atatürk Devri Hatıraları.* 2 Cilt. Istanbul: Dünya Yayınları, No. 5, 1958.

————*Atatürk'ün Hatıraları: 1914-1919.* Türkiye İş Bankası Kültür Yayınları. Ankara, 1965.

Axford, B., *The Global System,* Cambridge, Polity Press, 1995.

Avcıoğlu, Doğan. *Milli Kurtuluş Tarihi: 1938'den 1995'e.* 3 Cilt. Istanbul: Istanbul Matbaası, 1974.

Aydemir, Şevket Süreyya. *Tek Adam: Mustafa Kemal.* 3 Cilt. Istanbul: Yükselen Matbaası, 1966-67.

———— *İkinci Adam: İsmet İnönü.* 3 Cilt. Istanbul: Yükselen Matbaası, 1966-68.

———— *İnkılâp ve Kadro.* 2. Baskı. Ankara: Başnur Matbaası, 1968.

Bahrampour, Firouz. *Turkey: Political and Social Transformation.* Brooklyn, N.J.: Theo Gaus' Sons, Inc., 1967.

Barber, Bernard ve Inkeles, Alex (eds.). *Stability and Social Change.* Boston: Little, Brown and Co., 1971.

Baydar, Mustafa (ed.). *Atatürk'le Konuşmalar.* Varlık Yayınları. Istanbul: Ekin Basımevi, 1960.

———— *Atatürk ve Devrimlerimiz.* Türkiye İş Bankası Kültür Yayınları, Istanbul: Çeltüt Matbaacılık Kol. Şti., 1973.

Başer, Ahmet Hamdi. *Atatürk'le 3 Ay ve 1930'dan Sonra Türkiye.* Istanbul: Tan Matbaacılık, 1945.

Belen, Fahri. *Büyük Türk Zaferi.* Ankara: Doğuş Ltd. Şti. Matbaası, 1962.

———— *Atatürk'ün Askeri Kişiliği,* Istanbul: Milli Eğitim Basımevi, 1963.

Bendix, Reinhard. *Nation-Building and Citizenship.* New York: Wiley, 1964.

Berkes, Niyazi. *İki Yüz Yıldır Neden Bocalıyoruz?* 2. Baskı, Istanbul: Istanbul Matbaası, 1965.

————— *Türkiye'de Çağdaşlaşma.* Ankara: Bilgi Basımevi, 1973.

Binder, Leonard et al. *Crisis and Sequences in Political Development.* Princeton, New Jersey: Princeton University Press, 1971.

Black, C. E. *The Dynamics of Modernization.* New York: Harper and Row, 1966.

Bowie, Norman, E. and Simon R. L. *The Individual and the Political Order: An Introduction to Social and Political Philosophy.* Englewood Cliffs, N. J.: Prentice-Hall Inc. 1977.

Boyer, R. and Drache D., (eds.), *States Against Markets,* London, Routledge, 1996.

Bozkurt, Mahmut Esat. *Atatürk İhtilâli,* Istanbul: As Matbaası, 1967.

Brinton, Crane. *The Anatomy of Revolution.* New York: Vintage Books, 1959.

Burley, John ve Traeger, Peter. *African Development and Europe.* New York: Pergamon Press, 1970.

Cebesoy, Ali Fuat. *Moskova Hatıraları.* Istanbul: Vatan Neşriyatı, 1955.

Cicero, Marcus Tullius, 1977, *De res publica,* Stuttgart 1977.

Chalmers, Douglas A. (ed.). *Changing Latin America: New Interpretations of its Politics and Society.* The Academy of Political Science. Columbia University. Vermont, Montpelier: Capital City, 1972.

Chirot, Dantel. *Social Change in the Twentieth Century.* New York: Harcourt Brace Jovanovitch, Inc., 1977.

Clausen, John A. (ed.). *Socialization and Society.* Boston: Little, Brown and Company, 1968.

Cohn, Edwin J; *The Development o f a More Prosperous and Open Society: Turkish Economic, Social and Political Development 1948-1968.* Ankara: 1968 (copy).

Coleman, James S. (ed.). *Education and Political Development.* Princeton, N.J.: Princeton University Press, 1965.

Curle, Adam. *Educational Strategy for Developing Societies.* London: Tavistock Publications, 1970.

Çavdar, Tevfik et al. *Türkiye'de Toplumsal ve Ekonomik Gelişmenin 50 yılı.* Başbakanlık Devlet İstatistik Enstitüsü Yayını. Ankara: Devlet İstatistik Enstitüsü Matbaası, 1973.

Çiller, Selahaddin. *Atatürk İçin Diyorlar ki.* Varlık Yayınları, Istanbul: Ekin Matbaası, 1965.

Dahl, Robert A. *Polyarchy: Participation and Political Change.* New York: Praeger Publishers, 1970.

Demirkan, Selâhaddin. *Bir Milletin Yarattığı Lider: Mustafa Kemal Atatürk,* Istanbul: Gün Matbaası, 1972.

Deutsch, Karl W. *Politics and Government: How People Decide their Fate.* Boston: Houghton Mifflin Co.: 1970.

————— *The Nerves of Government: Models of Political Communication and Control.* New York: The Free Press, 1966.

————— *Nationalism and Social Communication: An Inquiry into the Foundations of Nationality.* Cambridge, Mass.: The M.I.T. Press, 1953.

————— and Foltz, William. *Nation-Building.* New York: Atherton Press, 1963.

Djilas, Milovan. *The New Class.* 9. baskı. New York: Frederick A. Praeger, 1958.

Di Palma G. *Apathy and Participation: Mass Politics in Western Society.* New York: The Free Press, 1970.

Dodd, C. H. *Democracy and Development in Turkey.* Manchester: Manchester University Press, 1979.

———— *Political Development.* London: Macmillan, 1972.

———— *Politics and Government in Turkey.* Manchester: Manchester University Press, 1969.

Ecevit, Bülent. *Atatürk ve Devrimcilik.* Tekin Yayınevi. Ankara: Yaylacılık Matbaası, 1976.

Eisenstadt, S.N. *The Political Systems of Empires.* New York: The Press of Glencoe, 1963.

———— (ed.). *Max Weber: On Charisma and Institution-Building.* Chicago: The University of Chicago Press, 1968.

———— *The Protestant Ethic and Modernization.* New York: Basic Books, Inc., 1968.

———— (ed.). *Readings in Social Evolution and Development.* New York: Pergamon Press, 1970.

———— *Tradition, Change and Modernity.* New York: John Wiley and Sons, 1973.

———— *Revolution and the Transformation of Societies: A Comparative Study of Civilizations.* New York: The Free Press, 1978.

Eldem, Vedat. *Osmanlı İmparatorluğu'nun İktisadi Şartları Hakkında Bir Tetkik.* Türkiye İş Bankası Kültür Yayınları. Ankara: Tisa Matbaacılık Sanayii, 1970.

Elliot, Henry G. *Some Revolutions and other Diplomatic Experiences.* London: John Murra, 1922.

Ellul, Jacques. *Autopsy of Revolution.* Alfred. Knopf, 1971.

Emerson, Ruppert. *From Empire to Nation: The Rise to Self-Assertion of Asian and African Peoples.* Cambridge, Mass.: Harvard University Press, 1960.

Emre, Ahmet Cevat. *Atatürk'ün İnkılâp Hedefi ve Tarih Tezi.* Istanbul: Ekin Basımevi, 1956.

Erikan, Celâl. *Komutan Atatürk,* 2 Cilt, 2. Baskı. Türkiye İş Bankası Kültür Yayınları. Ankara: Tisa Matbaacılık Sanayii, 1972.

Eroğlu, Hamza. *Devlet Kurucusu Atatürk.* Ankara: Emel Matbaacılık Sanayii Ltd. Şti., 1973.

Eroğul, Cem. *Demokrat Parti: Tarihi ve İdeolojisi.* 3. baskı. Ankara: İmge Kitabevi, Ekim 1998.

———— *Türk Devriminin Milli Değeri.* Ankara: Emel Matbaacılık Sanayii Ltd. Şti., 1973.

Escobar, Arturo, *Encountering Development: The Making and Unmaking of the Third World,* Princeton, N.J.: Princeton University Press, 1994.

Fiechter, George Andre. *Brazil since 1964: Modernization under a Military Regime.* New York: John Wiley and Sons, 1975.

Field, G. Lowell. *Comparative Political Development: The Precedent of the West.* London: Routledge and Kegan Paul Limited, 1967.

Fink, Z.S., *The Classical Republicans: An Essay in the Recovery of a Pattern of Thought in Seventeeth Century England,* Evanston, III, 1962.

Finkle, Jason L., Gable, Richard W. *Political Development and Social Change.* New York: John Wiley and Sons, Inc., 1968.

Fishman, Joshua A. *Language and Nationalism.* Rowley, Mass.: Newbury House Publishers, 1972.

Frey, Frederick W. *The Turkish Political Elite.* Cambridge, Mass.: M.I.T.Press,1965.

Friedland, William H. and Rosberg, Carl G. *African Socialism.* Stanford, California: Stanford University Press, 1964.

Gedikoğlu, Şevket. *Kemalist Eğitim İlkeleri, Uygulamalar.* Çağdaş Yayınları, Istanbul: Edini Basım ve Yayınevi, 1978.

Getizon, Paul. *Mustafa Kemal, ou l'Orient en march.* Paris: Bossard, 1929.

Giddens, Anthony (ed.). *Positivism and Sociology.* London: Heinemann, 1975.

———— *The Consequences of Modernity,* Cambridge, Polity Press, 1990.

Greider, J., *One World Ready or Not? The Manic Logic of Global Capitalism,* New York, Simon and Shuster, 1997.

Giritlioğlu, Fahir. *Türk Siyasi Tarihinde Cumhuriyet Halk Partisinin Mevkii.* 2 cilt. Ankara: Ayyıldız Matbaası, 1965.

Gorz, Andre. *Socialism and Revolution.* New York: Anchor Press, 1973.

Gökalp, Ziya. *Turkish Nationalism and Western Civilization.* (tr.: Niyazi Berkes). New York: Columbia University Press, 1959.

Gönlübol, Mehmet and Cem Sar. *Atatürk ve Türkiye'nin Dış Politikası.* Istanbul: Milli Eğitim Basımevi, 1963.

Greenberg, Edward G. (ed.). *Political Socialization.* New York: Atherton Press, 1970.

Güvenç, Bozkurt, *Türk Kimliği,* T.C. Kültür Bakanlığı Yayınları, Ankara, 1993.

Harrison, David, *The Sociology of Modernization and Development,* London: Routledge, 1993.

Held, D., *Democracy and World Order,* Cambridge, Polity Press, 1995.

Hirst, P. and Thompson, G., *Globalization in Question,* Cambridge, Polity Press, 1996.

Heyd, Uriel. *Foundations of Turkish Nationalism.* London: Luzac and Harvill Press, 1950.

Howard, Harry N. *The Partition of Turkey: A Diplomatic History, 1913-1923.* Norman: University of Oklahoma Press, 1931.

Hunter, Guy. *Modernizing Peasant Societies: A Comparative Study in Asia and Africa.* New York: Oxford University Press, 1969.

Hunter, Robert E. and Reilly, John E. *Development Today.* New York: Praeger Publishers, 1972.

Huntington, Samuel P. *Political Order in Changing Societies.* New Haven: Yale University Press, 1968.

İnan. Afet, *Atatürk Hakkında Hatıralar ve Belgeler.* 2. Baskı. Türkiye İş Bankası Kültür Yayınları. Ankara: Ajans Türk Matbaacılık Sanayii, 1968.

———— *M. Kemal Atatürk'ten Yazdıklarım,* Istanbul: Milli Eğitim Basımevi, 1971.

———— *Devletçilik İlkesi ve Türkiye Cumhuriyetinin Birinci Sanayi Planı: 1933.* Ankara: Türk Tarih Kurumu Basımevi, 1973.

———— *Türkiye Cumhuriyetin İkinci Sanayi Planı: 1936.* Ankara: Türk Tarih Kurumu Basımevi, 1973.

İstanbul İktisadi ve Ticari İlimler Mezunları Derneği, *Atatürk Döneminin Ekonomik ve Toplumsal Tarihiyle İlgili Sorunları,* Istanbul: Murat Matbaacılık Koli. Şt., 1977.

İstanbul İktisadi ve Ticari İlimler Akademisi, *Atatürkçülüğün Ekonomik ve Sosyal Yönü Semineri,* İ.İ.T.İ.A.'nin Cumhuriyete 50. Yıl Armağanı, Istanbul, 1973.

İstanbul Üniversitesi Tıp Fakültesi Talebe Cemiyeti. *Atatürk: Görüşler ve Hatıralarla,* Istanbul Üniversitesi Tıp Fakültesi Yayınları. Istanbul: Büyük Kervan Matbaası, 1962.

İstanbul Üniversitesi Atatürk Devrimleri Araştırma Enstitüsü. *Atatürk Devrimleri I. Milletlerarası Sempozyumu Bildirileri,* Istanbul: Sermet Matbaası, 1975.

Jackh, Ernest. *The Rising Crescent: Turkey Yesterday, Today and Tomorrow.* New York: Farrah and Rinehart, 1944.

Jaguaribe, Helio. *Political Development: A General Theory and a Latin American Case Study.* New York: Harper and Row Publishers, 1973.

Jäckhe, Gotthard. *Die Türkei in Den Jahren 1933 und 1934.* Berlin: Walter de Gruyter, 1936.

————— *Die Türkei in Den Jahren 1935-1941.* Leipzig Otto Harrassowitz, 1943.

————— *Die Türkei in Den Jahren 1935-1941.* Leipzig Otto Harrassowitz, 1955.

————— and Pritsch, Erich. *Die Türkei Seit Dem Weltkriege (1918-1928).* Berlin: Reichfruekerei, 1929.

Jameson, R., *Post Modernism or The Cultural Logic of Late Capitalisme,* London, Verso, 1991.

Johnson, Dale L. *The Sociology of Change and Reaction in Latin America.* New York: The Bobbs-Merril Company, Inc. 1973.

Kadro: 1932, cilt: I (Cem Alpar, ed.). Ankara İktisadi ve Ticari İlimler Akademisi Yayını. Ankara: Kalite Matbaası, 1978.

Kadro: 1934, cilt: 3 (Cem Alpar, ed.). Ankara Kalite Matbaası, 1978.

Kadro: 1934, cilt: 3 (Cem Alpar, ed.). Ankara Kalite Matbaası, 1980.

Karal, Enver Ziya. *Türkiye Cumhuriyeti Tarihi (1918-1960).* Istanbul: Milli Eğitim Basımevi, 1962.

————— *Atatürk'ten Düşünceler.* Ankara: Türk Tarih Kurumu Basımevi, 1956.

————— et al. *Atatürk, Din ve Laiklik,* Istanbul: Menteş Matbaası, 1968.

Kautsky, John H. (ed.). *Political Change in Underdeveloped Countries: Nationalism and Communism:* New York: Random House, 1960.

Kaynar, Reşad. *Yakın Tarihimizin Işığı Altında Atatürkçülüğün Üzerine Bir İnceleme Denemesi.* Istanbul: Fatih Yayınevi Matbaası, 1973.

Kazamias, Andreas, M. *Education and the Quest for Modernity in Turkey.* Chicago: The University of Chicago Press, 1966.

————— and Massialas, Byron G. *Tradition and Change in Education: A Comparative Study.* Englewood Cliffs, N.J.: Prentice-Hall, Inc., 1965.

Kedourie, Elie. *Nationalism.* London: Hutchinson, 1961.

Kerr, Clark, Dunlop, John-Harbison, F.H. Myers, Charles. *Industrialism and Industrial Man.* Cambridge, Mass.: Harvard University Press, 1960.

Kidd, John B., ve Richter, Frank-Jurgen, *Development Models, Globalization and Economies: A Search for the Holy Grail?,* New York: Palgrave Macmillan, 2006.

Kili, Suna. *Atatürk Devrimi: Bir Çağdaşlaşma Modeli.* 10th ed. Türkiye İş Bankası Kültür Yayınları. Istanbul: Şefik Matbaası, 2006.

————— *Türk Devrim Tarihi.* 10th ed. Türkiye İş Bankası Kültür Yayınları. Istanbul: Şefik Matbaası, 2006.

————— and Gözübüyük, Şeref. *Sened-i İttifaktan Günümüze Türk Anayasa Metinleri.* 3rd ed., Türkiye İş Bankası Kültür Yayınları. Istanbul: Şefik Matbaası, 2006.

————— *Cumhuriyet ve Küreselleşme* (editor). T.C. Kültür Bakanlığı Yayını. Ankara: Sistem Ofset, 2002.

————— *Dünya ve Türkiye Açısından Atatürk.* Yapı Kredi Yayını,1996.

————— *Osmanlı ve Türk Anayasaları.* Boğaziçi Üniversitesi Yayını. Istanbul: Boğaziçi Üniversitesi Matbaası, 1980.

————— *Bugünkü Türkiye ve Kemalizm,* Istanbul: Deniz Harp Lisesi Yayını, 1980.

————— *Çayırhan: Bir Orta Anadolu Köyünde Toplumsal Değişme ve Siyasal Davranış.* Boğaziçi Üniversitesi Yayını, Istanbul: Boğaziçi Üniversitesi Matbaası, 1978.

————— *Atatürk ve Devrimleri,* Istanbul: Deniz Harp Lisesi Yayını, 1977.

————— *Cumhuriyet Halk Partisinde Gelişmeler: Siyaset Bilimi Açısından Bir İnceleme.* Boğaziçi Üniversitesi Yayını, Istanbul: Çağlayan Basımevi, 1976.

————— *Turkish Constitutional Developments and Assembly Debates on the Constitutions of 1924 and 1961.* Robert College Research Center. Istanbul: Menteş Matbaası, 1971.

————— *Kemalism.* Robert College Publication. Istanbul: Menteş Matbaası, 1969.

————— *Turkey: A Case Study of Political Development.* Robert College Publication. Istanbul: Menteş Matbaası, 1968.

————— *Türk Anayasa Metinleri: Tanzimat'tan Bugüne Kadar.* Ankara Üniversitesi Siyasal Bilimler Fakültesi, İdari Bilimler Enstitüsü Yayın No. 2. Ankara: Ajans Türk Matbaası.

Kilson, Martin (ed.). *New States in the Modern World.* Cambridge, Mass.: Harvard University Press, 1975.

Kinross, Lord. *Atatürk: Bir Milletin Yeniden Doğuşu.* (Ayhan Tezel, tr.). 6th ed. Sander Yayınları, Istanbul: Sümbül Basımevi, 1978.

Kohli, Atul, *State-Directed Development: Political Power and Industrialization in the Global Periphery,* New York: Cambridge University Press, 2004.

Kohn, Hans. *A History of Nationalism in the East.* (Margaret L. Green, tr.). New York: Harcourt, Brace, 1929.

————— *Revolutions and Dictatorships.* Cambridge: Harvard University Press, 1939.

————— *The Idea of Nationalism: A Study in the Origin and Background.* New York: Macmillan, 1961.

Kongar, Emre. *Toplumsal Değişme Kuramları ve Türkiye Gereceği.* 2nd ed. Bilgi Yayınevi. Ankara: Çağdaş Basımevi, 1979.

Koopmans, R.R. *The Limits of Modernization: Turkey.* Doctoral Thesis presented to the University of Amsterdam, Institute of Applied Sociology. Amsterdam, 1978.

Köymen, Oya. *A Comparative Study of the Anglo-Turkish Relations: C. 1830-1879 and 1919-1939.* Doctoral Thesis presented to the University of Strathclyde (Glasgow), Department of Economics, 1967.

Krüger, Karl. *Kemalist Turkey and the Middle East.* London: George Allen and Unwin Ltd., 1932.

K.S., Jomo, *The Pioneers of Development Economics : Great Economists on Development,* New Delhi: Tulika Books; London; New York: Zed; New York: Distributed in the USA exclusively by Palgrave, 2005.

Kuran, Ahmet Bedevi. *Osmanlı İmparatorluğunda İnkılâp Hareketleri ve Milli Mücadele,* Istanbul: Çeltüt Matbaası, 1959.

LaChapelle, Guy, and Trent, John (eds.), *Globalisation, Governance and Identity: The Emergence of New Partnerships,* Montreal: Les Presses de l'Université de Montreal, 2000.

Landau, Jacob M. *Tekinalp: Bir Türk Yurtseveri (1883-1961).* Istanbul: İletişim Yayınları, 1996.

————— *Pan-Turkism: From Irredentism to Cooperation.* Bloomington University of Indiana Press, 1995.

————— *Radical Politics in Modern Turkey.* Leiden: E.J. Brill, 1974.

————— (Ed.), *Atatürk and the Modernization of Turkey,* Boulder, Colo.: Westview Press; Leiden, the Netherlands: E.J. Brill, 1984.

Lapalombara, Joseph and Weiner, Myron (eds.). *Political Parties and Political Development.* Princeton, N. J.: Princeton University Press, 1966.

Latimer, Jr. Frederick P. *The Political Philosophy o f Mustafa Kemal Atatürk: As Evidenced in his Published Speeches and Interviews.* Unpublished Doctoral Thesis presented to Princeton University, Department of History, 1960. Ann Arbor, Michigan, University Microfilms, Inc., 1960.

Lengyel, Emil, *Turkey.* New York: Random House, 1941.

Lerner, Daniel. *The Passing of Traditional Society.* Glencoe, 111.: The Free Press, 1958.

Levey, Marion J. *Modernization and the Structure of Societies.* (2 volumes). Princeton: Princeton University Press, 1966.

Lewis, Bernard. *The Emergence of Modern Turkey.* London: Oxford University Press, 1966.

Lewis, Godfrey. *Turkey,* 3rd ed. New York: Frederick, A. Praeger, 1965.

Lindsay, A.D. *The Modern Democratic State. I.* London: Oxford University Press, 1947.

Lipset, Seymour Martin. *Political Man.* New York: Doubleday and Co., Inc., 1960.

Madison, James and Hamilton, Alexander, Jay, John, 1787-1788, *The Federalist,* New York.

Malinowski, B. *The Dynamics of Cultural Change.* New Haven: Yale: University Press, 1945.

Manisalı, Erol. *Türkiye-Avrupa İlişkilerinde Sessiz Darbe.* 2 basım. Istanbul: Der İn Yayınları, 2002.

McMichael, Philip, *Development and Social Change: A Global Perspective (Sociology for a New Century Series),* 2. printing. California: Pine Forge Press, 2000.

Melzig, Herbert. *Thus Spoke Atatürk.* Ankara: Sümer Basımevi, 1942.

Mesthene, E.G. *Technological Change: Its Impact on Man and Society.* Cambridge, Mass.: Harvard University Press, 1970.

Migdal, Joel S. Peasants, *Politics and Revolution.* Princeton: Princeton University Press, 1974.

Milis, C. Wright. *The Power Elite.* New York: Oxford University Press, 1959.

Misen, Richard Von. *Positivism: A Study in Human Understanding.* New York: George Braziller, Inc., 1956.

Morgenthau, Hans J. *Politics Among Nations.* New York: Alfred A. Knopf, 1966.

Nettl, J.P., Robertson, Roland. *International Systems and the Modernization of Societies.* London: Faber and Faber, 1968.

Nieuwenhuijze, C.A.O. Van. *Development: A Challenge to Whom?* The Hague: Moutton, 1969.

————— Development: The Western View. The Hague: Mouton, 1972.

O'Dunnell, Guiilermo A. *Modernization and Bureaucratic Authoritarianism: Studies in South American Politics.* Berkeley: University of California, Institute of International Studies, 1973.

OECD. *The Mediterranean Regional Project: Turkey.* Organization for Economic Co-Operation and Development. Paris, 1965.

Ohmae, Kenichi, *Ulus-Devletin Sonu: Bölgesel Ekonomilerin Yükselişi,* trans. Zülfü Dicleli, Türk Henkel Dergisi Yay., Istanbul, Flash Yay., 1996.

Olaylarla Türk Dış Politikası (1919-1965). A.Ü. Siyasal Bilgiler Fakültesi Dış Münasebetler Enstitüsü Üyeleri. Ankara: Dışişleri Bakanlığı Matbaası, 1968.

Oran, Baskın. *Azgelişmiş Ülke Milliyetçiliği.* A.Ü. Siyasal Bilgiler Fakültesi Yayını. Ankara: Ankara Üniversitesi Basımevi, 1977.

Ostrolog, Leon. *The Angora Reform.* London: University of London Press, Ltd., 1927.

Ökçün, A. Gündüz. *Türkiye İktisat Kongresi, 1923 İzmir.* 2nd ed. A.Ü. Siyasal Bilgiler Fakültesi Yayını, no. 262. Ankara: Sevinç Matbaası, 1971.

Öymen, Onur. *Silahsız Savaş: Bir Mücadele Sanatı Olarak Diplomasi.* 2. basım, Istanbul: Remzi Kitapevi, 2002.

————— *Turkish Challenge.* Istanbul: Remzi Kitapevi, 2002.

————— *Geleceği Yakalamak: Türkiye'de ve Dünyada Küreselleşme ve Devlet Reformu,* l. basım, Istanbul: Remzi Kitapevi, 2000.

———— *Turkey's Challenge: Turkey, Europe and the World Towards the 21 st Century.* 2nd. ed.

Nicosia, Northern Cyprus: Rustem. Printed in Great Britain by Cambridge University Press, 2000.

———— *Türkiye'nin Gücü.* 3. basım, Istanbul: Doğan Kitapçılık, 1999.

Öztürk, Kâzım. *Türkiye Büyük Millet Meclisi Albümü: 1920-1973.* Ankara: Önder Matbaası, 1973.

———— *Türkiye Cumhuriyeti Hükümetleri ve Programları,* Istanbul: Baha Matbaası, 1968.

———— *Türkiye Cumhuriyeti Anayasası, 3 vol.* Türkiye İş Bankası Kültür Yayınları. Ankara: Ajans Türk Matbaacılık, 1966.

Palmer, Monte. *The Dilemmas of Political Development.* Itasca, Illinois: F.E. Peacock Publishers, Inc. 1973.

Paneth, Philip. *Turkey: Decadence and Rebirth.* London: Richard Madley,1943.

Peker, Recep. *İnkılap Tarihi Notları.* Ankara, 1935.

Petras, James (ed.) *Latin America: From Dependence to Revolution.* New York: John Wiley and Sons, Inc., 1973.

Pettit, Philip, *Republicanism: A Theory of Freedom and Government,* Oxford, 1997.

Price, Clair. *The Rebirth o f Turkey.* New York: Thomas Seltzer, 1923.

Pye, Lucian W. (ed.). *Communications and Political Development.* Princeton: Princeton University Press, 1963.

———— *Politics, Personality and Nation-Building.* 4th ed., New Haven: Yale University Press, 1966.

———— and Verba, Sidney (eds.) *Political Culture and Political Development.* Princeton: Princeton University Press, 1965.

Rawls, J., *Political Liberalism,* New York, 1993.

Reidy, David A., *Universal Human Rights: Moral Order in a Divided World (Philosophy and the Global Context),* Lanham: Rowman & Littlefield Publishers, Inc., 2005.

Riggs, Fred W. *Administration in Developing Countries: The Theory of Prismatic Society.* Boston: Houghton Mifflin, 1964.

Robins, Robert. *Political Institutionalization and the Integration of Elites.* Beverly Hills, California: Sage Publications, 1976.

Robinson, Richard D. *The First Turkish Republic: A Case Study in National Development.* Cambridge, Mass.: Harvard University Press, 1963.

Robock, Stefan, H. *Brazil: A Study in Development Progress.* Lexington, Mass: Lexington Books, D.C. Heath and Company, 1975.

Rodrick, Dani, *Has Globalisation Gone Too Far?,* Washington: Institute for International Economics, 1997.

Roos, Leslie L. Jr. and Ross, N.P. *Managers of Modernization: Organizations and Elites in Turkey (1950-1960).* Cambridge, Mass.: Harvard University Press, 1971.

Rosenau, J., *Along the Foreign-Domestic Frontier,* Cambridge, Cambridge University Press, 1997.

———— *Turbulence in World Politics,* Brighton, Harvester Wheasheaf, 1990.

Rustow, Dankwart, A. *A World of Nations: Problems of Political Modernization.* Washington, D.C.: The Brookings Institution, 1967.

———— *Politics and Westernization in the Near East.* Princeton: Center of International Studies, 1956.

Seminar Report: International Solidarity and Globalisation, a seminar arranged by the Swedish Government and the Columbian Presidency of the Non-Aligned Movement, Stockholm, October 27-28, 1997, Stockholm: Tryckeri AB Smaland, 1998.

Sander, Oral. *Balkan Gelişmeleri ve Türkiye (1945-1965)*. Ankara: Sevinç Matbaası, 1969.

Scharpf, E., *Crisis and Choice in European Social Democracy*, New York, Cornell University, 1991.

Selek, Sabahattin. *Milli Mücadele*. 2 vol. Istanbul: Dilek Matbaası, 1971.

———— *Anadolu İhtilâli*. 4th ed. Istanbul: Istanbul Matbaası, 1968.

Seliger, M. *Ideology and Politics*. New York: The Free Press, 1976.

Seligson, Mitchell A. ve Passé-Smith, John T., *Development and Underdevelopment*ent: *The Political Economy of Global Inequality*. Boulder, Colo. : Lynne Rienner Publishers, 2003.

Sellers, M.N.S., *Republican Principles in International Law: The Fundamental Requirements of a Just World Order*, New York: Palgrave Macmillan, 2006.

Seton-Watson, Hugh. *Nations and States: An Enquiry into the Origins of Nations and the Politics of Nationalism*. Boulder, Colorado: Westview Press, 1977.

Shaw, Stanford, J. *From Empire to Republic: The Turkish War of National Liberation, 1918-1923: A Documentary Study*. 5 volumes. Ankara: Türk Tarih Kurumu Basımevi, 2000.

———— and Shaw, Ezel Kural. *History of the Ottoman Empire and Modern Turkey: Reform, Revolution and Republic, the Rise of Modern Turkey, 1808-1975*. 2. cilt. Cambridge: Cambridge University Press, 1977.

Shils, Edward. *Political Development in New States*. The Hague: Mouton, 1962.

Sigelman, Lee. *Modernization and the Political System: A Critique and Preliminary Empirical Analysis*. Beverly Hills, Calif.: Sage Publications, 1971.

Sigmund, Paul, E. (ed.). *The Ideologies of the Developing Nations*. New York: Frederick A. Praeger, 1963.

Sklair, Leslie, *Globalization: Capitalism and its Alternatives*, Oxford; New York: Oxford University Press, 2002.

Silvert, K.H. (ed.). *Expectant Peoples: Nationalism and Development*. New York: Random House, 1963.

Smith, Anthony D. *Theories of Nationalism*. London: Gerlad Duckworth and Co. Ltd., 1971.

Smith, Elaine.D. *Turkey: Origins of Kemalist Movement*. Washington, D.C.: Judd and Detweiler, 1959.

Sinanoğlu, Suat. *L'humanisme à venir*. Ankara: Türk Tarih Kurumu Basımevi, 1960.

Sinha, R.K. *Mustafa Kemal ve Mahatma Gandhi*. Milliyet Yayınları. Istanbul: Latin Matbaası, 1972.

Sunstein, Cass R. *The Partial Constitution*, Cambridge, MA, 1983.

Szyliowicz, Joseph, S. *Education and Modernization in the Middle East*. Ithaca: Cornell University Press, 1973.

Talas, Cahit. *İçtimai İktisat*. 2. Baskı. A.Ü. Siyasal Bilgiler Fakültesi Yayını. Ankara: Ajans Türk Matbaası, 1961.

Taneri, Aydın. *Türk Devlet Geleneği: Dün ve Bugün*. Ankara: Ankara Üniversitesi Basımevi, 1975.

Tekinalp, M.C. *Kemalizm*, Istanbul: Cumhuriyet Matbaası, 1986.

Tengirşenk, Yusuf Kemal. *Türk İnkılâbı Dersleri: Ekonomik Değişmeler*. Istanbul: Resimli Ay Basımevi, T.L.S., 1935.

Tessler, Mark A.; O'Barr, William M.; Spain, David. *Tradition and Identity in Changing Africa*. New York: Harper and Row Publishers, 1973.

Thomas, Lewis V. and Frye Richard N. *The United States and Turkey and Iran*. Cambridge, Mass.: Harvard University Press, 1952.

Timur, Taner. *Türk Devrimi - Tarihi Anlamı ve Felsefesi.* A.Ü. Siyasal Bilgiler Fakültesi Yayını. Ankara: Sevinç Matbaası, 1978.

Touraine, A. *La Société Post-Industrielle.* Paris: Editions Denoel, 1969.

Toynbee, Arnold J. *The Western Question in Greece and Turkey.* Boston: Houghton Mifflin, 1922.

————— and Kirkwood, Kenneth P. *Turkey.* New York: C. Scribners, 1927.

————— A *Study of History.* (An abbreviated version of volumes I-IV, D.C. Somerville). New York: Oxford University Press, 1947.

————— and Kirkwood, Kenneth P, *Turkey,* New York: Scribners, 1927.

Tunaya, Tarık Z. *Türkiye'de Siyasi Partiler: 1859-1952.* Istanbul: Doğan Kardeş, 1952.

————— *Osmanlı İmparatorluğundan Türkiye Büyük Millet Meclisi Hükümetine Geçiş,* Istanbul: İsmail Akgün Matbaası, 1956.

————— *Türkiye'nin Siyasi Hayatında Batılılaşma Hareketleri,* Istanbul: Yedigün Matbaası, 1960.

————— *Devrim Hareketleri İçinde Atatürk ve Atatürkçülük,* Istanbul: Baha Matbaası, 1964.

Tuncay, Mete. *Türkiye'de Sol Akımlar (1908-1925).* Bilgi Yayınevi. Ankara: Başnur Matbaası, 1967.

Turan, Şerafettin, *İsmet İnönü'nün Yaşamı, Dönemi ve Kişiliği,* T.C. Kültür Bakanlığı Yayını, Ankara, 2000.

Türk Dil Kurumu. *Bugünün Diliyle Atatürk'ün Söylevleri, (Behçet Kemal Çağlar).* Türk Dil Kurumu Yayını. Ankara: Ankara Üniversitesi Basımevi, 1968.

Türk İnkılap Tarihi. Genelkurmay Harp Tarihi Başkanlığı Yayını. Ankara: Genelkurmay Basımevi, 1971.

Türk İnkılap Tarihi Enstitüsü. *Atatürk Önderliğinde Kültür Devrimi.* Ankara: Ankara Üniversitesi Basımevi, 1972.

Türk Tarih Kurumu. *Cumhuriyetin 50. Yıl Dönümü Semineri: Seminere Sunulan Bildiriler.* Ankara: Türk Tarih Kurumu Basımevi, 1975.

Türkiye İş Bankası. *Papers And Discussions: International Symposium on Atatürk (17-22 May, 1981).* Türkiye İş Bankası Publication. Ankara: Tisa Matbaacılık, 1984.

Türkoğlu, Pakize, *Tonguç ve Enstitüleri,* 2. ed., Türkiye İş Bankası Kültür Yayınları, Istanbul, 2000.

Tütengil, Cavit Orhan. *Atatürk'ü Anlamak ve Tamamlamak,* Istanbul: Baha Matbaası, 1975.

Ulam, Adam. *The Unfinished Revolution.* New York: Random House, 1960.

Ulağ, Naşit. *Halifeliğin Sonu.* Türkiye İş Bankası Kültür Yayınları. Istanbul: Baha Matbaası, 1975.

Understanding Globalisation: The Nation-State, Democracy and Economic Policies in the New Epoch, Essays by John Eatwell, Elisabeth Jelin, Anthony Mc Grew and James Rosenau, The Swedish Ministry of Foreign Affairs, Stockholm: Tryckeri AB Smaland, 1998.

Valyi, Felix, *Spiritual and Political Revolutions in Islam,* London: Kegan Paul, Trench, Trubner, 1925.

Velidedeoğlu, Hıfzı Veldet. *Bir Lise Öğrencisinin Milli Mücadele Anıları.* Varlık Yayınevi, Istanbul: Dilek Matbaası, 1971.

Von Kral, August Ritter. *Kemal Atatürk's Land: The Evolution of Modern Turkey.* Translated by Kenneth Benton. Wien: Wilhelm Braumüllter, 1938.

Wallerstein, Immanuel, *The Modern World-system,* New York: Academic Press, 1974.

Wallerstein, Immanuel, *Unthinking Social Science: The Limits of Nineteenth-Century Paradigms*, Cambridge, MA: Polity Press in association with B. Blackwell, 1991.

Ward, Barbara. *Nationalism and Ideology.* New York: Norton, 1966.

Turkey. London: Oxford University Press, 1942.

Ward, Robert and Dankwart, A. Rustow (eds.). *Political Modernization in Japan and Turkey.* Princeton: Princeton University Press, 1964.

Webster, Donald, E. *The Turkey of Atatürk: Social Process in the Turkish Reformation.* Philadelphia: American Academy of Political and Social Science, 1939.

Weiker, Walter, F. *Political Tutelage and Democracy in Turkey: The Free Party and its Aftermath.* Leiden: E.J. Brill, 1973.

Weissberg, Robert. *Political Learning, Political Choice and Democratic Citizenship.* Englewood Cliffs, N.J.: Prentice Hall, Inc., 1974.

Welch, Claude E. (ed.). *Political Modernization: A Reader in Comparative Political Change.* Belmont, California: Wadsworth Publishing Company, Inc., 1967.

Wilber, Charles (Editor), *The Political Economy of Development and Underdevelopment*, New York: McGraw Hill Publishing Co., 1987.

Woo-Cumings, Meredith, *The Developmental State*, Ithaca, N.Y.: Cornell University Press, 1999.

Yale, William. *The Near East: A Modern History.* Ann Arbor: The University of Michigan Press, 1958.

Zolberg, Aristied, R. *Creating Political Order.* Chicago: Rand McNally and Co.,1966.

ARTICLES

Ake, Claude. "Charismatic Legitimarion and Political Integration." *Comparative Studies in Society and History,* IX (1967), pp. 1-13.

Aksoy, Muammer. "Atatürk'ün Işığında Tam Bağımsızlık İlkesi." *Abadan'a Armağan.* A.Ü. Siyasal Bilgiler Fakültesi Yayım. Ankara: Sevinç Matbaası, 1969, pp. 689-799.

Alexander, Robert J. "Nationalism, Latin America's Predominant Ideology." *Journal of International Affairs.* XV, 2 (1961), pp. 108-114.

Anderson, Arnold C. "The Modernization of Education," *Modernization: The Dynamics of Growth.* (ed.: Myron Weiner). New York: Basic Books, 1966, pp. 68-80.

Andrain, Charles. "Democracy and Socialism: Ideologies of African Leaders." *Ideology and Discontent.* (ed.: David E. Apter). New York: Free Press of Glencoe, 1964, pp. 155-219.

Apter, David. "Why Political Systems Change." *Government and Oppression.* (Fall 1968), pp. 411-27.

Baykal, Bekir Sıtkı. "Atatürk Devrimlerinde Tarihin Rolü." *Atatürk Önderliğinde Kültür Devrimi. Türk İnkılap Tarihi Enstitüsü 'Yayınları.* Ankara: Ankara Üniversitesi Basımevi, 1972, pp. 95-98.

Bellah, Robert N. "Religious Aspects of Modernization in Turkey and Japan." *American Journal of Sociology,* LXIV (July 1958), pp. 1-5.

Bendix, Reinhardt. "Tradition and Modernity Reconsidered." *Comparative Studies in Society and History,* IX, No. 2 (April 1967), pp. 292-346.

Berkes, Niyazi. "Atatürk'ün Yöntemi ve Yönetimi." *Cumhuriyet,* 26 January 1979-16 February 1979.

———— "Ziya Gökalp and His Contribution to Turkish Nationalism." *Middle East Journal,* VII (Fall 1954), pp. 375-90.

Binder, Leonard. "Ideology and Political Development." *Modernization: The Dynamics of Growth.* (ed.: Myron Weiner). New York: Basic Books, Inc., 1966, pp. 192-204.

————— "National Integration and Political Development." *American Political Science Review,* LVIII, 3, (September 1964), pp. 622-31.

Black, Cyril E. "Change as a Condition of Modern Life." *Modernization: The Dynamics of Growth.* (ed.: Myron Weiner). New York: Basic Books, Inc., 1966, pp. 17-27.

Bose, Nirmal. "The Politics of Development and System Change." *Participation,* II, No. 3 (1978), pp. 43-48.

Bowles, Donald B. "Soviet Russia as a Model for Underdeveloped Areas." *World Politics,* XIV, No. 3 (April 1962), pp. 483-504.

Brezezinski, Zbigniew. "The Politics of Underdevelopment." *World Development,* IX, No. 1 (October 1956), pp. 55-75.

Curtight, Philips. "National Political Development: Measurement and Analysis." *American Sociological Review* (April 1963), pp. 253-64.

Dahl, Robert A. "The Concept of Power." *Behavioral Science* II (July 1957), pp. 201-5.

De Schweinitz Jr., Karl. "Growth, Development and Political Modernization." *World Politics,* XXII (July 1970), pp. 518-40.

Debray, Régis, "Etes-vous démocrate ou républicain?", *Le Nouvel Observateur,* 30 November-6 December, 1989.

Dettman, Paul R. "Leaders and Structures in "Third World" Politics: Contrasting Approaches to Legitimacy." *Comparative Politics,* VI (January 1974), pp. 245-69.

Deutsch, Karl W. "Social Mobilization and Political Development." *American Political Science Review,* LV (September 1961), pp. 493-514.

Eisenstadt, Samuel N. "Sociological Theory and Analysis of the Dynamics of Civilizations and Revolutions." *Daedalus,* II (Fall 1977), pp. 59-78.

————— "Post-Traditional Societies and the Continuity and Reconstruction of Tradition." *Daedalus,* 102 (Winter 1973), pp. 1-27.

————— "Initial institutionalization Patterns of Political Modernization." *Political Modernization: A Reader in Comparative Political Change.* (ed.: Claude E. Welch, Jr.). Belmont, California: Wadsworth Publishing Co., Inc., 1967, pp. 246-66.

————— "Modernization and Conditions of Sustained Growth." *World Politics,* XVI, No. 4 (July 1964), pp. 576-94.

————— "Breakdowns of Modernization." *Economic Development and Cultural Change,* XII, No. 4 (July 1964), pp. 345-67.

————— "Institutionalization and Change." *American Sociological Review,* XXIX, No. 2 (April 1964), pp. 235-47.

Emerson, Rupert. "Nationalism and Political Development." *Journal of Politics,* XXII, No. I (February "960), pp.3-28.

Emre, Ahmet Cevat, "Amele ve Köylü Kitleri Nasıl Fırka Teşkil Eder? (translated into modern Turkish by Zafer Toprak). *Toplum ve Bilim,* (Spring-Summer 1980), pp. 103, 121.

Fallers, Lloyd. "Equality, Modernity and Democracy in the New States." *Old Societies and New States: The Quest for Modernity in Asia and Africa.* (ed.: Clifford Geertz). New York: Free Press of Glencoe, 1963, pp. 158-219.

Foltz, William J. "Building the Newest Nations: Short-run Strategies and Long-run Problems." *Political Modernization: A Reader in Comparative Political Change* (ed.: Claude E. Welch). Belmont, California: Wadsworth Publishing Co., Inc., 1967, pp. 307-21.

Frey, Frederick W. "Political Development, Power and Communications in Turkey." *Communications and Political Development* (ed.: Lucian W. Pye). Princeton: Princeton University Press, 1963, pp. 298-326.

———— "Education and Political *Development in Turkey.*" *Education and Political Development* (ed.: J.S. Coleman). Princeton: Princeton University Press, 1965.

Geertz, Clifford, "The Integrative Revolution: Primordial Sediments and Civil Polities in the New States." *Political Modernization: A Reader in Comparative Political Change.* (ed.: Claude E. Welch, Jr.). Belmont, California: Wadsworth Publishing Co., Inc., 1967, pp. 167-88.

———— "After the Revolution: The Fate of Nationalism in the New States." *Stability and Social Change* (ed.: Bernard Barber and Alex Inkeles). Boston: Little, Brown and Co., 1971, pp. 357-376.

———— "Ideology as a Cultural System." *Ideology and Discontent.* (ed.: D. Apter). New York: The Free Press, 1964, pp. 57-76.

Huntington, Samuel P. "The Change to Change." *Comparative Politics* (April 1971), pp. 283-322.

———— "Political Development and Political Decay." *Political Modernization: A Reader in Comparative Political Change,* ed. Claude E. Welch. Belmont, California: Wadsworth Publishing Co., Inc., 1967, pp. 207-46.

Inkeles, Alex. "The Modernization of Man." *Modernization: The Dynamics of Growth.* ed. Myron Weiner. New York: Basic Books, Inc., 1966, pp. 138-50.

İnalcık, Halil. "Atatürk Devrimleri." *Çeşitli Cepheleriyle Atatürk.* Robert Kolej yayınları. No. l. Istanbul: Istanbul Matbaası, 1964, pp. 64-73.

Karlsson, Mats, "Solidaric or Captured Globalisation", *Address at India Centre for International Cooperation,* New Delhi, 10 March 1997.

Kili, Suna. "Kimlik Sorunsalı", *Türk Kültürü ve Kimliği,* İstanbul Kültür Üniversitesi Yayını. Istanbul: Mas Matbaacılık A.Ş., 2006. p. 22-37.

———— "Ulusal Gücün Öğeleri Açısından Atatürk Döneminin Bir Değerlendirmesi", *Cumhuriyetin 80. Yıldönümü Armağanı.* Atatürkçü Düşünce Derneği Mersin Şubesi Yayını, 2004. p. 7-20.

———— "Turkish Constitutional Developments: An Evaluation", *Essays in Honour of Georgios I. Kassimatis.* Athens, Berlin, Bruxelles, Ant. N. Sokkoulos, Berliner Wissenschafts, Bruylant, 2004. p. 121-140.

———— "Role of the Military in Turkish Society: An Assessment from the Perspective of History, Sociology and Politics", in *Military Rule and Democratization: Changing Perspectives.* (Ed.: Asha Gupta). New Delhi: Deep and Deep Publication PVT. LTD: 2003, s. 45-83.

———— "Sunuş" ve "Cumhuriyet, Atatürkçülük ve Küreselleşme", *Cumhuriyet ve Küreselleşme.* T.C. Kültür Bakanlığı Yayını. Ankara: Sistem Ofset, 2002. s. IX-XVI ve s. 177-199.

———— "Cumhuriyet ve Demokrasi", *Cumhuriyet ya da Demokrasi.* T.C. Kültür Bakanlığı Yayını. Ankara: Ofset Basımevi, 2002. s. 25-39.

———— "Küreselleşme ve Kemalizm." *Müdafaa-i Hukuk,* 30 Mayıs 1999, Sayı 10, pp. 14-21.

———— "Geleceğe Yönelme ve 21. Yüzyılda Atatürkçü Kültür Politikası." *Çağdaş Türk Dili-Söylev Özel Sayısı,* Sayı 116/117, 1997, pp. 2-10.

———— "Islam and Secularism in Contemporary Turkey." *Voice of ASA,* Year 2, No. 2. Washington, D.C., February 1997.

————— "Modernity and Tradition: Dilemmas of Political Education in Developing Countries." *Aspects of Globalization and Internationalization of Political Education* (ed.: B. Claussen). Hamburg: Kramer, 1995, pp. 102-14.

————— "Atatürk, Uygarlık ve Dünya Ulusları." *Cumhuriyet'in 70. Yılında Atatürk'e Armağan. Geçmişten Geleceğe Atatürk.* Çağdaş Yaşamı Destekleme Derneği yayını, Istanbul, 1993, pp. 93-8.

————— "Turkish Constitutional Developments: An Appraisal." *Capital University Law Review,* vol. 21, no. 4, 1993, pp. 1059-80.

————— "Turkey and Europe: An Assessment of Past Conflicts and Present Commitments." *Perceptions of Europe in East and West* (eds.: Rüdiger Meyenberg and Henk Dekker. European Studies, no. 2. Oldenburg: Library and Information System – University of Oldenburg, 1992, pp. 79-94.

————— "The Turkish Revolution, Developed and Developing Countries", in *Papers and Discussions: Türkiye İş Bankası International Symposium on Atatürk, 17-22 May 1981.* Türkiye İş Bankası Cultural Publications. Ankara: Tisa Matbaacılık Sanayi, 1984. p. 73-105.

————— "Kemalism in Contemporary Turkey." *International Political Science Review,* I, No. 3 (July 1980), pp. 381-404.

————— "Politikacı Atatürk." *Boğaziçi Üniversitesi Dergisi: Sosyal Bilimler,* VII, 1979, pp. 37-54.

————— "1876 Anayasası'nın Çağdaşlaşma Sorunları Açısından Değerlendirilmesi." *1876 Anayasası 100. Yıldönümü Armağanı,* A.Ü. Siyasal Bilgiler Fakültesi Yayını, Ankara: Sevinç Matbaası, 1978, pp.191-212.

————— "Türkiye Örgütleşme Sorunu ve Örgütsel Dengesizlik." *Boğaziçi Üniversitesi Dergisi,* IV-V, 1977, pp. 63-77.

————— "Tarih Açısından Kemalizmin Özü ve Oluşumu." *Atatürk Devrimleri. I. Milletlerarası Sempozyumu,* Istanbul: Sermet Matbaası, 1975, pp. 22-32.

————— "Türk Dil Devriminin Yenileşme Çabamızdaki Yeri." *Bilimsel Bildiriler - 1972.* Türk Dil Kurumu Yayınları. Ankara: Ankara Üniversitesi Basımevi, 1975, pp. 55-65.

Krugman, Paul R, "Competitiveness: A Dangerous Obsession."*Foreign Affairs,* Vol. 73, March-April 1994, pp. 28-44.

Lapalombara, Joseph, "Distribution and Development." *Modernization: The Dynamics of Growth,* ed., Myron Weiner. New York: Basic Books, 1966, pp. 218-29.

Lenczwoski, George, "Radical Regimes in Egypt, Syria and Iraq: Some Comparative Observations on Ideologies and Practices." *Journal of Polities,* XXVIII, No. I (February 1966), pp. 25-56.

Lerner, Daniel. "Towards a Communication Theory of Modernization." *Communication and Political Development.* (ed.: L.W. Pye). Princeton: Princeton University Press, 1963, pp. 327-51.

————— and Robinson, Richard D. "Swords and Ploughshares: The Turkish Army as a Modernizing Force," *World Polities,* XIII (October 1960), pp. 19-44.

Levy, Jr. Marion J. "Patterns (Structures) of Modernization and Political Development." *The Annals of the American Academy of Political and Social Science,* 358 (March 1965), pp. 29-40.

Lewis, Bernard. "History Writing and National Revival in Turkey," *Middle Eastern Affairs,* IV (June-July 1953), pp. 218-227.

————— "Speech Delivered by Bernard Lewis On the Occasion of his Receipt of the ASA 'Atatürk Award', *Voice of Atatürk.* Year 7, No. 18, November, 2002.

Lipset, Seymour Martin. "Political Cleavages in "Developed" and "Emerging" Polities." *Mass Polities: Studies in Political Sociology.* (ed.: Erik Allardt and Stein Rokkan). New York: The Free Press, 1970, pp. 23-44.

———— "Some Social Requisites of Democracy: Economic Development and Political Legitimacy." *American Political Science Review,* 53 (March 1959), pp. 69-105.

Lowi, Theodore J. "Our Milleiinium: Political Science Confronts the Global Corporate Economy", *Opening Address of Theodore J. Lowi, President of IPSA, at the 18th World Congress of IPSA.* Quebec, Canada. August 2000.

M.I.T. Study Group. "The Transitional Process." *Political Modernization: A Reader in Comparative Political Change.* (ed.: Claude E. Welch Jr.). Belmont, California: Wadsworth Publishing Co., Inc., 1967, pp. 22-48.

MacFarquhar, Roderick. "The Chinese Model and the Underdeveloped World." *Political Modernization: A Reader in Comparative Political Change.* (ed.: Claude E. Welch, Jr.). Belmont, California: Wadsworth Publishing co., Inc., 1967, pp. 373-82.

Mazrui, Ali A. "Africa Between the Meiji Restoration And the Legacy of Atatürk: Comparative Dilemmas of Modernization", in *Papers and Discussions: Türkiye İş Bankası Symposium on Atatürk (17-22 May 1981).* Türkiye İş Bankası Cultural Publications. Ankara: Tisa Matbaacılık, 1984. p. 379-412.

———— "From Social Darwinism to Current Theories of Modernization, A Tradition of Analysis." *World Politics,* XXI, No. I (October 1968), pp. 69-83.

McClelland, David, C. "The Impulse to Modernization," *Modernization: The Dynamics of Growth.* (ed.: Myron Weiner). New York: Basic Books, 1966, pp. 28-39.

Medding, Peter, Y. "Elitist Democracy: An Unsuccessful Critique of a Misunderstood Theory." *The Journal of Politics,* 31 (August 1969), pp. 641-54.

Melson, Robert and Wolpe, Howard. "Modernization and the Politics of Communalism: A Theoretical Perspective." *The American Political Science Review,* LXIV (December 1970), pp. 1112-1130.

Millikan, Max. "Equity vs. Productivity in Economic Development." *Modernization: The Dynamics of Growth.* (ed.: Myron Weiner). New York: Basic Books, Inc., 1966, pp. 307-320.

Nove, A. "The Social Model and Underdeveloped Countries." *Political Modernization: A Reader in Comparative Political Change.* (ed.: Claude E. Welch, Jr.). Belmont, California: Wadsworth Publishing Co., Inc., 1967, pp. 363-372.

Lowi, Theodore, J. "Our Millenium: Political Science Confronts the Global Corporate Economy", *Opening Address of Theodore J. Lowi, President of IPSA, at the 18th World.*
———— *Congress of IPSA,* Quebec, Canada. August 2000.

Öymen, Onur. "Avrupa Türkiye'yi Neden Otuz Yıldır Kapıda Bekletti", *Büyükelçi Onur Öymen ile Söyleşi. Cumhuriyet.* 21 Temmuz 2002.

Payaslıoğlu, Arif. "Political Leadership and Political Parties: Turkey." *Political Modernization in Japan and Turkey.* (ed.: Robert E. Ward and Dankwart A. Rustow). Princeton: Princeton University Press, 1964, pp. 411-33.

Pfaff, Richard H. "Disengagement from Traditionalism in Turkey and Iran." *Political Modernization: A Reader in Comparative Political Change.* (ed.: Claude E. Welch, Jr.). Belmont, California: Wadsworth Publishing Co., Inc., 1967, pp. 105-25.

Pye, Lucian P. "The Concept of Political Development," *The Annals of the American Academy of Political and Social Sciences,* 358 (March 1965), pp. 1-13.

———— "Communication Patterns and the Problems of Representative Government in Non-Western Societies." *Public Opinion Quarterly,* XX (Spring 1956), pp. 249-57.

Reed, Howard A. "Secularism and Islam in Turkish Politics." *Current History*, XXXII (June 1957), pp. 333-38.

Rivkin, Arnold. "The Politics of Nation-Building: Problems and Preconditions." *Journal of International Affairs*, XVI, No. 2 (1962), pp. 131-143.

Rosenau, James N. "Global World Order and Political Space: Changing Dimensions of Sovereigny and the Nation-State", *Seminar Report: International Solidarity and Globalization. In Search of New Strategies*. Swedish Ministry of Foreign Affairs. Stockholm: Tryckeri Ab Smaland, 1998. pp. 85-92.

Roth, Guenther. "Personal Rulership, Patrimonialism, and Empirebuilding in the New States." *World Politics*, XX (January 1968), pp. 194-206.

Rustow, Dankwart A. "Atatürk's Political Leadership." *Near Eastern Round Table 1967-68* (ed.: R. Bayly Winder). New York: New York University Near East Center, 1969, pp. 143-55.

———— "Devlet Kurucusu Olarak Atatürk," *Abadan'a Aramağan*. A.Ü. Siyasal Bilgiler Fakültesi Yayını, Ankara: Sevinç Matbaası, 1969, pp. 573-643.

———— "Turkey: The Modernity of Tradition." *Political Culture and Political Development* (ed.: Lucian W. Pye and Sidney Verba). Princeton: Princeton University Press, 1965, pp. 171-98.

———— "The Politics of the Near East, Southwest Asia and Northern Africa." *The Politics of the Developing Areas* (ed.: Gabriel A. Almond and James S. Coleman). Princeton: Princeton University Press, 1960, pp. 369-454.

———— "The Army and the Founding of the Turkish Republic." World Politics, XI, No. 4 (July 1959), pp. 513-52.

Sartori, Giovanni. "Politics, Ideology and Belief Systems." The American Political Science Review, LXIII (June 1969), pp. 398-411.

Seligman, Lester G. "Political Elites Reconsidered: Process, Consequences and Values." Comparative Polities, VI (January 1974), pp. 299-314.

Sellers, Mortimer, "Republicanism, Liberalism and the Law", *Kentucky Law Journal*, vol. 86, no: 1, 1997-98, pp.1-30.

Shils, Edward. "Demagogues and Cadres in the Political Development of New States." *Communication and Political Development* (ed.: L.W. Pye). Princeton: Princeton University Press, 1963, pp. 64-78.

———— "The Intellectuals in the Political Development of New Nations." *World Politics*, XII, No. 3 (April 1960), pp. 329-68.

Silvert, K. H. "Parties and the Masses." *The Annals of the American Academy of Political Social Science*, 358 (March 1965), pp. 101-108.

———— "The Strategy of the Study of Nationalism." *Expectant Peoples: Nationalism and Development* (ed.: K.H. Silvert). New York: Random House, 1963, pp. 3-38.

Smelser, Neil J. "The Modernization of Social Relations." *Modernization: The Dynamics of Growth* (ed.: Myron Weiner). New York: Basic Books, Inc., 1966, pp. 110-21.

Spengler, Joseph J. "Breakdowns of Modernization." *Modernization: The Dynamics of Growth* (ed.: Myron Weiner). New York: Basic Books, Inc., 1966, pp. 321-33.

Staley, Eugene. "The Role of State in Economic Development." *Modernization: The Dynamics of Growth*. (ed.: Myron Weiner). New York: Basic Books, Inc., 1966, pp. 294-306.

Sunstein, Cass R., "Beyond the Republican Revival", 97 *The Yale Law Journal*, 1988.

"Symposium: The Republican Civic Tradition", *The Yale Law Journal*, special edition, 1988.

Szyliowicz, Joseph S. "Political Participation and Modernization in Turkey." *Western Political Quarterly,* XIX (1966), pp. 266-84.

Torres, Jose Arsenio. "The Political Ideology of Guided Democracy." *Political Modernization: A Reader in Comparative Political Change* (ed.: Claude E. Welch, Jr.). Belmont, California: Wadsworth Publishing CO., Inc., 1967, pp. 346-63.

Trimberger, Ellen Kay. "A Theory of Elite Revolutions." *International Development,* VII, No. 3 (Fall 1972), pp. 191-207.

Tunaya, Tarık Z. "Doğu-Batı Politikası Arasında Türkiye." *Abadan'a Armağan.* A.Ü. Siyasal Bilgiler Fakültesi Yayını. Ankara: Sevinç Matbaası, 1969, pp. 51-61.

Webster, Donald E. "State Control of Social Change in Republican Turkey." *American Sociological Review,* IV (April 1939), pp. 247-56.

Weiner, Myron. "Political Integration and Political Development." *Political Modernization: A Reader in Comparative Political Change.* (ed.: Claude E. Welch, Jr.). Belmont, California: Wadsworth Publishing Co., Inc., 1967, pp. 150-66.

———— "Political Participation and Political Development." *Modernization: The Dynamics of Growth* (ed.: Mayron Weiner). New York: Basic Books, 1966, pp. 205-17.

Welch, Claude E. Jr. "The Comparative *Study of Political Modernization." Political Modernization: A Reader in Comparative Political Change.* (ed.: Claude E. Welch, Jr.). Belmont, California: Wadsworth Publishing Co., Inc., 1967, pp. 1-17.

Willner, Ruth and Dorthy Willner. "The Rise and Role of Charismatic Leaders." *The Annals of the American Academy of Political and Social Science,* 358 (March 1965), pp. 77-88.

Wriggens, Howard. "National Integration." *Modernization: The Dynamics of Growth.* (ed.: Myron Weiner). New York: Basic Books, Inc., 1966, pp. 181-191.

Wright, Walter Livingston. "Truths About Turkey", *Foreign Affairs,* XXVI. January, 1948.

Yalman, Nur. "Some Observations on Secularism in Islam: The Cultural Revolution in Turkey." *Daedalus,* 102 (Winter 1973), pp. 139-168.

NAMES INDEX

SUBJECTS AND CONCEPTS INDEX